AQA

AS Business Studies

2ND EDITION

John Wolinski & Gwen Coates

Philip Allan Updates, an imprint of Hodder Education, part of Hachette Livre UK, Market Place, Deddington, Oxfordshire OX15 0SE

Orders

Bookpoint Ltd, 130 Milton Park, Abingdon, Oxfordshire OX14 4SB
tel: 01235 827720
fax: 01235 400454
e-mail: uk.orders@bookpoint.co.uk

Lines are open 9.00 a.m.–5.00 p.m., Monday to Saturday, with a 24-hour message answering service. You can also order through the Philip Allan Updates website: www.philipallan.co.uk

ISBN 978-0-340-95935-0

First printed 2008
Impression number   5 4 3
Year   2013   2012 2011   2010 2009   2008

This textbook has been written specifically to support students studying AQA AS business studies. The content has been neither approved nor endorsed by AQA and remains the sole responsibility of the authors.

All efforts have been made to trace copyright on items used.

All web addresses are correct at the time of going to press but may subsequently change.

Design by Juha Sorsa

Printed in Italy

Hachette Livre UK's policy is to use papers that are natural, renewable and recyclable products and made from wood grown in sustainable forests. The logging and manufacturing processes are expected to conform to the environmental regulations of the country of origin.

Contents

The Sheffield College
Hillsborough LRC
Telephone: 0114 260 2254

Operations management

Marketing and the competitive environment

Introduction

This textbook has been written specifically to meet the needs of students taking AQA AS business studies. It provides comprehensive coverage of the subject content of the AQA AS specification, unit by unit, section by section, as it is laid out in the specification document.

Up-to-date examples and illustrations from actual organisations and situations are used throughout the book in order to help you to recognise the dynamic and changing nature of business studies and its relevance to society.

Course coverage and how to use this book

Terminology

The A-level specification uses the following terms:
- **Subject content** is a body of learning (i.e. the topics that are included in the specification).
- The **scheme of assessment** describes the aims of the examinations and the methods of assessment — the AS and A2 courses are assessed 100% by examinations.
- **Transferable skills** are abilities that will be acquired and/or enhanced by studying this course. These skills are intended to prepare you for both employment and higher education.

Structure

This book follows the order of the AQA AS business studies (1131*) specification. (*1131 is the AQA code used to describe the AS award. The A2 award is referred to as 2131 and the overall A-level award (AS + A2) is coded as 2130.)

The specification is divided into two units, each of which is split into further parts. Unit 1 is 40% of the AS examination (20% of the A-level). Unit 2 is 60% of the AS examination (30% of the A-level).

Unit 1 — BUSS1 is concerned with 'Planning and financing a business'. The first part of Unit 1 is 'Starting a business', which introduces the range of activities involved in setting up a small business. These topics are covered in Chapters 1–10.

The second part of Unit 1 looks at 'Financial planning'. This considers the key financial concepts essential for the planning of small businesses and the assessment of a business start-up. These topics are covered in Chapters 11–15.

Unit 2 — BUSS2 is concerned with 'Managing a business'. The core theme of Unit 2 is 'improving the effectiveness of the business'. It examines the growing business, focusing on regional or national (but not international) businesses. The core theme of effectiveness is evaluated through measurements of a business's effectiveness and how effectiveness is improved through the actions of a business's four main functional areas: finance, people/human resource management, operations management, and marketing. The study of how these functional areas contribute to the effectiveness of the business forms the core of Unit 2:

- Finance: Chapters 16–18
- People in business: Chapters 19–22
- Operations management: Chapters 23–27
- Marketing and the competitive environment: Chapters 28–34

For each unit, the order of the chapters in this book provides a logical progression of business development, with Unit 1 looking at the start-up of a business and Unit 2 looking at how the efficiency of the business is maintained and improved as it develops.

The order of the chapters also provides a logical progression of learning, with the later chapters building on the theory and understanding acquired in the earlier chapters. Some questions at the end of chapters also assume an understanding of work done in previous chapters.

The view of the authors is that it is advisable to follow the order of the specification and start with Unit 1 for three main reasons:

- The sequence of learning is most logical, as Unit 1 deals with a business *before* it begins trading, although many elements can be taught in the context of a recently formed start-up business.
- The 'lower-level' skills (knowledge and application) are tested to a greater extent in this unit, making the transition to AS easier.
- The structure of the AQA AS business studies course has been designed so that 40% of the content is contained in Unit 1, leaving 60% for Unit 2. This division of content enables you to sit the Unit 1 (BUSS1) examination in January of your AS year. This relieves the pressure facing you in the summer of your AS year, as only Unit 2 (BUSS2) will need to be taken at this time. Most other AS subjects are likely to focus on summer examinations, so taking Unit 1 in January is a logical decision that spreads the examination workload.

However, this is not a clear-cut decision and your teacher will decide on the most appropriate sequence of chapters for your learning and the optimum time for sitting the examinations.

Chapters 13, 14, 16 and 17

It may be advisable to amend the sequence of chapters for these topics. Chapters 13 and 14 are Unit 1 (BUSS1) chapters entitled 'Using cash-flow forecasting' and 'Setting budgets' respectively. These two topics form the two penultimate chapters of Unit 1. Chapters 16 and 17 are the opening topics of Unit 2 (BUSS2) and follow on logically from Chapters 13 and 14. Chapter 16 ('Using budgets') takes the budgets that were planned in Chapter 14 and uses them to assess the effectiveness of budgeting in the organisation. Similarly, Chapter 17 ('Improving cash flow') draws on the planning of cash flow from Chapter 13 in order to see how an organisation can improve its performance in this area.

Because of these links, it is logical to treat these two chapters as 'pairs', with Chapter 13 being followed immediately by Chapter 17 and Chapter 14 being followed by Chapter 16. Chapter 15 should come next, as it should not precede Chapters 13 and 14.

If both the Unit 1 and 2 examinations are being taken in the summer, this sequence is strongly advised.

If the Unit 1 examination is being taken in January and the Unit 2 examination is being taken in the summer, the situation is less clear-cut. Early study of Unit 2 material (Chapters 16 and 17) will affect the amount of time available for revision of Unit 1 in December and January. However, it may mean that Unit 2 is completed earlier, giving more time for Unit 2 revision in the summer.

At the time of going to press, there are no confirmed dates for the examinations in the summer of 2009 and beyond, but there are suggestions that AS examinations will be taken in May. If this is the case, it is advisable to cover Chapters 16 and 17 earlier, as the greatest time pressure for revision is likely to arise in the summer. If the summer examinations are in June, the authors' advice is to delay Chapters 16 and 17 until after the Unit 1 examination has been taken in January.

Chapters 29–33

These chapters cover the marketing mix and are presented in the order in which they are laid out in the AQA specification. Chapter 29 deals with 'Designing an effective marketing mix'. Chapters 30–33 cover the individual elements of the marketing mix (the four Ps): product, promotion, price and place. It is the view of the authors that, in order for you to understand how to design an effective marketing mix, the four Ps should have been covered fully beforehand.

Consequently, Chapter 29 should be read after Chapters 30–33. Chapter 29 has been written on the assumption that Chapters 30–33 have already been read.

Special features

This book contains several special features designed to aid your understanding of the requirements of the AQA AS business studies course.

Key terms

These are clear, concise definitions of the main terms needed for the course. In Unit 1, every term in the AQA specification is included as a key term to enable you to respond accurately to the early questions that require terms to be explained. An accurate understanding of the definitions of key terms will reduce the chances of you producing irrelevant answers in both units.

Examiner's voice

Both authors have over 20 years' experience of examining and have used this to provide snippets of advice that will help you to present your ideas effectively and to avoid potential pitfalls. Some of this advice is specific to a particular topic; the remainder is general advice on how you should approach the examinations.

Fact files

Topical examples from the world of business are included at regular intervals to help you develop your application skills by showing how the business ideas you have studied can be applied to real-life situations. The fact files will also increase your awareness of current developments and practices.

Did you know?

These boxes are placed throughout the book; they provide useful insights into the ideas and concepts covered in the AS course and their use in businesses. The comments will help you to improve your understanding of business activities.

What do you think?

On occasions, facts or comments on business activity are presented in the form of a challenge — what do you think? There is often a range of possible solutions to business problems or many differing consequences to an action. These boxes will get you thinking about possible alternative solutions or consequences.

Group exercises

These are included when a part of the specification lends itself to discussion or a cooperative approach to study.

Practice exercises

In the 34 chapters of this book, there are 50 different practice exercises that are provided to help you check your understanding of the topics you have covered in each chapter. Most of these exercises are geared towards testing knowledge, but several are based on relevant information or articles. You can use the latter type to test your higher-level skills, such as evaluation. Although individual questions in a practice exercise may match the style of AQA AS questions, overall the practice exercises do not adopt the AQA examination style — the case studies perform this role.

With three exceptions the practice exercises are placed, with the case studies, at the end of each chapter. This is to allow your understanding of the chapter contents to be tested immediately after completing the topics. The three exceptions to this rule are Chapters 19, 21 and 22. These three chapters cover a great deal of material and have been divided into identifiable topic areas. Consequently, some of the practice exercises and case studies in these three chapters have been placed in the body of the chapter, at the point at which a particular topic area has been completed. As a result, you will be able to test your understanding immediately after completing that topic rather than waiting until the end of the chapter.

Case studies

A common problem facing both teachers and students is finding suitable material for examination practice. The examinations are based on the whole specification and so, on completion of a particular topic, it is not possible to find a past examination paper that sets a realistic challenge. To fill this gap, 51 examination-style questions have been included in this book. The heading 'case study' is used wherever the style of the questions is the same as in the AQA AS examinations.

It is not practical to replicate full 75-minute or 90-minute examination case studies on a topic from a single chapter, as there is usually insufficient material involved. For this reason, 'case studies' within the book are designed to include the types of individual question that will be set in the actual examinations, based on the sort of articles that will be used as stimulus material by AQA. However, they do not match the overall format of a 75-minute examination for Unit 1 or a 90-minute examination for Unit 2.

As indicated earlier, the case studies are placed *at the end of each chapter*, with the exceptions of Chapters 19, 21 and 22. In these chapters, some case studies are incorporated in the body of the chapter, at the point at which a particular topic has been completed.

Unit 1 (BUSS1)
In the Unit 1 (BUSS1) examination there are two stimulus-response (sometimes known as data-response) questions, worth 20 and 40 marks respectively. Both questions are based on the same stimulus material, which is an article of approximately 550–600 words, and are designed to cover a business start-up and its initial financial planning.

Question 1 consists of shorter questions, focusing on testing knowledge and application skills.

Question 2 comprises (probably three) longer questions, enabling you to show the full range of your skills; these questions will include analysis and evaluation.

Unit 2 (BUSS)

The Unit 2 (BUSS2) examination is based on two stimulus-response (sometimes known as data-response) questions. There will be two separate articles, each of approximately 300–350 words, featuring information covering the four functional areas of medium- to large-scale businesses. These questions will focus on the four skills of knowledge, application, analysis and evaluation. However, it is anticipated that there will be few, if any, questions focused solely on knowledge, such as definitions. Instead, the shorter questions will require some application of knowledge, and the more extensive questions will require analysis and evaluation. However, a good understanding of basic terms is still essential for the more extensive questions, as a failure to understand a term may mean that a much higher mark is lost because the answer lacks relevance.

CD-ROM

The enclosed CD-ROM contains sample student responses to specimen examination questions. The answers are followed by examiner comments that explain the strengths and weaknesses of the student's approach and indicate how they would be assessed by the examiner.

Assessment

The hierarchy of skills

Every mark that is awarded on an AS paper is given for the demonstration of a skill. The following four skills are tested:

- **Knowledge and understanding** — demonstrating knowledge and understanding of the specified content of the course, such as giving the definition of a business term or stating the advantage of a particular method.
- **Application** — relating or applying your knowledge and understanding to a specific organisation or situation. An example might be advising a business to target a particular segment of consumers, based on recognising the most relevant consumers for that organisation.
- **Analysis** — using business theory to develop a line of thought in relation to the solution of a business problem. An example might be showing how improvements in the quality of a product may cause cash-flow problems in the short term but lead to more satisfied customers, and therefore more sales revenue, in the long run.
- **Evaluation** — making a judgement by weighing up the evidence provided and, possibly, recognising the strength, quality and reliability of the evidence before making a decision.

All questions are marked according to this hierarchy of skills, with knowledge being the easiest and evaluation being the most difficult.

- An AS (Unit 1) question that requires you to define a term will only reward **knowledge** — do not waste time on showing the importance or application of this concept.

- A question asking you to explain will test **application** — both knowledge and application are needed.
- Questions requiring **analysis** will have marks allocated for knowledge, application and analysis.
- **Evaluation** questions will award marks for all four skills. You cannot evaluate (make a judgement) effectively without showing knowledge, applying it to the situation and then developing the argument (analysing).

To reflect the relative difficulties of these skills, most AS and A2 examinations allow for progression, with AS papers placing more emphasis on the skills of **knowledge** and **understanding**, and A2 papers testing **evaluation** to a greater extent.

However, despite the natural progression of skills in this hierarchy, in AQA AS business studies examinations, students tend to find **application** more difficult than **analysis**. They are often able to show their ability to use theory and business logic (analysis), but are less skilled in applying this theory to the business in the stimulus material or case study (application). Always ensure that your answers are linked to the situation in the stimulus material or case study. This will gain you application marks and will also make it easier for you to evaluate, as evaluation marks are gained by assessing the particular situation in the question.

Recognising the skills required

There are two ways in which you can identify the skills that are being tested by any particular question:
- trigger words
- mark allocations

Trigger words

In AQA AS business studies examinations, specific 'trigger' words tend to be used to show you when you are required to demonstrate application, analysis or evaluation (this is not the case with the A2 examinations).

Please note that AQA has indicated that it will *not* be following rigid rules, so trigger words other than those shown here may be used. However, it is probable that the majority of questions will use these words.

Knowledge and understanding

There are no prescribed trigger words for knowledge and understanding. The mark allocation for each question is the best guide for this (see p. xii). However, questions testing only knowledge will usually ask you to 'define' or 'explain the meaning of the term', or will start with 'what is meant by'. It is also possible that you will be asked to 'state' or 'identify'. Both AS papers guarantee that at least one question (and probably more) will require you to demonstrate numerical skills.

Application

The main trigger words for application are:

■ 'Explain…'   ■ 'Outline…'   ■ 'Calculate…' (or some indication of a calculation)

Analysis

The following trigger words will be used at AS when you are being asked to analyse:

■ 'Analyse…'   ■ 'Examine…'   ■ 'Explain why…'

Evaluation

The following trigger words will be used at AS when you are being asked to evaluate:

■ 'Evaluate…'   ■ 'Discuss…'   ■ 'To what extent…'   ■ '…Justify your view.'

Mark allocations

In general, the more marks allocated to a question, the more skills it is testing. There is no set pattern for every question, but Tables 1 and 2 show how 'typical' questions on the AS examination papers might be assessed in terms of the skills required.

Unit 1 (BUSS1) examination papers have two questions worth 20 marks and 40 marks respectively. The first question will usually be subdivided into five or six parts requiring a mixture of definitions, calculations and short answers. The second part will usually be split into three large questions, the first one testing analysis and the second and third ones requiring evaluation.

Table 1 Typical skills requirements based on mark allocations for Unit 1 (BUSS1) questions

Number of marks	Skill(s) required
2–3 marks	Knowledge only
3–7 marks	Knowledge and application
8–12 marks	Knowledge, application and analysis
12–18 marks	Knowledge, application, analysis and evaluation

Unit 2 (BUSS2) examination papers have two questions, each based on separate stimulus material. These two questions test all four functional areas (finance, people, operations and marketing), and will usually be subdivided into four or five parts. There are likely to be a couple of questions covering just knowledge and application, with about three questions requiring analysis. It is probable that four of the questions will require evaluation. In effect, between 40 and 50% of the questions are likely to require evaluation.

Table 2 Typical skills requirements based on mark allocations for Unit 2 (BUSS2) questions

Number of marks	Skill(s) required
2–3 marks	Knowledge only
3–6 marks	Knowledge and application
6–10 marks	Knowledge, application and analysis
11–16 marks	Knowledge, application, analysis and evaluation

AQA has stated that it will not follow a rigid policy and that examination papers will 'evolve' over time. However, it is likely that changes from the specimen papers issued with the specification will be gradual. The marks awarded for the questions and the overall weighting of the assessment objectives for the specimen papers is shown in Tables 3 and 4.

Question	Skills				Total
	Knowledge	Application	Analysis	Evaluation	
1(a)	2				2
1(b)	2				2
1(c)	2				2
1(d)	2	2			4
1(e)	2	4			6
1(f)	2	2			4
2(a)	3	3	4		10
2(b)	3	3	4	5	15
2(c)	3	3	4	5	15
Totals	21	17	12	10	60

Table 3
Mark allocations for Unit 1 (BUSS1) specimen paper

Question	Skills				Total
	Knowledge	Application	Analysis	Evaluation	
1(a)	2	2			4
1(b)	2	3	4		9
1(c)	3	2	3	4	12
1(d)	3	3	4	5	15
Subtotal	10	10	11	9	40
2(a)(i)	2				2
2(a)(ii)	2	3	1		6
2(b)	2	2	4		8
2(c)	2	2	3	4	11
2(d)	3	2	4	4	13
Subtotal	11	9	12	8	40
Totals	21	19	23	17	80

Table 4
Mark allocations for Unit 2 (BUSS2) specimen paper

Demonstrating the skills required

Avoid the temptation to show off your knowledge by listing many different points. The AQA examinations reward quality, not quantity. As a general rule, it is best to focus on two or three points and to develop them in depth. Typically, for an evaluation question, you should identify two or three relevant ideas, explain their relevance (wherever possible using arguments that are specific to the situation or organisation in the question), and then draw a conclusion/make a decision based on your arguments. If, and only if, time

permits, you can add and develop further ideas. In short, you should move up the skills levels from knowledge to application and analysis, and on to evaluation as quickly as possible.

The AS examinations

Scheme of assessment

Each unit is tested in a separate examination:

- **BUSS1 'Planning and financing a business' (40% of AS; 20% of A-level)**
  Unit 1 is tested in BUSS1. This is a 75-minute paper with a maximum of 60 marks. It features short-answer questions and extended responses based on a mini case study.

- **BUSS2 'Managing a business' (60% of AS; 30% of A-level)**
  Unit 2 is tested in BUSS2. This is a 90-minute paper with a maximum of 80 marks. It features compulsory multi-part data-response questions based on two articles.

Unit 2 has a higher weighting because it builds on some of the topics covered in Unit 1 and has a greater level of content.

BUSS1 is designed as an initial foundation paper; BUSS2 is designed to be taken at a time when the more challenging skills (notably evaluation) have been developed more fully. Consequently, in comparison with BUSS2 the marks allocated in BUSS1 are slightly higher for knowledge (35% of the total in comparison with 27% for BUSS2) and slightly lower for evaluation (17% of the total in comparison with 22% for BUSS2).

The skills demonstrated in Unit 1 (BUSS1) are marked out of 60; the skills demonstrated in Unit 2 (BUSS2) are marked out of 80.

Table 5 shows the AQA guidelines for the number of marks to be awarded for each skill in the two papers.

Table 5 Marks awarded
for each skill at AS

Paper	Knowledge	Application	Analysis	Evaluation	Total
BUSS1	21	17	12	10	60
BUSS2	21	19	23	17	80

(Skills: Knowledge, Application, Analysis, Evaluation)

Your 'quality of language' is awarded a mark according to the skills/quality identified in your answer to those questions that require evaluation.

The case studies in this textbook are designed to reflect the AQA examinations. Thus the case studies in Unit 1 should provide a challenge comparable with that in the Unit 1 examination; similarly, Unit 2 questions requiring evaluation are pitched at the level demanded in the Unit 2 examination.

Unit 1

This is a 60-minute stimulus-response paper, based on a single mini case study of between 550 and 650 words. You will not see the stimulus material or questions before the examination.

The examination consists of two questions, both of which will be based on the material provided:

- Question 1 is worth 20 marks and consists of approximately six short questions, requiring definitions, calculations and explanations.
- Question 2 is worth 40 marks and consists of a relatively long analysis question and two questions requiring evaluation.

Unit 2

The examination consists of two sets of stimulus material, each about 300–350 words in length. These may be a written article, or may take the form of graphical or numerical data. Each is followed by four or five questions based on the material provided. It is likely, but not certain, that one of the articles will be based on a real-life business or situation.

The aim of the examination is to test the four sections of the Unit 2 specification (finance, people, operations management and marketing). However, there is no guarantee that there will be an even weighting of these four sections in any one paper. The specification encourages you to see business studies as an integrated whole, so you are advised to try to identify links between the four elements.

The structure of this book means that in Unit 2 a series of 'finance' questions is followed by a series of 'people' questions and so on through operations management and marketing. The actual examinations will not follow this pattern. Although the two articles (stimulus-response material) will incorporate elements of all four functional areas, there will be no formulaic approach so an article may feature all four functional areas or focus predominantly on one or two areas.

During your revision you are advised to practise answering actual past papers. AQA AS business studies past papers are available (in PDF format) from the AQA website (www.aqa.org.uk). Mark schemes for these examinations can also be downloaded.

How to approach the course and examination
Study advice
Keep up to date

This book contains many topical examples for you to use, but business studies is constantly changing. Although a textbook provides you with the theory,

reading newspapers and magazines, and using other topical media such as the internet, will help you to keep pace with changes. One thing is guaranteed: the business environment will have changed between the beginning and the end of your AS course, so there is no substitute for keeping an eye on the latest business news.

Build your own business studies dictionary

As you progress through this book, build up your own glossary/dictionary of terms. This will ease your revision and help to ensure that you can define terms clearly. Knowing the exact meaning of terms will also allow you to write relevantly on the other, non-definition questions.

Read each chapter thoroughly

On completion of each topic, make sure that you have read each page of the relevant chapter and use the questions at the end of each chapter to test yourself. If you adopt this approach for every chapter of the book, your revision will be just that: revising what you have already learned rather than learning material for the first time.

Complete the practice exercises and case studies

Tackle the practice exercises and case studies at the end of each chapter, even if not asked to do so by your teacher. Completion of the practice exercises will help you to check that you have understood the basic ideas in the chapter. Completion of the case studies will give you useful examination practice and help you to learn what you can achieve in the examination. It will also help you to develop the best approach to answering business studies questions.

Develop your communication and data-handling skills

There is no need to have studied GCSE business studies before starting the AS course; the AQA AS specification assumes that you have no prior understanding of the subject. However, the AS course does expect you to have already developed certain skills during your general GCSE programme. These skills are communication and the ability to use, prepare and interpret business data. You should be able to understand and apply averages (the mean, median and mode); prepare and interpret tables, graphs, histograms, bar charts and pie charts; and use index numbers.

Focus on the higher-level skills

It is tempting to focus chiefly on the facts when you are revising. Remember, the really high marks are given for the depth of your answers. Include scope for this in your revision so that you are able to earn marks for analysis and evaluation. Try to think of ways to apply your learning. For example, as people become richer they buy more products, but some firms (those making luxuries) will probably benefit more than those providing necessities.

Read the Chief Examiner's report

This report will alert you to the strengths and weaknesses shown by previous students and will help you to refine your approach. Along with previous examination papers and mark schemes, these reports are available in PDF format from the AQA website (www.aqa.org.uk).

Examination advice

Advice is provided throughout the book in the 'examiner's voice' boxes. Some of the key points are noted here:

- **Practice makes perfect.** Examination practice will help you to establish the best approach for you to take in the exam itself.
- **Plan the length of your answers.** After allowing for reading time, you will have about 1 minute for every mark awarded. Use this as a guide to the timing of your answers (6 marks = 6 minutes; 10 marks = 10 minutes etc.)
- **Use the trigger words and mark allocations.** Use these to determine the skills that you need to show in answering each question.
- **Move up the hierarchy of skills as quickly as possible.** Do not spend an excessive amount of time stating points when analysis and evaluation are required.
- **Read the wording of the question carefully.** Half a minute spent on deciding exactly what the examiner requires can save you 10 minutes of wasted effort.
- **Do not be tempted to display unnecessary knowledge.** Be prepared to accept that your favourite topic is not relevant to this examination if there are no questions on it.
- **State the obvious.** Some explanations might seem to be too easy, but they need to be included in your answer. The examiner can only reward what you have written.
- **Leave a space at the end of each answer.** If time permits, you can then add more detail at the end of your answer.

We wish you well in your studies and examinations, and hope that this book helps to provide you with the understanding needed to succeed. Good luck!

Acknowledgements

The authors would like to express their thanks to numerous individuals who have contributed to the completion of this book. Particular gratitude is shown to Philip Cross for the initial idea, unstinting support, good humour and patience.

John owes a debt of gratitude to Yvonne for her stoicism and tolerance during the writing, and to Lara, Nina, Dave, Marje, Tricia and Martin for their support over many years.

Gwen is grateful to John and Jessica, both of whom are always calm, relaxed and supportive, allowing her the time and space to complete this work.

Unit 1: Planning and financing a business

Starting a business

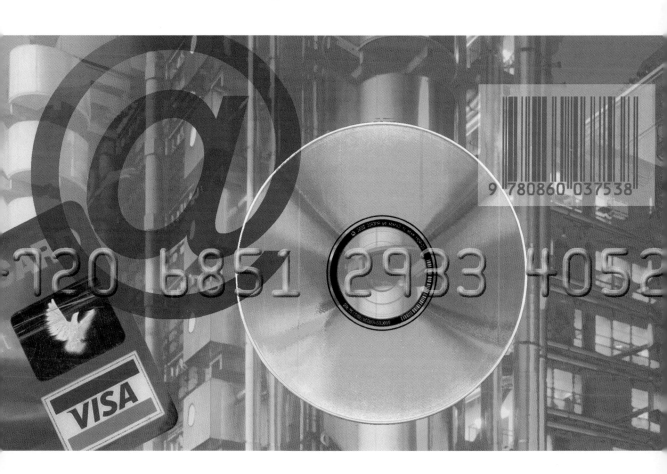

9 780860 037538

Enterprise

This chapter explains what is meant by the term 'enterprise' and the important contribution it makes to the development of a growing economy. It considers the motives for becoming an entrepreneur, the characteristics of successful entrepreneurs and the importance of their role in establishing new businesses. The importance of risk and rewards such as profit is examined, and the notion of opportunity cost is explained. Finally, government and other support for enterprise and entrepreneurs is identified.

Enterprise and entrepreneurs

Enterprise is an important concept that is being actively promoted by the UK government, through, for example, its support for start-up businesses and its curriculum requirements in schools. Reality television programmes, such as *The Apprentice*, *Dragons' Den*, *Mary Queen of Shops* and *Badger or Bust*, have encouraged a much wider interest in entrepreneurial activity. The fact that people have seen actual entrepreneurs succeed and make large amounts of money, often in quite short periods of time, has reinforced this interest.

Richard Branson

KEY TERMS

enterprise: almost any business or organisation can be called an enterprise but the term usually refers to the process by which new businesses are formed and new products and services created and brought to the market. Enterprises are usually led by an entrepreneur (see below).

enterprise skills: skills that allow an individual or organisation to respond effectively to changing market situations, including problem-solving skills, thinking and acting innovatively and creatively, and understanding the importance of risk and uncertainty. The definition of enterprise capability used by the Department for Children, Schools and Families includes innovation, creativity, risk management, risk taking and a 'can do' attitude.

entrepreneurs: individuals who have an idea that they develop by setting up a new business and encouraging it to grow. They take the risk and the subsequent profits that come with success or the losses that come with failure.

DID YOU KNOW?

The factors of production are the various elements (inputs) needed to produce goods or services (outputs). In economics, these are defined as land, labour, capital and enterprise. Land includes physical land on which to base the productive activity and also any necessary raw materials needed to produce the final product or service. Labour includes the contribution of all types of employee to the production of the finished product or service. Capital includes all machinery and buildings (i.e. factors made by people) that assist in the production of a finished product or service. Enterprise involves entrepreneurs identifying business projects to be undertaken and organising the other factors of production in order to produce goods and services.

The Sheffield College
Hillsborough LRC
Telephone: 0114 260 2254

FACT FILE

Social enterprises

In the private sector, there are both commercial or business enterprises and social enterprises. Social enterprises use business skills to solve social and environmental problems. They are usually charitable trusts, are founded for a social purpose, reinvest their profits in the company or the community, and attempt to change lives for the better. Examples are *The Big Issue* magazine and Jamie Oliver's 'Fifteen' restaurant. There are at least 55,000 social enterprises from the smallest community groups to larger businesses. Social enterprises operate in what has become known as the 'third sector' (i.e. neither the public nor the private sector). In May 2006, the prime minister announced a new Office of the Third Sector with a new minister for the third sector.

The characteristics of successful entrepreneurs include:
- determination and persistence
- passion
- the ability to spot and take advantage of opportunities
- relevant skills and expertise
- vision, creativity and innovation
- motivation to succeed and not be daunted by failure
- willingness to take risks — possibly the most important quality of an entrepreneur

The fact files in this and the next chapter illustrate all these characteristics. However, to be successful a business must have both a market and a comparative advantage (i.e. its product or service is in some way better or cheaper than what is already out there).

DID YOU KNOW?

Bill Gates, founder of Microsoft, dropped out of Harvard University less than halfway through his IT degree. Despite this, his drive, imagination, business acumen and obsession for detail turned Microsoft into one of the world's most successful companies and him into the world's richest man.

DID YOU KNOW?

Jordan Kensington, chief executive officer (CEO) of the Invincible Media Group, founder of the Urban Music Awards and promoter of British Music Week, suggests that 'there are two types of people in the world — doers and dreamers. The doers think of something and act now, which is what you have to do if you want to succeed' (www.invinciblemag.com).

FACT FILE

How many entrepreneurs?

Figures released by Barclays Bank in 2006 showed a substantial increase in the number of entrepreneurs. Estimates show that 110,300 new businesses started up in the first quarter of 2006 — almost a quarter more than in the same period in 2005 (88,800).

CHAPTER 1   Enterprise

Having an entrepreneurial attitude is vital in today's job market. Individuals change jobs more often, management structures have become less hierarchical, and working methods have become more network-orientated. All these factors require individuals and employees, in both small and large businesses, to be able to spot opportunities, take initiatives and adapt to changing circumstances. An understanding of what it means to be entrepreneurial is especially important for young people when they are weighing up decisions about their future.

The importance of risk and rewards such as profit

In the UK, people tend to be risk averse, with over one-third of those surveyed in the Global Entrepreneurship Monitor in 2006 saying that they are afraid of failure. As the majority of new businesses fail, such fears are well placed. Failure occurs for a number of reasons:

- lack of finance
- poor infrastructure
- skills shortages
- complexity of regulations or red tape

However, the ability to evaluate the risks and uncertainty that are an integral part of almost all business decisions is an important element of successful entrepreneurship. The fact files in this and the next chapter demonstrate that most entrepreneurs are happy to take risks if the potential rewards are great enough. Of course, this depends on them doing their research to ensure that all reasonable steps are taken to minimise the probability of failure. The outcome of successful risk-taking will be a profitable venture.

According to Andrew Davidson, author of *Smart Luck: The Seven Other Qualities of Great Entrepreneurs*, it is more than talent, ambition and drive that makes people like Richard Branson and Alan Sugar so successful: it is 'smart luck', which Davidson defines as taking a gamble when you know the odds. Many of the entrepreneurs he writes about, including Brent Hoberman of Lastminute.com, and Simon Woodroffe of Yo! Sushi, appeared to get started through coincidence and chance more than design or strategy. The fact file on Chris Carey's Collections provides another example of how being in the right place at the right time can lead to business success — if the entrepreneur is prepared to take a risk.

 FILE

Chris Carey's Collections

Chris Carey has built a £4 million business from scratch by buying the second-hand clothes that even charity shops cannot sell, washing and repairing them, and then sending them to places such as Africa, where they are sold in street markets. She even manages to make money from the clothes she cannot sell in this way — she passes them on to a company in Sweden that turns them into wadding for car seats and sofas.

On leaving school, Carey worked in a factory where she was taught how to use a sewing machine. She later ran stalls in London street markets, selling second-hand clothing that she had washed and repaired. After about 12 years of doing this, she was approached by a man who asked if she had enough clothes to fill a container to export to Africa. She did and has not looked back since.

Carey and her husband invested in a machine that pressed clothes into small bales so that more could be exported in one container. This was a risk and they mortgaged their house in order to do it. But it paid off and the business grew from there. The business now employs 140 staff and deals with up to 80 tonnes of clothing and bedding every day. The secret of her success is determination. Her advice is simple: 'If you have a dream, follow it. Don't ever let anyone put you down.'

Source: adapted from Bridge, R. (2007) 'Clothes recycling venture turned rags into riches. How I made it: Chris Carey, founder of Chris Carey's Collections', *Sunday Times*, 14 January.

The 'dragons' in the *Dragons' Den* programme are prepared to risk their own money by investing in a business, but only if they feel that there is a good probability that the venture will succeed and they will reap a reward. In this case, the reward is an increase in the value of a business that they will partly own, as well as the annual return on their investment.

Of course, sometimes the 'dragons' get it wrong and a business that they see as too risky may prove to be otherwise. Andrew Gordon's stabletable business is a case in point (see the fact file on p. 6).

A characteristic of most successful entrepreneurs is the ability to learn from their mistakes and try again. Simon Woodroffe, the founder of Yo! Sushi, said: 'I looked at what every entrepreneur has in common and I found one thing: they all make mistakes, lots of them.' The fact file on Tyrrells Crisps (p. 6) provides an example of risk-taking followed by failure, followed by further risk-taking that eventually resulted in success — a cycle that is common to many successful entrepreneurs.

CHAPTER 1 Enterprise

 FILE

Stabletable

When Andrew Gordon unveiled his invention for propping up wobbly table legs on *Dragons' Den* in 2005, the panel of business experts dismissed it with howls of laughter. The plastic device, which can be adjusted according to the extent of the wobble, was branded 'the most ridiculous idea' she had ever heard of by Rachel Elnaugh, the founder of the failed Red Letter Days business. Despite this, the business is proving to be a success and sales of the stabletable product have passed the £1 million mark.

In the UK, the business has recently won an order from the Exam Officers' Association for 200,000 stabletables. It is also negotiating with Tesco, ASDA, IKEA and B&Q to get its device in their stores, and even Kensington Palace has bought some for its tearooms. Outside the UK, it has received orders for 300,000 devices from China, and Gordon has struck a deal with

The Dollar Chest, a discount chain in the USA, where the device will be renamed 'WobbleWizard'.

Gordon says he came up with the idea after seeing tables in a pub propped up with beer mats and napkins. He started collecting pieces of cardboard from cereal packets and seeing which shapes and thicknesses worked best. He then arranged a company in China to manufacture them.

The stabletable is a simple design with eight plastic leaves pinned together. It retails online for £1. Gordon said, 'I think I've got a 3-year window to do as well as I can.' Elnaugh, the *Dragons' Den* expert, said: 'I'm really glad Andrew's done well, but if you're investing, you want to be seeing a return in 6 months, not 3 years.'

Sources: www.stabletable.co.uk; Bale, J. (2007) '"Ridiculous" idea has last laugh in the Dragons' Den', *The Times*, 20 April; Hawkes, S. (2007) 'Inventor out to crack America with wobble-buster the dragons rejected', *The Times*, 22 August.

 FILE

Tyrrells Potato Chips

William Chase took on the family farm when he was 19 years old and ran it for 8 years before debt and badly judged deals with supermarkets took him under. After bankruptcy, he spent 10 years as a potato trader. At the age of 40, he had an inspirational idea to produce and market up-market, 'sustainable' crisps. It worked — so much so that Chase had to fight off Tesco, which wanted to sell Tyrrells' products under its own brand. Chase is the only UK crisp-maker to carry out the process from seed to bag. The crisps, made

from root vegetables as well as potatoes, are hand-fried in small batches. It was a hard decision saying no to Tesco, which has 31% of the UK grocery market. 'When you're offered the chance to expand a business that you've raised from nothing, your instinct is to say yes. But I knew going into the mass market would take the edge off the brand. I'd lose my major suppliers such as Selfridges. Going bankrupt...makes you braver. I know how failure tastes and it's not the end of the world.'

Source: adapted from Shephard, A. (2007) 'The Antripreneurs', *The Times magazine*, 3 February.

The notion of opportunity cost

 TERM

Opportunity cost: the 'real cost' of taking a particular action or the next best alternative forgone, i.e. the next best thing that you could have chosen but did not.

Resources, including time and money, are scarce, so choosing to pursue one thing inevitably results in forgoing something else. For example, the time you have available in the evenings and at weekends is limited and you may have to choose between going out with friends or, say, revising a business topic for a class test. The 'real cost', as opposed to the monetary cost, of spending an evening out with friends may thus be your failure to understand the business topic and your resulting low mark in the test. Alternatively, the 'real cost' of an evening spent revising could be the missed opportunity of attending a concert.

Unit 1: Planning and financing a business

This 'real cost' is known as the **opportunity cost** and is the next best alternative forgone, i.e. the next best thing that you could have chosen but did not.

Opportunity cost is a vital concept in business because there are always alternative decisions that could be made. With a limited budget, a school may have to decide whether to refurbish the canteen or build an all-weather games pitch. The real cost of choosing to build the games pitch is the ongoing problems of the old, overcrowded canteen. If the founders of Innocent Drinks had decided to remain in their original jobs rather than pursuing the smoothie venture, the opportunity cost would have been the chance they had of developing a highly successful business and the large amount of wealth they have subsequently made (see fact file). The opportunity cost that William Chase of Tyrrells faced on taking the risk of deciding to remain independent was the guaranteed sales that he would have made if he had entered into a contract with Tesco (see fact file).

e EXAMINER'S VOICE

Ensure that you understand fully the concept of opportunity cost as it is relevant to most business decisions and therefore to most areas of the AS specification.

Motives for becoming an entrepreneur

The UK is becoming an increasingly entrepreneurial place and more people are interested in setting up businesses. Possible reasons for this include:

- long-term low interest rates that make it easier to borrow money to start a business
- a change in the political climate so that the government supports enterprise and the entrepreneurial spirit
- increasing affluence, which often means that people start to look for meaning in their lives — one way of doing this is to try to fulfil the dream of starting their own business

Entrepreneurs are extremely diverse: they include men and women, young and old, and those from differing ethnic, social and educational backgrounds. However, statistics suggest that most successful entrepreneurs start to build their businesses before the age of 44, and many start their entrepreneurial activities while still at school. All the fact files in this and the next chapter support this and most of the best-known entrepreneurs are renowned for starting young. While still at school, Sir Alan Sugar, the owner of Amstrad and star of *The Apprentice* made more money than his father through enterprising projects. Sir Richard Branson began his first Virgin project soon after leaving school.

Entrepreneurs engage in entrepreneurial activity for a variety of reasons. Most will want to make money. Some will want to gain more freedom at work, or sustain a going concern such as a family business. Others may be concerned with providing employment for the local community, sometimes in the form of social enterprises.

Alan Sugar

 FILE

Rich list

The information in Table 1.1 illustrates just how successful many entrepreneurs have been. It is taken from the 2007 Times Rich List, which identifies, in order, the wealthiest 500 people in the UK.

Government research indicates that a typical entrepreneur in the UK is most likely to be a white man aged around 36 years, who has some form of vocational training or secondary-school qualification. He will probably be motivated by the freedom that running his own business offers him, or the desire to make money.

Position	Name	Business information
2	Roman Abramovich	Oil billionaire and owner of Chelsea football club. Started out in Moscow making cheap plastic products.
7	Sir Philip Green	Retailing. Owner of Bhs and the Arcadia group (including Burton, Dorothy Perkins, Topshop, Topman, Miss Selfridge, Outfit, Evans and Wallis). Entrepreneur of the Year in 2002. In 2007, employed Kate Moss to design and launch a collection for Topshop.
11	Sir Richard Branson	Virgin transport, mobile phones, internet and holidays.
49	Sir Stelios Haji-Ioannou	easyGroup, including aviation and shipping. Knighted for 'services to entrepreneurship' in 2006. Says his favourite business is 'the next one'.
59	Sir James Dyson	Household appliances, particularly the Dyson bagless vacuum cleaner.
74	Charles Dunstone	Carphone Warehouse — mobile phones.
84	Sir Alan Sugar	Amstrad electronics and property. Stars in the reality television show *The Apprentice*.
280	Toni Mascolo	Toni and Guy hairdressing salons.
343	Kirit and Meena Pathak	Food products. Their Lancashire business produces Patak's curry products that are sold in 75 countries.
351	Duncan Bannatyne	Nursing homes, children's nurseries and fitness clubs. One of the entrepreneur 'dragons' on *Dragons' Den*.
414	Bernard Matthews	Turkey farming. Business has been seriously affected by the discovery of the bird flu virus in some of its products in 2007, and by Jamie Oliver's campaign to get Turkey Twizzlers removed from school dinner menus.
438	Peter Jones	Mobile phones. Entrepreneur 'dragon' on *Dragons' Den*.

Table 1.1 Selected entrepreneurs on the Times Rich List 2007

Government support for enterprise and entrepreneurs

The government believes that an environment that encourages enterprise and supports people who take opportunities and risks is crucial for improving productivity. A strong entrepreneurial base is essential for encouraging growth and prosperity in a modern economy. New and more dynamic businesses increase competitive pressures in markets, and facilitate the introduction of new ideas and technologies and more efficient working practices.

A successful enterprise culture, in the form of small and medium-sized enterprises (SMEs), boosts an economy's productivity by increasing competitive pressure. This forces existing businesses to increase their efficiency in order to stay in the market. If existing businesses are unable to match the productivity of new or rapidly growing SMEs, either they are forced to leave the

market or their market share is reduced. This then increases the productivity of the market as a whole. In addition, any efficiency gains can be passed on to consumers through lower prices and greater choice.

Despite the rapid growth of the SME sector since the 1970s, rates of entrepreneurial activity in the UK remain moderate by international standards, particularly when compared with the USA. As a result, the government has introduced measures to make it easier to start up and run a business, and to support a growing business. It has done this by:

■ reducing business taxes and trying to establish and maintain a modern and competitive business tax system
■ reducing the regulatory burden on enterprises
■ reducing barriers to raising finance for small businesses
■ improving the support for small and new businesses
■ promoting a change in the UK's enterprise culture (see the fact file on Enterprise Insight)
■ encouraging business start-ups in economically deprived regions of the UK
■ introducing legislation to promote competition
■ funding projects to raise awareness of enterprise among under-represented groups of people
■ reviewing how to encourage unemployed people to move into self-employment
■ giving financial support to voluntary and not-for-profit organisations that are carrying out excellent work

 FILE

Enterprise Insight

The government supports a major national campaign by Enterprise Insight to create a significant shift in the enterprise culture of the UK, including national Enterprise Weeks. Enterprise Insight is a campaign coalition, founded by the UK's leading business organisations, education bodies and Regional Development Agencies. The campaigns focus on young people, providing inspirational role models and peer networks to encourage them to be enterprising.

The Enterprise Directorate (previously the Small Business Service) in the Department for Business, Enterprise and Regulatory Reform (BERR, formerly the Department of Trade and Industry) is the government's expert policy unit on small-business issues. In most regions, government support in terms of Regional Economic Development Agencies, Economic Development Units and Business Links is available. Other local and national organisations, such as local city councils and the Prince's Trust, exist to help entrepreneurs develop their ideas, by providing advice and funding. In addition, many university students have started their own businesses, benefiting from university enterprise centres, where they gain advice, help in developing entrepreneurial skills and business planning, and sometimes office accommodation.

CHAPTER 1   Enterprise

 DO YOU THINK?

The government believes that equipping young people with vital skills is a way of securing the future economic success of the UK. This is not just about developing the next generation of entrepreneurs, but about encouraging young people to develop valuable enterprise-related skills for their futures. Since September 2005, all Key Stage 4 students have had an entitlement to the equivalent of 5 days' activity each year to develop their enterprise capability. In the Budget of April 2007, the government announced further funding of £180 million over the next 3 years to encourage this development in schools.

How valuable has the enterprise education you have received been in developing your entrepreneurial skills?

DID YOU KNOW?

Young Enterprise is a national charity that runs a number of schemes to encourage enterprise in schools and colleges. The Young Enterprise mission is to 'inspire and equip young people to learn and succeed through enterprise'. Students involved in the Young Enterprise scheme set up their own companies, sell shares to raise finance, appoint directors and report to their investors at the end of the year. Many of you may get involved in this scheme and apply the business knowledge you gain during your course to making your enterprise a success.

FACT FILE

Enterprising Britain

Enterprising Britain is a nationwide competition to find the most enterprising place in the UK — the city, town, place or area in the country that is best improving economic prospects and encouraging enterprise. It was introduced in 2004/05 and developed in partnership with Regional Development Agencies. It aims to:

- identify and recognise successful activities and initiatives undertaken to promote enterprise and entrepreneurship
- showcase and share examples of best practice in enterprise policy and implementation
- create more awareness of the importance of enterprise in society

DO YOU THINK?

Having worked through this chapter, you should now be more aware of the importance of enterprise. To what extent do you think student debt, pressures to get on the housing ladder and the necessity of saving for retirement stifle risk-taking? Could the government, whether in terms of taxation, funding or other measures, play a bigger role in encouraging youth enterprise?

FACT FILE

SMEs among underrepresented groups

In terms of business ownership in the UK, two large sections of society are not represented to the extent that might be expected, given their numbers in the population: women and certain minority ethnic groups.

Source: *Annual Small Business Survey 2005*, BERR.

QUESTIONS FOR DISCUSSION

Having read the information and fact files in this chapter, try to answer the following questions. The questions can be used as written exercises or as the basis for discussion about important issues related to enterprise and entrepreneurs.

1 To what extent are passion and determination sufficient for business success?

2 Are there certain characteristics that all successful entrepreneurs have?

3 What appear to be the main reasons for becoming an entrepreneur?

4 Is the ability to cope with uncertainty, make mistakes and take risks an essential characteristic of a successful entrepreneur? Illustrate your answer with actual examples.

5 Should the government provide more money to support start-up businesses? If so, how might it judge which entrepreneurs or businesses to support?

6 Can government agencies ever be really effective in providing advice for entrepreneurs?

PRACTICE EXERCISE   Total: 40 marks (30 minutes)

1 Define the term 'enterprise'. *(2 marks)*

2 What is an entrepreneur? *(3 marks)*

3 Give three examples of successful entrepreneurs. *(3 marks)*

4 Identify four characteristics of successful entrepreneurs. *(4 marks)*

5 Explain why the ability to take risks is important in developing a successful business. *(4 marks)*

6 Define the term 'opportunity cost' and give examples of how it might apply to you as a student, to your school or college, and to a business. *(8 marks)*

7 Suggest three reasons why an individual might want to become an entrepreneur. *(3 marks)*

8 Why are an enterprising culture and people with entrepreneurial skills important for the UK economy? *(5 marks)*

9 Explain three ways in which the government supports enterprise and entrepreneurs. *(6 marks)*

10 State two organisations other than central government that provide support for new businesses. *(2 marks)*

CASE STUDY   Creating an enterprise culture

The data in Table 1.2 are taken from the report, *Creating an Enterprise Culture*, by HM Treasury (January 2004). The table shows the percentage of 'yes' or positive responses to questions about attitudes to enterprise. Study the table and answer the questions that follow.

Table 1.2
Attitudes to
enterprise

	Are there good start-up opportunities? (%)	Do you have the skills to start up? (%)	Do you fear failure? (%)	Is being an entrepreneur a good career? (%)	Do entrepreneurs have high status? (%)
UK	39.0	54.2	31.7	51.2	71.0
East Midlands	37.3	53.3	30.4	48.4	70.6
East of England	42.7	56.3	30.5	47.8	67.8
London	38.1	56.1	32.4	51.0	71.3
North East	33.3	50.0	33.8	53.5	76.5
North West	34.1	49.2	31.1	54.4	70.4
South East	46.5	56.7	31.5	47.7	64.0
South West	43.2	57.4	28.4	51.1	69.7
West Midlands	36.5	55.8	32.0	55.5	72.4
Yorkshire and Humberside	34.4	52.0	35.0	51.0	75.9
Northern Ireland	35.7	47.2	38.1	58.7	76.8
Scotland	39.3	53.2	30.3	50.3	73.4
Wales	37.0	53.4	32.3	52.0	73.8

Questions

Total: 35 marks (45 minutes)

1 a Which area of the UK has the best start-up opportunities? *(2 marks)*
  b In which area of the UK are people least likely to fear failure? *(2 marks)*
  c Using the data, decide which area of the UK is likely to be the best place to start a business and explain the reasons for your answer. *(6 marks)*

2 a Study the results for the area in which you live. Analyse the reasons for the survey results for that area. *(10 marks)*
  b Identify reasons why some areas of the UK might be more favourable than others for starting a business. Evaluate which of these reasons might be the most important. *(15 marks)*

9 780860 037538

Generating and protecting business ideas

This chapter considers the sources of business ideas for small businesses with limited resources. It also focuses on franchising as a means of getting into business. In this context, it includes a discussion of the formation and operation of franchises, and the benefits and pitfalls of operating them. The chapter concludes with a consideration of how business ideas are protected using copyright, patents and trademarks.

Sources of business ideas

As we saw in Chapter 1, people who start businesses have many different motivations. Some are motivated by a desire for independence or the possibility of receiving high profits. If someone has been made redundant and has received a substantial lump-sum redundancy payment, he or she may see it as an opportunity to do something different. Others may be motivated by a commitment to an idea or product, or the development of a hobby or creative talent. A profitable opportunity could arise if an invention can be made into a commercial opportunity, or from the purchase of a franchise or by spotting a gap in the market. Whatever the motivation behind it, every entrepreneurial success story starts with an idea.

Finding a good idea that will be profitable is not easy. Given that approximately one-third of all new businesses fail in their first 3 years, an entrepreneur has to think carefully about the idea for a new business and the likelihood of its success. Ideas can be generated by the process of brainstorming or can come from the entrepreneur's own personal and/or business experience. Research suggests that there are four major sources of ideas for entrepreneurs, as listed below.

INGRAM

Spotting trends and anticipating their impact

This was the approach adopted by Innocent Drinks, the business that makes fruit smoothies. The company, which was launched in 1999, tapped into the growing desire for healthier lifestyles (see fact file on p. 4).

Identifying a market niche

This involves noticing something that is missing from the market or that can be improved on. Rachel Elnaugh spotted a gap in the market when

she could not find any interesting presents to buy for young professional people, who could afford to buy most things themselves. She created Red Letter Days, a business selling extraordinary experiences, such as a champagne hot-air balloon flight, a trip in a powerboat or a session in a recording studio, as gifts. (Red Letter Days eventually collapsed, but it has been copied by many other companies since.) Oliver Bridge set up the shoe company Bigger Feet Ltd

in September 2004 at the age of 15. Having size 13 feet and not being able to find shoes in this size, he realised that there was a gap in the market. James Murray Wells set up Glasses Direct, offering spectacles online at little more than cost price, after buying a pair of glasses from one of the large high-street chains and being shocked at how expensive they were (this is the case study at the end of this chapter).

Copying ideas from other countries

Many entrepreneurs have found and copied successful ideas from abroad. For example, Howard Schultz of Starbucks did not invent the espresso coffee machine or the coffee bar, but he saw the coffee bar culture in Italy and thought that it could be introduced in the USA. In a different way, Ali Clabburn spotted an idea in Germany for car sharing that he has adapted and introduced in the UK (see fact file).

FACT FILE

Liftshare

Thirty-year-old Ali Clabburn set up his innovative car-sharing scheme while he was in his final year of university. His aim was to help alleviate congestion and pollution in the UK, while offering people the chance to save money on fuel bills. He first saw car sharing in action when he was travelling through Germany in his gap year. He discovered a network of car-sharing bureaux at major train stations that provided a cheaper way of getting around than public transport.

Clabburn travelled frequently between his home town of Norwich and university in Bristol. Taking the train was expensive, and he knew that someone must be making the same journey in a car who would appreciate being able to share the costs. He realised that this was a whole market that no one was servicing. Around this time the internet was beginning to take off, and he saw its potential.

In 1999, Glastonbury Festival got in touch. Thousands of people descend on Glastonbury every summer for the festival, and it was causing a great deal of congestion on the local roads. The organisers asked him to build them a branded car-share website so that people travelling to the festival could share lifts. It was a huge success and has saved an estimated 15,000 car journeys to the festival each year.

Glastonbury was also a breakthrough for Liftshare; it showed how the organisation could make money and highlighted the importance of finding people with a common link. This has served as the basis of the business model: allowing the public to sign up free to the national car-sharing scheme, while earning revenue from clients who pay a one-off sum plus a regular licence fee for setting up a scheme for their employees or customers. The organisation has now grown substantially and works with almost 600 clients across the UK, including local authorities, hospitals, universities, schools and communities, building branded and private car-share schemes.

Source: www.liftshare.org

Taking a scientific approach

Entrepreneurs sometimes work in a laboratory or university to invent original new products. As a third-year computer science student, Richard Jones of Last.fm developed the Audioscrobbler that eventually made him a millionaire (see fact file). James Dyson developed the Dyson bagless vacuum cleaner through technical research, having recognised that traditional vacuum cleaners did not suck up the dirt effectively. He is reputed to have made 5,127 prototypes of the product before he perfected the final design. Inventors like James Dyson, who start a business on the strength of a new invention, have the benefit of a short-term market niche, until the 'me-too' products start to appear. The fact file about Dyson's fight against Hoover illustrates the importance of taking out patents to protect such ideas (see p. 20).

 FILE

Last.fm

Felix Miller, Martin Stiksel and Richard Jones, the three entrepreneurs behind Last.fm, the music and social networking website launched in 2003, became internet millionaires in June 2007, receiving windfalls of nearly £20 million each after selling their business.

Last.fm — an online radio station that creates personal playlists — has about 20 million members in 200 countries. The site can create the playlists by tracking and analysing users' listening habits using software called Audioscrobbler, developed by 24-year-old Richard Jones, a computer science graduate. The site was tipped as the next big thing after MySpace in the sphere of music and social networking online. It was named in the belief that its founders could create a music stream personalised to each listener, so that there would be no need for anyone to struggle to find a music station that met their needs.

Stiksel, 32, an Austrian former DJ, developed the original idea for the site with 30-year-old Miller, from Germany, before teaming up with Jones in 2003. Richard Jones is the youngest of the three founders and the only Briton. He joined up with the other two after finishing his degree. When Stiksel and Miller heard about Audioscrobbler, they immediately took a train to Southampton to convince Jones to join the venture. He moved to London, becoming chief technical officer and taking a 15% stake.

EXAMINER'S VOICE

Business ideas and opportunities come from a variety of sources, but all require a great deal of hard work and clear thinking. Although some look as if they were a case of having the right idea at the right time (i.e. luck), most are '5% inspiration and 95% perspiration'. When planning answers to questions in this area, be aware of the importance of thinking through exactly what needs to be considered in assessing a business idea.

EXAMINER'S VOICE

All business decisions include an element of risk. In your answers to questions on this area, do not assume, as many students do, that if a business venture or opportunity is risky, it should be abandoned. The most profitable opportunities are often the riskiest. Risk needs to be assessed and taken into account but, unless extreme, it should not necessarily deter action.

Franchising

KEY TERM

franchise: when a business (the franchisor) gives another business (the franchisee) the right to supply its product or service.

In addition to developing their own business ideas, people wishing to set up in business can purchase a franchise. Instead of setting up a business from scratch, a franchise allows an individual to use a proven business idea, to trade under a well-known brand name, and to gain help and support. Well-known businesses that offer franchises include Prontaprint, Dyno-Rod and Burger King.

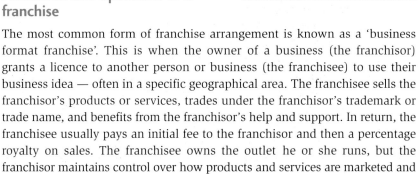

Formation and operation of a franchise

The most common form of franchise arrangement is known as a 'business format franchise'. This is when the owner of a business (the franchisor) grants a licence to another person or business (the franchisee) to use their business idea — often in a specific geographical area. The franchisee sells the franchisor's products or services, trades under the franchisor's trademark or trade name, and benefits from the franchisor's help and support. In return, the franchisee usually pays an initial fee to the franchisor and then a percentage royalty on sales. The franchisee owns the outlet he or she runs, but the franchisor maintains control over how products and services are marketed and sold, and how their business idea is used.

FACT FILE

Franchising survey

The British Franchise Association, in conjunction with the NatWest bank, produces an annual survey about franchising. Its 2007 survey provides the following statistics about the franchise industry:
- industry turnover: £10.8 billion
- total franchisees: 33,900
- total employment: 371,600
- average investment: £50,500
- profitability: 93% of all franchisees claim to be profitable after 5 years

Source: NatWest/BFA Franchise Survey 2007.

FILE

Other types of franchise

Other types of sales relationship may sometimes be referred to as franchises. These include:

- Distributorship and dealership, where the franchisee sells the products but does not usually trade under the franchise name. In this case, the franchisee has more freedom over how his or her business is run. This is common in car sales, where a particular showroom may be the main dealership for a particular make of car (e.g. Toyota).
- Agency, where the franchisee sells goods or services on behalf of the supplier (franchisor).
- Licensing, where the franchisee has a licence giving him or her the right to make and sell the licensor's product. As in distributorships and dealerships, there are usually no extra restrictions on how the business is run.

Benefits of operating as a franchise

Franchises offer the following benefits to franchisees:

- They involve the least amount of risk for a start-up business and, as a result, a high percentage of them are successful. For example, while approximately 75% of new businesses last for more than 2 years, for franchise businesses the figure is closer to 95%. As indicated in the fact file on p. 16, 93% of franchises claim to be profitable after 5 years.
- Franchise businesses usually have established brand names, which means the franchisee is investing in a business with a proven track record of success.
- Financing the business may be easier because banks are often more willing to lend money to someone wishing to buy a franchise with a proven reputation than to an unknown, new business.
- The franchisee is likely to incur lower advertising and promotional costs, as the business is likely to benefit from national advertising or promotion by the franchisor.
- The franchisee usually has exclusive rights in his or her area, as the franchisor will not sell any other franchises in the same region.
- Relationships with suppliers are likely to have been established by the franchisor.
- The franchisor offers support and training, usually funded by an ongoing management service fee paid by the franchisee. The franchisor helps in setting up the business, including putting together the business plan, assisting the franchisee in gaining suitable funding for the business, selecting a site, and giving operational and technical support where relevant. As franchisees gain more experience, they usually require less advice and guidance from the franchisor. As a result, many franchisors provide intensive initial support followed by more general ongoing support and advice once the business is up and running successfully.

DID YOU KNOW?

In the USA over half of all retail sales are generated through franchised outlets.

FACT FILE

Benefits of operating a franchise for the franchisor

- The franchisor receives a regular reward for the value of the intellectual property and concept that has been developed, while the franchisee provides the capital for expansion into other sites and locations, and takes on the risk involved.
- Rapid expansion is easier to achieve with franchising than it is with the more traditional company-owned expansion. The franchisor does not need to invest in additional premises or staff, and can instead focus on developing the business idea.
- By speeding up expansion, franchising enables the franchisor to achieve higher economies of scale

earlier, a stronger brand awareness and a larger share of the market more quickly. It may also allow the franchisor to establish market leadership more easily than if he or she had used a non-franchising format.

- Unlike licensing and other distribution agreements, the franchisor retains control over the quality of the products and services, and the way they are marketed and distributed. Under the franchise agreement, the franchisee is required to maintain a specified standard of service, which can be monitored through mystery shoppers, client feedback and field visits.

Possible pitfalls of operating as a franchise

- There is always a possibility that the franchisor has not researched the business carefully, and has not tackled teething problems, set up robust systems and procedures, or built a sufficiently strong brand image.
- Costs may be higher than expected. As well as the initial costs of buying the franchise, a franchisee must pay ongoing royalties to the franchisor in the form of a percentage of turnover, and may have to agree to buy all its supplies from the franchisor. This will limit a franchisee's ability to earn high profits.
- Other franchisees could give the brand a bad reputation and this may have an adverse impact on all franchisees.
- The franchise agreement usually includes restrictions on how the business should be run. Therefore, a franchisee may not be able to make changes to suit the local market or, in general, use its initiative in making decisions as much as an independent business could.
- Franchisees are required to sign non-competition clauses, agreeing not to set up competing businesses in the franchisor's industry for a significant period after the end of the franchise agreement.
- Franchisees must be approved by the franchisor, so an existing franchisee may find it difficult to sell the franchise.
- If the franchisor goes out of business or changes the way it does things, this will have a direct impact on the franchisee's business.

Protecting a business idea

Business ideas can be protected by using copyright, patents and trade marks.

Copyright

KEY TERM

copyright: legal protection against copying for authors, composers and artists.

If a business creates or employs someone to create an original piece of literary, dramatic, musical or artistic work, it automatically holds the copyright on the work. The material could range from books, information leaflets and films, to computer programs and sound recordings. The material cannot then be copied without permission from the owner of the copyright. The law allows the owners of the copyright to decide whether it can be copied and adapted, and allows them to charge a royalty or licence fee.

In general, copyright protection for literary, dramatic, musical and artistic works lasts until 70 years after the death of the creator, but copyright in sound recordings, broadcasts and cable programmes lasts 50 years. See the fact file below for the impact of this on pop singers. Unlike patents, there is no requirement to register an author's copyright. The law on copyright is governed by the Copyright, Designs and Patents Act 1988. Copyright is indicated by the symbol ©.

 FILE

Musicians' copyright pleas fall on deaf ears

The music industry has reacted with outrage to the government's rejection of pleas to extend the period that musicians get royalties from their tracks beyond the current 50 years. The Who's lead singer, Roger Daltrey, was one of the first artists to attack the government's stance. 'Thousands of musicians have no pensions and rely on royalties to support themselves. These people helped to create one of Britain's most successful industries, poured money into the British economy and enriched people's lives. They are not asking for a handout, just a

fair reward for their creative endeavours,' he said.

The campaign for a longer copyright period in the UK has recently gathered pace as the fruits of the late-1950s explosion of UK rock'n'roll will start falling out of copyright soon. A broad coalition of industry groups and artists including Cliff Richard, whose earliest recordings will be among the first to drop out of copyright from 2008, have loudly campaigned for the copyright term to be extended to 95 years.

Source: Allen, K. (2007) *Guardian Unlimited*, 24 July.

Patents

If an individual invents a new process, piece of equipment, component or product, he or she may apply for a patent in order to prevent other people copying the invention and then making, selling, importing or using it without permission. To register a patent, the inventor must provide full drawings of the invention for the UK Intellectual Property Office (UK-IPO), demonstrate that the ideas have original features, and promise that the ideas are his or her own. The Copyright, Designs and Patents Act 1988 gives patent holders the monopoly right to use, make, license or sell the invention for up to 20 years after it has been registered.

The following issues need to be considered in relation to patenting an idea:

■ Holding a patent allows the product or process to be developed further, to be positioned in the market, and to reap benefits in terms of revenue and profits.

 TERM

patent: an official document granting the holder the right to be the only user or producer of a newly invented product or process for a specified period.

CHAPTER 2

Generating and protecting business ideas

- Having a patent means that the invention becomes the property of the inventor, which means that it can be bought, sold, rented or licensed — and can therefore be a useful bargaining tool when trying to persuade manufacturers and investors to help the business.
- Purchasing a small business that has an existing patent might be an attractive proposition for a large business, simply in order to obtain the patent.
- Although a patent can be a valuable asset for a business, taking a patent application through to completion can be a complex and expensive process. As a result, the cost of effectively developing and launching a product for which a patent is held may be too high for a small business and the business may sell the patent. Although filing an initial application for a patent in the UK is free, further fees are payable at each stage of the process and the greatest expense is for the services of a patent agent, whose fees can run into thousands of pounds. Moreover, if a business is planning to sell its product abroad, the cost will be much higher — the UK-IPO suggests about £32,000 for patent protection across Europe.
- Although a patent grants the inventor rights that can be valuable, there is no agency for enforcing patents. Therefore, the holder has to be willing to take those who infringe the patent to court (see the fact file on *Dyson* v *Hoover*). An individual inventor is unlikely to be able to afford the legal costs and hence new patents are often sold on to larger businesses.

 FILE

Dyson v *Hoover*

The inventor who sparked the vacuum cleaner wars with his revolutionary bagless machine won a multimillion-pound court battle yesterday. A High Court judge ruled that Hoover was guilty of stealing ideas from James Dyson and had infringed the patent on bagless cleaners...In March 2000, Hoover brought out its own version, the Vortex, using a new 'triple cyclone' machine. Mr Dyson claimed that it was a blatant copy of the cleaner he had spent 20 years developing...Mr Dyson...said after the hearing: 'I spent 20 years developing the technology and I am very pleased to see Hoover, who made a lot of false claims about their product, have been found guilty of patent infringement. I am also pleased on behalf of other small businesses and inventors, who should be encouraged to take out patents by the result of this case.'

Source: adapted from an article in *The Times*, October 2000.

 FILE

Virgin v *Contour*

In the cut-throat battle for business-class airline passengers, any competitive advantage is jealously guarded — even the shape of the seats. Virgin Atlantic is understood to have started legal proceedings to protect the design of its Upper Class seat after competitors started to roll out suspiciously similar seats. Industry sources said that Sir Richard Branson's airline was suing Contour, a Wales-based

seat manufacturer, for breach of patents. Virgin spent £50 million developing the herringbone shape and layout for its Upper Class seat, and introduced it with great fanfare in 2003.

Business-class tickets, which generate most of an airline's profits, are sold on features such as the flattest bed and best in-flight entertainment. The largest airlines develop their own seats in order to have a unique sales proposition. Virgin has two patents covering the shape and configuration of the seats and the technology used to lower the seat into a bed. Contour built Virgin's seats, but the company has also supplied herringbone-shaped seats to Delta, Cathay Pacific, Air Canada and JetAir. Virgin is thought to be seeking damages from Contour and demanding that these other airlines remove their seats, which could cost them millions of pounds in lost revenue.

Virgin has always sought to differentiate itself from large competitors by developing innovative service ideas. Upper Class passengers have a bar area on board and can get massages at their seat. Ticket prices for an Upper Class seat from London to New York are about £4,000 return and the airline is jealously protective of this market.

Source: adapted from Robertson, D. (2007) 'Airliners in the hot seat over Virgin's Upper Class patents', *The Times*, 22 October.

FACT FILE

Disposable contact lenses

Ron Hamilton, the Scottish entrepreneur who invented daily disposable contact lenses, used a patent agent to help him put together his patent application and ensure it was sufficiently precise and watertight. He also entered into an agreement with British Technology Group, which markets bright ideas. He assigned the patent to the group in return for 50% of the ensuing income. The total cost of getting all the international patents granted eventually ran to £200,000, a sum that Hamilton would never have been able to afford.

Once the patent was granted, Hamilton was able to get additional investment and within 3 years he was able to sell the business, including the intellectual property, to Bausch and Lomb, the eyewear company, for £33 million.

He said, 'Patents are central to creating value in a business. Intellectual property runs right through every aspect of the business — it is not an add-on. You can develop the business without a patent, but it will be valueless because it can be replicated. You must give yourself a competitive advantage and to do that you must look at every aspect of protecting your intellectual property: for example, making sure that it features in your conditions of employment. Without a patent agent the intellectual property would have been pinched, there is no question about that. You need to include specific terms to give your patent the solidity it needs. I believe it is a misconception that you can file a patent for £200. You probably can — but you will lose it in about 2 years because you get what you pay for.'

Source: adapted from Bridge, R. (2007) 'See how vital patents can be', *Sunday Times*, 14 January.

EXAMINER'S VOICE

Think of patents as barriers to entry: i.e. strategic tools that protect businesses from possible competitors entering the market.

Trademarks

Trademarks can be powerful marketing tools, helping customers to recognise the products of a business, and distinguishing them from those of competitors. In order to prevent rivals from copying a symbol or style of wording, the trademark must be registered at the UK Intellectual Property office (or UK-IPO). Once the trademark has been registered, the company has exclusive rights to its use. Trademarks are indicated by the symbol ®.

DID YOU KNOW?

The phrase 'Have a break, have a KitKat' was first used in a television advert in 1957. In a recent survey, when prompted with 'Have a break', 98% of Britons responded with 'Have a KitKat'. Despite this, Nestlé, the chocolate bar's Swiss maker, was refused a trademark for the slogan in May 2002. The case then went to the High Court, where it was decided that the slogan 'Have a break' on its own was not distinctive enough. The High Court therefore decided that Nestlé could not claim that it owned the phrase. This meant that Nestlé's rival, Mars, was free to begin a confectionery war by launching its own new product called 'Have a Break'. Clearly, Nestlé feared that shoppers would confuse Mars's new bar with the KitKat.

Source: adapted from an article in *Metro*, December 2002.

FACT FILE

Louboutin shoes

The red soles on Christian Louboutin shoes make them instantly recognisable. As a result, Louboutin is seeking to protect his designs from copycats by applying to have them trademarked in both the USA and the UK. He said, 'The shiny red colour of the soles has no function other than to identify to the public that the shoes are mine.'

Source: adapted from an entry in *Grazia* magazine, October 2007.

WHAT DO YOU THINK?

Taking into account the information, fact files and case studies you have read in this and the previous chapter, to what extent is it luck or judgement that determines whether a new idea becomes a successful business?

DID YOU KNOW?

Intellectual property includes the business's name, logo, designs and inventions — all the aspects covered by copyright, patents and trademarks. All businesses have some form of intellectual property, which is likely to be a valuable asset that can:

- set the business apart from competitors
- be sold or licensed, forming an important source of income
- offer customers something new and different
- form an essential part of marketing or branding

PRACTICE EXERCISE

Total: 45 marks (35 minutes)

1 State four possible sources of business ideas or opportunities, and identify one business example to illustrate each of these four sources. *(8 marks)*

2 Define the term 'franchise'. *(3 marks)*

3 Outline two benefits of operating a franchise compared with starting a new business. *(6 marks)*

4 Why might it be easier for a business to expand as a franchise organisation rather than as a traditional business organisation? *(4 marks)*

5 Explain two problems of operating a franchise compared with starting a new business. *(6 marks)*

6 Explain the meaning of the term 'copyright'. *(3 marks)*

7 What is a patent? *(3 marks)*

8 Explain one benefit that a patent could provide for a business. *(3 marks)*

9 Explain why many small businesses sell their patents to larger businesses. *(4 marks)*

10 What is a trademark and how might it benefit a business? *(5 marks)*

CASE STUDY   What a spectacle!

The following case study provides information on how two very different businesses, both providing customers with spectacles, were set up. Read the case study and answer the questions that follow.

The franchise

Entrepreneur and trained optometrist Stephen Halpin always intended to run his own business. In his chosen market, the high-street optical services sector, a franchise seemed like a good way to get a head start. After considering the options, Stephen bought one of the first Boots Opticians franchises in Northwich, Cheshire:

> The retail optical services market is highly competitive and starting an outlet in your own name is a risky affair. A franchise made sense, because it reduces some — not all — of the risks. Also, because I was applying for one of the first Boots Opticians franchises, there was more scope to get involved in developing the operational systems. This was important to me — I found that longer-established franchisors had a less flexible attitude.

With the help of an accountant, I put together a detailed business plan. The store I wanted to take on had been trading as a Boots Opticians for several years so it had financial records to assess. Other factors I considered were the store location, local competitors and current operational practices. Without a clear idea of how much the business could make and how much cash I needed, it would have been impossible to tell if the franchise agreement on offer was worthwhile.

The business plan also formed the basis of the presentation I gave to Boots' management. This was a key part of the process of being accepted for the franchise. The presentation and plan also gave me the information I needed to negotiate a contract.

Once I had been accepted for the franchise, Boots drew up a franchise agreement setting out terms, conditions and fees. I got advice from specialist franchise solicitors before signing. One of my key objectives was to ensure that the agreement benefited both parties, that I made money and so did Boots.

Source: www.businesslink.gov.uk

The web-based business

Twenty-two-year-old James Murray Wells revolutionised the spectacle-buying market by offering glasses online at little more than cost price, thereby saving the consumer substantial amounts of money. He got the idea after buying a pair of glasses from one of the large high-street chains, the price of which (£149.99) shocked him — it was more than half a month's rent. He thought he could provide them at lower prices, saving students — and everyone else — a great deal of money.

Murray Wells was studying for his finals in English at the University of the West of England. He started with a lot of research and test orders, and spent quite a bit of time deliberating until he was absolutely confident the business model would succeed. He posted a job advertisement on the university notice board for fellow students to come on board and help him design the website. Initially, financing came from a student loan. He officially opened Glasses Direct on 1 July 2004 and since then has had over 1.5 million visitors to the website and more than 21,000 customers.

It costs around £7 to make a pair of glasses and Murray Wells suggests that opticians try to maintain their high-street prices at an average of around 20 times the cost of manufacture. The business is planning to consolidate the UK market and follow with an international rollout. Murray Wells believes in the following maxim: 'Start small, grow big. Start big, go bust.' He started from his living room with £1,000 and learned that it is best to minimise risk while testing the concept in a 'cottage business'.

Source: www.glassesdirect.co.uk

Questions
Total 44 marks (55 minutes)

1 What is meant by the term 'franchise'? *(2 marks)*

2 Apart from franchising, identify two sources of business ideas. *(2 marks)*

3 Explain two benefits to Stephen Halpin of taking on a Boots franchise business. *(6 marks)*

4 If it costs £7 to make a pair of glasses, how much are opticians likely to charge, according to Murray Wells? *(4 marks)*

5 Discuss the differing levels of risk that Halpin and Murray Wells are likely to have faced when developing their business idea. *(15 marks)*

6 To what extent might the web-based Glasses Direct business have more potential to grow than the Boots franchise? *(15 marks)*

CHAPTER 3

Transforming resources into goods and services

This chapter introduces the resources (inputs) that make up the factors of production. It looks at ways in which organisations transform these inputs into outputs, and how they try to do this in the most efficient way possible. The division of outputs into primary, secondary and tertiary production is then considered in the context of the UK economy. The chapter concludes by examining the concept of adding value and how it can be achieved through the production process.

Resources (inputs)

In order to produce goods and services a business will need to use resources. These resources are the inputs into the production process, but are more commonly known as the **factors of production**.

The factors of production

The four factors of production are as follows:

- **Land.** The term 'land' incorporates all the natural resources that can be used for production. Clearly, land in the traditional sense is included under this heading. However, as a factor of production, 'land' also includes natural and mineral resources such as coal, oil and gravel, and livestock such as sheep, pigs and cows. It also includes the sea and resources contained within it, e.g. fish.
- **Labour.** This describes both the physical and mental effort involved in production. It therefore ranges from people providing personal and commercial services, such as accountants and window cleaners, to those providing manual effort in producing finished goods, extracting raw materials or harvesting crops.
- **Capital.** This means goods that are made in order to produce other goods and services. Examples are machinery, computer systems, shelving, lorries, forklift trucks, factories, shops and office blocks.

■ **Enterprise.** This is the act of bringing together the other factors of production in order to create goods and services. Enterprise is carried out by the entrepreneur, who makes decisions and provides the finance. The entrepreneur takes the financial risk and therefore earns the profit that can be made from converting inputs into outputs.

WHAT DO YOU THINK?

Some people say that there are only three factors of production, arguing that enterprise is not a separate factor. Their logic is based on the argument that decision making is just a highly skilled form of labour. This debate has come from studies of large public limited companies, in which decisions are taken by highly paid managers (labour). However, in a sole trader business, the person making the critical decisions and taking the financial risk can usually be clearly identified as one person — the entrepreneur.

Does the entrepreneur play a significantly different role from employees of a business?

Improving the efficiency of the factors of production

An organisation that can use the factors of production efficiently, in order to generate the maximum possible output, is likely to become more profitable. Its efficiency will enable it to produce goods and services more cost-effectively, and so it might be able to increase its sales by reducing its prices. Alternatively, it may keep its price the same and therefore increase the difference between its revenue and its costs of production.

There are a number of ways in which the efficiency of factors of production can be improved. Examples are:

■ **Improving the fertility of land.** Modern agricultural techniques enable farmers to achieve greater output per acre. Similarly, factory farming can enable a farmer to generate greater productivity from livestock farming.

■ **Using renewable or recyclable resources.** Many factories are now designed to minimise waste and improve energy efficiency so that resources are used more effectively.

■ **Greater education and training of the workforce.** This can lead to much greater output from labour, which is particularly important in the UK as the skills of the labour force are an essential element in allowing UK businesses to compete with countries that have lower wage levels.

■ **Increasing the level of investment in capital equipment.** High-quality capital goods, such as modern machinery, can greatly enhance the efficiency of a labour force. Businesses that are able to update constantly their machinery and technology will be able to operate much more efficiently and provide goods and services that meet the ever-changing requirements of customers.

■ **Improvements in entrepreneurial skills and a willingness to take risks by entrepreneurs.** These may greatly improve efficiency because factors of production will be converted into goods and services that meet customer needs.

■ **Combining the factors of production in a balanced way.** This can help a business to avoid problems, such as the diminishing return, that may arise if one factor of production is overused in comparison with the other factors.

■ **Extending the overall scale of production.** This should lead to greater efficiencies, such as bulk buying and the ability to use large-scale production techniques.

The nature of output

The process by which inputs of factors of production are transformed into outputs is known as **production**.

It is important to note that the customer may be another business that requires a product (e.g. sheet metal or cloth) which will in turn be used to make further products. Customer requirements may also be for a service rather than a good. The vast majority of production in the UK takes the form of services rather than goods.

Inputs to outputs: the transformation process

The purpose of a business is to produce goods or services profitably. In order to achieve this purpose, a business must acquire inputs, convert them into outputs, and ensure that these outputs reach the customer. All of these activities are part of the transformation process.

Some inputs are used up in the process of creating goods or services; others assist the transformation process but remain intact.

In general, land in the form of raw materials is used up during the transformation process. In contrast, capital equipment remains intact, but constant processing means that it will eventually need to be replaced. The other factors of production — land (in its traditional sense), labour and enterprise — all remain active, ready to be used in further production. However, the business must be careful that it does not overuse these resources, as this may lead to lower levels of efficiency in the future.

In the tertiary sector, the transformation process focuses directly on the consumer. No physical product emerges at the end of the process but the consumer may emerge from the nightclub with a happy smile, or leave the hairdresser with a new hair colour and style.

KEY TERMS

production: the process whereby resources (factors of production) are converted into a form that is intended to satisfy the requirements of potential customers.

output: the finished products resulting from the transformation process.

Figure 3.1
The transformation process

Production can vary significantly in terms of the mix of labour and capital that make up the inputs. Technical operations depend largely on capital; personal services may rely mainly on labour.

Classifying outputs

The main outputs of the transformation process are classified in three different ways, as:

- natural resources
- semi-finished and finished goods
- services

These are respectively referred to as **primary production**, **secondary production** and **tertiary production**. Collectively, these three types of production (output) make up the three sectors that form the structure of industry.

> ### KEY TERMS
>
> **primary sector:** those organisations involved in extracting raw materials (e.g. farming, fishing, forestry and the extractive industries such as oil exploration, mining and quarrying).
>
> **secondary (manufacturing) sector:** those organisations involved in processing or refining the raw materials from the primary sector into finished or semi-finished products (e.g. paper mills, oil refineries, textile manufacturers, food processors and vehicle manufacturers).
>
> **tertiary sector:** those organisations involved in providing services to customers and to other businesses, in either the public or the private sector (e.g. education, health, hairdressing, retailing, financial services, restaurants and leisure services).

TOPFOTO

Production in the primary sector

In primary production, the final output is a natural resource. Consequently, the transformation process is quite simple. In agriculture, it takes the form of the conversion of seed to the finished crop, or the care of livestock. In other areas of primary production, it usually involves the extraction of a natural resource, such as coal and gold. Although the process of primary production is simple, extraction of some resources, such as oil, can be an expensive undertaking.

Production in the secondary sector

Secondary production describes the process of converting primary products into finished goods. These finished goods may, in turn, act as inputs for businesses producing a more complex end product. For example, Michelin purchases a primary product — rubber — as the main input into making tyres. Subsequently, these tyres may be one of the inputs into a car made by Volkswagen.

Production in the tertiary sector

The provision of services is known as 'tertiary production'. Services are classified in two ways:

■ commercial — where the service is provided for another business, such as advertising agencies and delivery services

■ personal — where the service is provided directly to the individual, such as hairdressing, plumbing and retailing

In some cases, it is possible for a service to be either commercial or personal. Banking and insurance are examples of services that could be commercial (a loan to a company) or personal (an individual insuring a car).

Many transformation processes produce both goods and services. For example, the work done in a restaurant provides a service, but also leads to the production of a good (the meal) from raw materials (the ingredients).

As well as the resultant goods and services, production may also lead to undesirable outputs, such as pollution and waste, or unacceptable processes, such as the exploitation of child labour. Increasingly, businesses are being held responsible for these outputs through pressure groups, consumer action or government laws and regulations.

Feedback

The final part of the transformation model in Figure 3.1 (p. 27) is feedback. Feedback of information is used to adjust the process in the future. For example, a retailer relies on feedback from its customers about the quality of its goods and services. Adverse feedback on a product might lead to the retailer switching to a different supplier; favourable feedback on customer care may encourage the retailer to maintain its customer care training programme.

Structure of industry in the UK

The tertiary sector is the largest sector in terms of contribution to GDP and employment in the UK. As economies develop, the secondary sector tends to grow faster than the primary sector, and in well-developed economies such as the UK, the tertiary sector tends to grow faster than the secondary sector. In general, as people become more affluent, they want more manufactured products and, as their wealth increases still further, they desire more services.

 YOU KNOW?

GDP means gross domestic product. It is the total value of a country's output over the course of a year.

Tables 3.1 and 3.2 indicate the changing importance of these three sectors in the UK economy, in terms of their contribution to GDP and to employment.

Sector	1964	1969	1973	1979	1990	1995	1999	2006
Primary	5.7	4.5	4.2	6.7	3.9	4.2	3.0	2.5
Secondary	40.6	42.2	40.9	36.7	31.6	28.2	27.2	21.2
Tertiary	53.7	53.3	54.9	56.6	64.5	67.6	69.8	76.3

Table 3.1 The structure of UK industry (% share of GDP)

Source: adapted from ONS (2000) and Blue Book (2007).

Table 3.2 The structure
of UK industry (% of total
employment)

Source: adapted from ONS
(2000) and Blue Book (2007).

Sector	1964	1969	1973	1979	1990	1995	1999	2006
Primary	5.2	3.4	3.0	3.0	2.1	1.7	1.6	1.6
Secondary	46.9	42.3	38.5	35.5	26.6	22.7	21.9	17.7
Tertiary	47.9	54.3	58.5	61.5	71.3	75.6	76.5	80.7

The extent to which services are increasing their dominance of, and
importance to, the UK's economy can be seen in Figure 3.2. Figure 3.3 shows
the impact that this is having on different regions of the UK.

Figure 3.2 Increasing
value of services to the
UK economy

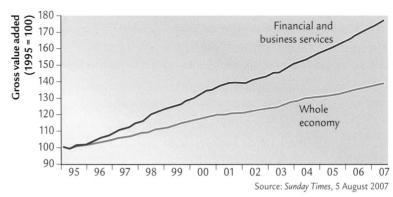

Source: *Sunday Times*, 5 August 2007

Figure 3.3 Regional
impact of service
expansion in the UK

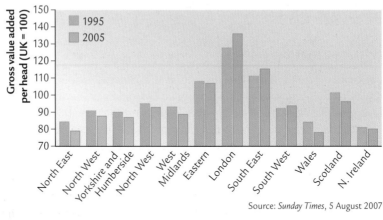

Source: *Sunday Times*, 5 August 2007

Measuring output

How is output measured? This might seem to be an
obvious question — if Toyota produces a car that is
sold for £12,000, then the value of its output is
£12,000.

However, parts of this car (e.g. the radiator and the
tyres) might have been manufactured by another
company and sold to Toyota as a component.
Therefore, the true value of the car is its selling price
minus the value of goods and services bought in by
Toyota. This is known as **value added**.

Adding value

Adding value is the process of increasing the worth of resources by modifying them. The production process is seen to be a major factor in adding value. For example, the transformation of various components into a television set adds value, as people place a higher value on the television set than on the parts used to make it. Similarly, distribution and retailing add value by bringing the product within easier reach of the customer. Other services, such as marketing, also add value by:

- creating a unique selling point/proposition (USP) — this may be real, such as a different design or different components, or it may be based on image and branding
- identifying an attractive mix of design, function, image and service

If a business can improve customer awareness and goodwill by using the transformation process to make its product different from rival products, it may be able to increase both its sales volume and its price. It may also acquire loyal customers who are less likely to stop buying the business's product.

In order to make a profit, businesses need to add value to the resources that they possess. As discussed earlier, this can be carried out through different elements of the transformation process. For example, a restaurant such as McDonald's might aim to minimise costs by using low-cost inputs and/or transforming them in a cost-effective way. This allows McDonald's to make high profits by achieving relatively low levels of added value but selling vast quantities, as customers are attracted to the low prices. In contrast, the Ritz Hotel can sell afternoon tea at a high price (and high added value) by concentrating on the quality of its service and products.

The case study at the end of this chapter looks at how burger companies are increasingly focusing on quality in order to achieve high levels of added value.

Changes in output in the UK

As shown in Figures 3.1 and 3.2, certain sectors and regions of the UK are experiencing different levels of growth. Financial and business services — the latter including accounting, advertising, architects, estate agents, lawyers and others — drive the UK's economy. In the year to the first quarter of 2007, the financial sector of the UK saw its gross value added rise by 10%, compared with a 2.8% rise for the economy as a whole. Financial and business services have nearly doubled their share of economic output in the UK since 1980, from under 15% then to almost 29% in 2007. The sector has expanded at three or four times the rate of the rest of the economy over the past decade. In London and southeast England, the increase has been from 20% to more than 42%. The share of financial and business services in UK employment has risen from 11% to almost 21%. In London and the southeast, these services employ 28% of workers, compared with just 15% in 1980.

KEY TERMS

adding value: the process of increasing the worth of resources by modifying them.

value added (added value): sales revenue *minus* the cost of bought-in materials, components and services.

unique selling point/proposition: a feature of a product or service that allows it to be differentiated from other products.

This trend has major implications. The strength of financial and business services has made a significant contribution to the dominance of London and the southeast. However, as Sir John Gieve, one of the Bank of England's two deputy governors, pointed out recently, if one sector of the economy, and one region, is doing disproportionately well, the effect may be to reduce output and employment in others.

Looking forward, the growth in London and the southeast will outstrip the rest of the UK by between 0.5 and 0.75% a year over the next decade. This is owing not just to the expected strength of financial and business services, but also to factors such as construction work linked to the 2012 Olympics and other infrastructure projects.

FACT FILE

North Sea oil and gas

A quick look at Table 3.1 gives an idea of the impact of North Sea oil and gas on primary production in the UK. In the late 1970s, the size of the primary sector increased rapidly as a result of the discovery of oil and gas in UK waters, but it has declined significantly since the extraction of most of the oil.

However, a glance at Table 3.2 shows that there was little impact on employment in the primary sector. This is because the technology involved was so advanced that few workers were needed to extract the oil and gas.

WHAT DO YOU THINK?

Michael Blastland and Andrew Dilnot's book *The Tiger That Isn't: Seeing Through a World of Numbers* (Profile Books, 2007) is about numbers and misconceptions about them. Included in it is a series of questions asked of senior civil servants. They did badly. Can you do better? See if your class can outscore the mandarins.

1 What is the share of income tax paid by the top 1% of earners?
   a 5%   **b** 9%   **c** 13%   **d** 17%   **e** 21%

2 What joint income, after tax, would a childless couple need to be in the top 10% of earners?
   a £35,000   **b** £50,000   **c** £65,000   **d** £80,000   **e** £100,000

3 Approximately how much bigger is the present output of goods and services in the UK economy, compared with what it was in 1948?
   a 50%   **b** 100%   **c** 150%   **d** 200%   **e** 300%

The answers are given on p. 34.

PRACTICE EXERCISE Total: 50 marks (45 minutes)

1 Define the term 'resources'. *(2 marks)*

2 Define the term 'land'. *(2 marks)*

3 Define the term 'capital'. *(2 marks)*

4 Explain how a business can improve the efficiency of its:
   a capital   *(3 marks)*   **b** labour   *(3 marks)*

5 What is the fourth factor of production? *(1 mark)*

6 Draw a labelled diagram to show the transformation process. *(5 marks)*

7 Explain two undesirable outputs that might arise from a transformation process. *(4 marks)*

8 Distinguish between the primary, secondary and tertiary sectors. *(6 marks)*

9 Identify three industries in each of the following sectors (nine industries in total):
   a primary *(3 marks)*   **b** secondary *(3 marks)*   **c** tertiary *(3 marks)*

10 Explain why the tertiary sector is the largest sector of industry in the UK. *(5 marks)*

11 Define the term 'adding value'. *(2 marks)*

12 Re-read the section 'Changes in output in the UK' on pp. 31–32. Why is growth expected to be higher in southeast England and London than other regions of the UK? *(6 marks)*

CASE STUDY   Fast food goes posh

Paul Campbell took a seat a few weeks ago by the window of the newly opened branch of Gourmet Burger Kitchen (GBK) in the Festival Square shopping mall in Basingstoke.

The site, one of 24 branches of the chain owned by the company that Campbell heads, was the first to open directly opposite a Burger King outlet and the boss wanted to see how shoppers reacted.

He was pleasantly surprised. 'I watched people as they wandered through the mall and were looking at both,' he said. 'A fair percentage came into GBK. The site is performing better than we expected.'

GBK is the market leader in a wave of upmarket burger bars that have sprung up, mainly in southeast England, in recent years. Since opening in March 2001, it has been joined by Hamburger Union and Fine Burger Company, both of which were launched in 2003, and by Ultimate Burger and Natural Burger Company. All of them serve better-quality food in a smarter environment than a traditional fast-food outlet.

Collectively, these new eateries amount to about 50 outlets, insignificant next to the 1,800 or so operated by the sector's giants, McDonald's and Burger King, and have made barely a dent in the £11 billion UK market. But the upstarts are about to get a lot bigger —

GBK hopes to get to 100 sites within 3 years — and the big boys are waking up to the fact that unless they respond they could start to lose customers.

It is not just hamburger joints where staple fast-food fare is being reinvented. Fish and chips has lent itself particularly well to being taken upmarket. Mini-chains, such as Sea Cow, are springing up, while chefs such as Rick Stein and Tony Allan have launched fish-and-chip outlets in Cornwall and Surrey respectively.

'Business is booming,' said Allan, 'now that customers have got their heads around the extra cost. People don't mind paying £8 for a pizza that cost 30p to put in a box,' he said. 'Initially it was a bit of a problem getting them to pay £7 for fish and chips that cost £3.50 to serve, but these days people don't mind paying for a bit of quality.'

These upmarket versions of mainstream foods have been gaining in popularity over the past 2 or 3 years. Some cite the success of chains such as Pret A Manger and Pizza Express as paving the way. But the rise of the posh burger bar is the most notable.

In part it is a symptom of the so-called 'flight to quality' prevalent in much of the UK's food culture.

'It's been happening in supermarkets with the success of labels such as Taste the Difference at

Sainsbury's and Finest at Tesco, and with Marks and Spencer and Waitrose doing well,' said Jeffrey Young at the marketing consultancy firm, Allegra.

Consumers have become increasingly concerned about eating more healthily and are more interested in the quality of their food. While they still want to enjoy the odd burger or fish and chips, they want to be confident that the food is of good quality. Robert Tame, founder of Fine Burger Company, believes 'It's not just about the product, it is also the environment you are presenting the burgers in.'

To date, the new wave of fast-food outlets has been a London phenomenon, but that is beginning to change. Fine Burger Company, for example, has opened an outlet in Swindon, which Tame says is doing 'very well'. Tame is also looking to acquire property elsewhere in the UK. In addition to its Basingstoke outlet, GBK also has restaurants in Bristol and Brighton.

Some question whether people in many parts of the UK will be prepared to pay £8 for a burger, but Young believes that upmarket fast food will prove as sustainable as coffee shops, which were once written off as a fad. 'This is going to be a permanent shift,' he said.

Source: adapted from an article by Matthew Goodman in the *Sunday Times*, 6 May 2007.

Questions

Total: 55 marks (65 minutes)

1 This question looks at the resources being used by Gourmet Burger Kitchen (GBK).
   a Identify two examples of 'land' that are used by GBK. *(2 marks)*
   b Identify two examples of 'capital' that might be used by GBK. *(2 marks)*
   c Is Paul Campbell an example of labour or enterprise? Justify your choice. *(5 marks)*

2 Is GBK mainly involved in primary production, secondary production or tertiary production? Explain your reasoning. *(5 marks)*

3 How might GBK use 'feedback' in order to improve its efficiency? *(4 marks)*

4 Based on the figures in the article, calculate the level of added value on a pizza. *(2 marks)*

5 Analyse three ways in which GBK might improve the efficiency of its factors of production. *(10 marks)*

6 Analyse the reasons why GBK can achieve higher levels of added value than McDonald's. *(10 marks)*

7 Jeffrey Young believes that the move towards 'upmarket burgers' in the UK is a permanent shift. To what extent do you agree with this view? *(15 marks)*

Answers to *What do you think?* questions on p. 32

1 e 19% of senior civil servants got the correct answer.
2 a 10% of senior civil servants got the correct answer.
3 e 3% of senior civil servants got the correct answer.

Developing business plans

This chapter considers the purpose of business plans, identifies their essential content, and analyses the benefits and the problems of such plans for a business. The sources of information and guidance available for new small businesses are also discussed.

Purpose of a business plan

Drawing up a business plan is an important step in setting up a new business. The following points indicate the benefits of a business plan and highlight some of the problems involved for a small business.

KEY TERM

business plan: a report describing the marketing strategy, operational issues and financial implications of a business start-up.

Benefits

- A business plan is useful in helping entrepreneurs to clarify their objectives and to consider their business idea thoroughly from every perspective, which should improve the likelihood of its success.
- It enables the owners to know precisely what needs to be done in order to meet their business objectives, including targeting specific customer groups, product pricing, costing, sales forecasts and marketing.
- It is an essential document in persuading lenders to invest capital in the business by demonstrating why it is likely to succeed. Banks insist on seeing such a plan before granting loans or overdrafts.
- A business plan should not be produced simply for a third party, such as a bank manager, when trying to raise finance, but should be viewed as a valuable tool to help in running the business. In this way, the plan becomes a working document with clearly defined objectives against which the business can monitor its progress. It should be reviewed regularly and updated whenever the circumstances of the business change significantly.

Problems

- For a business plan to be a valuable tool and a persuasive document, it needs to be accurate and realistic. It should not only show strengths and

opportunities, but also document weaknesses and any threats the business will face.

- Many business plans underestimate how much it will cost to get the business off the ground, and find that operating costs often turn out to be more than the amount budgeted for.
- Business plans often take an overly optimistic view of the potential of a business. They make assumptions about the size of the market without any supporting market research evidence, and/or are vague about identifying competitors and their products and prices.
- Many business plans tend to be overly optimistic in their sales forecasts and unrealistic about when payment can be expected. For example, they often assume that the business will receive payment from customers as soon as it sends out an invoice, and thus do not allow for delays and the effect these will have on cash flow. From a lender's point of view, providing accurate and realistic financial information is vital, as he or she will want to know when to expect repayment of the loan, and will want to assess carefully the risks involved.

Content of a business plan

A start-up business plan needs to explain clearly and concisely the nature of the business and its market. It should provide financial forecasts and details of any financial requirements the business has, as well as details of how the business will be managed. Templates are widely available from banks and from small business advisory agencies such as Business Link.

The main sections of a business plan are as follows:

- **Details about the business.** These include its name and location, its legal structure, and a description of the product or service.
- **Personal information.** The plan should include personal information about the owner and those who will be managing the business, as well as their CVs and an account of their business skills, experience and financial commitments. Details about any support they are receiving, including mentors and other advisory agencies, should be listed, together with any training they have received or are undergoing. The plan should also include key staff and staffing requirements.
- **Objectives.** The objectives of the business or what it is aiming to achieve should be stated as quantifiable or SMART targets.
- **Marketing plan.** This should show the gap in the market that the business start-up is intended to fill; the results of any market research that has been done; the type, size and location of the market; a description of potential customers (such as their age, gender, location, income and the price they are prepared to pay); a comparison of the business's products/services with those of its competitors; and their respective strengths and weaknesses. The marketing plan should also include information about what makes this

DID YOU KNOW?

SMART targets or objectives are those that are specific, measurable, agreed, realistic and time-bound.

product or service unique (and therefore more likely to succeed), details of promotion and selling techniques to be used, and how the product or service will be priced.

- **Production plan.** This should detail how goods and services will be created, including the day-to-day practical activities involved; the materials, staff and equipment needed; and the scale of production.
- **Fixed assets.** Details of fixed assets such as premises and equipment should be given, including those needed to fulfil immediate plans and how these are to be financed. For example, the plan should state whether the entrepreneur intends to purchase or rent premises or work from home, and whether he or she intends to purchase or rent any essential equipment and machinery.
- **Financial forecasts.** Sales and cash-flow forecasts, a projected profit and loss account, and a balance sheet for the end of the first year and for the next 2–3 years need to be included, together with details of pricing and break-even level. Cash-flow forecasts allow the entrepreneur to analyse the cash coming in and going out of the business, and thus to identify those periods when an overdraft will be necessary. This will involve a detailed consideration of all the costs involved: for example, rent and rates, electricity, telephone and postage, stock and materials, insurance, IT equipment, vehicle and travel expenses, wages and salaries.
- **Details of finance needed and repayment.** The plan should specify how much, when and in what form the finance is needed, and what it will be used for. The forecast speed of repayment or rate of return on the investor's capital should also be included.
- **Collateral offered.** With most business start-ups, the entrepreneur is likely to rent premises or work from home, rather than own business premises. In this case, the owners will have to offer their own personal assets (usually their home) as security.
- **Long-term plans.** The business plan should include a brief account of the long-term forecasts and plans of the business.
- **SWOT analysis.** This should explain how the business intends to build on its strengths in order to exploit opportunities, and reduce its weaknesses in order to overcome any threats.

DID YOU KNOW?

The 2005 Annual Small Business Survey suggested that home was the main business or work premises for over 40% of small businesses.

ⅇ EXAMINER'S VOICE

Most of the issues considered in this chapter are covered in more detail elsewhere in the AS specification. This highlights the importance of taking an integrated view of business studies and thinking broadly about issues such as small business start-ups.

DID YOU KNOW?

'SWOT' stands for strengths, weaknesses, opportunities and threats. Strengths and weaknesses are internal characteristics of the business; opportunities and threats are external aspects that can have an impact on the business. Strengths provide opportunities for a business: for example, having a product of superior quality (a strength) might allow a business to win customers from a competitor that has an inferior product (an opportunity). Weaknesses can pose a threat: for example, a business that is dependent on a single customer (a weakness) could collapse if that customer goes bust or decides to take its business elsewhere (a threat).

CHAPTER 4   Developing business plans

 FILE

Klein Caporn

Klein Caporn is a business selling fresh pasta sauces, set up by Paddy Klein and Ed Caporn. According to Paddy Klein:

> Creating the business plan forced us to research our customers, competitors and market thoroughly. It also helped us establish the precise costs of design, packaging and distribution.

> One of the difficulties in starting a business is that you won't know which questions will cause you the biggest headaches. You may have hunches, but they can be wrong. We found ours to be very wrong indeed. For example, our biggest practical issue proved to be finding a packaging company with the machinery to apply our labels to our pots! This was something we both thought would be an easy task. Writing a detailed business plan forces you to look at questions as practical as this!

It is probable that you will need to find many other companies to help you deliver your offering. For example, we need designers, packers, printers, distributors, manufacturers, wholesalers, butchers and retailers, to name a few. The business plan will help you to get your list together.

What if something goes wrong? It will and you will have to deal with it. You should think about any problems that may arise as early as possible. Again, a business plan can help. Include a section on risk — this should list everything that could go wrong and what you would do about it. Think about your initial assumptions here: what effect would it have on your business if your assumptions were wrong — too high, too low or too expensive?

Source: adapted from Klein, P. (2006) 'Klein Caporn: a new business', *Business Review*, Vol. 13, No. 1, pp. 2–3.

 FILE

GHD — Good Hair Day

In 2001 Martin Penny was approached by a hairdresser friend who showed him a hair-styling iron he had been sent by a Korean inventor and asked him what he thought. Penny tried it out on his wife's hair and thought it was such a good product that it might be worth trying to turn it into a business.

When Penny asked his bank for a loan to start a business selling the hair-styling irons, the bank manager refused his request and told him he was completely mad to think of doing such a thing. He asked another friend to join them. The three of them wrote a business plan, put in £15,000 each and took a one-third share each in the company.

Instead of approaching shops, they took the unusual decision to sell the styling iron — mostly used for straightening hair — through hair salons, using the experience of the hairdressers to help them. 'There are about 38,000 hair salons in the UK, so we thought there was a big market to go for,' said Penny. They began approaching top salons in the West End of London to see if they were interested in selling the styling iron to their clients for about £100.

In the first year, sales were only £400,000, a far cry from the optimistic £1.8 million they had forecast in their business plan. But in the second year everything changed. Word about the iron started to get about and soon a number of celebrities, including Victoria Beckham, Madonna, Gwyneth Paltrow and Jennifer Aniston, were reported to have bought one.

By the end of the second year, sales had leapt to £11.7 million, all without doing any advertising. Penny said, 'I think if you ever tried to write a business plan saying that, people wouldn't take you seriously.'

All the irons are still made by the Korean inventor, who now has six factories. The business sells over 2 million styling irons a year to hair salons and direct to consumers. Its average sales growth has been over 360% per year since it was set up in 2001. Annual sales are currently worth over £40 million. GHD is now launching a range of 30 haircare products under the brand name nu:u.

Source: Bridge, R. (2007) 'Hair-brained idea grew into a winner', *Sunday Times*, 25 June.

Sources of information and guidance

Starting and managing a new business involves many challenges and making difficult decisions. Small businesses do not have large management teams; most do not have a financial director to advise on money matters or a marketing manager to advise on marketing issues. Most entrepreneurs do not have the skills necessary both to plan and run a business, and need to seek specialist advice on a range of issues, including drawing up a business plan and financial matters.

There are many sources of information and guidance for a new business, including a range of small business advisory services as well as the more traditional sources of advice, accountants and bank managers. Accountants and bank managers tend to provide advice and guidance on how to manage a business financially and when and how to obtain finance, both at the start-up stage and later when the business wants to expand.

Business Link is a government-funded service that provides the information, advice and support needed to start, maintain and grow a business. It helps businesses with their start-up business plan and with raising finance by providing information on loans and grants that they may be able to access. Business Link provides advice on a whole range of issues, including what type of computer to purchase, the most appropriate bank accounts to open, information on trademarks and advice on exporting. Its advisers even accompany entrepreneurs to meetings with their bank managers.

Business Link does not provide all this help and advice itself, but directs its clients to the experts they need. The service it provides is delivered through advisers in local areas, and is supported by a single national website (**www.businesslink.gov.uk**) and phone line. New entrepreneurs can also be directed to a business mentor (an experienced and successful business person who can listen to ideas and give advice).

Other sources of advice and support include local enterprise agencies, chambers of commerce and local trade associations. Many of these provide opportunities for entrepreneurs to meet and network with people with similar business interests and concerns. For entrepreneurs aged 18–30, The Prince's Trust offers help and often funding, while at the other end of the age range, the Prince's Initiative for Mature Enterprise (PRIME) helps the over-fifties.

Interestingly, the 2005 Annual Small Business Survey suggests that 26% of new businesses had not sought advice from anybody before starting up, and a further 22% had consulted only their friends, family or informal contacts.

 YOU KNOW?

The Prince's Trust provides help and support for unemployed young people aged 18–30 who have an idea for a business but cannot raise all the cash they need from

elsewhere. It provides low-interest loans and sometimes grants, and ongoing advice from a business mentor. Its website, www.princes-trust.org.uk, includes interesting case studies of young people who are running successful businesses as a result of the help they have received.

The Prince's Initiative for Mature Enterprise (PRIME) helps people over the age of 50 to set up in business. Like the Prince's Trust, it was founded by the Prince of Wales. It offers a sympathetic ear, free information and help, workshops and business networking events, and refers people to properly accredited advisers for free business advice.

PRACTICE EXERCISE   Total: 30 marks (25 minutes)

1 What is a business plan?   *(2 marks)*

2 Explain two purposes of a business plan.   *(4 marks)*

3 Outline two ways in which an unrealistic or inaccurate business plan could lead to problems.   *(6 marks)*

4 List four important sections of a business plan and describe in detail the type of information that should be provided in each section.   *(12 marks)*

5 Identify and explain two sources of advice and information for a start-up business.   *(6 marks)*

CASE STUDY   **Prashad**

Prashad was set up in Bradford in the mid-1990s by Mr and Mrs Patel. It sold Indian sweets and Bombay mixes. Although reasonably successful, it lacked a business plan and there was no sense of progress in the business. Mr and Mrs Patel's son, Bobby, began working for the business on graduating with a degree in business studies. In 2004, the family decided to move the business forward by opening a small restaurant that made more use of Mrs Patel's cooking skills.

They developed a business plan with the help of Asian Trade Link, Business Link West Yorkshire and West

Yorkshire Ventures. In developing their business plan, it was important to show they had a well-informed understanding of their business, the competition and potential customers. They found the SWOT analysis particularly useful. Listing their strengths made them feel more confident, helped them to identify opportunities and enabled them to develop a strategy for capitalising on them. Similarly, thinking about their weaknesses enabled them to spot or guard against any threats they might face. Although their costs were low, they guarded against overly optimistic financial projections by slightly

over-estimating their costs and being conservative about income.

It took the Patels about 2 months to research and finalise their first business plan, but it was time well spent. They refer to their plan regularly and update it when necessary. As a result, their business has prospered and their new venture has been a success.

Source: www.businesslink.gov.uk

Questions

Total: 40 marks (50 minutes)

1 What is meant by the term 'business plan'? *(2 marks)*

2 State four items that you might expect to see in Prashad's business plan. *(4 marks)*

3 Explain why a business plan might have helped Prashad develop further. *(4 marks)*

4 Explain how any start-up business might benefit from an organisation such as Business Link. *(5 marks)*

5 Analyse why the Patels might have decided to over-estimate their costs slightly and to be conservative about their income when drawing up their business plan. *(10 marks)*

6 To what extent might a business plan improve the possibility of success for a new start-up business and for an existing business such as Prashad? *(15 marks)*

CHAPTER 5

Conducting start-up market research

Start-up businesses need to understand their market. The purposes of market research are introduced in this chapter, and comparisons are made between primary and secondary market research and between qualitative and quantitative research data. The final topic that is considered in this chapter is the need for sampling, including the different methods of sampling, the factors that influence the choice of sampling method, and the size of the sample.

Purposes of market research

Market research is undertaken for descriptive, explanatory, predictive and exploratory reasons.

Descriptive reasons

The collection and analysis of data allows organisations to identify a number of important pieces of information. Examples include:

- **Achieving objectives.** Has the firm achieved its target sales figure or its desired percentage market share?
- **Identifying trends.** Are sales rising or falling? Is the trend stable or unpredictable?
- **Comparisons.** How are the firm's sales performing relative to a competitor? Is its advertising expenditure matching its rivals? Is it appealing to the same market segments?

Explanatory reasons

Market research can help an organisation to investigate why certain things occur. For example:

- Does the weather affect sales? If so, how big is the impact and is it consistent?
- Is the brand name attractive to the targeted consumers?
- What are the main reasons why customers buy the product? How can this information be used in the business's marketing?
- Why was a promotional campaign unsuccessful?

Predictive reasons

Information can be used to predict trends and find links between sets of data. This will help the business to predict what will happen in the future.

KEY TERMS

marketing: the anticipation and satisfying of customers' wants in a way that delights consumers and also meets the needs of the organisation.

market research: the systematic and objective collection, analysis and evaluation of information that is intended to assist the marketing process.

Typical uses include:

- calculating the extent to which advertising influences sales volume
- discovering whether introducing a new flavour affects the sales of existing flavours
- predicting whether a new price will boost sales value
- examining the likely effect of the arrival of a new competitor on profit levels

Exploratory reasons

On occasions, such as when a new product is introduced, there will be no existing information to guide an organisation. In this situation, a business may conduct research into the probable consumer reaction to a product or its marketing. This may help the business to assess factors such as:

- the probable level of demand
- the most suitable market segments to be targeted
- the ideal price level
- the best ways of promoting the product

Types of market research

Market research is classified in two ways, according to:

- how the data are collected (primary or secondary)
- the content of the data (quantitative or qualitative)

Primary market research

There are two sources of information: primary and secondary.

Although called 'primary', primary research actually comes second — it should only be used to complete the gaps that cannot be filled by secondary data. Because researchers often need to go out (into the field) to collect primary data, it is frequently called field research.

There are several methods of conducting primary research, each with its own benefits and drawbacks.

Experiment

An organisation experiments with a particular approach in certain areas or for a certain time. If successful, it then uses this approach nationally or on a more long-term basis. For example, Mothercare experimented with different promotional offers in different stores. The offers that appeared to be most successful in these experiments were then adopted for use in stores throughout the country.

The benefits of experiment are as follows:

- It is a relatively cheap way of finding out customer preferences.
- It considers actual customer behaviour rather than opinions given in a questionnaire.

> **KEY TERMS**
>
> **primary market research:** the collection of information first-hand for a specific purpose.
>
> **secondary market research:** the use of information that has already been collected for a different purpose.

The drawbacks of experiment are as follows:
- Consumer behaviour may not be the same throughout the country.
- It may delay the introduction of a potentially successful strategy.

Observation

Stores watch customers while they are shopping and gather information on customer reactions and thought processes. This enables the stores to gain useful data, such as the displays or offers that seem to attract the most interest. Psychologists are employed to offer opinions on customer reactions,

The benefits of observation are as follows:
- The layout of displays can be modified if observation reveals any problems. For example, supermarkets used to place small packages of products on the top shelves, as they yielded lower profits, until observations showed that many of these products were required by elderly customers who were unable to reach them.
- Observation examines actual customer behaviour in detail and can sometimes show what customers are thinking.

The drawbacks of observation are as follows:
- It is expensive to employ specialist psychologists to observe relatively limited behaviour.
- It shows what is happening rather than why it is taking place.

Focus groups

A group of consumers is encouraged to discuss their feelings about a product or market. Typically, focus groups meet at times convenient to their members, such as weekends and evenings.

The benefits of focus groups are as follows:
- They enable a firm to gather detailed information on why consumers react in the way that they do, and can help a business to modify products according to these comments, or to identify gaps in the marketplace.
- These groups also help to uncover new ideas on how to market products or services.

The drawbacks of focus groups are as follows:
- There is sometimes an element of bias in focus groups, as the groups consist of people who have a particular interest in the product and may also want to please the company. Consequently, their views may be less critical than those of the average consumer.
- They are expensive to operate. A single focus group can often cost between £2,000 and £4,000.

Surveys

Consumers are questioned about the product or service. Surveys can take a number of forms, but usually involve the completion of a questionnaire that

is designed to collate the characteristics and views of a cross-section of consumers. The main types of survey are listed below.

Personal interviews

These are conducted face-to-face, with the interviewer filling in the answers given by the interviewee.

The benefits of interviews are as follows:

- A wide range of information can be obtained because questions can be either closed, where a limited choice of answers is allowed, or open, where the interviewee chooses what to say. Closed questions are easy to collate and compare; open questions are better if *qualitative* information is needed.
- The interviewer can explain any uncertainties in the wording of the question to the interviewee, thus avoiding the possibility of answers that are misleading because of misinterpretation.

The drawbacks of interviews are as follows:

- Personal interviews can be time-consuming, particularly as members of the public may be reluctant to answer questions.
- The person responding may give false answers to please the interviewer.
- The interviewer may not select an unbiased cross-section of the public.

Postal surveys

These surveys are posted to the addresses of potential customers, who are then expected to complete them at home and return them, usually in a prepaid envelope.

The benefits of postal surveys are as follows:

- This method is cheap, especially if the surveys are posted by hand rather than through the mail.
- It allows more specific targeting of geographical areas.
- It may avoid the possible bias from a personal survey.
- As respondents have more time to answer the questions, much more detail can be put into the survey.

The drawbacks of postal surveys are as follows:

- Response rates are usually low (often less than 2% are returned if no incentive is given).
- There is no guarantee that the responses are representative, as people completing them may have a strong opinion (or a great deal of spare time).
- Businesses often offer gifts or competition entries to encourage more replies, thus adding to the expense.

Telephone interviews

A market researcher telephones members of the public, seeking their answers to certain questions. Telephone interviews are particularly popular with

EXAMINER'S VOICE

Make sure that you do not confuse 'telephone interviews', which are a method of gaining market research data, with 'telesales', which are a form of direct selling. These two concepts are easily confused because telesales are invariably introduced to the customer as market research, but the telephone caller then attempts to persuade the customer to buy a product or service.

businesses that are seeking to get an opinion, and they often involve questions related to the recent purchase of a consumer durable such as a car or white good (e.g. a refrigerator or washing machine).

The benefits of telephone interviews are as follows:

- Telephone calls are cheap and can be targeted directly at known customers.
- They are also used because they 'get entry into the house' — whereas postal surveys are often considered to be 'junk mail' and discarded, relatively few people will refuse to answer the telephone.

The drawbacks of telephone interviews are as follows:

- Detailed questions are impossible, as interviewees are reluctant to give too much time on the telephone.
- The increased use of unpopular telesales (often initially disguised as a survey) has led to customer resentment.

Internet surveys

Questionnaires on internet sites enable customers to express their views about a product, service or company, thus giving valuable information to the business whose website is visited.

The benefits of internet surveys are as follows:

- It is relatively inexpensive to place a questionnaire on a website.
- They target those most likely to be interested in buying the product, as these people have made a conscious decision to visit the website. Therefore, response rates are much higher than for postal surveys.
- The surveys can be updated frequently, generating excellent topical data for the firm.
- It may be possible to use a detailed questionnaire, particularly if the respondent has an incentive to complete it.

The drawbacks of internet surveys are as follows:

- The sample will tend to be biased towards people with a particular interest in the product or service.
- They will be less relevant for organisations whose target market does not use the internet.

Test marketing

By launching a product in a limited part of a market, usually a geographical area, a firm can discover customer opinions. For example, Northern Foods tested new flavours of muffins in Sainsbury's stores, in order to compare their popularity with that of the original flavours.

The benefits of test marketing are as follows:

- The results of test marketing are a relatively accurate predictor of future popularity, as they are based on actual purchases made by customers.
- It is a useful way of gauging the popularity of a product without incurring the expense of a national launch. This is especially useful in markets where there are high failure rates for new products.

The drawbacks of test marketing are as follows:

- Fewer firms now use test marketing because it can lead to 'me-too' products (copies) being produced by rivals. Thus it can reduce the time during which a firm benefits from being the only producer.
- In rapidly changing markets, the delay in launching a product nationally may endanger the chances of making a profit from a new launch.

 FILE

Market research and marketing

Market research is also used to see if marketing has been successful:

- Cadbury knows that its sponsorship of *Coronation Street* was successful because its 'before' and 'after' surveys showed that people who watched *Coronation Street* now buy more chocolate than they did before the sponsorship began.
- Six months after the launch of the Kate Moss range of clothing, Topshop recorded a 10% growth in sales revenue. Early estimates attribute 5% of its profits to the range.
- A recent Marks and Spencer advertisement featuring hot chocolate puddings led to a 288% increase in sales.

- Black Circles, a chain of Scottish tyre fitters, analyses the success of its advertisements in different magazines by calculating the sales that have been generated by each advert. If advertising in a particular magazine is not creating sales, the adverts are stopped. As a result of this strategy, the owner of the firm estimates that 70% of his advertising converts into sales.

Secondary market research

Secondary information is found by examining published documents (i.e. through desk research). Firms may be able to save a great deal of money by using data that have already been compiled. As market research is never going to be 100% reliable, it is often more cost-effective to accept cheap, reasonably accurate and fairly relevant secondary research than to spend money on primary research. Primary research can then be used to fill any gaps.

Secondary research data can take many forms. Firms will select data that suit their particular purposes. Some key sources are as follows:

- **Government publications.** The Office for National Statistics (ONS) provides information on economic and social trends, so that firms can investigate the implications for their business. Detailed surveys on individual industries are also prepared. The Census of Population provides a detailed survey once every 10 years.

- **Newspapers.** Broadsheet newspapers such as *The Times* and *Guardian* contain articles on specific industries and more general features.
- **Magazines.** Publications such as *The Economist*, *Media Week* and *Grocer Today* can provide helpful data through articles and surveys.
- **Company records.** The company's own records, sales figures, accounts and previous surveys are an easily accessible source and have no cost attached (they are secondary sources because they are not going to be used for their original purpose).
- **Competitors.** Brochures, promotional materials, company reports and investor information can help a firm to study its rivals' actions.
- **Market research organisations.** In addition to conducting primary research, organisations such as Mintel and Dun & Bradstreet produce detailed secondary surveys, the results of which can be purchased by firms.
- **Loyalty cards.** Cards such as Nectar allow a range of businesses to identify the spending patterns of consumers and target them with relevant promotions.
- **The internet.** This is a rapidly increasing source of secondary data, but it should be treated with caution as it may lack the reliability of the other sources listed.

Benefits of secondary market research

The benefits of secondary market research to a business vary according to the relevance and detail of the data, and whether it is reliable and up to date. Beyond these factors, the main benefits are as follows:

- The information is already available, so quick decisions can be taken based upon it.
- It is cheaper than primary research; for some government research and the company's own information, it will be free. Market research organisations usually charge for their general research, but the expenses are shared between different organisations, making the cost cheaper.
- Secondary surveys are often conducted regularly, so the information obtained is particularly helpful in identifying trends over time.

Drawbacks of secondary market research

- The information may be dated and therefore could be misleading.
- Since the information is available to other firms, it is unlikely to give the organisation any advantages over its competitors.
- There may be no relevant secondary data to meet the specific needs of the firm.
- As the data are collected by other organisations for their own use, the secondary user may not know the level of accuracy and reliability of the data. Consequently, there is a danger that over-reliance on these data could lead to poor marketing decisions.

DID YOU KNOW?

The faster the pace of change, the more useful it is to conduct primary research, but the information becomes out of date more quickly.

AQA

 FILE

Gecko Headgear

A useful source of market research is feedback from customers. Gecko Headgear Ltd, a manufacturer of safety helmets that employs seven people in Cornwall, started as a supplier to surfers. Since it began supplying helmets to the Royal National Lifeboat Institution (RNLI), business has boomed. Constant feedback from the RNLI has led to 'ten different versions of the original safety helmet', according to founder, Jeff Sacree. He also confirms that 'partnerships with suppliers have been another key to success as their suggestions have led to improvements in products'. A new adhesive that is resistant to salt water is one such improvement.

EXAMINER'S VOICE

For questions that are based on market research data, it is always worth looking at the quality of the data before drawing firm conclusions:

- Is there a possible bias in the sample, the questions or the person conducting the survey?
- Is the sample large enough to be statistically significant?
- Is the survey recent and are opinions likely to have changed since it was conducted?

Content of data

Qualitative market research

As we saw earlier, market research may be classified in terms of its content, into qualitative or quantitative research.

Qualitative research deals with issues such as 'why?' or 'how?' With this information, Yorkshire Television might be able to see why people watch *Emmerdale*: is it the quality of the acting, the stunning scenery or the brilliance of the story lines? An organisation can use this information to plan appropriate strategies. For example, Sky has been able to attract more advertisers to its football programmes as a result of market research showing that football matches were watched by larger groups than other programmes. The normal measure of demand (the number of sets being used) therefore underestimated the number of people actually watching the programme.

KEY TERMS

qualitative market research: the collection of information about the market based on subjective factors such as opinions and reasons.

quantitative market research: the collection of information about the market based on numbers.

Benefits of qualitative market research

- By examining why consumers behave in a certain way, the business can gain a greater insight into what it needs to do to appeal to its consumers. Similarly, qualitative market research can be used to appeal to new potential customers in order to increase a firm's sales.
- This research can highlight issues that the business was not aware of, so it can take action to overcome problems or seize opportunities that might not have been considered before.
- Qualitative research can give detailed insights into customers' thinking processes when they buy products. This can enable a business to modify its marketing strategies and methods in order to persuade customers to buy more.

Drawbacks of qualitative market research

- It is expensive to gather qualitative information, as it usually requires skilled personnel to interpret it. Consequently, most qualitative research is conducted on a small scale. This can lead to bias or unrepresentative opinions.

from the services provided by, for example, hairdressers and sports centres. The same logic applies to services provided in the home by plumbers and electricians, who tend to be local businesses.

The vast majority of goods purchased in person by the consumer will also be bought in a local market, as customers are reluctant to travel long distances, because of the costs and time involved.

Traditionally, the local market was centred on the high street of a particular town or city, but in recent decades there has been a growing tendency for out-of-town shopping centres to develop. It should be noted, however, that although the markets may be local, the companies operating in city centres and out-of-town centres are invariably national companies and, in some cases, multinational organisations.

National markets

A national market can be defined in one of two ways. First, a company would see itself as operating in a national market if it sold its products or services across all or most of the country. Consequently, organisations such as British Home Stores (Bhs), Ford and Lloyds TSB see themselves as operating in a national market, although their individual outlets tend to compete locally for the customers in a particular geographical area.

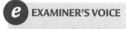

EXAMINER'S VOICE

International markets are not examined, as it is unlikely that they will be targeted by a start-up business.

Second, many industrial and primary products, such as building materials, gravel, machine parts and electronic equipment, are traded on a national or even international scale. The organisations that produce these products mainly deal in providing products that are components of consumer goods made by other organisations. Therefore, they compete in a national market in order to persuade companies that make consumer goods to buy their components or materials.

 FILE

Perishable goods

Where components are perishable or expensive to transport, a local market may be used in preference to a national market. Many supermarkets purchase fresh fruit and vegetables locally for this reason. The supermarkets have also found that this policy improves their image, as they are seen to be supporting the local community.

Physical and non-physical markets

This classification is based on the way in which products are bought and sold.

Physical markets

This is the traditional view of a market. In a physical market there is an actual place where buyers and sellers meet. This can be a marketplace, a shop, a garage or a business's own premises. Invariably, the product itself can be seen,

so the purchaser can make a well-reasoned decision about whether it is worth the price being charged.

Non-physical (electronic) markets

For many goods and services, the traditional, physical market is being replaced by marketplaces that take advantage of the opportunities presented by modern technology. Telephone sales have been used for some products over a long period of time. In the last decade there has been a rapid increase in the use of the internet as a marketplace. For firms producing certain goods and services, these electronic methods of buying and selling present both opportunities and challenges. Electronic markets are of particular significance to business start-ups because they allow small firms to compete in a national market without the high levels of capital that were previously required.

Other classifications of markets

- Markets can also be classified in accordance with the type of customer. This is known as **market segmentation** and will be dealt with later in this chapter (see pp. 63–67).
- Markets may also be classified according to the level of competition in the market. This is dealt with in Chapter 34.

The nature of the market

Firms need to recognise the nature of the market that they are in. TGI Friday's sees itself as being in the entertainment industry rather than as a 'restaurant'. A similar view is held by McDonald's, which aims to make eating out a social rather than a culinary experience. By redefining their market, these and other companies have seen a rapid increase in 'eating out'. In 2007 44% of all food expenditure was on meals provided by restaurants and takeaways, compared with less than 20% 20 years ago.

In a similar way, many DIY companies are promoting do-it-yourself as a leisure activity as well as a means of home improvement, in order to try to increase the size of their market. Garden centres are including more facilities in their premises, so that a visit can be more of a leisure pursuit than a shopping expedition.

 FILE

Choosing a target market

The choice of market to target depends on the nature of the product, the customers and the strategies of the entrepreneur. Young entrepreneur Fraser Doherty started making 'Super Jam' at the age of 14. He focused initially on the local market near Edinburgh, capitalising on the strong demand for local produce in the area. However, a deal with Waitrose has now started the move to a national market as his target.

Louis Barnett, who set up his confectionery company, Chokolit, at the age of 13, has moved quickly into the international market. His unique selling point is the fact that the chocolates are in a box that is itself made of chocolate. Having quickly extended beyond the Midlands into over 300 Sainsbury's stores, Chokolit has now set up an international distribution system to target the European market, as a result of the level of interest received through the internet.

Demand

It is important for a business to understand the nature of the demand for its products and how this demand is affected by different factors.

Factors influencing the demand for a product

The factors influencing demand vary according to the product or service that is being considered. However, there are a number of factors that influence the demand for most products or services.

Price

As the price of a product rises, the demand for it will usually fall. This is partly because consumers will think more carefully about whether the product is required, but also because alternative products will appear more attractive in comparison with the initial product.

For products that are necessities and have no close alternatives (substitutes), an increase in the price will make little difference to the quantity demanded. In contrast, if the product is not a necessity and has many close substitutes, an increase in the price can lead to a quite dramatic fall in the quantity demanded. The extent to which the price influences the demand for a product is known as the **price elasticity of demand**. This is considered in more detail in Chapter 32.

The same logic applies to a fall in price. A fall in price will lead to a rise in demand. The degree of change in demand will depend on factors such as the level of necessity and the existence or non-existence of close substitutes.

Income and wealth of consumers

The demand for a product is connected not only to consumers' *willingness* to purchase the product, but also to their *ability* to purchase it. To some extent this ability depends on the price of the product, but it also depends on the income and wealth of the consumer. As consumers' incomes increase, their overall demand for products also rises. Furthermore, the pattern of consumers' demand changes, as they purchase more luxuries but fewer basic goods.

One of the keys to Tesco's success in recent years has been its wide provision of goods, from its 'Value' range (targeted mainly at people on low incomes) to its 'Finest' range (aimed at wealthier consumers). This means that people will always be able to find products that appeal to them, regardless of their income level.

Tastes and fashion

Over time, fashion and people's tastes change. Such changes affect the demand for products and services. Changes in work patterns tend to mean that fewer families sit down in the evening for a traditionally produced family meal, often because of a lack of time. Consequently, people are now more likely to buy takeaway meals or convenience food, as opposed to ingredients for meals that take some time to prepare. In contrast, people now tend to spend more time shopping and are therefore more likely to spend time relaxing in a coffee shop or restaurant while on a shopping trip.

Some items, notably (but not exclusively) clothing, are also prone to swings in demand, according to what is perceived to be fashionable at the time. Consequently, businesses in these industries must keep a close eye on the latest consumer trends in order to cater for any changes in demand. Good market research can be the key to success in such cases.

Prices of other goods

Sometimes, the demand for a product can be influenced by the price of a totally different product. This occurs in two instances — when the products are either substitutes or complements:

- **Substitutes.** These are goods that are close alternatives to a particular product. If the price of the substitute increases, the original product will appear to be much better value for money in comparison. Therefore, the demand for this product will increase. Similarly, a fall in the price of a substitute will lead to a fall in demand for the product.
- **Complements.** Complementary products are ones that are used alongside each other, such as fish and chips, or shampoo and conditioner. If the demand for one of these products increases, the demand for the complement will also increase and vice versa. For example, if fish becomes more expensive, people will be less likely to buy it, so the demand for chips will fall, even though the price of chips remains the same.

 FILE

Innocent smoothies and McDonald's

In 2007 Innocent Drinks agreed to supply their beverages to McDonald's. This was designed to support McDonald's attempts to become more strongly associated with healthy food, while giving Innocent a boost in sales by providing it with a major new outlet and a new complement (McDonald's meals). However, Innocent is seeking feedback from customers about this, as the company is concerned that loyal customers may dislike the link to McDonald's.

Demographic factors

Demographic factors are those related to population. The UK population has grown in recent years and this has led to an increase in overall demand. Alongside this overall increase there have been changes to the geographical

spread of the population, its ethnic balance, the size of households and the age distribution of the population.

These have all led to changes in patterns of demand. For example, changes in the geographical spread of the population have increased the demand for supermarkets in the southeast of England. Immigration has led to the growth of products such as Indian food in the UK. The growing number of individuals living alone has led to an increase in the building of flats rather than houses. An ageing population has caused an increase in the demand for leisure cruises.

Marketing and advertising

Successful marketing and promotion can have a major impact on the demand for a good or service. Innocent Drinks believes that clever use of advertising and public relations has greatly helped its growth. In autumn 2007, Cadbury's released an advert featuring a gorilla playing the drums. It was hailed as a great success and has increased brand awareness.

The creation of a strong brand can also lead to consumers being prepared to pay a higher price for a product, as well as purchasing more of it. Consequently, the business can increase its sales volume, its value added and its sales value.

Competitors' actions

The demand for a product will also be influenced by the strategies of a competitor. In addition to price changes (see prices of other goods), a competitor may introduce a new product or increase the popularity of an existing product through effective marketing. These actions will lead to a decrease in demand for the rival firm's products.

The reverse also applies. Ineffective actions by a competitor may help a business to benefit from an increase in demand for its products.

Seasonal factors

The time of year has a significant impact on demand. Products such as porridge and ice cream experience huge fluctuations in demand between summer and winter. Businesses may try to overcome these fluctuations by providing a range of goods (e.g. a clothing store will change its stock according to the season) so that demand is more evenly spread throughout the year. However, it is difficult to ensure that there are no seasonal fluctuations in demand.

Government action

The government can influence the demand for a product in a number of ways.

In order to encourage demand, the government can subsidise a product to reduce its price. Alternatively, it can introduce its own advertising campaigns to encourage the purchase of a product that it regards as being desirable for people to buy. In some cases, such as seat belts in cars, the government can make it compulsory for a product to be used.

If the government wishes to reduce the demand for a product, it can do this through taxation. For example, cigarettes are taxed heavily and this leads to a much higher price. The government may also use advertising to discourage purchase of the product. Finally, it can introduce legislation (laws) to restrict the advertising or use of a product, or to ban it altogether. In 2007, sales of cheese were hit by the inclusion of cheese on the list of unhealthy products that cannot be advertised during children's television programmes.

The ban on smoking in public, introduced throughout the UK between 2006 and 2007, has led to a fall in sales of cigarettes. However, it has also hit other businesses, such as bingo halls, as the lack of opportunity to smoke discourages some customers from visiting.

WHAT DO YOU THINK?

Some people believe that the government intervenes too much in order to influence the demand for certain products. They argue that markets should be allowed to operate freely so that people can buy the products they most want. Other people argue that the government should intervene more, citing examples such as global warming as instances where the market economy encourages the purchase of goods and services (e.g. air travel) that may cause permanent damage to the environment.

e EXAMINER'S VOICE

There are many factors that can affect demand. Look for clues in the articles and case studies in examination papers, as changes do not always fit neatly into the main categories identified. Some recent changes in demand in the UK illustrate this:

- Between February and May 2007, ASDA sold 1.2 million more clothes pegs than during the same period in 2006, as a result of environmentally conscious customers cutting back on the use of tumble dryers.
- With approximately 600,000 Poles now living in the UK, sales of Polish products have increased. For example, 10 million pints of the Polish beer Tyskie were sold in 6 months at the end of 2006.
- Annual sales of stockings have halved from £10 million to £5 million in the last 4 years. During the same period, sales of footless tights have increased by £5 million.

Market segmentation

Types of market segmentation

A number of different ways of segmenting a market may be identified. The AQA A-level business studies specification only requires an understanding of

KEY TERM

market segmentation: the classification of customers or potential customers into groups or sub-groups (market segments), each of which responds differently to different products or marketing approaches.

KEY TERM

segmentation analysis: where a firm uses quantitative and qualitative data or information to try to discover the types of consumer who buy its products and why.

e EXAMINER'S VOICE

Remember that market segmentation is based on customers rather than markets or products. It is a method of putting different customers into categories, to help a firm market its products.

demographic and **geographic segmentation**. Two alternative approaches have been noted at the end of this section for information only.

Demographic segmentation

The main forms of demographic segmentation are age, gender and social class, although residential/housing methods are also popular.

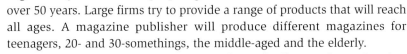

- **Age.** For many products and services, age is a crucial influence on demand, so firms will segment on this basis. Holidays are a classic example: Club 18–30 targets its holidays at a specific age range, while Saga holidays are aimed at people aged over 50 years. Large firms try to provide a range of products that will reach all ages. A magazine publisher will produce different magazines for teenagers, 20- and 30-somethings, the middle-aged and the elderly.
- **Gender (sex).** Some products are targeted specifically at males or females. The market for perfume is dominated by females, while attendance at sporting events has been dominated by male customers. However, in both these cases, firms have recognised the potential for growth by targeting the other gender.
- **Social class.** This method classifies families according to occupation:

I/A	Professional
II/B	Managerial and technical
IIIN/C1	Skilled: non-manual
IIIM/C2	Skilled: manual
IV/D	Partly skilled
V/E	Unskilled

In general, social class influences purchasing habits because class A receives more income than class B and so on. However, there are some activities that may appeal to particular social classes regardless of income: for example, golfers are more likely than football supporters to be from the middle classes, A, B and C1.

- **Residential.** One of the main residential methods is ACORN (A Classification Of Residential Neighbourhoods). This segments the market according to types of housing. Over 30 different categories of housing are identified by this technique. Families in suburban detached houses are expected to have very different tastes from those living in terraced houses in rural areas. Postcodes can be used to identify these segments, helping firms to target their marketing.

Geographic segmentation

Although regional variations in taste are becoming less significant, there are still major differences in tastes and purchasing behaviour based on geographical features. Rambling, surfing, theatre visits and night-clubbing are all activities that are influenced by the place where someone lives. Geographic variations may be linked to regions (e.g. differences in tastes between the north and south), to the differences in spending patterns in urban as opposed to rural areas, and to geographical features such as the terrain and climate.

Other segmentation methods

- **Lifestyle.** This type of segmentation is becoming more popular as businesses can use credit card and loyalty card records to identify the pattern of individuals' expenditure. Family food purchases are classified into categories according to the tendency to buy takeaways, organic food, economy brands, health foods etc. Leisure pursuits are also used to segment customers for marketing purposes.
- **Usage/frequency of purchase.** Some customers, known as 'early adopters', like to be the first to try new products; in contrast, 'followers' are more cautious. Awareness of these customer types allows a firm to target the right people. Similarly, consumers can be classified according to how often they purchase products. A frequent purchaser will have a different view of a product from an occasional, casual user.

 **EXAMINER'S VOICE**

Market segmentation is becoming much more sophisticated because databases can now provide firms with quite detailed data on consumers. Loyalty cards and credit or debit card transactions also enable firms to identify potential customers more accurately. This has led to an increase in direct mail promotions to customers.

What type of segmentation?

The exact type of segmentation used depends on the business or the product. For example, in the case of clothing, gender is important and so is age, especially for children's clothing. Not every type of segmentation is used by every business. In general, organisations identify the market segment or segments that are relevant to their products and services. Products, services and the organisation's approach to marketing is then geared to the targeted segments.

FACT FILE

Market segmentation of social networks in the UK

In the USA, Facebook is reputed to appeal to richer people from 'higher' social classes. Does this feature apply to UK users too? This is vital information as advertisers want to know who their adverts are reaching so that they can target customers effectively.

Table 6.1 shows the breakdown of the three leading social networks, all of which tend to target younger age groups.

Table 6.1 *Profile of social network users in the UK*

Source: Nielsen/Net Ratings, July 2007.

	Bebo (%)	Facebook (%)	MySpace (%)
Age			
2–17	32	5	15
18–34	33	66	46
35–49	23	14	24
50+	12	15	15
Household income			
Under £30,000 p.a.	46	40	45
£30,000–£49,999	27	25	26
£50,000 and over	20	28	22
Education			
Still at primary school	11	2	5
At secondary school	23	6	13
Completed secondary school	12	9	13
In further education	30	34	36
Taking degree course or completed	24	49	34

Benefits and drawbacks of market segmentation

The benefits and drawbacks of market segmentation apply generally to all the types of segmentation. However, the extent to which a particular organisation might benefit from segmentation depends on the degree to which:

- a particular segment can be easily identified
- consumer behaviour varies according to market segmentation
- the firm is able to reach that segment directly in its marketing and market research

Benefits of market segmentation

There are several benefits for businesses that use market segmentation:

- **To increase market share.** An organisation can identify market segments that have not been reached and adapt its products and marketing to reach those segments. For example, Mothercare extended the age range of its products to attract older children and mothers.
- **To assist new product development.** Gaps in market segments can be used to indicate the scope for introducing new products. Originally, software offered with new computers tended to be games. These offers have been extended to appeal to more segments by including Microsoft Office, photographic processing, music and educational software.
- **To extend products into new markets.** Mobile phones were initially targeted at business users before being extended to teenagers and then whole families.
- **To identify ways of marketing a product.** A company that recognises its customers' characteristics can target its advertising to media used by that market segment. For example, someone in social class A is most likely to read *The Times*, whereas someone in social class E has a greater tendency to read the *Star*. Similarly, promotional methods and messages can be

modified to suit specific segments — for instance, young people prefer different images from older consumers.

 EXAMINER'S VOICE

In questions on market segmentation, identify and focus your arguments on the market segment or segments that are relevant to the product or business in the case study. For example, suppose that the target market is young males. In this case, the firm should place advertisements in magazines read by young males, using messages or characters that will excite their interest. The features of the product should be those that will appeal to young men.

Drawbacks of market segmentation

Segmentation analysis may involve the following problems:

- **Difficulty in identifying the most important segments for a product.** Successful segmentation requires market segments to be identifiable, reachable and distinct. In practice, a business may be unable to categorise its customers. Some segments, such as gender, are easy to identify, but it is more difficult to put consumers of bread, household cleaners and pillows into categories.
- **Reaching the chosen segment with marketing.** Lifestyle categories in particular are difficult to identify or locate. Which media would you use to attract primary school parents on a national scale? In general, socioeconomic class tends to be the most difficult of the demographic segments to target.
- **Recognising changes in the segments interested in the product.** Markets are dynamic and businesses cannot assume that an existing segment will always stay loyal to a product. Thus businesses must constantly research their market segments.
- **Meeting the needs of customers not included in the chosen segment.** Emphasis on market segmentation may lead to a business ignoring other potential customers. This may prevent a business from attracting the mass market.

 YOU KNOW?

Sometimes it is important to identify the *buyer* rather than the *consumer* when segmenting a market. Surveys show that women buy more male underwear than men.

Similarly, when it comes to selling make-up to young girls, up to the age of 12, mothers are most likely to make the decision; from age 13 onwards, they have less say.

Such information can make a big difference to the way in which a product is marketed.

 EXAMINER'S VOICE

Use the mark allocation as a guide to the length of your answer. After allowing for reading and planning time (15 minutes on BUSS1), AQA A-level business studies papers tend to use the same formula: a mark a minute.

Market mapping

Market mapping is a technique that uses market segmentation to look at the features that distinguish different products or firms. In the case of the car market, people may buy cars because they are:

- suitable for family use (e.g. they are large enough to carry a pram or to seat three children)
- cheap to buy and/or run (e.g. replacement parts are cheap, so garage bills should be cheaper)
- environmentally friendly (e.g. they have efficient consumption of fuel to limit emissions)
- capable of fast speeds (e.g. they accelerate quickly and so appeal to 'boy racers')
- safe and secure (e.g. off-road vehicles protect the passengers in case of an accident)

Interestingly, in relation to the last point some people would argue that off-road vehicles can cause more injuries to other road users, but for the person making the decision to buy, this is not such an important consideration. For a similar reason, cigarette companies were unsuccessful when they developed a smokeless cigarette because it was not smokers who disliked cigarette smoke, and so they did not buy the new product.

Features such as those listed can be 'mapped' in order to identify the extent to which an individual car possesses them. An example, featuring the market for female clothing, is illustrated in Figure 6.1 on p. 72. A computer-based model or map could examine any number of factors at the same time, but for convenience it is normal to show the two most important factors in a market map. For the female clothing market, these could be price and fashion. A firm or product at the centre of the map would not be seen to possess either feature significantly. In this market, Karen Millen represents a brand that is considered to be set at a premium price (often a measure of quality) and offers fashionable products. Peacocks provides functional (non-fashionable) clothing that is relatively cheap to buy.

Benefits of market mapping

Market mapping has the following benefits:

- It helps firms to identify their closest rivals, in order to plan suitable competitive strategies.
- It helps to identify gaps or niches in the market that could be filled by the introduction of a new product or image.
- If carried out through market research, it can help a firm to discover the public's view of it as a business/brand.
- It may help a firm that needs to reposition itself in a market (e.g. Skoda).

Market size, growth and share

How is a market measured?

Many markets are measured by *volume* because it is easier for people to identify with an item than with a sum of money. For example, in the car market it is easier to picture 2.5 million cars being sold than a value of

e **EXAMINER'S VOICE**

Remember the trigger words in any question. 'Analyse', 'examine' and 'explain why' require analysis — developing a line of argument. 'Evaluate', 'discuss', 'to what extent' and 'justify your view' require evaluation — weighing up your answer and making a judgement.

KEY TERM

market size: the volume of sales of a product (e.g. the number of computers sold) or the value of sales of a product (e.g. the total revenue from computer sales).

£30 billion. However, in some markets (e.g. hair care products, dog food and deodorants) there are many different products with huge variations in price. In these cases, it is easier to measure the market in terms of the *value* of goods sold.

Market growth

Market size can increase as a result of extra sales of goods or persuading customers to pay higher prices. Trainers and other markets with premium brands are good examples of this latter point.

KEY TERM

market growth: the percentage change in sales (volume or value) over a period of time.

The market size indicates the potential sales for a firm. In a car market worth £30 billion a year, a car manufacturer can earn huge revenue even if it is only small in comparison with its competitors.

The volume of car sales fell by 3.5% between 2005 and 2006 (see Table 6.2 on p. 70). Declining markets are likely to lead to falling sales for an individual manufacturer, but they also discourage competition. This can allow a dominant company to 'milk' its 'cash cows' to boost its profits.

In growing markets, there is more scope for increased sales, but competition is likely to become fiercer. In 2006 the growth rate in the car market was below the average growth rate in the UK. Cars are often purchased on credit and fears of higher interest rates and a slowing of economic growth made people more cautious.

Factors influencing market growth

Market growth is largely outside the control of individual firms. However, a business should be aware of the factors that influence growth, so that it can predict future trends and make sure that it is taking advantage of the potential for growth in certain markets (or avoiding the problems faced in declining markets). Key factors are as follows:

- **Economic growth.** If a country's wealth is growing by 3% per annum, then sales are likely to rise in any given market.
- **The nature of the product.** Markets dealing with luxury products, such as jewellery or investments, tend to grow more rapidly when growth is high, but often suffer more severe cutbacks when people are worried about their living standards.
- **Changes in taste.** As lifestyles change, new products become more popular while others decline. This is a factor that firms can influence through good marketing.
- **Social changes.** The way in which people live may influence product sales. A greater tendency to stay at home will assist sales of digital televisions, while longer working hours have led to fewer people preparing their own meals.
- **Fashion.** Recent television programmes highlighting the delights of home cooking, garden design and do-it-yourself are likely to influence the number

of people pursuing those activities. Note how the market for home cooking is being increased by this factor but reduced by the previous influence.

Market share

KEY TERM

market share: the percentage or proportion of the total sales of a product or service achieved by a firm or a specific brand of a product.

Market share is usually measured as a percentage, calculated by the formula:

$$\text{market share} = \frac{\text{sales of one product or brand or company}}{\text{total sales in the market}} \times 100$$

Market share is an excellent measure of a company's success because it compares a firm's sales with those of its competitors. A company's market share can increase only if the company is performing better than some of its rivals.

> **𝑒** **EXAMINER'S VOICE**
>
> When defining terms in an examination, try not to repeat words that are used in the question: for example, by saying that 'market share is the share of the market owned by a company'. This is a correct statement but is just paraphrasing the question. A better answer is 'market share is the percentage of total sales of a product achieved by one company'.

In 2006 Peugeot's car sales decreased, but only by 0.1% (see Table 6.2). Because total sales in the car market fell more rapidly, by 3.5%, Peugeot's overall share of the market rose by 0.2%. Audi's sales fell by 3.5%, the same as the fall in total car sales in 2006. Consequently, its market share remained the same as the year before. Businesses often aim to be the market leader, taking the largest share of the market.

PRACTICE EXERCISE 1 — Total: 45 marks (45 minutes)

Read the information in Table 6.2 and, using your knowledge of business, answer the questions that follow.

Table 6.2 *Analysis of the UK market for new cars, 2006*

Source: The Society of Motor Manufacturers and Traders (SMMT), January 2007.

Manufacturer	Cars sold 2005	Cars sold 2006	% change	Market share 2005 (%)	Market share 2006 (%)
1 Ford	347,551	344,408	–0.9	14.3	14.8
2 Vauxhall	317,353	301,679	–4.9	13.1	12.9
3 Volkswagen	185,519	189,959	+2.4	7.7	8.1
4 Peugeot	144,332	144,132	–0.1	6.0	6.2
5 Renault	174,743	138,094	–21.0	7.2	5.9
6 Toyota	122,534	117,819	–3.8	5.1	5.1
7 BMW	111,666	115,616	+3.5	4.6	5.0
8 Honda	98,344	97,728	–0.6	4.1	4.2
9 Citroën	99,576	95,578	–4.0	4.1	4.1
10 Audi	85,494	82,496	–3.5	3.5	3.5
Other makes	737,785	703,842	–4.6	30.4	30.2
Total market	**2,424,897**	**2,331,351**	**–3.9**	**100.0**	**100.0**

1 How large was the market for new cars in the UK in 2006? *(1 mark)*

2 Which company was the market leader? *(1 mark)*

3 **a** Between 2005 and 2006, which firm had the largest increase in the number of cars sold? *(2 marks)*
   b Between 2005 and 2006, which firm had the largest percentage increase in its sale of cars? *(1 mark)*

4 How was it possible for Honda to have a decrease in sales and yet increase its market share? *(4 marks)*

5 Analyse two possible reasons why Ford sales are greater than the sales of other car manufacturers. *(6 marks)*

6 Volkswagen occupies third place in terms of UK market share. However, Volkswagen is part of a business that also owns Audi, Skoda and Seat (tenth, fourteenth and eighteenth in the market). Explain why a firm might use different brand names for different cars in this way. *(6 marks)*

7 Why might the use of volume (the number of cars sold) give a misleading impression of the market share of a car manufacturer? *(4 marks)*

8 Analyse three factors that might influence the demand for new cars in the UK. *(9 marks)*

9 Evaluate the usefulness of the information in Table 6.2 to a small business that wishes to set up a franchise selling new cars. *(11 marks)*

PRACTICE EXERCISE 2   Total: 50 marks (40 minutes)

1 What is meant by the term 'market segment'? *(3 marks)*

2 Identify a product for which 'age' would be a useful way of segmenting the market. Justify your choice, indicating the specific ages that would be targeted. *(4 marks)*

3 Name four products for which 'gender' would be used to segment the market. *(4 marks)*

4 Explain three benefits of using market segmentation for a clothing retailer. *(9 marks)*

5 Examine two problems for a furniture manufacturer when trying to use segmentation analysis. *(6 marks)*

6 Why is 'social class' such a popular method of market segmentation? Support your answer with real-life examples. *(6 marks)*

7 How might market segmentation influence the media (television, radio, newspapers etc.) that
a business uses for its advertising? *(5 marks)*

8 In what circumstances is market segmentation unlikely to be helpful to a business? *(6 marks)*

9 How might a supermarket use information from a loyalty/reward card to assist its marketing? *(4 marks)*

10 What is an 'early adopter'? *(3 marks)*

Choosing the right legal structure for the business

This chapter explains the terms 'unincorporated' and 'incorporated' businesses, and the concepts of unlimited and limited liability. It then examines the various legal structures that businesses in the private sector can adopt, focusing particularly on sole traders, partnerships, and private and public limited companies. The chapter also considers the characteristics and significance of not-for-profit businesses.

Unincorporated and incorporated businesses

The range of legal structures in the private sector is illustrated in Figure 7.1. Two important classifications are unincorporated and incorporated businesses, and limited and unlimited liability.

Figure 7.1 Legal structures of business in the private sector

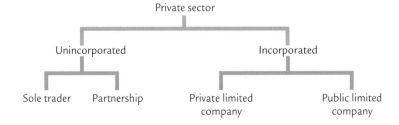

KEY TERMS

unincorporated business: there is no distinction in law between the individual owner and the business itself. The identity of the business and the owner is the same. Such businesses tend to be sole traders or partnerships.

incorporated business: this has a legal identity that is separate from the individual owners. As a result, these organisations can own assets, owe money and enter into contracts in their own right. Such businesses include private limited companies and public limited companies.

The distinction between unincorporated and incorporated businesses can be illustrated as follows. If you have a part-time job with Tesco plc, your employer, with whom you have a contract of employment, is Tesco and not the shareholders (owners) of Tesco. If, however, you have a part-time job with the local newsagent's, known (say) as Robinson's, which happens to be run as a sole trader by the owner, Mary Robinson, then your employer is the individual who owns the business, Mary Robinson. Similarly, if you had an accident on the premises of Tesco and were advised to sue, then you would sue Tesco plc, not the shareholders (owners) of Tesco. If, however, you had an accident on the premises of Robinson's newsagent, you would sue Mary Robinson, the owner.

Limited and unlimited liability

Unlimited liability is a characteristic of businesses that are unincorporated, meaning that there is no distinction in law between the owners and the business. If the debts of the business are greater than the personal assets of the owners, they may be forced into bankruptcy. The main types of business with unlimited liability are sole traders and partnerships.

In contrast, if a business with **limited liability** goes into liquidation because it cannot pay its debts, the shareholders (owners) have no responsibility for further payments as long as they have paid in full for the shares they have purchased; their personal assets cannot be used to pay the debts of the business. Legally, such a business has 'died' and so its debts 'die' with it. Limited liability is a feature of incorporated businesses, where the identity of the owners and the business are separate in law. The main types of business with limited liability are private limited companies and public limited companies. Limiting the amount of shareholders' liability is an important factor in encouraging people to invest, as they will be aware of the level of risk that they face.

> **DID YOU KNOW?**
>
> **Insolvency** occurs when the liabilities of a business are greater than its assets and it is unable to meet its financial obligations. Where this happens, it is likely that the business will go into **liquidation** — i.e. it will turn its assets into cash, for example by selling the firm or its assets, in order to pay creditors. The terms insolvency and liquidation are applied to incorporated businesses with limited liability. For individuals and for unincorporated businesses, with unlimited liability, the situation when liabilities cannot be paid in full is called **bankruptcy**.

Types of legal structure

Sole trader

Sole traders usually have little capital for expansion and are heavily reliant on their own personal commitment to make their business a success. Because of its unincorporated status, if the business is unsuccessful, there is no protection from limited liability, i.e. the firm's finances are inseparable from the owner's. Sole traders are most commonly found in the provision of local services, e.g. newsagents, plumbers and hairdressers.

> **KEY TERMS**
>
> **unlimited liability:** a situation in which the owners of a business are liable for all the debts that the business may incur.
>
> **limited liability:** a situation in which the liability of the owners of a business is limited to the fully paid-up value of the share capital.

> **e EXAMINER'S VOICE**
>
> Ensure that you are absolutely clear about the distinction between limited liability and unlimited liability, so that you do not confuse the two in your answers.

> **KEY TERM**
>
> **sole trader:** a business owned by one person. The owner may operate on his or her own or may employ other people.

CHAPTER 7   Choosing the right legal structure for the business

Partnership

The Partnership Act 1890 forms the basis of partnership law in the UK. Partners normally have unlimited liability, which means that each partner is liable for the debts of the other partners. A partnership agreement usually sets down the rights and responsibilities of the partners and how profits will be allocated. In the absence of an agreement, profits are shared equally among all partners. A partnership allows more capital to be used in the business than is the case with a sole trader and enables the pressures of running the business to be shared. It also gives partners more personal freedom to take holidays etc. However, unlike private or public limited companies, partners retain major responsibilities for the success of the organisation, and their ability to raise finance remains rather limited.

Under the Limited Partnership Act 1907, a **limited partnership** can be formed when at least one partner assumes responsibility for managing and running the business and has unlimited liability, and at least one partner contributes finance but has no involvement in the management or running of the business. Partners with unlimited liability are often called 'general partners' or 'active partners', and those with limited liability are often called 'limited partners' or 'sleeping partners'. In return for their investment, limited partners normally receive a dividend.

In 2000, the Limited Liability Partnership Act came into force and introduced a new form of business known as the **limited liability partnership** (LLP). This was created in response to pressure from large professional partnerships, such as accountancy and law firms, which were concerned about the unlimited liability of partners for very large legal claims, particularly for professional negligence. The LLP is designed for professional or trading partnerships. It enables partners who are actively involved in the business of their partnership to limit their liability for the partnership's debts. However, at least two partners, known as 'designated members', have additional responsibilities placed upon them. Partnerships that choose to become LLPs lose the privacy enjoyed by general partnerships in relation to their financial affairs and must, for example, register with Companies House, like private and public limited companies.

Private limited company

Public limited companies are often the most high-profile organisations but the significance of private limited companies should not be ignored. Most companies are privately owned and they contribute enormously to the economy.

Features of a private limited company

■ A private limited company can keep its affairs reasonably private and thus the owners can determine their own objectives without the pressure to achieve short-term profit that is so common for public limited companies.

KEY TERM

partnership: a form of business in which two or more people operate for the common goal of making a profit.

EXAMINER'S VOICE

Note the distinction between a limited partnership, which must include at least one partner with unlimited liability, and a limited liability partnership (LLP), where all partners have limited liability.

KEY TERM

private limited company: a small to medium-sized business that is usually run by the family or the small group of individuals who own it.

- Private companies are funded by shares that cannot be sold without the agreement of the other shareholders, which means that their shares cannot be traded on the Stock Exchange.

 FILE

The Stock Exchange

The Stock Exchange is a market where second-hand shares (i.e. shares that have already been issued by public limited companies) can be bought and sold. When a public limited company wishes to raise finance, it does this by issuing (selling) shares to the public. Once these have been issued, the owners can sell them on the Stock Exchange. The Stock Exchange assists companies in raising finance, since people would be more reluctant to buy shares if they could not easily offload them when required.

- The share capital of private companies may be less than £50,000, although many have much higher levels of share capital.
- Private limited companies generally tend to be limited in size.
- A private limited company must have 'Ltd' after the company name to warn people that its owners (shareholders) have limited liability.

 FILE

Changing legal structure to suit the circumstances

Samantha Hale has run her sports-products business, Advance Performance UK, as a sole-trading operation, a partnership and a limited company. Founded in 1996, the company first traded from a back bedroom but now has its own shop and is growing at a rate of over 20% a year. According to Hale:

When I started, I was selling sports products and my then-husband was coaching athletes. I started small, operating from home, and never needed outside funding, so being a sole trader seemed the simplest option.

But when I decided to get retail premises, things grew quickly and the expense of stocking and marketing the shop meant a strain on cash flow. So, a few months into having the shop, my husband and I formed a partnership. That way we could offset the initial 'start-up' losses from the shop against the profits from the coaching side of the business.

When my marriage and business partnership collapsed, I immediately changed the business to a limited company so I could protect my personal assets.

There are two people who really make this business run now, myself and the company secretary. He's worked his socks off since the shop opened, so going incorporated allowed me to give him 20% of the company's shares as a reward for his commitment.

When I set up my partnership with my ex-husband, I did it all on trust. I never thought things could go wrong. This caused enormous problems when the marriage broke up. It took 15 months and lots of negotiations to resolve.

If I was doing things again, I'd have everything in a written contract, with clauses saying exactly what happens should the partnership break down.

Source: **www.businesslink.gov.uk**

FACT FILE

The UK's biggest private limited companies

Each year the Oxford-based research company Fast Track produces a league table of the largest private businesses in the UK.

In 2007, top of the table was the Ineos Group, a chemical manufacturer based in Hampshire with sales of £18,134 million. In just 9 years, the firm has quietly built a global chemical giant by picking up unwanted subsidiaries from large companies such as BP and ICI.

At number two in the league table was the John Lewis Partnership, which has 26 John Lewis stores, 185 Waitrose stores and a 33% share in the online delivery business Ocado. Sales for the John Lewis Partnership were £5,698 million. In 2006, the business announced the appointment of its first non-executive directors — people who sit on the board of directors but do not have a full-time role in the company. Non-executive directors can offer less biased views of decisions and can bring more experience of other industries and firms.

The third largest private business was Somerfield, the supermarket chain, which changed from public to private company status in December 2005. It used to include the KwikSave chain, but these stores have now been rebranded as Somerfield. Sales at Somerfield were worth over £5,249 million.

Other well-known businesses in the 2007 league table were as follows (positions are given in brackets):
- Virgin Atlantic — airline and tour operator (10)
- Arcadia — fashion retailer including Dorothy Perkins, Burton and Topshop (13)
- Iceland — frozen-food retailer (15)
- JCB — construction equipment (20)
- Matalan — retailer (29)
- C & J Clark — Clarks shoes (34)
- Specsavers — optician (37)
- New Look — fashion retailer (39)
- Bhs — department store (41)
- Kwik-Fit — car repair (42)
- The AA — motor services (43)
- Thresher Group — off-licence (44)
- River Island — fashion retailer (46)
- Welcome Break — motorway services (59)
- Peacock Group — retailer (62)
- Trailfinders — travel agency (74)
- Odeon 8 UCI Cinemas Group — cinema operator (85)
- Dyson — vacuum cleaner maker (88)

Public limited company

 EXAMINER'S VOICE

As both private limited companies and public limited companies are incorporated businesses and have limited liability, ensure that you are clear on the distinction between them and do not confuse them in your answers.

 KEY TERM

public limited company: a business with limited liability; a share capital of over £50,000; at least two shareholders, two directors, a qualified company secretary; and, usually, a wide spread of shareholders. It has 'plc' after the company name.

The shares of public limited companies are traded on the Stock Exchange, which enables these businesses to raise finance more easily. Private limited companies sometimes change to public limited companies, usually to obtain extra funds for growth. However, 'going public' has disadvantages:

- It involves a loss of control, as the business moves away from the ownership and support of a family or close-knit group of individuals, and becomes responsible to shareholders, including institutional investors.
- It subjects the business to constant scrutiny by the financial press.
- It may cause the business to focus on short-term profits for shareholders and maintaining share prices in order to avoid takeover pressure, which detracts from long-term decision making.

YOU KNOW?

Institutional investors are pension funds, insurance companies and other financial organisations that invest huge sums of money in the shares of public limited companies quoted on the Stock Exchange. They are by far the largest group of investors in company shares and therefore have huge influence on companies. Critics suggest that it is pressure from institutional investors, which are seeking to maximise their funds and profits, that forces businesses to focus on short-term profits (known as **short-termism**) rather than on long-term performance.

e EXAMINER'S VOICE

Ensure that you understand the effect that becoming a public limited company with a quotation on the Stock Exchange can have on a company, as this is a crucial factor for a company that wants to grow.

These disadvantages are such that a number of large, successful private limited companies resist becoming public limited companies, while other successful public limited companies revert back to private limited company status. The number of public limited companies on the London Stock Exchange has declined sharply from almost 1,600 in 1997 to fewer than 1,000 in 2007. Well-known companies that have gone private include Debenhams, Arcadia, Selfridges, Harvey Nichols, Hamleys, New Look, Fitness First, Cannons, Esporta and Pizza Express.

Surprisingly, fewer than 10% of the companies that ceased trading as public limited companies suffered financial failure. Most chose to go private for a number of reasons, including the excessive cost of meeting the regulatory requirements for public limited companies, the continual dissection of public limited companies' performance by market analysts, and the relative privacy of the private limited company structure. A sharp rise in the amount of capital available to private companies is a major reason for the decline in the number of companies becoming public limited companies. Given the level of backing on offer, one of the greatest benefits of listing on the stock markets is no longer so compelling. Another key advantage of joining the stock market — share liquidity — has also become less persuasive and, indeed, is sometimes regarded as unnecessarily risky because predators can easily snap up shares and put pressure on management to make changes it may not agree with.

FACT FILE

The private equity boom

In recent years, private equity takeovers have played an important part in UK business. Private equity firms are made up of private investors who take over a company and work closely with the managers to turn the business around. Their aim is to make it profitable and then sell it. Therefore, they look for businesses that are undervalued and can be improved. Private equity firms often buy public limited companies, make them private, improve them and then sell them back to the public.

When public limited companies are listed on the Stock Exchange, managers often find that the investors are interested only in short-term rewards. This can make it difficult to invest in longer-term projects or to take risks in decision making. Radical, daring or innovative decisions may be shelved in favour of conservative and potentially uninspiring choices.

Reporting to many different investors also takes up a lot of management time. When a private equity company takes over a public limited company, it

empowers the managers to run the business and make the right decisions, even if they are risky or take years to pay off. The private equity firm is closely involved in the running of the business and in developing the right strategy.

However, private equity takeovers are usually financed by debts, so they carry a high risk. Some private equity firms have been accused of being asset strippers — buying a company to squeeze out whatever profit they can get before selling it on. In general, private equity is perceived as representing the short-term interest of between 2 and 5 years — quite different from the longer-term perspective taken by most family-based private limited companies.

Structure	Advantages	Disadvantages
Sole trader	<ul><li>easy and cheap to set up</li><li>few legal formalities</li><li>able to respond quickly to changes in circumstances</li><li>owner takes all the profit and hence there is good motivation</li><li>independence</li><li>more privacy than other legal structures, as financial details do not have to be published</li></ul>	<ul><li>unlimited liability</li><li>limited collateral to support applications for loans</li><li>limited capital for investment and expansion</li><li>difficulties when the owner wishes to go on holiday or is ill</li><li>limited skills as the owner needs to be a 'jack of all trades'</li></ul>
Partnership	<ul><li>between them, partners may have a wide range of skills and knowledge</li><li>partners are able to raise greater amounts of capital than sole traders</li><li>the pressure on owners is reduced, as cover is available for holidays and decisions are made jointly</li></ul>	<ul><li>control is shared among the partners</li><li>arguments are common among partners</li><li>there is still an absolute shortage of capital — even 20 people can only raise so much</li><li>unlimited liability (unless a limited liability partnership)</li></ul>
Private limited company	<ul><li>limited liability and the business has a separate legal identity</li><li>access to more capital than unincorporated businesses</li><li>more privacy than a plc, as it is only required to divulge a limited amount of financial information</li><li>more flexible than a plc</li></ul>	<ul><li>shares are less attractive, as they cannot be traded on the Stock Exchange and hence could be difficult to sell</li><li>less flexible if expansion needs finance, which is more difficult to raise than for a plc</li><li>there are more legal formalities than for an unincorporated business</li></ul>
Public limited company	<ul><li>limited liability and the business has a separate legal identity</li><li>easier to raise finance as a result of its Stock Exchange listing</li><li>greater scope for new investment</li><li>can gain positive publicity as a result of trading on the Stock Exchange</li><li>suppliers tend to be more willing to offer credit to public limited companies</li></ul>	<ul><li>must publish a great deal of financial information about its performance</li><li>greater scrutiny of activities</li><li>significant administrative expenses</li><li>founders of the firm may lose control if their shareholding falls below 51%</li><li>a stock exchange listing means pressure from investors may lead to more emphasis on short-term financial results, not long-term performance</li></ul>

Table 7.1 Advantages and disadvantages of different legal structures

The advantages and disadvantages of each type of organisation considered in this chapter are summarised in Table 7.1.

Divorce of ownership and control

Traditionally, entrepreneurs have two functions: **ownership** and **control**.

In a sole trader business, the owner and manager are likely to be the same person, so these functions remain with that one person, the entrepreneur.

However, in public limited companies, the owners (shareholders) vote for a board of directors, who in turn appoint managers to control and manage the business. In this case, the two functions of ownership and control are separated or divorced.

The functions have been separated for a number of reasons. In order to raise finance for further growth, many private limited companies become public limited companies. In turn, large public limited companies attract shareholders, who may only be interested in the dividends they can earn on their shares or in the capital gain they can make from buying and selling shares. They often have little or no real interest in the management of the company or its long-term performance.

The fact that managers and shareholders become more separated as the company grows can mean that shareholders find it difficult to access the information needed to challenge or judge the quality of managers' decisions. The more autonomy managers have, the more likely they might pursue objectives that benefit themselves rather than shareholders, such as furthering their own careers or increasing their job satisfaction.

A more positive view of the divorce of ownership and control is that shareholders have too narrow a focus on short-term finance and also have less understanding than management of the needs of the other stakeholders. Figure 7.2 illustrates this issue.

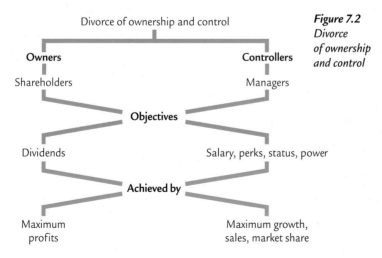

Figure 7.2
Divorce of ownership and control

KEY TERMS

ownership: providing finance and therefore taking risks.

control: managing the organisation and making decisions.

KEY TERM

stakeholders: any group of individuals with an interest in a business. This includes employees, customers, shareholders and the local community.

_e_ EXAMINER'S VOICE

Ensure you understand the difference between shareholders and stakeholders. Stakeholders include shareholders, but also include other groups with an interest in a business, such as employees, customers, the local community and suppliers.

Corporate governance

Corporate governance refers to the systems and mechanisms established by a firm to protect the interests of its owners (shareholders). In theory, the board of directors is elected to represent shareholder interests, determine strategy and ensure that the firm acts legally. But how do shareholders make sure that the directors actually do a good job? Most of the information they receive will

be from the directors themselves, so how can investors make sure that the directors are not being negligent or that they are not being misled?

The challenge of making sure that companies are run in the best interests of their owners is a complex one. Shareholders do not want to know everything that happens in the business — this would simply lead to an information overload and the directors must be given some freedom to do their job. On the other hand, the shareholders do own the company and so should be kept informed of relevant issues — but how do they know this is happening and that the directors are presenting the information truthfully? While there is no doubt that an independent, questioning approach is desirable to keep a check on a firm's actions, there is also the need for strong leadership and good-quality directors who have a deep inside knowledge of the business. So what is the right mix?

The delicate relationship between shareholders, directors and managers has been reviewed in the UK several times at the request of the government. The Cadbury Report (1992), the Hampel Report (1998) and the Higgs Report (2003) have made numerous recommendations for UK companies, mainly focusing on the need for public limited companies to have more **non-executive directors**, i.e. directors who do not have a full-time job in the business. The argument is that these non-executive directors will be more independent and provide a better check on managers' behaviour than executive directors, who are in effect checking on themselves. Allowing managers to police themselves might mean that issues are not examined from enough perspectives — the right questions do not get asked, so the right solutions are not found.

In the UK, and more recently in the USA, much greater pressure is now being put on directors to be more accountable to their shareholders. However, investors still cannot be sure that their money is being used in the way they want or that power is not being abused.

Not-for-profit organisations

Not-for-profit organisations include a large and diverse group that are increasingly known as the **third sector** (i.e. neither the commercial nor the public sector). This sector includes voluntary and community organisations, charities, social enterprises, pressure groups, cooperatives, mutual societies and trusts. There are an estimated 400,000 not-for-profit organisations, of which approximately 180,000 are charities registered with the Charity Commission.

Although the organisations vary, they share the following common characteristics:
- They are non-governmental organisations.
- They have a governing body responsible for managing their affairs.
- They are value driven and have social, environmental, community, welfare or cultural aims and objectives.

FACT FILE

Shaw Trust

Shaw Trust is a national charity that provides training and work opportunities for people who are disadvantaged in the labour market owing to disability, ill health or other social circumstances. It is the largest voluntary-sector provider of employment services for disabled people in the UK.

- They are usually established for purposes other than financial gain, with any profits or surpluses being reinvested in the organisation in order to further its objectives.
- Many use volunteer staff in addition to paid employees.

These organisations may make profit, but their objective is not to maximise profit for their shareholders and owners. They can operate under a number of different legal structures, including charities, trusts and companies limited by guarantee.

FACT FILE

While most private limited companies are owned by their shareholders and are limited by shares, it is also possible to set up a private company limited by guarantee. Such an organisation has a defined legal identity and limited liability status. Shelter, for example, is a charity and has a limited company for its trading activities, and AQA, your examining board, is a company limited by guarantee.

By taking up limited liability status, a charity limits the liability of its management or trustees in respect of any financial losses that it may sustain. The directors of the organisation give a nominal guarantee (usually of £1), and are not personally liable for any losses beyond that amount. A charitable company limited by guarantee is forbidden from distributing profits to its directors or members and so complies with the 'not-for-profit' classification. Some charitable organisations divide themselves into a number of associated parts, each with a different legal status, such as a company limited by guarantee and an educational trust. In this way, each part can benefit from different legal or tax benefits.

Conclusion

A number of factors affect the choice of legal structure. These include the need for finance in order to expand; the size of the business, and the level and type of investment required; the need for limited liability; the degree of control desired by the original owners; the nature of the business; and the level of risk involved.

For example, a manufacturing business requiring heavy investment in plant and equipment before anything can be sold may need limited liability in order to raise sufficient funds. On the other hand, a business that requires much less investment and therefore very little borrowing will involve relatively little financial risk, and there may be no need for limited liability. In other cases, image might be vitally important and the word 'Ltd' after a name may add status, and 'plc' even more so.

PRACTICE EXERCISE   Total: 40 marks (30 minutes)

1 What is meant by the term 'incorporated business'?   *(2 marks)*

2 What is meant by the term 'unincorporated business'?   *(2 marks)*

3 Explain the implications of a business having unlimited liability.   *(3 marks)*

4 Explain the implications of a business having limited liability. *(3 marks)*

5 Explain two advantages and two disadvantages of a sole trader as compared with a partnership. *(8 marks)*

6 Distinguish between a limited liability partnership and an ordinary partnership. *(4 marks)*

7 Distinguish between a private limited company and a public limited company. *(4 marks)*

8 Identify two advantages of a private limited company over a public limited company. *(2 marks)*

9 Identify three disadvantages of a private limited company as compared with a public limited company. *(3 marks)*

10 State and explain three factors that are likely to influence the choice of legal structure. *(9 marks)*

CASE STUDY Staying private

A number of large, high-profile, public limited companies have made the decision to revert back to private limited company status in order to reduce media scrutiny and pressure and the accompanying emphasis on short-termism. Other expanding companies have made the decision to remain as private limited companies. In 2003, the family-owned shoe repairer, Timpson, bought Minit UK, which owns Sketchley cleaners, Supasnaps and Mister Minit.

Timpson now controls more than 1,000 retail outlets nationwide. John Timpson, the group's chairman, said at the time of the purchase that he was in the process of integrating the various divisions, but he added: 'We only have one firm plan, which is that we will not float the business. We think staying private is the best way to run the business.'

Source: adapted from an article in the *Financial Times*, May 2003.

Questions

Total: 45 marks (50 minutes)

1 William Timpson opened his first shop in Butler Street, Manchester, in 1865. His business structure is likely to have been a sole trader, or possibly a partnership. State two advantages and two disadvantages of a partnership over a sole trader. *(4 marks)*

2 Distinguish between a private limited company and a public limited company. *(4 marks)*

3 As a private limited company, Timpson had limited liability. Identify and explain one implication of limited liability in comparison with unlimited liability from the following points of view:
   a Timpson's customers *(3 marks)*
   b Timpson's suppliers *(3 marks)*
   c Timpson's workforce *(3 marks)*
   d Timpson's shareholders *(3 marks)*

4 Analyse the factors that can influence the most appropriate legal structure that a business should adopt. *(10 marks)*

5 Discuss the factors that John Timpson might have taken into account in judging that 'staying private is the best way to run the business'. *(15 marks)*

CHAPTER 8

Raising finance

All organisations need to be able to access funds in order to start up and then continue to operate. This chapter describes the main sources of finance available to a start-up business, showing how these sources can be classified according to the length of time for which they are acquired (long term, medium term and short term) and the reasons for this categorisation. The features of the main sources of finance are described, and the main advantages and disadvantages of each source are compared.

Sources of finance

The owner of a business start-up will need to put together a business plan. This plan describes how the business will operate and includes financial forecasts. These forecasts help the owners to recognise the levels of finance they need to raise.

The main sources of finance for a start-up business include the following:
- personal sources
- ordinary share capital
- venture capital
- loan capital, such as bank loans
- bank overdrafts

The order in which the sources of finance are described in this chapter is in accordance with the AQA business studies specification. Note that most businesses will not use all of these sources and some sources will provide much larger sums than others.

Personal sources tend to be the first form of finance used by very small firms, so you may want to study these first (see p. 91). Larger organisations that require much more finance will almost certainly need to use ordinary share capital. Similarly, a firm may use a bank overdraft if it needs short-term cash but a bank loan if it has a specific item to buy. If a firm requires short-term money to buy a specific item, it can use both a loan and an overdraft at the same time.

DID YOU KNOW?

A major source of finance for any business is the retained profit of that business. However, as this section of the specification examines the setting up of a *new* business, this source of finance is unavailable. Once the business is operating, retained profits invariably become a major (if not *the* major) source of finance. With high start-up costs, it may be some time before a business is able to benefit from this source.

EXAMINER'S VOICE

Unit 1 (BUSS1) in the AQA AS specification is about *planning* a business start-up. Your answers should take into consideration the fact that the organisation is new and will be in either the planning stage or the early stages of operating as a new business.

Unit 2 (BUSS2) is concerned with *improving* the business and how it can be made more efficient.

Ordinary share capital

DID YOU KNOW?

People who are owed money are known as creditors. A shareholder who gives money to a company in order to buy shares is not classified as a creditor because a shareholder is a part-owner of the company. Creditors are organisations or individuals that have lent the company money or provided materials on credit, and have not yet been paid.

 DID YOU KNOW?

If an individual, such as a sole trader, is unable to pay debts, he or she can be declared 'bankrupt'. A limited company in the same situation will go into 'liquidation' – limited companies are not declared 'bankrupt'.

In the case of small private limited companies, raising money to purchase the ordinary shares of the business is a process similar to that described under 'personal sources' later in the chapter. What follows here is more applicable to large private companies or public limited companies (plcs).

Features of ordinary share capital

- Ordinary shares are known as **risk capital** or **equity capital**. Ordinary shareholders receive no promises from a company. If the business is successful, each shareholder receives a **dividend** (a share of the profits). A shareholder owning 1% of a company's ordinary shares receives 1% of the profit that is given to shareholders, and gets 1% of the votes at the annual general meeting (AGM). The shareholders themselves decide at the AGM what dividend will be paid, but there is no guaranteed level of dividend. In profitable years, a high dividend may be paid, but creditors must be paid first and sometimes the future of the firm could depend on profits being retained in the business to finance capital expenditure. In these circumstances, no dividend may be paid at all.

- Ordinary share capital appeals to investors who are prepared to take a risk in return for (usually) higher rewards. If a business goes into liquidation and ceases to exist because it cannot pay its debts, money invested by shareholders will only be returned to them if every debt has been paid in full. On the other hand, because profitable companies can borrow at low interest rates, shareholders can get high returns when things go well.

- In the case of liquidation, the shareholder is protected by the limited liability provided by limited companies. This means that shareholders can only lose the paid-up value of their shares and cannot be asked to pay any more money.

- Ordinary shares are often known as **permanent capital**, as the business will always have shareholders who own these shares. (There are rules that allow a business to buy back some of its shares, but businesses can only do this in a limited way.) For this reason, ordinary share capital is used as a *long-term source of finance*, to set up the firm in the first place or for major expansion plans that cannot be financed from other sources.

- For expansion plans, companies will often use a **rights issue**, where the new shares are sold to existing shareholders. This reduces the administrative costs that are an element of issuing ordinary share capital, as the new shares are often sold in proportion to the existing number of shares (e.g. one share for every five already owned).

 FILE

Share dealing

The Stock Exchange deals mainly in second-hand shares. When shares are first issued, they are sold directly to the original shareholders by the company (helped by a specialist bank known as an issuing house). If a shareholder no longer wants the shares, he or she can use the Stock Exchange to sell them. The company itself is not involved, but will just change its records so that the dividend is paid to the new owner. The price of shares at the Stock Exchange does not affect a firm directly, because it has already received the original value. However, if a company wants to issue more shares, it may be able to sell them at the current Stock Exchange price, and so a high share price helps a company to raise more money in a cost-effective way.

Advantages of ordinary share capital

The advantages of using ordinary share capital are as follows:
■ Limited liability encourages shareholders to invest in the business, as it restricts the amount of money they can lose.
■ It is not necessary to pay shareholders a dividend if the business cannot afford these payments. This contrasts sharply with loans — interest must be paid on these, regardless of the success or failure of the business.
■ Bringing new shareholders into a small business can add further expertise. This usually applies when the additional share capital is being provided by a business angel or venture capitalist.
■ Increasing ordinary share capital can make it easier to borrow more funds from a bank, as the share capital can help to pay for assets that can be used as collateral.
■ Ordinary share capital is permanent, so the business will never be required to gather together sufficient funds to repay it; the money stays permanently in the business.

Disadvantages of ordinary share capital

The disadvantages of using ordinary share capital are as follows:
■ In profitable years, ordinary shareholders will expect good dividends and this is likely to be more expensive than the interest charged on a loan.
■ The original aims of the business may be lost as new shareholders may not have the same values as the original owners.
■ As the business grows through this source of finance, it is probable that the percentage shareholding of the original owner(s) will decline. This can ultimately lead to a smaller share of the profit and even a loss of control of the business.

 FILE

Business angels are wealthy individuals who invest in high-growth businesses. In addition to money, business angels often make their own skills, experience and contacts available to the business.

 FILE

A controlling stake

Because ordinary shareholders are usually given one vote for each share, ownership of 51% of the shares in a company guarantees overall control of that company.

> ### DID YOU KNOW?
>
> When the late Dame Anita Roddick needed money to open her second Body Shop in 1976, the bank refused to give her a loan. She borrowed £4,000 from a friend, Ian McGlinn, in exchange for a half-share of the company. In 2006 Roddick sold the business to L'Oréal for £652 million. McGlinn, who still held 22.4% of the shares, received £146 million. This was much more expensive than repaying a £4,000 loan, but without that £4,000 the company might never have taken off.

Loan capital

> ### KEY TERMS
>
> **loan capital:** money received by an organisation in return for the organisation's agreement to pay interest during the period of the loan and to repay the loan within an agreed time.
>
> **bank loan:** a sum of money provided to a firm or an individual by a bank for a specific, agreed purpose.

Providers of loan capital are known as **creditors**. They charge interest on the loan and must be paid before any dividends are received by shareholders. Similarly, if a business goes into liquidation (closes down), the money raised from the sale of its assets must be paid in full to creditors before any payment is made to the shareholders.

> ### *e* EXAMINER'S VOICE
>
> The AQA AS business studies specification requires the study of loan capital from *banks*: this takes the form of bank loans or bank overdrafts. There are alternative sources of loan capital, but these are not required for AS.

Bank loans

The terms of a bank loan usually specify the purpose, the interest rates and the repayment dates. The business receiving the loan is required to provide a form of security, such as the deeds to a property, and will repay the loan and interest on a regular basis over an agreed period of time. Bank loans tend to have fixed rates of interest, but this is not always the case and flexible rates are possible, particularly if the loan is for a long period of time. All banks have a base interest rate, and the rate actually charged will be a set percentage above this base rate, depending on how much of a risk the bank is taking. New and small firms usually pay higher rates of interest than larger organisations.

> ### DID YOU KNOW?
>
> Banks take security, usually in the form of property (known as **collateral**), so that they can eliminate the risk of a loan not being repaid. If the loan is not repaid, they can sell the property and collect the sum that is owed to them.

Bank loans are useful because they can be set for any length of time, to suit the needs of the firm. They are normally used as a *long-term or medium-term source of finance*.

Advantages of bank loans

The advantages of using bank loans are as follows:

- The interest rate and therefore the repayments are fixed in advance, making it easy to budget the schedule for repayments.
- Interest rates are normally lower because of the security provided, although it is possible to get unsecured loans at a higher interest charge if the business cannot provide collateral.

- The size of the loan and the period of repayment can be organised to match the exact needs of the firm.

Disadvantages of bank loans

The disadvantages of using bank loans are as follows:

- The size of the loan may be limited by the amount of collateral that can be provided rather than by the amount of money needed by the business.
- There is less flexibility in a bank loan, so the business will tend to pay interest for the agreed period, even if it gets into a position where it can pay off the loan early. It may be possible to repay the loan earlier, but often a fee must be paid for doing this.
- Loans are more expensive than alternatives such as personal finance. This is particularly true for start-ups, which are charged higher rates of interest because they are unable to provide the guarantees that the bank prefers.

 FILE

The Small Firms Loan Guarantee

Start-ups often find it difficult to provide the security needed for a loan. In recognition of this, the Department for Business, Enterprise and Regulatory Reform (BERR) has established a scheme called the Small Firms Loan Guarantee (SFLG). The scheme applies to businesses that have been trading for less than 5 years and have a turnover of less than £5.6 million. The main features of the scheme are as follows:

- BERR guarantees to cover 75% of the loan provided to a small business by a lender, such as a bank.
- The business pays a 2% premium to BERR to help fund this guarantee.
- BERR will pay the lender up to £250,000 for loans for up to 10 years, where the business has been unable to repay the loan.

Bank overdrafts

Overdrafts are widely used and flexible, and can overcome the cash-flow problems suffered by businesses whose sales are seasonal or which need to buy materials in advance of a large order. The rate of interest is nearly always variable and only charged daily on the amount by which the account is overdrawn. As with a bank loan, the interest rate depends on the level of risk posed by the account holder. Security is not usually required, so interest rates tend to be higher.

Although the terms of most overdrafts allow banks to demand immediate repayment, this is rare. In practice, overdraft agreements are often renewed and are treated as a reliable source of finance. A bank manager will get to know the nature of a customer's finances and will be able to recognise times when an overdraft is required.

Bank overdrafts are mainly used to ease cash-flow problems, sometimes being needed for just a few days to fund a major payment, so they are a *short-term source of finance*.

KEY TERM

bank overdraft: when a bank allows an individual or organisation to overspend its current account in the bank up to an agreed (overdraft) limit and for a stated time period.

Advantages of bank overdrafts

The advantages of using overdrafts are as follows:

- They are extremely flexible and can be used on a short-term basis (even just for a single day) if the business has a temporary cash-flow problem.
- Interest is only paid on the amount of the overdraft being used rather than the maximum level allowed.
- They are particularly useful to seasonal businesses, which are likely to experience some cash-flow problems at certain times of the year.
- Security is not usually required.

Disadvantages of bank overdrafts

The disadvantages of using overdrafts are as follows:

- The interest rate charged is usually higher than for a loan.
- Banks can demand immediate repayment (although this is rare).
- Cash-flow forecasts and other evidence are usually needed to show the bank manager why an overdraft is needed.

Venture capital

Venture capital commonly involves sums of between £50,000 and £100,000, which are provided by individuals (often known as **business angels**) or merchant banks. It can take the form of loans or payment in return for share capital (or a mixture of the two). Venture capitalists take a risk, but small/medium high-risk companies can produce excellent returns.

Venture capital is used to fund expansion plans, so it is a *long-term source of finance*, although in rapidly changing industries it can be offered as a *medium-term loan*.

Advantages of venture capital

The advantages of using venture capital are as follows:

- It is often provided to businesses that are unable to get finance from other sources because of the risk involved.
- Venture capitalists sometimes allow interest or dividends to be delayed, as they recognise the need for the start-up to become established before it pays out large rewards to its backers.
- Venture capitalists often provide advice, to help the business (and their investment) succeed.

> **KEY TERM**
>
> **venture capital:** finance that is provided to small or medium-sized firms that seek growth but which may be considered as risky by typical share buyers or other lenders.

> **FILE**
>
> **Reggae Reggae Sauce**
>
> In 2007 an episode of *Dragons' Den* on BBC2 saw reggae singer and producer and chef Levi Roots ask the 'dragons' for £50,000 in return for a 20% share in his business. Levi had been selling his own special hot sauce, named 'Reggae Reggae Sauce', for 15 years at the Notting Hill festival and wanted some money to take it to a larger market.

'Dragon' Peter Jones offered half the amount for 20% of the business's equity, and Richard Farleigh chipped in with the remaining £25,000 for another 20%. This left Levi with just 60% of the business but, crucially, with the money he needed to expand and the expertise of two successful entrepreneurs to help.

Disadvantages of venture capital

The disadvantages of using venture capital are as follows:

■ Venture capitalists often demand a significant share of the business in return for their investment. Levi Roots had initially been prepared to offer 20% of his business in return for £50,000, but had to settle for giving up 40% for the same investment.

■ In return for the high risks involved, venture capitalists often want high interest payments or dividends, potentially undermining the future growth prospects of the firm.

■ Venture capitalists may exert too much influence and so the original owner could lose his or her independence.

 FILE

Community development finance institutions

If a start-up is setting up in a deprived area of the country, or in a sector that is under-served by lenders, it might be able to get a loan from a Community Development Finance Institution (CDFI). These loans can be used to finance the purchase of property, equipment or marketing campaigns, or as working capital. The loans vary in size from £50 to £1 million.

Personal sources

For small business start-ups, such as sole traders or partnerships, personal sources are often the most practical way of raising finance for a new business, particularly if the owner has no previous experience of running a business and is therefore unlikely to be able to get a loan.

The main sources of personal finance are described on the following pages, together with their advantages and disadvantages.

Personal savings

An important personal source of finance is the savings that the entrepreneur accumulated before starting up the business.

Advantages

■ Savings are a cheap form of finance as they do not involve paying any interest. Although interest would have been received on the savings, organisations such as banks tend to pay lower rates of interest to savers than the rates charged to borrowers, so the **opportunity cost** (see Chapter 1) is low.

 TERM

personal sources of finance: money that is provided by the owner(s) of the business from their own savings or personal wealth.

- Using savings enables the owner to keep control of the business. This is especially valuable to those owners who are choosing to run a business partly so that they can enjoy the independence it gives them.

Disadvantages

- Setting up a new business is always risky. With high failure rates among new businesses, there is a good chance that an entrepreneur will quickly lose savings that have taken a long time to accumulate.
- Many entrepreneurs do not have sufficient savings to finance a new business. Older people are more likely to have accumulated savings, but it is often the young who have the most innovative ideas.

Mortgages

If the business owner(s) already own a property, a second mortgage can be taken out to raise additional finance to establish the business.

Advantages

- To many people their property is their major financial asset and a second mortgage can enable them to raise enough money to set up a reasonable-sized business.
- The interest rates charged on mortgages tend to be lower than those on other loans because the collateral provided (a property) is very secure. Therefore, lenders see a mortgage as a low-risk loan.

Disadvantages

- If the business is unsuccessful, the owner(s) may lose their property, even though it was purchased from wealth accumulated before the business was set up.
- Many entrepreneurs do not own a sufficiently valuable property or may be reluctant to take such a high-level risk.

Borrowing privately from friends and family

In this instance, the money is lent to the individual entrepreneur and not to the business, and is therefore paid back from the individual's own wealth (although this may eventually be from the dividends or wages received by the owner from the business).

Advantages

- Friends and family may be prepared to lend money when a bank would refuse because of the owner's lack of collateral (security).
- Friends and family often provide easier repayment terms, such as an interest-free loan.
- The additional money raised through friends and family may encourage a bank to offer a further loan.

Disadvantages

- Borrowing in this way can add to the stress felt by the new entrepreneur, particularly if the business gets into difficulties.

■ It can undermine friendships, as there may be disputes about when and how much money should be repaid, and whether some share of the profit should be given to the lender.

Selling private assets

In this instance, the money is raised by selling a valuable item, such as a property or a car.

Advantages

■ An asset that was previously of no real use to a person can be used productively.
■ It is possible that the asset can be leased back by the owner and still used. If the business is successful, the profits can easily cover the rent or leasing costs.

Disadvantages

■ Selling private assets can cause family tensions, as the business may be seen to be benefiting at the expense of the family, particularly if the asset was used regularly by the family. For example, selling the family car may upset family members if it means they have to catch the bus everywhere.
■ It is unlikely that large sums of money can be raised by selling off assets that are not needed by an individual.

FACT FILE

Advice for small businesses

There are a range of organisations that assist small businesses, although often this assistance takes the form of advice rather than financial support. These organisations include:
● local chambers of commerce
● Prowess — an organisation that provides support for women in business
● the Asian Business Development Network (ABDN), which provides support for Asian entrepreneurs
● the Black Business Initiative (BBI), which helps the black and minority ethnic business community

Capital expenditure and revenue expenditure

When considering sources of finance, the most critical factor is the length of time for which the finance is needed. Finance is used to fund:

■ **Capital expenditure.** This is spending on items that can be used time and time again (**fixed assets**). It may take a long time before these items generate enough revenue to pay for themselves, so a *long-term source of finance* is ideal. For items that pay for themselves more quickly, such as computer

TOPFOTO

equipment, medium-term finance is most relevant. The long term is normally greater than 5 years, while the medium term is usually between 2 and 5 years.

■ **Revenue expenditure.** This is spending on current, day-to-day costs such as the purchase of raw materials and payment of wages. Such expenditure provides a quick return, so the company should rely for this on a *short-term source of finance*, usually repayable within 1 year, but possibly 2 years.

Table 8.1 classifies the main sources of finance in terms of the usual time period for which the finance is needed.

Table 8.1 *Classification of sources of finance by time period*

Long-term	Medium-term	Short-term
Personal sources	Personal sources	Personal sources
Ordinary share capital		
Loan capital/bank loan	Loan capital/bank loan	
		Bank overdraft
Venture capital	Venture capital	

Choosing a source of finance

The relative importance of the different sources of finance may vary according to the specific context and circumstances facing the business. When deciding which source of finance to use, a business person will weigh up the following factors:

■ **The legal structure of the business.** Private limited companies and public limited companies sell shares; sole traders and partnerships rely on personal finance.

■ **The use of the finance.** As indicated earlier, the purchase of fixed assets must come from one of the sources of long-term finance, but if the business needs working capital, an overdraft or personal finance is more appropriate. The basic rule is that the length of time that it takes the business to earn the money to repay the source should match the length of time the business is given to repay the money.

■ **The amount required.** The larger the sum, the less likely it is that the owner(s) will be able to generate enough finance from internal sources. Larger sums therefore often mean that loans or share capital are needed. In practice, lenders want to see that the receiver of a loan is also taking a risk, so large loans may depend on a combination of internal and external finance.

■ **The firm's profit levels.** A very profitable firm will have its own money and may not need external help, although banks and other lenders will be happy to lend it money. Ironically, unprofitable firms are those most likely to need a loan but least likely to be able to receive one.

■ **The level of risk.** If an enterprise is viewed as risky, firms will find it harder to attract loans, although venture capital may be a possibility. High-risk activities, especially among small firms, therefore tend to rely more on personal sources.

■ **Views of the owners.** Shareholders or owners may be reluctant to lose control of a firm, so they may reject shares and venture capital, for reasons of control rather than on financial grounds. Many small firms value their independence and will not want 'outsiders' to be a part of the decision-making process. Even if they are only providing a loan, some venture capitalists insist on having a say in how the business is run. Some owners will value these opinions and want venture capital support, but others will take the opposite view.

 EXAMINER'S VOICE

Sources of finance are a popular way of testing analysis and evaluation in the examination. Each source of finance has its own benefits and problems, so analysing the reasons for choosing a particular source (or evaluating/judging the best source is a good test of a student's understanding of a business's finances. Always look for clues in the background information on the business and its situation. The owners may want to keep control or may lack security for a loan, so certain sources may not be available.

FACT FILE

RTL Games

Deciding on a source of finance is not just about numbers. Rachel Lowe appeared on *Dragons' Den* in 2005. The 'dragons' refused to back her, but the publicity surrounding her appearance boosted sales of 'Destination', the board game that she invented.

'I didn't want to sell shares in the business,' she says. 'I was borrowing from friends and family [£115,000 of her £180,000 debt was from them] and ended up in a right pickle because of the cash flow being seasonal.' It was a very stressful period.

'I'd listened to advisers who said borrow from friends and family. Don't, because £25,000 in business is nothing but it can be an individual's life savings.'

The secret to making it, she says, was taking on limited liability and both financially and psychologically separating herself from the business. This has eased the pressure considerably.

'I've learned to separate RTL Games from Rachel Lowe. The investors have a say in RTL Games, but do not have control over me as a person.'

Source: BBC website

PRACTICE EXERCISE · Total: 45 marks (35 minutes)

1 Identify three sources of personal finance. *(3 marks)*

2 Explain two problems of using personal finance as a source of finance. *(4 marks)*

3 Identify two sources of short-term finance. *(2 marks)*

4 What is venture capital? *(3 marks)*

5 Describe the main differences between a bank loan and a bank overdraft. *(6 marks)*

6 What is meant by 'ordinary share capital'? *(3 marks)*

7 Explain two advantages of using ordinary share capital. *(6 marks)*

8 Identify three sources of long-term finance.   *(3 marks)*

9 Explain one reason why a firm should choose a short-term source of finance.   *(3 marks)*

10 Explain one disadvantage of using a bank loan as a source of finance.   *(3 marks)*

11 Analyse three factors that might influence the source of finance chosen by a business.   *(9 marks)*

CASE STUDY 1 A golden opportunity

James van der Beek was the youngest of seven children. Initially, James worked in the family business as a goldsmith and became highly skilled in making gold jewellery and ornaments.

5   James intended to set up his own business using his savings and some venture capital, but could not raise enough money. When the family heard of his attempt, they offered their support. His father and uncle provided the ordinary share capital in return for 70% of
10 the shares, with James given 30% as an incentive. A private limited company was set up with James as chief executive and his girlfriend, Katie Holmes, established as company secretary.

The business grew quickly and 7 years later James
15 was employing ten goldsmiths. James was based in Leeds but planned to expand into retailing elsewhere.

The business had made high levels of profit, but these had been retained in the business and used to expand the premises in which the jewellery was made. There was also always a large amount of money tied up in 20 stocks of finished jewellery and work in progress (partly finished pieces). This was a particular problem in the run-up to Christmas when stock levels were high in readiness for the increased demand for jewellery. Over 50% of the firm's sales were in the 8 weeks leading up 25 to Christmas.

James's goldsmiths had produced a number of unusual items of jewellery at the request of clients, and these speciality pieces were becoming a much larger part of the business. Some basic market research 30 informed James that there was a gap in the retail market for unusual pieces of jewellery, but the main customer base was in London, and a store in Regent Street would be needed. A goldsmith with an unusual range of products would be successful there, according 35 to James's research.

James and Katie estimated that they would need £900,000 to establish the new store in London. They believed that it would take 3 years before the London store made a profit, but after that time a profit in 40 excess of £500,000 per annum could be made. However, as jewellery is a luxury, there was a risk that the venture might fail to make a profit if the economy did not grow.

Questions   **Total: 30 marks (35 minutes)**

1 Explain the meaning of the term 'venture capital' (line 6).   *(2 marks)*

2 Explain two reasons why the business will need short-term finance. When will this be necessary?   *(6 marks)*

3 Is the money needed to open the London store an example of capital expenditure or revenue expenditure? *(2 marks)*

4 James planned to raise £900,000 to open the London store. Analyse two problems of using a bank loan to finance this plan. *(8 marks)*

5 Discuss the arguments for and against James seeking financial assistance from venture capitalists in order to raise the £900,000 finance needed to open the shop in London. *(12 marks)*

CASE STUDY 2 Frozen meals firm took years to hot up

Edward Perry's frozen and ready meals business, Cook, took 10 years to make a profit, and for the first 2 years as a sole trader he did not even bother keeping accounts because the figures were so bad.

In 1996, at the age of 25, he persuaded a chef — Dale Penfold — to help him pursue his vision. With no savings Perry took out a £15,000 bank loan and borrowed a further £5,000 from his parents. Penfold borrowed £5,000 and they used the money to rent a small kitchen in Kent and a small shop in Farnham for £10,000 a year.

By 1999, with sales worth £500,000, Perry realised he needed further investment in order to move to a larger kitchen. The bank refused to lend any money. Perry was convinced the business had potential and decided to talk over the problem with his younger brother, James. James was running his parents' coffee shop and bakery business, which had a turnover of £1.5 million. In 2000 his parents sold the coffee shops and cake business for £1 million and invested the proceeds in Cook.

'My parents made an enormous leap of faith because Cook was just a tiny business that was losing money and they had built up a nice business that was doing quite well,' said Perry. However, after investment in larger kitchens and more shops, Cook took off. Two years ago, in 2005, the family sold 12% of the business for just over £1 million. Cook now has 21 shops and this year will have sales of £14 million. The business has also started selling its frozen ready meals through concessions in farm shops.

Source: adapted from Perry, E. (2007) 'How I made it', *Sunday Times*, 24 June.

Questions

Total: 35 marks (40 minutes)

1 Identify two examples of 'personal sources' of finance from the article. *(2 marks)*

2 What is meant by the term 'bank loan'? *(2 marks)*

3 Based on the evidence in the article, why is it unusual for Perry to have received a bank loan in 1996 but to have been refused one in 1999? *(6 marks)*

4 Analyse one reason why Perry might have refused investment from a venture capitalist and one reason why a venture capitalist might have refused to invest in Cook. *(10 marks)*

5 Discuss the factors that Perry's family might have considered when agreeing to sell a profitable business 'that was doing quite well' and invest in a 'tiny business that was losing money'. *(15 marks)*

Locating the business

This chapter discusses the business approach to decisions on location. The key factors that influence business location — technology, costs, infrastructure, the market and qualitative factors — are considered, and their relative importance assessed.

> **𝑒 EXAMINER'S VOICE**
>
> The AQA AS business studies specification focuses on factors influencing *start-up* location decisions. Although these factors are similar to those influencing larger, more established businesses, the relative importance of the different factors can vary quite considerably. For example, while technology is applicable to firms of all sizes, it is more likely to influence the location of start-ups and small firms than large businesses, as it opens up the opportunity for working from home or 'virtual working' (working in such a way that contact is made remotely through communication systems such as computers and mobile phones).

Main factors influencing business location

Business decisions concerning location are influenced by a range of factors.

Technology

> **KEY TERM**
>
> **teleworking:** working in a location that is separate from a central workplace, using telecommunication technologies.

This is an important factor for many small firms. With the development of communication technologies such as mobile phones, personal computers and the internet, it is becoming increasingly feasible for people to work from home or in locations that are away from centralised office, distribution or production bases. This type of working arrangement is known as **teleworking** — over 3 million people in the UK are classified as teleworkers.

Most of these jobs do not mean that the person stays at home for the whole day. They are often jobs involved in IT, consultancy, building, transport and distribution, or the provision of personal services where the person does not need an office or factory base. In all these cases, the essential element is the ability to communicate through technology at certain times during the day.

Of the estimated 3.3 million teleworkers in the UK, 62% are self-employed. In total, only 4% of employees are classified as teleworkers. Consequently, this communication technology is a much more crucial factor for small businesses, such as start-ups, than it is for large, established businesses — 41% of self-employed people in the UK are teleworkers.

Technology is also a factor in the location of small manufacturing businesses, although for these firms it has a different impact. In manufacturing, if

FILE

Benefits of the 'virtual' working environment

A survey by Yac in July 2006 reveals that 36% of start-up businesses preferred a 'virtual working' environment rather than a physical location separate from the owner's home. Yac asked start-up business owners the main reasons why they did not have a physical location outside the owner's home. The three main reasons for this choice were:

- flexibility — allowing the business to operate from anywhere via communication technologies, and to change location easily if necessary (81% of start-ups gave this reason)
- reduced costs/lack of overheads (69% of start-ups)

- time flexibility, enabling the business and its staff to work outside normal office hours (62% of start-ups)

Ian Osborne, chief executive of Yac, said:

It is evident from our research that creating a stable virtual environment is a key factor for many start-ups. With the technology available today, small businesses can easily stay connected with their customers, giving them the ability to work from home, an office, or when on the move, without jeopardising the service they deliver.

The survey also indicated that start-ups felt that technology made it easy for businesses to increase in size and take on new staff, who might be part-time or tele-workers.

technological equipment is needed, it is highly unlikely that a small business will be able to operate from the owner's home. Consequently, location tends to be an industrial estate or similar factory premises.

Costs of factors of production

The main assumption made about decisions concerning the costs of factors of production is that firms will locate at the **least-cost site**.

For start-ups and small businesses, it is vital that costs are kept to a minimum to allow the business to compete with larger competitors, which are more likely to be able to keep their costs low. If the selling price is vital in achieving sales, the least-cost site will greatly increase the competitiveness of the business. Although many small firms tend to compete on the basis of quality and other criteria, such as personal service and flexibility, low costs are required to give the business a chance of making a reasonable profit.

 TERM

least-cost site: the business location that allows a firm to minimise its costs (and hence its selling price).

 FILE

Effect of costs on start-ups

The Yac survey referred to above indicated that 85% of owners of start-ups stated that they did not have the funds to set up a permanent base outside their home.

According to Ian Osborne:

For start-ups especially, setting up a traditional office environment can be expensive. The nature of being a start-up business, and the long hours this often requires, can be more conducive to flexible working. It is clear that employees too value the ability to work outside the traditional office. Recent research on the market has shown that this approach helps staff loyalty and motivation.

The main costs influencing the location of businesses are discussed in the following pages.

CHAPTER 9 Locating the business

GROUP EXERCISE: LOCATING SMALL BUSINESSES

(If preferred, this exercise can be completed individually rather than as a group.)

Somerwall

Task 1

Where in Somerwall would you locate the following businesses? The eight possible sites are identified by the numbers 1–8 on the following map. Each location should be used once only.

a farmer (needs arable land)

b pottery (needs to attract tourists)

c fisherman (needs a port, but low costs)

d fashion retailer (needs to be in a main shopping centre)

e caravan park (needs to be close to tourists, but on cheaper land if possible)

f garden centre (needs to be on a main road, close to centres of population)

g restaurant for tourists

h warehouse for computing equipment

Task 2

Identify those places where a *hotel* could be sited. Explain the largest markets for your hotels and the reasons for the chosen location.

Additional notes:

- The most expensive land is in the tourist area and the larger towns.
- The tourist area between W and X has the vast majority of tourist restaurants.
- Land becomes cheaper as you move away from the coastline.
- The most arable land is close to the water.

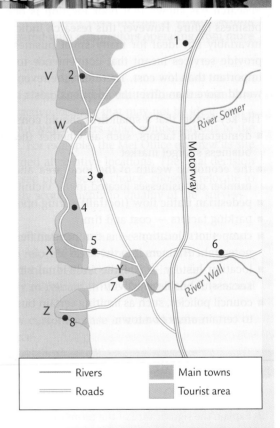

| | Rivers | | Main towns |
| | Roads | | Tourist area |

CASE STUDY **Wladek's gym**

The local council was trying to improve the local infrastructure to assist the new shopping centre. Unfortunately, this meant that Wladek's gym was going to be demolished. His landlord had given him the option to transfer his gym and its 190 members to an alternative city-centre location with the same facilities. However, after researching the market Wladek had discovered that a disused warehouse near to his house had been converted into a large gym, but was never used. It was available to rent cheaply, as the owner was desperate to earn some revenue. Unlike the

Unit 1: Planning and financing a business

FILE

Benefits of the 'virtual' working environment

A survey by Yac in July 2006 reveals that 36% of start-up businesses preferred a 'virtual working' environment rather than a physical location separate from the owner's home. Yac asked start-up business owners the main reasons why they did not have a physical location outside the owner's home. The three main reasons for this choice were:

- flexibility — allowing the business to operate from anywhere via communication technologies, and to change location easily if necessary (81% of start-ups gave this reason)
- reduced costs/lack of overheads (69% of start-ups)

- time flexibility, enabling the business and its staff to work outside normal office hours (62% of start-ups)

Ian Osborne, chief executive of Yac, said:

It is evident from our research that creating a stable virtual environment is a key factor for many start-ups. With the technology available today, small businesses can easily stay connected with their customers, giving them the ability to work from home, an office, or when on the move, without jeopardising the service they deliver.

The survey also indicated that start-ups felt that technology made it easy for businesses to increase in size and take on new staff, who might be part-time or tele-workers.

technological equipment is needed, it is highly unlikely that a small business will be able to operate from the owner's home. Consequently, location tends to be an industrial estate or similar factory premises.

Costs of factors of production

The main assumption made about decisions concerning the costs of factors of production is that firms will locate at the **least-cost site**.

For start-ups and small businesses, it is vital that costs are kept to a minimum to allow the business to compete with larger competitors, which are more likely to be able to keep their costs low. If the selling price is vital in achieving sales, the least-cost site will greatly increase the competitiveness of the business. Although many small firms tend to compete on the basis of quality and other criteria, such as personal service and flexibility, low costs are required to give the business a chance of making a reasonable profit.

 TERM

least-cost site: the business location that allows a firm to minimise its costs (and hence its selling price).

 FILE

Effect of costs on start-ups

The Yac survey referred to above indicated that 85% of owners of start-ups stated that they did not have the funds to set up a permanent base outside their home.

According to Ian Osborne:

For start-ups especially, setting up a traditional office environment can be expensive. The nature of being a start-up business, and the long hours this often requires, can be more conducive to flexible working. It is clear that employees too value the ability to work outside the traditional office. Recent research on the market has shown that this approach helps staff loyalty and motivation.

The main costs influencing the location of businesses are discussed in the following pages.

Land costs

For small firms land costs can represent a large percentage of total costs. For this reason, many retailers choose to locate away from town centres in order to benefit from lower rents. Firms may also be discouraged from locating in expensive areas, such as London. When locating in town centres, small firms are often forced to locate on the outskirts of the shopping area, where rents are lower. However, as indicated earlier, many small firms can now benefit from being based at home. This can considerably reduce the costs and help to make a small business competitive. Ultimately, if the business wishes to expand, land costs can be a major stumbling block.

Land may also be a factor if an industry has special requirements. For example, farms require relatively large areas of land. As many towns have expanded, agricultural land has been swallowed up because large commercial firms could afford to offer high prices for the land. For farmers it was more sensible to sell their land and purchase a larger farm away from the town.

DID YOU KNOW?

The latest government survey (August 2007) on new businesses reveals that Northern Ireland is the best location in the UK for starting a business, with 79% of start-up businesses still trading after 3 years. London has the lowest survival rate, with 67% of start-up businesses still trading after 3 years. Apart from Northern Ireland, the top seven locations for start-up survival were all in the north of England. The report attributed this to the lower costs of land and labour in those areas (and government support in Northern Ireland). Although demand was more buoyant in London, there was also greater competition and small businesses tended to lose out to larger, more established firms.

Labour costs

In the UK there are significant variations in wage levels between regions. The southeast of England is the most expensive region and those areas that are the furthest from London generally have the lowest wage levels. On its own, this factor would suggest that low-wage areas should be the least-cost sites. However, labour costs are not the only important factor. A highly skilled labour force may compensate for slightly higher wage levels through greater labour productivity. Ultimately, the labour cost per unit produced is more important than the wage level. This factor is a key aspect of decisions to relocate overseas. Many small firms source their materials from abroad because the lower labour costs help to keep their prices low and competitive.

Firms basing their location decisions on labour costs also need to consider the quality and reliability of the product or service produced. A firm selling its products on the basis of craftsmanship should locate itself in an area where the workforce is highly skilled and not necessarily where wage levels are low. A growing area of small firm development is that of consultancy — consultants generally require high levels of education, training and knowledge in their

particular field, and therefore it is the quality of the work rather than the labour cost that is most important.

Transport costs

The location of raw materials is crucial for most primary industries. Extractive industries such as mining and quarrying must be located where the materials are found. However, the costs of extraction and transport to the market may determine whether it is economically worthwhile to operate at all.

Heavy industries — notably iron and steel — usually locate in close proximity to their raw material supplies. During the manufacturing process, a significant percentage of the raw materials is wasted, so the final product weighs much less than the raw materials. Therefore, it is cheaper to distribute the finished product to the market than it is to move the raw materials to the place of manufacture. For these **bulk-reducing** or **weight-losing** industries, the least-cost site tends to be close to the raw materials.

For some industries, such as brewing and soft drinks, the addition of large amounts of water means that the final product is bulkier to transport than the raw materials. These **bulk-increasing** or **weight-gaining** industries tend to locate closer to the market than to the raw materials. A growing number of small, local breweries are taking advantage of the fact that their lower transport costs enable them to compete quite effectively with large breweries that can brew the beer much more cheaply, but then incur relatively high transport costs to ship the goods nationwide.

In recent years, much of the UK's 'heavy' (weight-losing) industry has declined, so raw material supply has become a less important factor.

The location of suppliers may also influence business location. A manufacturer will reap the benefits of a location that is close to its suppliers, particularly if it is using just-in-time methods, where goods must be delivered quickly and at short notice to the customer. Therefore, a region such as Lincolnshire, with its abundance of agricultural suppliers, is an attractive location for a food manufacturer because the raw materials are fresh and cheap to transport. However, it should be noted that in most industries suppliers are more likely to locate near manufacturers than the other way round.

The clothing retailer Zara still produces its clothing in Europe because this enables it to distribute the products quickly to its main retailers. Rapid distribution is the company's unique selling point.

 FACT FILE

Transport costs for supermarket suppliers

For small businesses that supply the large supermarkets, transport costs are becoming relatively unimportant, as the large supermarkets can achieve better economies of scale by picking up the supplies themselves, rather than having them delivered by the supplier. However, speed of delivery is becoming much more important and supermarkets are buying a greater percentage of their fresh produce from local suppliers.

CHAPTER 9

Locating the business

Infrastructure

Infrastructure is vital for most companies. Transport links are the key factor, as the ability to move raw materials and finished products easily is crucial to the success of any business. It is also essential that the labour force can easily access the place of work. In addition, companies need basic services that allow them to operate normally, such as sewerage facilities and high-quality telecommunications systems.

The time and cost of transport are more important than distance. In the UK, road is the preferred mode of transport, as it provides flexibility. With the growth of containerisation, roads can be linked to other forms of transport more efficiently too. Therefore, the road network is a major influence on business location in the UK. Improvements in roads can create opportunities for the areas affected, as reduced travelling times lead to lower costs.

For small businesses, the local infrastructure may be more important than the regional or national infrastructure. The following questions would be of particular significance to a small business:

- Are parking spaces available nearby?
- How much does it cost to park?
- Is traffic flow good?
- Is the business on a bus route or close to a station?
- If the business is a shop, is it isolated or close to other shops too?
- Is it easy to receive deliveries?

In some areas and countries, canals, railway lines and air transport dominate location decisions. Air transport provides speed and, for products requiring high security, airport locations limit the chances of theft. Water and rail transport are effective means of transporting bulky, durable products.

The market

For retailers and other service industries, the market is the most important influence on location. The majority of small firms in the UK are tertiary providers rather than manufacturers, so for most of them the market is the major factor influencing location. Customers expect convenience and easy access, so firms such as electrical retailers, hairdressers and restaurants see this factor as particularly important.

In deciding on location, small retailers will look at the 'footfall' in an area (the number of potential customers walking past the shop). These firms will also research the types of customer in an area to see whether they are likely to be interested in their products. Organisations such as estate agents and charity shops often locate close to each other so that potential customers will be drawn to the area by competitors and are then likely to visit their premises.

Businesses must also understand the way in which their potential customers think and act. For example, coffee shops often locate next to the larger retailers because many customers want to relax after an intense period of shopping and browsing. Similarly, coffee shops are locating in bookstores because people enjoy reading while having a cup of coffee.

Organisations save transport costs if they locate close to their market. A company supplying raw materials to a manufacturer may find that transport costs represent a large percentage of the final costs. In this case, proximity to the manufacturer may be a key factor.

Many start-ups supply components for larger manufacturers. As just-in-time production grows in popularity among manufacturers, the ability to transport goods quickly becomes a key factor in the choice of suppliers. Therefore, small suppliers of components are likely to locate close to the large manufacturers that use their components.

Sometimes a business will locate where it believes it can enhance its revenue rather than merely cut costs. For example, a restaurant or a jewellery shop may pay a premium rate in order to locate in an exclusive area of town where people will be prepared to pay high prices.

 FACT FILE

The 'virtual' market

For many businesses in sectors such as retailing and financial services, proximity to the customer is still vital, but it is no longer an influence on physical location. In these businesses, the marketplace is via a telephone line or an internet connection. As a result, local branches are not needed. In the building trade, tradespeople often operate from a vehicle, maintaining contact with customers by mobile telephone.

Qualitative factors

Convenience

Ultimately, all business decisions are taken by individuals, often without access to perfect forecasts of the implications of the different choices available. Consequently, directors may base their choices on factors other than business criteria. For example, the Body Shop's head office is located in Sussex because Anita Roddick lived there at the time that she set up the business. Similarly, the head office of Alliance and Leicester plc is based in Leicester because its original founders lived there. For most small firms, the natural inclination of the entrepreneur is to start operating from the place where he or she lives. As the business develops, the tendency will be to remain where they are unless there are overwhelming reasons to move, as families will not want to experience unnecessary disruption to their lives.

> **KEY TERM**
>
> **qualitative factors:** based on the opinions and wishes of individuals. These factors can influence business decisions because an entrepreneur will want to include his or her own wishes and preferences in decisions taken.

Unique selling points

Unusual premises may also be an attractive feature of the business. For example, a gym based in a converted barn may provide a unique selling point for the business when compared with competitors operating from more traditional premises.

Quality of life

The quality of life in an area is also a factor that influences location. Entrepreneurs may choose an attractive location that may not be ideal from a 'least-cost' location perspective, but which offers other compensations to the business owner and the workforce. For example, the Met Office outgrew its site in Bracknell, Berkshire and examined alternative locations. The final decision was left to the workforce who, based on personal choice, chose to relocate to Exeter. As a city, Exeter consistently scores highly in 'quality of life' surveys.

Inertia

Industrial inertia is another factor that can influence location. Once established, a firm may be reluctant to relocate elsewhere, particularly in the case of a small business operating from home. Reasons for this include:

- the desire of the owner's family to remain in the same place for personal reasons
- difficulties in building up a new customer base in a new location
- loyalty to its existing labour force
- a desire to keep the same locally based suppliers
- a fear of change
- lower morale and productivity before the relocation, as a result of some staff probably losing their jobs
- the cost of relocation
- transitional difficulties while adjusting to the new location and processes

These problems need to be set against the benefits gained from the new location.

 EXAMINER'S VOICE

These are just some examples of qualitative factors. If an examination question requires you to consider qualitative factors, look for 'non-quantifiable' factors in the case study. There may also be reference to 'inertia' factors that can be instrumental in persuading the business to stay where it is.

FACT FILE

Government intervention

Government intervention plays a part in the location of businesses.

The government gives grants (gifts) to firms in Assisted Areas — parts of England that have relatively low levels of economic activity and high and persistent unemployment. These grants are paid as a contribution towards capital investment, but are only available in a limited range of industries and are subject to strict conditions. Consequently, government intervention is not seen as a key factor in the location of start-ups or small businesses.

Nevertheless, in 2006/07 the Small Firms Loan Guarantee (SFLG) scheme did support 2,702 loans to small businesses, guaranteeing loans that totalled over £211 million.

Locating small businesses

Research has shown that poor location is one of the main causes of small business failure. However, this research indicated that the least-cost site was invariably not ideal for many small businesses because their tendency to provide services meant that convenience to the customer was often more important than low cost. Therefore, the revenue generated by a good location would more than offset the additional costs of that location.

The key factors that a small firm should consider were found to be:
- demographic factors, such as whether the local population matched the business's target market
- the economic wealth of the local area and whether it could support the number of businesses located in the vicinity
- pedestrian traffic flow (footfall) during opening times
- parking factors — cost and time
- competitors' locations — is competition fierce or would competition attract potential customers into the area?
- location history — did the individual site have a good track record of successful business activity?
- council policies, such as limiting certain business activities (e.g. nightclubs) to certain areas of a town

PRACTICE EXERCISE
Total: 60 marks (50 minutes)

1 What is meant by the term 'least-cost site'? *(2 marks)*

2 Explain the significance of the term 'weight-losing' or 'bulk-reducing' with reference to the location of industry. *(4 marks)*

3 Explain three reasons why working from home is popular with start-up businesses. *(9 marks)*

4 Analyse four factors that might influence the location of a newsagent. *(12 marks)*

5 Briefly outline three reasons why a small shop might decide to locate away from a town centre. *(6 marks)*

6 Explain two reasons why a small shop might decide to locate in a town centre rather than away from the centre. *(4 marks)*

7 Explain two ways in which the local infrastructure might influence the location of a small firm. *(6 marks)*

8 Why are start-up firms more likely to survive in Northern Ireland than in London? *(6 marks)*

9 Why would the main factors influencing the location of a coffee shop be different from those influencing the location of an electrician? *(6 marks)*

10 Identify five factors that might be seen as qualitative influences on a decision about where to locate a business. *(5 marks)*

GROUP EXERCISE: LOCATING SMALL BUSINESSES

(If preferred, this exercise can be completed individually rather than as a group.)

Somerwall

Task 1

Where in Somerwall would you locate the following businesses? The eight possible sites are identified by the numbers 1–8 on the following map. Each location should be used once only.

a farmer (needs arable land)

b pottery (needs to attract tourists)

c fisherman (needs a port, but low costs)

d fashion retailer (needs to be in a main shopping centre)

e caravan park (needs to be close to tourists, but on cheaper land if possible)

f garden centre (needs to be on a main road, close to centres of population)

g restaurant for tourists

h warehouse for computing equipment

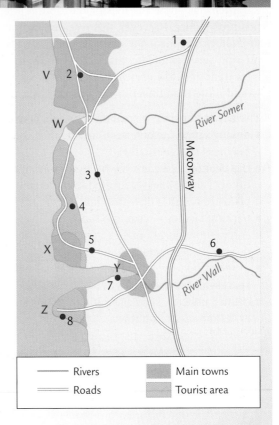

Task 2

Identify those places where a *hotel* could be sited. Explain the largest markets for your hotels and the reasons for the chosen location.

Additional notes:

- The most expensive land is in the tourist area and the larger towns.
- The tourist area between W and X has the vast majority of tourist restaurants.
- Land becomes cheaper as you move away from the coastline.
- The most arable land is close to the water.

CASE STUDY   Wladek's gym

The local council was trying to improve the local infrastructure to assist the new shopping centre. Unfortunately, this meant that Wladek's gym was going to be demolished. His landlord had given him the option to transfer his gym and its 190 members to an alternative city-centre location with the same facilities. However, after researching the market Wladek had discovered that a disused warehouse near to his house had been converted into a large gym, but was never used. It was available to rent cheaply, as the owner was desperate to earn some revenue. Unlike the

city centre, where members (and employees) had to pay £1 an hour to park, there was an extensive, free car park at this location.

Wladek calculated the least-cost site. However, he was not sure whether it was the more profitable site of the two. He was optimistic that he could increase membership if he took over the disused warehouse, but it was a less attractive site and members were less likely to spend money in the café after their training sessions. In contrast, members in his current city-centre

club often called in for a drink after work, even if they were not training.

Wladek felt a loyalty to his customers, all of whom had indicated that they would keep up their membership if his new gym was in the city centre. However, relatively few would stay if the disused warehouse were chosen, as most of the current members worked in the city centre.

The various factors involved in the location decision are summarised in Table 9.1.

Table 9.1 *Wladek's gym: factors in the location decision*

Factor	City-centre location	Disused warehouse
Size (capacity)	200 members	600 members
Technology	Lack of space would prevent installation of certain high-tech equipment	The warehouse would accommodate all the equipment needed

Total costs (per month) (based on expected membership):
   Monthly rent
   Labour costs
   Other costs (per member)
	
	 £1,520
	 £2,090
	 £1,330
		
		 £1,400
		 £4,000
		 £2,400

Expected membership	190 members	400 members
Building features	Modern and bright	Old-fashioned but spacious
Monthly membership price paid by members	£50	£30
Other factors	Popular at lunchtimes and throughout the day High spending in café/bar in gym Staff like the proximity to the shops during their breaks	Mainly evening and weekend customers Low spending in café in gym Staff value the fact that it is quicker to reach than the town centre

Questions

Total: 40 marks (50 minutes)

1 Based on Table 9.1, which is the 'least-cost site'? *(2 marks)*

2 Briefly explain how 'technology' might affect Wladek's decision. *(4 marks)*

3 What is meant by the term 'infrastructure'? *(3 marks)*

4 Explain how 'infrastructure' might influence Wladek's decision. *(4 marks)*

5 Based purely on financial information, analyse why the least-cost site might not be the best choice in this case. *(8 marks)*

6 State four qualitative factors that Wladek might consider in this location decision. *(4 marks)*

7 Evaluate the factors that Wladek should consider in making his choice, and use your evaluation to recommend which location he should choose. *(15 marks)*

CHAPTER 10

Employing people

This chapter describes the types of employees found in small businesses, including temporary, permanent, full-time and part-time, and the consultants and advisers who might be used. It considers the reasons for employing people or using consultants and advisers, and the drawbacks and difficulties of doing so.

Reasons for employing people

Entrepreneurs setting up a new business need to employ people for a number of reasons:

- Only in the smallest businesses does the owner have the capacity to carry out all the tasks necessary to provide the finished product or service. In most businesses, it is necessary to employ people. As a business grows, it needs to ensure that it can meet demand by increasing the number of staff it employs.
- An entrepreneur setting up a new business will not often have all the skills required to run a business. The same applies to a partnership, or even a limited company. Most businesses require specialist expertise in relation to the production of their goods or services, the marketing of them, and the management of their finance and will therefore need to employ appropriate people.

- Some businesses are seasonal in nature; the demand for their products will peak at certain times of the year and drop away at other times. Examples are strawberry growers (spring and summer), cafés and restaurants in tourist areas (summer), and gift shops (Christmas). A business needs to ensure that it can meet demand during the peak season by employing additional staff.
- A start-up business that wants to expand will need to consider outsourcing, training existing staff or taking on new staff.

Types of employee used in small businesses

People can be employed in a number of different ways and a business owner needs to think carefully about this in order to ensure that the business is run as efficiently as possible. Decisions depend on how constant the work is, how long the work will last and the number of hours of work required each week. They also depend on the level of responsibility and obligation that the business is willing to take on in relation to employing people. Contractually, the following options are available:

- **Permanent employees.** These can be full time or part time and they have an open-ended employment contract with the business, which has extensive obligations to them.
- **Temporary or fixed-term contract employees.** These have an employment contract with the business, but it is for a predetermined time or until a specific task has been completed.
- **Employees on zero-hours contracts.** Such contracts allow a business to have people on-call to work whenever necessary and mutually convenient. Generally, a business is not obliged to offer work, nor is there a responsibility for the worker to accept any work.
- **Employment agency staff.** These workers have contracts with the employment agency that supplies them, but the business still has certain legal responsibilities towards its agency workers.
- **Self-employed freelancers, consultants and contractors.** These give a business the minimum of employer obligations.

Permanent or temporary employees

An important decision for a new business is whether staff should be permanent or temporary. Staff who are required throughout the year and whose services are necessary to the day-to-day running of the business are likely to be permanent employees. This includes management, such as the sales or operational managers, factory operatives and sales assistants, and administrative staff. Permanent staff tend to be more loyal to the business and more motivated than temporary staff.

Where additional staff are needed — for example, to meet the seasonal demand for goods or services, or to complete a particular task or cover a particular event — they are more likely to be employed on a temporary basis. For example, many strawberry growers now employ large numbers of young people from eastern European countries such as Poland. They are hired for the season, and once this is over their employment contract ends. Similarly, a toy shop might take on additional staff for the 3 months running up to Christmas. It would be inefficient for a business to employ these staff on a permanent basis because for most of the year they would have little to do. Hiring temporary staff can also be useful when a business needs someone to cover the specific job of an employee who is on maternity leave.

Some businesses make use of temporary staff supplied by agencies. The worker supplied is usually under the control of the business that is employing them, but is paid by the agency. For example, office staff from an agency might cover the jobs of permanent employees while they are on holiday or ill.

Full-time or part-time employees

The business also needs to consider whether people should be employed on a full-time or part-time basis. This depends on the nature of the job and the

needs of the business, but it also depends on the individual employee. Some jobs clearly need to be full time, such as a machine operator in a factory, or a telephonist, but others might require only a few hours' work per week. For example, a cleaner would only be required for a few hours each morning or evening, so he or she might have a permanent post but one that is part time.

A business could also introduce **job sharing**, where two or more people share the responsibilities, pay and benefits of a full-time job in proportion to the hours they work. This may be an invaluable way of retaining staff who can no longer work full time and may otherwise wish to leave.

The advantages of employing part-time workers include the following:
- It is an efficient way to keep costs down in areas where full-time cover is not necessary.
- It is a way of building in flexibility, allowing a business to respond to changes in demand more easily.
- If part-time work suits employees, they may be more motivated, absenteeism and stress may be reduced, and productivity may increase.
- The availability of part-time work may create a wider pool of candidates for recruitment.
- The opportunity to work part time may mean the business is able to retain valued employees.

However, employing part-time staff may involve potentially higher staffing costs as a result of extra induction, training and administrative costs.

External consultants, contractors and advisers

In addition to employees, a business might hire the services of consultants, contractors and advisers. Since these people are self-employed or belong to a separate company, this is a useful way of benefiting from extra skills and labour without taking on many of the responsibilities of an employer. For example, except in a reasonably large business, an accountant is unlikely to be an employee of the business. A small business will probably hire the services of an accountant and pay them an hourly or annual fee for the services provided.

Other consultants might be brought in to give advice on a particular issue. For example, a design consultant might be hired to advise the business on particular aspects of packaging design, working with the business for a few weeks only. Similarly, an outside IT contractor might be hired to build a business website, or a freelance public relations (PR) consultant might be hired when a business needs to run a promotional campaign. Other advisers, such as Business Link and Prince's Trust mentors, provide their services free to start-up businesses.

***e* EXAMINER'S VOICE**

Ensure that you understand the distinction between permanent and temporary employees and between full-time and part-time employees, and that, for instance, someone could be a part-time permanent employee or a full-time temporary employee.

***e* EXAMINER'S VOICE**

Ensure that you understand the difference between temporary employees and external consultants or contractors.

Drawbacks and difficulties of employing people

Despite their obvious contribution to the successful operation of a business, employing people has drawbacks for a small business, which include the following:

- **The cost of employing people.** This is a major problem for small businesses. As well as the actual wage or salary paid, businesses also incur other costs, such as national insurance contributions, possible pension contributions and extensive administrative costs. These costs include the time that needs to be spent to ensure that payment systems, including tax deductions and national insurance contributions, are organised effectively.
- **Meeting the range of employment legislation requirements.** This is often seen as a real burden for small businesses, most of which do not have in-house human resources departments that can advise on their employment responsibilities under the various pieces of legislation. In addition to the requirements of employment legislation (such as contracts of employment, grievance and disciplinary procedures, equal pay and equal opportunities legislation, minimum wage and working time requirements), a business must also ensure that the working environment is safe and secure, and meets the requirements of health and safety legislation.
- **Managing staff.** Leading and managing staff effectively is important in ensuring that employees are well motivated and perform their jobs well. The entrepreneur in a start-up business will not necessarily have the skills or experience to do this.
- **Employee absence.** Because start-up businesses tend to employ few people, the absence of any one employee can have a significant negative impact on the business.

PRACTICE EXERCISE
Total: 35 marks (30 minutes)

1 Explain two reasons why small businesses might need to employ people. *(6 marks)*

2 Identify four different contractual relationships that a firm might have with its employees. *(4 marks)*

3 Under what circumstances might a business decide to employ people on a temporary rather than a permanent basis? *(5 marks)*

4 Outline two advantages of employing people on a permanent rather than a temporary basis. *(4 marks)*

5 Explain three advantages of employing people on a part-time rather than a full-time basis. *(6 marks)*

6 Give two examples of how external consultants or contractors might be of benefit to a business. *(4 marks)*

7 Explain three drawbacks or difficulties that a small firm is likely to encounter when employing people. *(6 marks)*

CASE STUDY Employing people at Haywood Associates Ltd

Haywood Associates Ltd is a small IT company providing integrated software services to companies and organisations. It is based in the Midlands, has been in existence for 4 years and has 20 permanent employees.

The managing director, Lesley Strand's own background is in IT and she recognised that despite her own technical and managerial expertise she had little experience of selling or of financial management. Her first priority, therefore, was to recruit a sales director who had the experience and skills she lacked and who would be committed to the company's success and future growth. She then recruited a finance manager to ensure that, as the company grew, it kept a tight hold on financial aspects. She suggests that 'The different skills and perspectives of the management team are great for business decision making.'

The business regularly uses skilled contractors and consultants on a short-term basis. According to Strand, this gives the business labour flexibility and allows management to bring in specialist skills as and when it needs them. She says, 'For example, we recently won a major contract to build a web portal for a large advisory agency. Part of this involved setting up and classifying large amounts of online content. The skills required to do this are highly specialised and our team was already working at full capacity on other projects, so we decided to employ a team of content editors on short-term contracts. We were very careful in our selection of the contracting team and ensured they were fully briefed about requirements, standards and company expectations. This allowed us to meet the project deadlines and quality standards without sacrificing any of our ongoing work commitments.'

Recently, the company hired a small firm of marketing consultants to advise the business on revamping its logos and generally improving the image of the company. The directors had tried to do this in-house but realised that they did not have the expertise and that it was better to spend money on hiring specialists, leaving the permanent workforce to focus on what they did best.

Most of the staff employed by the company are permanent and most are full time. However, one young man has recently been appointed on a temporary contract in order to cover the job of an employee who is on maternity leave. In addition, two of the IT technicians job-share. This arrangement was suggested by the employees themselves, both of whom have young families and wanted to cut back on their working hours, but who also wanted to stay with the company. Although slightly worried about this arrangement at first, Strand feels that it has been highly beneficial in enabling the company to retain skilled and experienced staff.

Questions

Total: 37 marks (45 minutes)

1 From the information provided, what type of legal structure is the business in the case study likely to have?

(2 marks)

2 Explain two benefits of employing people on a permanent rather than a temporary basis.

(4 marks)

3 Explain the drawbacks and difficulties encountered by a firm like Haywood Associates Ltd when employing staff.

(6 marks)

4 Analyse the advantages to Haywood Associates of using more part-time employees.

(10 marks)

5 Evaluate the benefits to Haywood Associates Ltd of hiring external consultants and contractors rather than employing more temporary staff.

(15 marks)

Unit 1: Planning and financing a business

Financial planning

CHAPTER 11

Calculating costs, revenues and profits

This chapter sets out the key concepts used in simple financial calculations. It looks at the basic calculation of profit (total revenue minus total costs) and examines the ways in which costs can be classified as fixed or variable. The relationships between cost, price, revenue and profits are outlined.

Price, total revenue and profit

> **KEY TERMS**
>
> **price:** the amount paid by a consumer to purchase one unit of a product.
>
> **total revenue:** the income received from an organisation's activities.
>
>   total revenue = price per unit × quantity of units sold
>
> (e.g. if price is £5 and 10 units are sold then total revenue is £5 × 10 = £50)
>
> **profit:** the difference between the income of a business and its total costs.
>
>   profit = total revenue − total costs

Price

Setting a price is a difficult task. Typically, a business must set a price that is high enough to cover the costs of making a product and leave a surplus that is profit. However, as shown in Chapter 6, the higher the price, the smaller the number of customers likely to buy the product. A full treatment of the impact of price on the quantity bought is provided in Chapter 32.

The business must find the ideal selling price — the one that helps the firm to make the most profit.

Total revenue

Total revenue may also be described by the following terms:
- income
- revenue
- sales revenue
- sales turnover
- turnover

Unit 1: Planning and financing a business

Total revenue (TR) can be calculated by multiplying the average selling price (p) by the quantity sold (q):

$TR = p \times q$

For example, if the selling price is £8 and 5 items are sold, total revenue is £40.

Similarly, if TR = £48 and the selling price = £4, the quantity sold is £48/£4 = 12 units.

Also, if TR = £60 and the quantity sold is 10 units, the selling price is £6 (£60/10).

If two of the variables in the equation $TR = p \times q$ are known, the third can be calculated.

Profit

Profit is a prime objective of most firms. In effect, there are two ways of improving profit:
■ increase sales revenue
■ decrease costs

A combination of both would be the ideal way of achieving additional profit.

Costs

Some functional areas of a business, such as production and administration, can help to achieve rising profits by reducing costs. If more efficient methods can be introduced, the business can increase profit by cutting down on staff or reducing the amount of wastage on the production line. However, the business must be careful that these cost savings do not reduce the quality of the good or service. If this is reduced, total revenue may be affected as customers will be less likely to buy the products.

Costs are therefore a major factor in determining the overall success of a firm, as measured by its profit. Organisations need to understand their costs if they wish to improve their profit.

Classifying costs

There are two principal reasons for classifying costs:
■ **To assess the impact of changes in output on the costs of production.** A firm can compare additional revenue from an increase in output to see if it exceeds the extra costs incurred. Regardless of its current profit level, a firm aiming to make profit should increase output if the extra revenue exceeds the additional costs of increasing output.
■ **To calculate the costs of making a particular product in a multi-product company.** It can be difficult to work out whether it is worthwhile making a

product. It is easy to calculate the sales income of a product, but many costs (e.g. office rent, canteen facilities) are not specific to any single product made by a firm.

KEY TERMS

fixed costs: costs that do not vary directly with output in the short run (e.g. rent).

variable costs: costs that vary directly with output in the short run (e.g. raw materials).

total costs (TC): the sum of fixed costs and variable costs.

Costs and output

A company can use the link between costs and output to calculate the financial *implications* of changing its level of output.

In reality, it is impossible to predict the exact change in each and every cost, so general classifications of costs are used to *estimate* the likely effect of output changes on individual costs. To simplify the calculations, costs are classified as fixed, variable and total.

If there is an $x\%$ rise in output, it is assumed that:
- fixed costs do not change
- variable costs change by the same percentage as the change in output (a rise of $x\%$ in this case)

This is an oversimplification of what actually happens in real life, but it is helpful to firms because it allows them to make fairly accurate predictions about how costs will change as output changes. In turn, this will assist them in making logical business decisions.

Fixed costs	Variable costs
Machinery	Raw materials
Rent and rates	Wages of operatives/ direct labour
Salaries	
Administration	Power
Vehicles	
Marketing	
Lighting and heating	

Table 11.1 Classification of costs by output

Table 11.1 shows how firms classify the costs they incur into fixed and variable costs. The logic behind these choices is that the costs of items in the first column are not affected by small changes in output. These fixed costs will, however, change in the long run if large increases in output are required. For example, if there were a significant increase in output, new machinery (a fixed cost) would have to be installed. The variable costs, shown in the second column, will change if output changes, even if it is only by a small amount.

Note that a distinction is made between **wages** (paid to operatives who make the product) and **salaries** (paid to staff who are not directly involved in production). Similarly, power to drive the machinery is a variable cost, while office lighting and heating are fixed (not related to output).

Semi-variable costs are costs that combine elements of fixed and variable costs. A worker may be paid a set wage plus a bonus for each item produced. The set wage would be a fixed cost and the bonus a variable cost.

> *e* **EXAMINER'S VOICE**
>
> Do not worry about the merits of individual categories, but accept the logic behind them when carrying out calculations. Analytical skills can then be demonstrated through pointing out the potential flaws in any calculations based on these general classifications.
>
> For example, many offices will employ temporary staff to cover changes in activity levels. Therefore, in practice, administration costs such as salaries will vary with output in the short run.
>
> Similarly, the likelihood of variable costs not increasing by the same percentage as output can be investigated. With bulk buying of raw materials, it is likely that variable costs will rise more slowly than output. However, as maximum capacity is approached it can become costly to increase output just by changing variable factors.

Effect of changes in output on costs

When asked to look at the effect of a change in output on costs, you must assume that variable costs change by the same percentage as output. If output doubles, variable costs will double; if output falls by 10%, variable costs will fall by 10%. In both cases, the fixed costs will stay the same.

For example, let us assume that output is 1,000 units, fixed costs are £5,000 and variable costs are £6,000. Therefore, total costs are £11,000. The fixed costs will not change if output changes. The variable costs of £6,000 will increase, but by how much? To calculate this we need to know the variable cost per unit. If 1,000 units cost £6,000 in variable costs, this is £6 per unit (£6,000 ÷ 1,000 units). If 1 more unit is produced, it will increase variable costs by £6 (to £6,006). If 50 more units are produced, variable costs will increase by £300 (50 × £6) to £6,300 (1,050 × £6). Fixed costs will stay at £5,000.

1 What happens to total costs if output doubles from 1,000 units to 2,000 units?

2 What happens to total costs if output falls by 10% from 1,000 units to 900 units? (Answers on p. 121)

> *e* **EXAMINER'S VOICE**
>
> All AQA examiners use a rule called the 'own figure rule'. This means that if you make a mistake in a calculation, you can only be penalised once. Therefore, it is

important to show all your working. In question 2 on p. 117, a student who calculated variable costs as 700 × £6 (instead of 900 × £6) would have reached an incorrect answer (£4,200 instead of £5,400 for variable costs, and thus £9,200 rather than £10,400 for total costs). Typically, this answer (with working) would achieve almost maximum marks, as only one small error has been made. However, an answer of £9,200 without working would receive zero marks because the examiner would not be able to see that the answer contained only one error.

Table 11.2 shows the link between monthly costs and output for a magazine producer. It illustrates why the magazine producer wants high monthly sales. If only 20,000 magazines are sold, the fixed costs are high as a percentage of total costs. However, if sales quadruple to 80,000 magazines, total costs increase by less than double (from £70,000 to £130,000) and the fixed costs are a much lower percentage of the total costs.

Table 11.2 Monthly costs and output for a magazine producer

Units of output (000s)	Fixed costs (£000s)	Variable costs (£000s)	Total costs (£000s)
0	50	0	50
20	50	20	70
40	50	40	90
60	50	60	110
80	50	80	130
100	50	100	150
120	50	120	170

EXAMINER'S VOICE

Finance and accounting questions can be quite daunting if you dislike numbers. However, number crunching is not the main skill that is being tested. The high-mark questions on an examination paper are based on evaluation (making a judgement). Numbers tend to give firm conclusions, so it is unlikely that evaluation questions will be based only on numerical answers — they are far more likely to ask you to comment on the usefulness of a method or the consequences or causes of a situation.

Relationship between costs and price

In many industries, increases in costs, such as raw materials and labour, are 'passed on' to the consumer in the form of higher prices. Although business theory suggests that higher prices will lead to a fall in the quantity demanded (and possibly in sales revenue), demand is less likely to fall if every business is increasing its prices. This is likely to happen when costs are increasing, because all firms will be affected in a similar way, and they will all be trying to maintain a profit margin (the difference between the selling price of an item and the cost of making or buying that item).

 FILE

Forecasting costs

In planning a small business, it is vital that costs are forecast accurately because small businesses are vulnerable to sudden rises in costs. Whereas large organisations may be able to find alternative supplies abroad, small firms are more likely to continue buying from local suppliers.

In 2007 many small firms suffered from enormous rises in raw material costs. Two very contrasting factors were behind these increases — local flooding in parts of the UK in the summer of 2007 and greater competition for materials in world markets, created by much greater demand from countries such as China.

As a result, the cost of wheat rose by 33% in the UK in August 2007. This was not an isolated case. Lehman Brothers' ingredients cost index — which covers cocoa, coffee, oats, tea, soya beans and milk, among other commodities — rose by 33.9% between July 2006 and June 2007. This was at a time when overall UK inflation was running at just over 2% per annum.

Rents also rose. In London, rents increased by just under 10% in the 3 months from April to June 2007 — possibly another reason why fewer start-ups succeed in London than anywhere else in the country.

Fortunately, energy prices (electricity and gas) fell by 10% over the same period, although they had risen dramatically in previous years.

It is difficult for a small firm to anticipate these changes, but incorrect forecasting may mean that a

business does not achieve the results that it needs to succeed (although it can also lead to larger than expected profits if costs are underestimated).

PRACTICE EXERCISE 1 — Total: 12 marks (8 minutes)

1 Identify three fixed costs and three variable costs from the list below:
- raw materials
- power
- stationery expenditure
- property rent
- advertising expenditure
- wages
(6 marks)

2 Calculate the missing figure in each of the following:
   a Average price per unit = £33 and quantity sold = 25 units. Total revenue = ? *(2 marks)*
   b Total revenue = £1,260 and quantity sold = 70 units. Selling price per unit = ? *(2 marks)*
   c Total revenue = £1,840 and selling price per unit = £23. Quantity sold = ? *(2 marks)*

PRACTICE EXERCISE 2 — Total: 20 marks (20 minutes)

A textile manufacturer sells 400 shirts at a price of £15 each. The costs of producing the 400 shirts are shown in Table 11.3.

Table 11.3 Costs for a textile manufacturer

Item	Cost (£)
Raw materials	1,600
Marketing costs	120
Power	80
Heating/lighting	60
Property/rent	400
Wages	2,220

1 Calculate the profit made from selling 400 shirts. *(4 marks)*

2 The retailers that buy the shirts have said that they will buy 600 shirts if the price is reduced to £13. Calculate the profit made if the textile manufacturer increases output and sales to 600 shirts, with the selling price at £13 per unit. *(6 marks)*

3 Using quantitative and qualitative factors, advise the manufacturer on whether it should charge a price of £13 or £15. *(10 marks)*

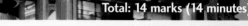

PRACTICE EXERCISE 3   Total: 16 marks (16 minutes)

A company makes and sells 100 units each of two products (A and B). The fixed costs and variable costs are shown in Table 11.4.

Table 11.4 *Fixed and variable costs*

	Product A	Product B
Fixed costs (£)	200	800
Variable costs (£)	800	200
Total costs (£)	1,000	1,000

1 Calculate the total costs of making:
  a 50 units of product A
  b 50 units of product B   *(4 marks)*

2 Calculate the total costs of making:
  a 150 units of product A
  b 150 units of product B   *(4 marks)*

3 Briefly explain why the change in total costs for product A is different from that for product B as output changes.   *(3 marks)*

4 Explain the implications that these figures have for a company that is deciding whether to replace its workers with machinery.   *(5 marks)*

PRACTICE EXERCISE 4   Total: 14 marks (14 minutes)

The table below shows some costs and revenue data at different levels of output.

Output level	Sales revenue	Fixed costs	Variable costs	Total costs	Profit
0	0				
1					
2					
3	75				
4		20			
5					
6			90		

1 What are the total fixed costs?   *(2 marks)*

2 What is the selling price of the product?   *(2 marks)*

3 What are the variable costs per unit?   *(2 marks)*

4 Using the above information, complete the table by filling in the gaps.   *(8 marks)*

PRACTICE EXERCISE 5   Total: 12 marks (12 minutes)

The following information applies to a paper manufacturer that produces and sells 1 million reams of paper a week. Its costs are as follows:
- fixed costs – £400,000
- raw materials – £500,000
- wages – £150,000

Assume that there are no other costs.

1 Calculate the costs per unit of a ream of paper.   *(2 marks)*

2 Calculate the variable costs per unit of a ream of paper.   *(2 marks)*

3 A ream of paper is sold for £1.50. Calculate the total weekly profit made by the firm.   *(4 marks)*

4 Calculate the weekly profit if 1.1 million reams are sold at a price of £1.50.   *(4 marks)*

CASE STUDY Gnomes United

Gnomes United is a small garden centre in Colchester. The owner, Jim Tavare, has successfully increased sales in recent years by widening the range of products and services offered. A total of 70% of the garden centre's revenue comes from the sale of plants and garden tools, but the opening last year of a nearby superstore led to a sharp reduction in sales of these items. Sales of plants have fully recovered, owing to quality problems at the superstore, but sales of garden tools are still low. Market research among his customers has led to Jim realising that the sale of garden tools in his garden centre is important, since customers see them as an essential element of any garden centre. Furthermore, Jim remembers how sales of plants at his cousin Jack's garden centre in Ipswich fell sharply when Jack decided to stop selling garden tools.

Sales records show that relatively few garden tools are bought in the run-up to Christmas.

Last year Jim experimented with selling some Christmas products, such as decorations, as many customers visit the centre once a year to buy their Christmas trees. The restaurant at the garden centre enjoys a boom time in the month before Christmas, and Jim's research shows that about 20% of his customers first came to the garden centre to buy Christmas products and have come back since for other products.

Jim is wondering whether to stock Christmas tree lights this year — an item that he has not previously sold. He has asked 50 customers and they seem to be keen on the idea. Their responses have led him to conclude that he will sell 200 boxes in December. A standard box of lights will sell for £19.99. The lights will cost £13.50 to buy from the supplier, but Jim estimates that he will need to increase the number of part-time hours worked by 4 hours in total, at a rate of £5 per hour. This estimate is based on asking the owners of three other local garden centres.

Questions

Total: 30 marks (35 minutes)

1 Name two other terms that also mean 'revenue'. (2 marks)

2 Identify four different examples of fixed costs for a garden centre. (4 marks)

3 Based on the figures in the case study, calculate the extra profit that Jim hopes to make from the Christmas tree lights. (6 marks)

4 Analyse one reason why it would be difficult to estimate the effect of stocking Christmas tree lights on the number of part-time hours needed. (6 marks)

5 Discuss the other factors that Jim should consider before deciding whether to stock the Christmas tree lights. (12 marks)

Answers to questions on p. 117

1 variable costs =
   2,000 × £6 = £12,000
   fixed costs = £5,000
   total costs = £17,000

2 variable costs =
   900 × £6 = £5,400
   fixed costs = £5,000
   total costs = £10,400

Note that in question 1, although output doubles, total costs increase by less than double their original amount. In question 2, although output falls by 10%, total costs fall by less than 10%. The fact that fixed costs do not change means that total costs will change by a smaller percentage than the change in output.

CHAPTER 12

Using breakeven analysis to make decisions

The concepts explained in Chapter 11 are used to show how firms can calculate contribution per unit and total contribution. The chapter then uses these concepts in order to conduct breakeven analysis, to compile simple breakeven charts, and to calculate or plot the breakeven output and the margin of safety. These are examined in the context of testing the feasibility of setting up a new venture. The chapter also considers the impact of changes in fixed costs, variable costs per unit and selling price on the breakeven output, profit levels and margin of safety of a business activity, with particular emphasis on the impact that such changes have on small businesses. The assumptions made in breakeven analysis are shown, and the strengths and weaknesses of breakeven analysis as a business technique are explained.

Contribution

Contribution is an important concept in business studies. It looks at whether an individual product (or activity) is helping the business to make a profit.

All firms need to pay their fixed costs in order to operate. These costs must be covered before a profit can be made.

Contribution ignores these fixed costs. Instead, it looks only at the variable costs of making the product. If the sales revenue from making the product is greater than the variable costs, the product is contributing towards either paying off the fixed costs or making a profit (if the fixed costs have already been covered).

For example, if the variable costs of making a pen are 7p and the pen sells for 18p, the contribution per unit is 11p (18p – 7p).

If the total contribution exceeds the fixed costs, the business is making a profit. If the fixed costs exceed the total contribution, the firm is making a loss. A firm will break even if the total contribution is equal to the fixed costs (or if *TR* = *TC*).

The total contribution of a product can be calculated in two ways:
- contribution per unit × number of units sold
- sales revenue – total variable costs

> **KEY TERMS**
>
> **contribution per unit:** selling price per unit – variable cost per unit
>
> **total contribution:** the difference between total revenue and total variable costs

Calculating contribution per unit and total contribution: an example

An entrepreneur is planning to set up a coffee shop. She predicts that her costs and revenue will be as follows:

- fixed costs (per week): £750
- variable costs: £0.90 per customer
- selling price (per customer): £2.75
- number of customers (per week): 700

The contribution per unit = £2.75 – £0.90 = £1.85.

Using the first of the two formulae on p. 122:

total contribution = £1.85 × 700 = £1,295

The same figure for total contribution is obtained using the second formula:

(700 × £2.75) – (700 × £0.90) = £1,925 – £630 = £1,295

weekly profit = total contribution – fixed costs = £1,295 – £750 = £545

What if variable costs increase to £1 per customer, the selling price increases to £2.80 and fixed costs increase to £800 per week?

The contribution per unit falls to £1.80 (£2.80 – £1), so the total contribution falls to £1,260 (£1.80 × 700).

weekly profit becomes £1,260 – £800 = £460

Note that the change in fixed costs affects the weekly profit but has no impact on the contribution.

GROUP EXERCISE

Table 12.1 shows the contributions made by four different 'water features' produced by a firm. The total of £971,000 is a contribution towards fixed costs and profit.

Look at the contributions made by each product.

1 What immediate action should you take to improve profit?

2 Which other product should be investigated to see if its contribution can be improved?

(Answers on p. 136)

Table 12.1 Contributions made by four different water features

Water feature	Price (£)	– Variable costs (£)	= Contribution per unit (£)	× No. of units sold (000s)	= Total contribution (£000s)
Cascade	30	25	5	40	200
Fountain	45	22	23	16	368
Stream	60	28	32	14	448
Waterfall	15	18	(3)	15	(45)

	Sales (£000s) –	Direct costs (£000s) =	Contribution (£000s)
Cascade	(30 × 40) 1,200	(25 × 40) 1,000	(5 × 40) 200
Fountain	(45 × 16) 720	(22 × 16) 352	(23 × 16) 368
Stream	(60 × 14) 840	(28 × 14) 392	(32 × 14) 448
Waterfall	(15 × 15) 225	(18 × 15) 270	((3) × 15) (45)
		Total contribution	**971**

KEY TERMS

breakeven analysis: study of the relationship between total costs and total revenue to identify the output at which a business breaks even (i.e. makes neither a profit nor a loss).

breakeven output: the level of output at which total sales revenue is equal to total costs of production.

Breakeven analysis

A business can use breakeven analysis to discover its breakeven output and the impact of changes in output on its profit levels.

Assumptions of breakeven analysis

A firm's costs and revenue must be investigated in order to discover the level of output needed to break even. As explained in Chapter 11, costs can be classified as either **fixed** or **variable**.

Fixed costs such as rent must be paid regardless of output. If a firm produces no units of output, it still has to pay its fixed costs. However, if output increases, it is assumed that these costs will not increase. For example, if fixed costs are £50,000, the firm must pay £50,000 whether it produces zero units, 1 unit, 10 units, 100 units or any other level of output.

Variable costs such as raw materials increase as output increases. It is normal to assume that variable costs stay at the same level per unit produced. Thus if 1 unit costs £5 in variable costs, then 2 units will cost £10, 10 units will cost £50 and so on.

Sales revenue follows a pattern similar to variable costs. If the price is £15, selling 1 unit earns £15, 2 units will earn £30, and 10 units will earn £150.

In practice, costs and revenue do not always behave in a set, predictable way. However, in order to study breakeven, certain assumptions are made:
- The selling price remains the same, regardless of the number of units sold.
- Fixed costs remain the same, regardless of the number of units of output.
- Variable costs vary in direct proportion to output.
- Every unit of output that is produced is sold.

These assumptions mean that objective comparisons can be made between different products or firms.

Calculating breakeven output

Breakeven output can be worked out in three different ways:
- using a table showing revenue and costs over a range of output levels
- using a formula to calculate the breakeven quantity
- using a graph showing revenue and costs over a range of output levels

Using a table

In Table 12.2 it can be seen that the breakeven output is 5,000 units. At this level of output, sales revenue is equal to total costs and profit is zero. Below 5,000 units, the firm makes a loss. Above 5,000 units, the firm makes a profit.

Using a formula

For each additional (marginal) item that the company produces, its extra revenue will equal the price of the item, but it will incur more costs (the variable costs only, such as raw materials and wages of operatives).

Units of output (000s)	Sales revenue (£000s)	Fixed costs (£000s)	Variable costs (£000s)	Total costs (£000s)	Profit (£000s)
0	0	50	0	50	(50)
1	15	50	5	55	(40)
2	30	50	10	60	(30)
3	45	50	15	65	(20)
4	60	50	20	70	(10)
5	75	50	25	75	0
6	90	50	30	80	10
7	105	50	35	85	20
8	120	50	40	90	30
9	135	50	45	95	40
10	150	50	50	100	50
11	165	50	55	105	60
12	180	50	60	110	70

Table 12.2 Deducing breakeven output

e EXAMINER'S VOICE

Keep a close eye on the units of measurement being used, as it is easy to make a mistake in examinations. A quick glance at Table 12.2 will tell you that the breakeven output is '5'. However, the unit of measure is '000s' (thousands). Therefore '5' means 5,000 units. Similarly, the '70' in the bottom right-hand corner of the table means that when 12,000 units are produced, the firm earns a profit of £70,000.

Remember:

contribution per unit = selling price per unit – variable cost per unit

This shows the amount of money that each unit provides (contributes) towards paying off the fixed costs (or creating a profit, once the fixed costs have been met). Thus a product with a selling price of £12 and variable costs per unit of £7 will contribute £5 per unit (£12 – £7), while a product with a price of £60 and variable costs per unit of £22 will contribute £38 per unit.

total contribution = contribution per unit × number of units sold

In the latter example above, 100 units would provide a contribution of £3,800 (£38 × 100) towards fixed costs and profit.

If each unit contributes £38 towards fixed costs and fixed costs were only £38, then only 1 unit would need to be produced in order to break even. If fixed costs were £76, then 2 units would be needed to break even (2 × £38). From this we can see that the formula for calculating breakeven output is as follows:

$$\text{breakeven output} = \frac{\text{fixed costs (£)}}{\text{contribution per unit (£)}}$$

Using the data in Table 12.2, the price is £15 and variable costs are £5 per unit, giving a contribution of £10 for every unit sold. At £10 per unit, 5,000 units would need to be sold in order to pay the fixed costs of £50,000, so 5,000 units is the breakeven output.

$$\text{breakeven output} = \frac{£50,000}{£15 - £5} = 5,000 \text{ units}$$

Note how the £ signs at the top and bottom of the equation have cancelled each other out. The answer is 5,000 units, *not* £5,000.

can survive the difficulties presented by the cash-flow cycle. This is the most critical stage for the business because there will be a delay before revenue is received from the sale of goods and yet considerable expenditure is needed to purchase the factors of production. This is particularly the case if fixed assets, such as buildings and equipment, are needed to get the business up and running. Even well-established businesses are subject to the difficulties presented by the cash-flow cycle, as products must always be made before revenue can be received from selling them. Consequently, the issues presented by the cash-flow cycle are continuous challenges facing any business.

- **The length of time required to convert inputs into outputs.** If a product or service can be produced quickly, the cash-flow cycle may not create problems for a business. For example, a baker may buy the ingredients at the beginning of the day, bake the bread and sell it all within the same working day. However, this does not overcome the difficulties that the baker might have faced in purchasing the ovens and other equipment necessary for the business. Some products can take a long time to construct.

  House builders, for example, are vulnerable to cash-flow difficulties because considerable expenditure must be incurred before it is possible to put the house on to the market and receive revenue.

- **Credit payments.** The analysis so far has assumed that all transactions use cash. In practice, a business may receive credit from its suppliers. In this instance, payment for the factors of production may actually take place *after* cash has been received from the customer in return for the finished goods or service. Therefore, the cash-flow cycle does not cause problems for the business. However, cash flow may be worsened if the business needs to give credit terms to its customers in order to boost sales. This will lead to a further delay in the receipt of cash and therefore cause greater problems with the cash-flow cycle.

The ways in which businesses can ease the problems of the cash-flow cycle are dealt with in Chapter 17.

Cash-flow forecasting

A cash-flow forecast attempts to predict the future, whereas a cash-flow statement describes what actually happened in the past. As predicting the future is not an easy task, constructing a cash-flow forecast may be quite difficult.

Sources for cash-flow forecasting

In order to compile a cash-flow forecast, a business uses a number of sources:
- **Previous cash-flow forecasts.** An established business can examine forecasts from previous years and, taking into consideration any recent changes in business activity, make a forecast for the next financial year.

> **KEY TERM**
>
> **cash-flow forecasting:** the process of estimating the expected cash inflows and cash outflows over a period of time. Cash flow is often seasonal, so it is advisable to forecast for a period of 1 year.

- **Cash-flow statements.** The most recent cash-flow statement describes what actually happened in the previous financial year and is therefore an excellent foundation for next year's forecast.

  (It should be noted that both of these sources are unavailable to a new business start-up — this is one of the main reasons why it is much harder for a start-up to produce a cash-flow forecast accurately.)

- **Consumer research.** It is advisable for all businesses, especially start-ups, to conduct some research into potential sales and prices that potential customers will deem to be acceptable. This information will allow the business to forecast its sales revenue. It may also enable the business to identify any special features, such as seasonal variations in sales revenue. Many new businesses fail to recognise that sales are unlikely to be spread evenly across the year, and such businesses can therefore get into cash-flow difficulties during months when sales are below average.

- **Study of similar businesses, such as competitors.** It may be possible to gain information from similar businesses, particularly those that are not competing in the same geographical area. Local business groups, such as chambers of commerce, may also have expertise which will enable a business to predict the type of sales revenue (and possibly costs) that are likely to be incurred by a business in that particular industry.

- **Establishing the level of resources needed.** Once the probable sales level of the business has been established, it is possible to calculate the resources that the business will need. The cost of these resources, such as machinery, rent and wages, can be built into the cash-flow forecast. It is vital that the costs of all these factors are researched carefully, so that estimates are neither too optimistic nor too cautious.

- **Banks.** Commercial banks have considerable expertise in supporting and handling the finances of small businesses. Invariably, local branches have expertise in relevant industries. For example, a bank located in a tourist area will have expertise in the hotel industry.

- **Consultants.** Consultancy is a growth industry in the UK. A business can use a consultancy in order to access expert opinion on how to forecast cash flow accurately. For small businesses, the government provides financial support towards the payment of consultancy fees in certain circumstances.

- **The cash-flow forecast itself.** It is important that early drafts of the cash-flow forecast are used to build up the final forecast. If an early draft indicates a difficulty, such as a shortage of cash at a particular time, then the business can take steps to rectify this problem. For example, it might get an overdraft from the bank or persuade a supplier to provide credit terms. Any changes of this nature must then be built into the final cash-flow forecast.

Problems in cash-flow forecasting

Potential problems that may cause inaccuracy in a cash-flow forecast include the following:

> **KEY TERM**
>
> **cash-flow statement:** a description of how cash flowed into and out of a business during a particular period of time.

INGRAM

- **Changes in the economy.** Changes in economic growth or unemployment levels might mean that consumers have less (or more) spending power. If unemployment is higher than expected, sales of most goods will be lower than predicted. Changes in inflation may affect both costs and sales revenue.
- **Changes in consumer tastes.** In a dynamic environment, customers often change their opinions. This happens in all markets but is a major peril in fashion and technologically advanced markets.
- **Inaccurate market research.** The research might target the wrong group of consumers, there might be interviewer bias in the questions or the sample might be too small. All these factors could lead to an incorrect sales forecast.
- **Competition.** New competitors may enter the market or a rival may be aiming to increase its market share. Competitors' actions cannot be predicted but will affect the business's level of success. (It is also possible that unsuccessful competitors will mean that the firm's predicted sales are lower than its eventual sales.)
- **Uncertainty.** Estimates of costs for new firms or major projects are often incorrect. Start-ups, in particular, often have problems forecasting cash flow because they lack experience of how the market works. Consequently, new businesses are much more likely to come across unexpected expenses than a well-established firm.

Structure of a cash-flow forecast

The details of cash-flow forecasts vary according to the type of business. However, the key items in constructing a cash-flow forecast are as follows:

- **Cash inflows.** This item usually contains details of income from sales. The timing of the entry depends on when the cash is received, so although cash sales are shown on the date that the sale is expected, goods that are expected to be sold on 60 days' credit terms in February will be shown as forecast cash receipts in April. Other cash inflows may be for items such as rent received, money borrowed in the form of loans, and sales of assets.
- **Cash outflows.** Many items of expenditure could be included here. Raw materials, wages, rent and bills for utilities such as electricity will all need to be forecast. However, some of the difficulties involved in cash-flow forecasting occur when a business fails to recognise the imminent need for major items or one-off payments, such as a new vehicle, some machinery or a tax bill.
- **Net cash flow.** The formula for net cash flow is:

$$\text{net cash flow} = \text{cash inflows} - \text{cash outflows}$$

This shows the monthly situation and will help the business to foresee months in which cash shortages may occur.

- **Opening balance and closing balance.** A company that starts a year with a cash surplus may be able to survive months with negative net cash flows. The final elements in constructing a cash-flow forecast are to show the opening cash and closing cash balances. The formula for closing balance is:

closing cash balance = opening cash balance + net cash flow

A simplified cash-flow forecast for Gideon Prewett for the first 6 months of 2009 is set out in Table 13.1.

	January	February	March	April	May	June
Opening balance	0	300	(220)	1,060	440	70
Sales income	2,000	3,600	5,000	3,300	3,750	5,000
Borrowings	6,000	0	0	0	0	0
Total inflows	8,000	3,600	5,000	3,300	3,750	5,000
Materials	4,000	1,500	1,100	1,150	1,500	1,800
Wages	2,200	2,200	2,200	2,200	2,200	2,200
Other costs	1,500	420	420	570	420	420
Total outflows	7,700	4,120	3,720	3,920	4,120	4,420
Net monthly balance	300	(520)	1,280	(620)	(370)	580
Closing balance	300	(220)	1,060	440	70	650

Table 13.1 Cash-flow forecast (£) for Gideon Prewett, January–June 2009

 EXAMINER'S VOICE

Organisations will often choose their own way of laying out a cash-flow forecast. Table 13.1 is one example of a layout but you will certainly come across alternative ways of presenting such information. However, all cash-flow forecasts must contain information on cash inflows and cash outflows and the opening balance of cash.

As long as you remember the formulae for net cash flow and closing cash balance, you will be able to understand any cash-flow layout.

Constructing a cash-flow forecast

In order to construct a cash-flow forecast, the business must gather data on all of the likely flows of cash into and out of the business over a period of time. A year is the most sensible choice, because for most businesses there will be some seasonal changes that can lead to significant changes in cash inflow (or cash outflow) at particular times of the year. For the sake of simplicity, we will construct a cash-flow forecast that covers July, August and September 2009 for Gideon Prewett.

The data needed to forecast the business's cash flow for July to September 2009 are as follows:
- Sales income is expected to be £6,600 in July and £7,000 in August, but to fall to £6,000 in September.
- Raw materials will cost £2,000 per month in July and August, but only £1,600 in September.

- Wages will remain the same at £2,200 per month.
- 'Other costs' will be £570 in July, falling to £420 in August and September.

Putting these data into a cash-flow forecast gives us the information shown in Table 13.2.

To complete the cash-flow forecast, we need to add 'sales income' and 'borrowings' in order to calculate 'total inflows'. As there is no mention of borrowing in the data, we can take it that this figure is zero.

total outflows = materials + wages + other costs

so we can insert the total outflows figures for each month.

The 'opening balance' for July 2009 is the same as the closing balance for June 2009 (Table 13.1 shows this to be £650).

We can now complete the remaining gaps using the following formulae:

net monthly balance = total inflows – total outflows

closing balance = opening balance + net monthly balance

The completed cash flow is shown in Table 13.3.

Table 13.2 *Cash inflows and cash outflows for Gideon Prewett, July–September 2009*

	July 2009	August 2009	September 2009
Opening balance			
Sales income	6,600	7,000	6,000
Borrowings			
Total inflows			
Materials	2,000	2,000	1,600
Wages	2,200	2,200	2,200
Other costs	570	420	420
Total outflows			
Net monthly balance			
Closing balance			

Table 13.3 *Completed cash-flow forecast for Gideon Prewett, July–September 2009*

	July 2009	August 2009	September 2009
Opening balance	650	2,480	4,860
Sales income	6,600	7,000	6,000
Borrowings	0	0	0
Total inflows	6,600	7,000	6,000
Materials	2,000	2,000	1,600
Wages	2,200	2,200	2,200
Other costs	570	420	420
Total outflows	4,770	4,620	4,220
Net monthly balance	1,830	2,380	1,780
Closing balance	2,480	4,860	6,640

***e* EXAMINER'S VOICE**

For practical reasons, examination questions are unlikely to show 12 separate months, simply because of the volume of data involved and the time that it will take for you to read through it during the examination. Therefore, you should practise by looking at smaller cash-flow forecasts — those that cover a few months or those that use quarters (e.g. January to March) rather than cash-flow forecasts that show 12 separate months. For the same reason, there are unlikely to be many examples of separate headings for items such as cash outflows, although a real-life cash-flow forecast will contain this detailed information.

(The same logic applies to the details in budgets, the topic of the next chapter.)

Why businesses forecast cash flow

The most liquid asset that a business can possess is cash. All firms, however profitable, must manage their cash and their working capital (which includes those items that can be converted into cash most easily) to guarantee their survival. Thus, in the short term, a business must manage its cash flow in order to remain liquid.

Cash-flow forecasts are important to a business because they enable it to foresee times in the future when the business will be short of liquidity. If shortages are anticipated far enough in advance, the business may be able to take measures to prevent the shortage from occurring.

The main reasons for forecasting cash flow are therefore as follows:

- **To identify potential cash-flow problems in advance.** The forecast can detect if current plans are going to lead the firm into a situation in which it cannot meet payments. This might involve a lack of funds at the end of the month to pay the wage bill or a shortage of cash when a tax bill is due.
- **To guide the firm towards appropriate action.** Once a potential problem has been identified, action can be taken to overcome the difficulty. The problem may be solved by a change of plans, such as not extending the office accommodation, if this was one of the decisions that led to the predicted cash shortage.
- **To make sure that there is sufficient cash available to pay suppliers and creditors and to make other payments.** By studying the cash-flow forecast, the organisation can plan inflows of cash in time to make payments that might have been difficult to meet. Usually, this will mean arranging financial help such as a bank overdraft for a temporary cash shortage or a long-term loan for equipment purchase.
- **To provide evidence in support of a request for financial assistance (e.g. asking a bank for an overdraft).** The cash-flow forecast should show the bank manager why help is needed, but it must also indicate how the overdraft can be repaid. An overdraft is intended to cover short-term problems, so the forecast must show that, eventually, the firm will be able to pay back the overdraft.
- **To avoid the possibility of the company being forced out of business (into liquidation) because of a forthcoming shortage of money.** It is estimated that as many as 30% of all companies that liquidate fail because they cannot get hold of cash, rather than because they are unprofitable. Profitable companies must check that they have cash, rather than having all their profit tied up in stock or buildings.
- **To identify the possibility of holding too much cash.** This probably means that a firm has less

KEY TERM

liquidity: the ability to convert an asset into cash without loss or delay.

machinery and stock than it could possess, which gives the firm less production and stock to sell, so it makes less profit. Although this is perhaps less of a problem than a cash shortage, it is not wise for a firm to have too much cash.

ⓔ EXAMINER'S VOICE

You should avoid using bullet points in the examination. They encourage brief explanations rather than detailed analysis.

FACT FILE

When Peter Spivack and his three partners opened their restaurant, Rendezvous, in Wallasey Village, Merseyside, in 2004 they knew that sound cash-flow management would be a key to success during that crucial first year. Peter took responsibility for cash-flow planning and management: 'My first year's cash-flow forecast helped me secure a start-up loan. To keep on top of things I reviewed the forecast monthly,' said Peter. The cash-flow forecast helped the business to set up and is now helping it to operate smoothly and successfully.

PRACTICE EXERCISE 1   Total: 40 marks (35 minutes)

1 Draw a diagram to show the cash-flow cycle. *(6 marks)*

2 Explain the meaning of the term 'cash-flow forecast'. *(2 marks)*

3 Identify five different sources of information for a cash-flow forecast. *(5 marks)*

4 Identify four different examples of cash inflows. *(4 marks)*

5 Complete the formula below:

.... = cash inflow – .... *(4 marks)*

6 Complete the formula below:

closing balance = ... + ... *(4 marks)*

7 Explain two reasons why an organisation should prepare a cash-flow forecast. *(6 marks)*

8 Explain two problems that a firm might have when trying to predict its cash flow. *(6 marks)*

9 What is meant by the term 'liquidity'? *(3 marks)*

PRACTICE EXERCISE 2   Total: 45 marks (55 minutes)

Fun for Kids Ltd

Siu Wan decided to set up Fun for Kids because she had found it difficult to find a safe place for her young children to play.

Banknotes plc had been a small, but very profitable banknote producer, but a merger with a US security printer had led to the closure of the factory. The premises were ideal for Siu's idea. The

landscaped grounds were a highly suitable outdoor play area, and she could not believe that there were air-conditioned warehouses until she visited the site. Luckily, some friends were also excited about the idea and agreed to put a lot of money into the business.

Fun for Kids was set up on 14 January 2008, with enough capital to purchase the lease and convert the warehouse and grounds into an exciting and colourful play park, with rides and attractions ideally suited to young children. By the end of April, the work had been completed, in time for the grand opening on 1 May 2008.

Siu was pleased to see that Fun for Kids still had an opening balance of £9,250 in its bank account on 1 May.

Fun for Kids agreed an annual rental of £60,000 per annum, being paid in two equal instalments in June and December. Siu estimates monthly costs as follows:

- Wages are expected to be £5,000 per month in the autumn and winter (September to February);

£5,500 in March, April and May; and £8,000 in June, July and August.
- Maintenance is expected to cost £200 per month. Administration is forecast at £3,800 per month.
- Electricity, gas and other costs are due in March, June, September and December. Siu estimates that these costs will be £2,500 per quarter.
- Siu is targeting a major £7,500 marketing campaign in the opening month (May). The main target market is local families, but Siu hopes to attract tourists in July and August, and is planning expenditure of £2,000 per month in June and July. In August and from September onwards, marketing is expected to cost £300 per month.
- Cash sales are expected to be £15,000 per month, except for July (£25,000) and August (£30,000).
- Credit sales will be accepted for 'party' bookings. These will be £2,500 per month, but payment to the firm will take place exactly 1 month after the sales were recorded, so no money will be earned from these sales in May.

Table 13.4 *Cash-flow forecast for Fun for Kids Ltd, May–December 2008*

	May	June	July	August	September	October	November	December
Opening balance								
Cash sales								
Credit sales								
Total inflows								
Wages								
Maintenance and administration								
Electricity, gas etc.								
Marketing								
Rent								
Total outflows								
Net monthly balance								
Closing balance								

Questions

1 Explain the meaning of the term 'closing balance'. *(2 marks)*

2 State two other items that could be included as 'outflows' in a cash-flow forecast. *(2 marks)*

3 Compile a cash-flow forecast for Fun for Kids on a separate sheet of paper, using the template shown in Table 13.4. *(12 marks)*

4 Explain two sources of information that would have helped Siu to construct this cash-flow forecast. *(6 marks)*

5 Analyse two arguments that Siu could use to persuade a bank manager to provide a bank overdraft, where necessary. *(8 marks)*

6 Evaluate the main reasons why this cash-flow forecast may be inaccurate. *(15 marks)*

CASE STUDY VKP Ltd

VKP Ltd is a private limited company that sells computer software. The case is based on a real firm whose name has been changed.

Background information

- The majority of VKP's sales are internet software; it also sells some CDs.
- Skilful design of the VKP website means that people using an internet search engine to find a certain type of software will usually find VKP listed on the first page of the search engine's list.
- VKP buys the software and adds on a sum of money in order to set the price that it charges its customers.
- Customers (mainly businesses) pay VKP for the licensing rights to use the software. Credit terms are not offered to customers.

- The manufacturers of the software supplied to VKP give 30 days' credit to VKP (although this was not given in its first year of trading). As supply is via the internet, VKP does not need to keep any stock. Orders to suppliers can be made directly on the day that a customer orders software, as the product is sent via the internet.
- Value-added tax (VAT) is included in the price charged to the customer. VKP forwards the VAT that it has collected to the government (HM Revenue and Customs) at the end of each quarter (i.e. the end of March, June, September and December).
- 'Drawings' (see Table 13.5) are payments made to the owners of the business for the work that they have done.

Table 13.5 Cash-flow forecast for VKP Ltd: year 2009 (£000s)

	Jan	Feb	Mar	Apr	May	June	July	Aug	Sept	Oct	Nov	Dec
Opening balance	0	10	56	33	51	77	50	29	19	68	74	100
Cash inflow (sales)	90	118	118	118	118	118	79	54	135	118	118	90
Purchases	64	64	84	84	84	84	84		38	96	84	84
Wages and drawings	4	4	4	4	4	4	4	4	4	4	4	4
Administrative costs	12	4	4	12	4	4	12	4	4	12	4	4
VAT payments to government	0	0	49	0	0	53	0	0	40	0	0	49
Cash outflows	80	72	141	100	92	145	100	64	86	112	92	141
Net inflow/(outflow)	10	46	(23)	18	26	(27)	(21)	(10)	49	6	26	(51)
Closing balance	10	56	33	51	77	50	29	19	68	74	100	

Questions

Total: 30 marks (35 minutes)

1 What is meant by the term 'cash outflow'? *(2 marks)*

2 Sales income (including VAT) is the only 'cash inflow' on VKP's cash-flow forecast (Table 13.5). Identify two other items that could be included under the heading 'cash inflows' in a cash-flow forecast. *(2 marks)*

3 Calculate:
  a VKP's predicted 'purchases' in August *(2 marks)*
  b VKP's closing balance in December *(2 marks)*

4 Analyse two reasons why VKP does not anticipate any cash-flow problems for most of the year. *(10 marks)*

5 At present VKP does not offer credit terms to its customers. Discuss the possible implications for VKP of a decision to offer credit terms to its customers. *(12 marks)*

Stage 1: **set objectives** — what are the various budgets attempting to achieve?

Stage 2: **carry out market research** to discover the probable level of sales volume and the market price for the product or products.

Stage 3: **carry out research into costs**, based on the sales volume expected.

Stage 4: **complete the sales (income) budget** — this will give the business an idea of how much needs to be produced.

Stage 5: **construct the expenditure budget** to find the costs that will be incurred in achieving the sales target.

Stage 6: **create an overall profit budget** by combining stages 4 and 5.

Stage 7: **draw up divisional or departmental budgets** — this should be done by managers responsible for each area of the business.

Stage 8: **summarise the detailed budgets in the master budget.**

Figure 14.1 Stages of budget setting

The first step in setting budgets is similar to that involved in creating cash-flow forecasts. In fact, the budgeting process will be a major influence on the forecasts for cash outflows and inflows, as the budgets represent the organisation's financial plans.

The stages of budget setting are shown in Figure 14.1. It should be noted that budget setting is not a one-way process, as results from one stage may lead the business to reconsider or recalculate an earlier stage. Furthermore, the process may need to be repeated every time the budgeting process is reviewed. This may be annually, quarterly, monthly, weekly or even daily.

In stage 1, it is vital to establish the business's targets before getting into detailed examination of any budgets. Research into costs, in stage 3, requires scrutiny of wage levels and the cost of materials and any items of equipment that the business is planning to purchase. Although the government's predicted inflation rate can be useful in estimating future costs, it is not always reliable. Fuel costs, for example, have risen much more rapidly than other costs in recent years, and many raw material costs increased by over 30% in 2007.

The greater the number of divisions/departments in an organisation, the greater the number of budgets required for stage 7. There will also be some budgets that operate centrally, such as capital budgets (to plan expenditure on major assets such as building and machinery or a project, as described earlier).

Completing budgets

The following examples, which cover a period of only 1 month, are provided merely to illustrate the process of completing a budget.

The income budget

As a general rule, it is sensible for a business to start with doing an income budget, as most items of expenditure will depend on the level of sales that are budgeted.

The data below show the budgeted sales for ABC Ltd for January 2009:

■ product A — sales of 100 units at a price of £32 each
■ product B — sales of 80 units at a price of £15 each

■ product C — sales of 30 units at a price of £60 each

Table 14.1 shows the budget arising from these targets.

Source of income	Income (£)
Product A	3,200
Product B	1,200
Product C	1,800
Total income	**6,200**

***Table 14.1** Income budget for ABC Ltd, January 2009*

The expenditure budget

The expenditure budget is based on these levels of sales. For example, if raw material costs are budgeted at one-quarter of the selling price of each product, we can estimate that raw materials will cost a quarter of £6,200, which equals £1,550. Similarly, if labour costs are £10 per product, regardless of whether product A, B or C is involved, then labour costs will be £2,100 because 100 + 80 + 30 = 210 units, and 210 × £10 = £2,100.

Table 14.2 shows estimates for expenditure, including these figures of £1,550 for raw materials and £2,100 for labour costs.

Item of expenditure	Expenditure (£)
Raw materials	1,550
Labour costs	2,100
Marketing expenditure	150
Administration	450
Rent	750
Capital costs	0
Total expenditure	**5,000**

***Table 14.2** Expenditure budget for ABC Ltd, January 2009*

Item of income/ expenditure	£
Total income	6,200
Total expenditure	5,000
Budgeted profit	**1,200**

***Table 14.3** Profit budget for ABC Ltd, January 2009*

The profit budget

profit = income – expenditure

Therefore, the profit budget is constructed by taking the income budget and subtracting the expenditure budget. Table 14.3 shows the result.

Amending budgets

What happens if the finances are budgeted to change? Consider the following scenario. ABC Ltd is planning a large marketing campaign in February 2009. This will lead to:
■ a trebling of marketing expenditure
■ a 50% increase in sales of products A and C
■ a 10% increase in sales of product B (the company is increasing its price to £25)

The business also expects a fall in rent to £700 per month but no change in administration costs and capital costs.

(Labour costs will still be £10 per product and raw material costs will be a quarter of sales income.)

Tables 14.4–14.6 show the resulting budgets for February 2009.

Source of income	Amendment	Income (£)
Product A	150 × £32	4,800
Product B	88 × £25	2,200
Product C	45 × £60	2,700
Total income		**9,700**

***Table 14.4** Income budget for ABC Ltd, February 2009*

Item of expenditure	Amendment	Expenditure (£)
Raw materials	25% of £9,700	2,425
Labour costs	283 × £10	2,830
Marketing expenditure	3 × £150	450
Administration	No change	450
Rent	Falls from 750	700
Capital costs	No change	0
Total expenditure		**6,855**

***Table 14.5** Expenditure budget for ABC Ltd, February 2009*

Item of income/ expenditure	£
Total income	9,700
Total expenditure	6,855
Budgeted profit	**2,845**

***Table 14.6** Profit budget for ABC Ltd, February 2009*

Methods of setting a budget

The stages involved in setting a budget will vary according to the method(s) used by a firm when setting its budget(s). The approach described above assumes that the budgets are being set according to the company's objectives. However, the approach may need to be modified if a different method of budgeting is used. The main methods of setting a budget are summarised here.

Budgeting according to company objectives

The more ambitious the objectives, the greater the budget that needs to be allocated. In 2007, Blackpool Pleasure Beach budgeted an additional £8 million in order to add a new attraction, the Infusion Ride. It is hoped that this ride will enable the organisation to turn round the fall in visitor numbers and bring the total back to over 6 million visitors again.

Budgeting according to competitors' spending

In order to stay competitive, a business may have to match the spending of its rivals. In 2007 Tesco mounted a campaign of price comparisons between the leading supermarkets. Other supermarkets introduced their own responses, leading to changes in both income and expenditure budgets throughout the sector. Budgeting according to competitors' spending is particularly popular with start-ups, which may be relatively unaware of typical levels of spending and income in their market. Matching their budgets to those of rival firms may therefore enable them to be competitive.

Setting the budget as a percentage of sales revenue

Although this is less scientific, it is frequently used because it is seen to be fair. It is a common method of allocating budgets to product managers in a business in which there is a variety of different products with their own budgets. It is also used in organisations such as supermarkets and banks, when allocating budgets to branches.

If a firm matches the national average by spending just under 2% of its sales revenue on advertising, a product with sales of £100 million per annum will be given a budget of just under £2 million and one with sales of £100,000 will receive just under £2,000. In the UK's liqueur market, advertising budgets for products such as Baileys and Tia Maria equate to 3% of sales revenue, while for Unilever, marketing costs are over 13% of its sales revenue (and much higher than this for its soaps and washing powders).

Zero budgeting/budgeting based on expected outcomes

In effect, this method allocates a budget on the strength of the case presented by the product manager. It is ideal for budgets such as marketing, and research and development, as the dynamic nature of these activities means that a budget can be quickly agreed to suit a sudden event. It is also used for one-off events such as the London Olympics in 2012. A £3.1 billion budget has been set aside for this project, based on the case presented by the organising committee, which undertook detailed research into the facilities needed and the cost of commissioning them.

There are three main advantages of zero budgeting. First, it encourages budget holders to plan thoroughly and carefully. Second, it helps to identify changes in the needs of an organisation, thus avoiding problems where declining areas accumulate high budgets and prevent the expansion of newer, more profitable areas of the business. Third, it can save money by enabling the business to cut costs where managers are unable to justify their spending.

However, there are disadvantages of zero budgeting. It can be very time-consuming, as detailed planning is needed. (The time spent on planning may cost even more than the budget savings.) Furthermore, it may lead to high allocations for those managers who are skilled at presenting their case, rather than for those who genuinely need the largest amount of money.

Budgeting according to last year's budget allocation

Although this is less scientific than the other methods, it is common practice in markets experiencing little change for budgets to be set according to last year's allocation plus an allowance for inflation. The logic behind this approach is that, if the budget was suitable last year, it will be suitable again this year. This method is used widely in public services such as the health service and education.

Reasons for setting budgets

Budgets serve a number of purposes:

- **To gain financial support.** A well-reasoned business plan, incorporating clear budgets that indicate a good chance of success, is vital in persuading potential backers to invest in a start-up business. The quality of the budget can therefore be critical, as without it the business may never start. This is one of the reasons why detail is so important in a budget — the more detail it contains, the more reassurance there is for backers looking for a carefully planned business venture.
- **To ensure that a business does not overspend.** Careful control of budgets will make sure that a firm's finances do not worsen unexpectedly, as a result of a failure to limit spending to agreed levels.
- **To establish priorities.** A budget is a plan for the future. Allocating a large budget to an activity can indicate the level of importance attached to a

particular policy or division, sending a clear message to stakeholders such as employees and customers.

■ **To encourage delegation and responsibility, and to motivate staff.** Budgets allow local or junior managers to become budget holders and make decisions on spending in areas of a business in which they are more know-ledgeable than senior managers. This improves the quality of the decisions and acts as a motivator for the budget holder.

■ **To assign responsibility.** The budget holder is the person who is directly responsible for any success or failure. This makes it much easier to trace mistakes or recognise to whom credit should be given. Budget control can be included in the appraisal of a manager's work.

■ **To improve efficiency.** Businesses can monitor and review budgets, and are able to establish standards and investigate the causes of any successes and failures. They can use this information to improve future decisions. The discipline of working to a limited budget encourages managers to seek more efficient methods.

 FILE

Karan Bilimoria, creator of Cobra Beer, believes that careful budgeting is essential and a potentially great motivator.

I will always remember the time in Bangalore — where Cobra was first brewed — when I prepared a spreadsheet. It was a 5-year target detailing month by month the exports of containers.
For any company it is always a question of not only looking 5 years ahead but also breaking those 5 years down into achievable bite-size chunks and targets you can go for. The [income budgets] were ambitious but we managed to beat them all in the end.

Problems of setting budgets

Setting budgets involves a number of potential pitfalls:

■ **Managers may not know enough about the division or department.** In this case they will find it difficult to plan a reasonable budget. This problem is particularly acute for new firms or new ventures.

■ **There may be problems in gathering information.** For a start-up business, it can be very difficult to get financial information from other firms. As a consequence, initial budgets may contain large elements of guesswork and therefore lack accuracy.

■ **There may be unforeseen changes.** Predicting the future is always difficult and unforeseen changes will undermine the budgeting process.

■ **The level of inflation (price rises) is not easy to predict.** Businesses tend to use the average inflation rate, but some prices can change by much greater levels. Farmers have been hit by falling prices, but property prices have gone up by more than most other prices.

■ **Budgets may be imposed.** A key principle of budgeting is that the budget holder should be involved in setting the budget level. Unfortunately, budgets are often set by senior managers who may misunderstand the needs of a certain area. The resulting budget may appear to be unfair, causing resentment and reducing morale. On the other hand, a budget determined solely by the manager responsible may ignore potential scope for efficiency gains and fail to take account of developments outside that area of the business. Ideally, both the senior manager and the budget holder should find the time to discuss the budget fully, but this does not always happen.

■ **Setting a budget can be time-consuming.** It may not be worth devoting too much time to agreeing budgets if only marginal improvements are made.

PRACTICE EXERCISE 1 — Total: 40 marks (30 minutes)

1 What is meant by the term 'budget'? *(2 marks)*

2 What is meant by the term 'management accounting'? *(4 marks)*

3 Identify five of the stages in setting a budget. *(5 marks)*

4 Explain three reasons why a firm sets budgets. *(9 marks)*

5 Explain three difficulties that a firm might have when trying to plan a budget. *(9 marks)*

6 Describe how budgets are set in a 'zero budgeting' system. *(4 marks)*

7 Identify one other method for setting a budget and describe how a budget would be set using this method. *(4 marks)*

8 What is an income budget? *(3 marks)*

PRACTICE EXERCISE 2 — Total: 12 marks (15 minutes)

Tables 14.7–14.9 show an example of a budget for a social event at Nottingham University.

Table 14.7 Income budget for social event

Income	Price (£)	Number	Total (£)
Dinner tickets	15.00	100	1,500.00
Entertainment tickets	5.00	25	125.00
Sponsorship (Deloitte)			500.00
Total			**2,125.00**

Table 14.8 Expenditure budget for social event

Expenditure (incl. VAT)	£
Publicity	25.00
Dinners	822.50
Welcome drinks	117.50
PA and lighting	176.25
Band	587.50
Sub-total	1,728.75
+ Contingency 10% of subtotal	172.88
Total	**1,901.63**

Rewrite the budget, taking into account the changes listed below:

● Ten students have asked to switch from 'entertainment tickets' to 'dinner tickets'.

● The expenditure budget changes to take into account the extra dinner tickets sold (these tickets also entitle the holder to a welcome drink).

● The band has negotiated an increase in its fee to £700.

● Publicity costs have risen to £35.

● Deloitte has agreed to increase its sponsorship by 15%.

Table 14.9 Profit budget for social event

Income	£2,125.00
Expenditure	£1,901.63
Profit	£223.37

Source: Nottingham University Students' Union.

CASE STUDY Frank Roseland, dairyman and newsagent

Frank has just taken over the family milk delivery business from his father. Frank found it difficult to work out whether the business was operating successfully, as his father had not kept very good financial records.

Frank needed to set a budget to see whether it was worthwhile continuing the business. He was earning £20,000 a year in his current job and thought that the business needed to make at least £25,000 profit to make it worthwhile. However, part of him was desperate to continue running the business, as the Roseland family had been delivering milk since 1927. He sifted through the records that his father had kept about payments from customers and the invoices from suppliers indicating the money that they required in return for the milk, newspapers and groceries. These latter two items are products that Frank delivers alongside the milk, to certain customers. Frank also asked for advice from the bank manager, his accountants and one or two other dairymen.

The dairymen in particular proved to be useful, because they explained that although sales were fairly consistent throughout the year, there were seasonal variations. They indicated that it was normal for milk to be sold at a price that was 60% higher than the cost of purchase (although this made the price much higher than supermarket milk), while newspapers had to be sold at the price listed on the front page. Food products could be sold at well over double the cost paid, as anyone buying the products from Frank's business was saving the delivery charges imposed by supermarkets.

Frank noticed that his father's records indicated that, although total sales had grown recently, sales of milk and newspapers were falling each year. All of the growth was coming from groceries.

He tried to gather market research on the milk market, but the only reports that he could find would

cost him over £1,000 to purchase, a price he was not prepared to pay. He carried out some primary research among his customers, which concluded that milk deliveries were still very popular.

Frank was pleased when he eventually completed his income, expenditure and profit budgets covering the next 3 years, and he felt sure that he could reach these goals. However, he realised that he lacked experience in the trade and he was looking forward to reviewing progress over the next few weeks to see if he was on target for the yearly budgets that he had set. The yearly budgets are presented in Tables 14.10–14.12.

Table 14.10
Income budget for Frank Roseland, 2009–11 (£000s)

Source of income	2009	2010	2011
Milk	160	155	150
Newspapers	18	(a)	16
Groceries	14	17	22
Total income	**192**	**189**	**188**

Table 14.11
Expenditure budget for Frank Roseland, 2009–11 (£000s)

Item of expenditure	2009	2010	2011
Supplies of milk	105	103	100
Newspaper purchases	13	13	12
Grocery purchases	9	10	11
Wages	11	11	(b)
Fridge rental	1	1	1
Marketing expenditure	0	0	6
Motor expenses	11	12	13
Administration	4	4	4
Capital costs	0	10	0
Total expenditure	**154**	**164**	**158**

Table 14.12
Profit budget for Frank Roseland, 2009–11 (£000s)

Item of income/ expenditure	2009	2010	2011
Total income	192	189	188
Total expenditure	154	164	158
Budgeted profit	(c)	25	30

Questions

Total: 45 marks (55 minutes)

1 Identify three sources of information for Frank's budgets. *(3 marks)*

2 Calculate the missing figures in the budgets at (a), (b) and (c). *(3 marks)*

3 Which method did Frank use to set his income budget? Explain your reasoning. *(4 marks)*

4 Analyse two reasons why Frank decided to set budgets. *(10 marks)*

5 Examine two reasons why Frank's budgets might be inaccurate. *(10 marks)*

6 To what extent do you think that Frank's budgets show that the business is likely to be successful? *(15 marks)*

CHAPTER 15

Assessing business start-ups

This chapter reviews the objectives of business start-ups, and the strengths and weaknesses of a business idea and/or plan. It also considers why start-ups can be risky and why so many fail.

Objectives of business start-ups

The objectives of business start-ups vary and depend very much on the individual entrepreneur's motivation. Chapter 1 identified the following motivations for starting a business: to gain more freedom at work; to make money; to sustain a going concern such as a family business; and to provide employment for the local community, sometimes in the form of social enterprises.

The government's 2005 Annual Small Business Survey suggested a wide variety of reasons for starting up a new business, but the most common, accounting for 28% of responses, was the entrepreneur's wish to be independent and to be his or her own boss. The same survey suggested that about half (44%) of all new businesses aimed to grow. The larger the business, the more likely it was to aim to grow during the coming 2 or 3 years.

Assessing the business idea and/or plan

INGRAM

In Chapter 4, business plans were considered. Such plans encourage entrepreneurs to consider a range of issues, and to ask themselves questions relating to their business idea in order to identify the strengths and weaknesses associated with it. Possible issues include:

- what their objectives are
- which product or service to provide and whether it can be produced and supplied profitably
- customers' needs and wants, and which market segment to target
- the possibility of competition, and an appropriate pricing and selling strategy
- finance for day-to-day and longer-term operations, and the timescales between start-up and breakeven
- who will be involved, what they will be doing, and what skills, expertise and experience they have
- the risks involved

Questions to consider include:

- Is there anything special, new or different about the product that would make it appeal to consumers?
- Could the product compete successfully with similar products on the market?

Why start-ups can be risky and why many fail

Approximately one in six new products succeed in the marketplace — in other words, the failure rate is 5 in 6 or over 80%. Given that most new products are launched by established, well-financed firms in existing markets, it is not surprising that, if such products have an 80% failure rate, many new firms actually fail.

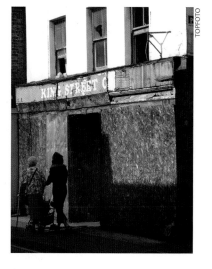

New businesses face a number of problems. Finding the right product for the right market niche is only one of them. Research into 65 businesses in liquidation found that marketing factors accounted for just 9 of the failures, 31 were for financial reasons, 13 were related to people management, 5 to operational problems, and 7 to external factors.

So it should come as no surprise that approximately one-third of all new firms fail to reach their second birthday. The miracle is, perhaps, that so many survive. The central problem for a new firm is its complete dependence on a single — and uncertain — income stream. For a new firm, poor sales during the first year would probably put so much pressure on cash flow that the business would have to close; there would be no other source of income for the firm to draw on.

The determinants of success or failure for a business venture depend upon the particular circumstances. One way to look at why start-ups are risky is to consider the main reasons for business failure. The most common are as follows:

- poor cash-flow management
- lack of effective market research
- lack of effective planning
- lack of skills needed to run a business and lack of business training
- problems in coordinating all the different aspects of the business
- failure to turn what looks like a good idea into a profitable business
- lack of finance to fund the business
- the actions of bigger competitors
- difficulties in developing a solid customer base
- difficulties in acquiring affordable premises
- unexpected changes in demand for the product or service
- unexpected changes in costs
- delays and unavailability of supplies

These reasons for business failure clearly translate into potential problems that business start-ups might encounter. For example:

- **finance** — raising funds, problems of cash flow, uncertainty about costs and profitability
- **marketing** — deciding on the product, forecasting demand and sales, deciding on the target market, conducting market research, deciding on a competitive price, choosing the most appropriate form of advertising and promotion
- **operations** — finding suitable premises, deciding on location and the most appropriate production methods, identifying reliable sources of supply, new technology
- **personnel and the organisation** — deciding on recruitment and selection strategies, organising appropriate training, deciding on the most effective organisational structure, quality of management and the skills needed to run a business
- **external factors** — complying with regulations, the impact of macroeconomic policies including interest rates and taxation, the competitive environment in which the business operates
- **personal problems** — suitability for self-employment, how the owner will provide cover for illness, what the opportunity cost of this business start-up is for the owner

We will look at some of these problems in more detail in the rest of this chapter.

 FACT FILE

Annual Small Business Survey

This is an annual survey carried out by the Department for Business, Enterprise and Regulatory Reform (BERR). It provides interesting information about new and small business issues. The latest survey, in 2005, found that 40% of new business owners said that they had not faced any real obstacles in starting up, and this fell slightly to 37% among new businesses with employees. Where problems had been encountered, financial difficulties were the most prominent, with 28% of recent start-ups reporting

obstacles in raising finance to start up their new businesses, and another 12% facing difficulties with their cash flow. Competition was mentioned by 4% as having been an obstacle to starting up the business, and the same proportion mentioned regulations as a constraint (4%, rising to 7% among new businesses with employees).

When asked what obstacles they faced in achieving business success, 20% of all businesses cited competition, 17% mentioned the economy (e.g. changing interest rates) and 12% cited regulations.

Financial difficulties

The main financial difficulties facing a start-up business are raising finance and managing cash flow.

Raising finance

Raising sufficient finance to get started is a major concern for most small businesses. Since a new business has no 'track record' or past success upon which lenders can judge its future potential, it is seen as much more of a risk than an established business. This is likely to lead to difficulties in finding suitable sources of finance. In addition, the finance that is available is likely to be expensive, with high interest rates being charged to balance the risk to the lender. This is why many small businesses are funded by their owners and by their relatives and friends, with owners often remortgaging their homes (using their homes as **security** for a loan) in order to raise funds, or using lump-sum retirement or redundancy payments.

Banks provide a majority of the external funds for small business start-ups, mainly in the form of loans and overdrafts. However, they expect **collateral** or security: that is, they want the owners to put up personal guarantees for any loans, offering their own assets, such as their homes or their business premises, as guarantees in case of default on the loan. In other words, if the borrower is unable to repay the loan, the lender will take the property (collateral or security) instead. In this way, the owner is taking the risk rather than the lender, which should ensure that the owner is highly motivated and works hard to make the business succeed.

Finance to cover two types of expense needs to be obtained: finance for equipment and premises (i.e. fixed capital) and finance to cover day-to-day expenses, including workers' wages, payments to suppliers etc. (i.e. working capital). Fixed capital costs are reasonably straightforward to estimate, but estimating working capital needs is much more complex. For this reason, cash-flow forecasting is essential for a business start-up in order to ensure that it has sufficient working capital to cover its trading needs.

Some 28% of start-up businesses in the government's 2005 Annual Small Business Survey said they had experienced difficulty in obtaining the finance they needed. The impact of this on a new business is likely to include one or more of the following:
- slow the growth of the business
- threaten the survival of the business
- affect the productivity of the business
- affect the ability of the business to invest — for example, in new machinery or premises
- take up management time in seeking sources of finance
- raise costs, perhaps because a lack of finance means that the business is not operating in the most efficient manner

Table 15.1
Changes in SME finance from external sources

Source of finance	1991–93	2000–02
Banks	60%	52%
HP leasing	16%	25%
Factoring	4%	6%
Partners/shareholders	8%	5%

Source: Griffiths, A. and Wall, S. (2007) *Applied Economics*, 11th edn, Pearson Education.

FACT FILE

External finance

According to Bank of England data, small and medium-sized enterprises (SMEs) are now much less reliant on external finance and are learning to access more varied sources of external finance (Table 15.1). Only 39% sought external finance in 2000–02 compared to 60% in the late 1980s.

Banks provide the main source of external finance for SMEs. The majority of this is by overdraft (59%), but it is increasingly in the form of medium- to longer-term loans. In 1992, the ratio of bank overdraft to loan finance was 48:52, but in 2003 it was 23:77. As a result, SMEs are now much less vulnerable to the economic cycle than in the past. The median cost of loans to small and medium enterprises is currently only around 2% above base rate.

Cash flow

Even firms that are profitable sometimes find it impossible to continue trading because they are unable to meet their current debts. Often cash is tied up in stock that cannot be used immediately to pay bills, or creditors are slow to pay their debts. (In the government's 2005 Annual Small Business Survey, 28% of all businesses thought late payment was a problem that might cause cash-flow problems.) It is essential, even for a very profitable business that has full order books and is working at full capacity, to ensure that enough cash is available for the business's working capital needs. In order to do this, it is usual for business start-ups to prepare a cash-flow forecast as part of their business plan. This shows the expected variation in working capital needs over a period of time and should indicate when overdraft facilities will be required to cover any shortfalls. (For a more detailed analysis of cash flow, see Chapters 13 and 17.)

Competition and the difficulties of building a customer base

The success of a business start-up will be determined by its ability to attract and retain customers. To do this, it will have to offer something more than any of its competitors. In the government's 2005 Annual Small Business Survey, 44% of all businesses thought competition in the market was an obstacle to their success, and 20% of businesses stated that this was their main obstacle. The issue of competition as a constraint on the success of a business was usually related to the fact that competitors were larger companies with more influence and resources.

Whether a business is a new start-up or an existing business, it needs carefully and constantly to research the extent and type of competition in the market. For example, it may seem unlikely that a new, small, local firm could compete successfully with an established, large, national firm. The large firm may have established and loyal customers, and it may be able to charge lower prices because, for example, it has an efficient operational process that benefits from economies of scale and has more bargaining power when negotiating prices with its suppliers. However, a small firm might be able to compete successfully and gain a significant share of the local market if it is able to provide customers with a more personal or more prompt service, even if the price is slightly higher. In this way, it may be able to build customer loyalty.

Satisfied customers are likely to recommend the business to others, and such recommendation is the most effective and least expensive form of advertising. However, customers will return to do business regularly only if they are satisfied with the goods and the service they are offered. Factors to consider when trying to encourage customer loyalty include:

- **Providing customers with service that is efficient and meets their expectations.** For example, products must be available in the quantities and the range intended by the business and expected by customers. A shop that is constantly out of stock of essential or popular items is unlikely to retain customers, who are more likely to go elsewhere.
- **Providing a good after-sales service and dealing effectively and positively with customer complaints.** For example, a restaurant that does not use customer complaints or comments as an opportunity to improve its provision is unlikely to encourage customers to return regularly.
- **Understanding customers' buying habits and ensuring that stock and staff availability are appropriate.** For example, hairdressers need to recognise which days of the week and times of the day are busy and which are slack in order to have sufficient staff available to meet demand. They can thereby ensure that people are not sitting around waiting for the stylist or colourist to finish with another client.
- **Ensuring that contact between customers and staff is always friendly and efficient.** Customers will remember this and be encouraged to continue to do business with the firm.

DID YOU KNOW?

Economies of scale are the advantages that an organisation gains because of an increase in size. These cause an increase in productive efficiency, which is the same as a decrease in the average cost per unit of production.

Regulations and 'red tape'

Small businesses often complain about the difficulties they encounter in dealing with 'red tape'. This usually refers to the many legal requirements facing a business, including those relating to legislation about employment, health and safety, consumer protection and environmental protection, as well as the requirements relating to taxation and other financial issues. For small businesses, most of which do not have, for example, specialist human resource, legal or finance departments, such regulation can be complex to comply with and costly, both financially and in terms of time.

In the government's 2005 Annual Small Business Survey, 32% of all businesses thought that 'regulations' placed obstacles in the way of their success, and for 12% this was their greatest obstacle. Among businesses with employees, regulations were more widely cited as an obstacle, with 39% of businesses identifying them.

FACT FILE

Age discrimination legislation

New legislation on age discrimination, which came into force in October 2007, adds another layer of red tape for small firms to deal with. Surveys in the few months before the introduction of the legislation suggested that 7 out of 10 employers were unaware that new age discrimination rules were about to come into force. Almost two-thirds said that they had previously discriminated against older people applying for jobs because they had concerns about whether people of their age were capable of doing the job.

The main provisions of the new Act are:

- prohibition of unjustified age discrimination in employment
- prohibition of harassment and victimisation on the grounds of age
- a default retirement age of 65 and a requirement for businesses that set their retirement age below that to provide objective justification for it or change it

ULRIKE PREUSS/PHOTOFUSION

- removal of the current upper age limit for unfair dismissal and redundancy rights
- changes to the way in which statutory redundancy pay and unfair dismissal basic awards are calculated

Employers also have a duty to consider an employee's request to continue working beyond retirement age.

WHAT DO YOU THINK?

Why do you think that the new legislation on age discrimination might cause problems for a small business?

e EXAMINER'S VOICE

Most of the issues considered in this chapter are covered in more detail elsewhere in the AS course. This highlights the importance of taking an integrated view of business studies and thinking broadly about issues such as small business start-ups.

PRACTICE EXERCISE   Total: 45 marks (35 minutes)

1 State three possible objectives of business start-ups. *(4 marks)*

2 Identify four issues a business would need to consider when assessing the strengths and weaknesses of its business idea. *(4 marks)*

3 Explain why unexpected changes in demand and in costs might lead to business failure. *(5 marks)*

4 Explain why the delays in, or the unavailability of, supplies might lead to business failure. *(3 marks)*

5 State and explain three reasons for business failure. *(9 marks)*

6 Explain two reasons why raising finance for a new business start-up can be difficult. *(6 marks)*

7 Explain how a business can fail despite being profitable. *(3 marks)*

8 Why might competition be a significant issue for a business start-up? *(4 marks)*

9 Identify and explain one factor that is vital in building a solid customer base for a new business. *(3 marks)*

10 Why might regulation and legislation create problems for a small business start-up? *(4 marks)*

CASE STUDY Tribal Woods

Bill Tribe had always been a talented woodworker, or wood sculptor, as he preferred to be described. His particular interest was in making an item out of a single piece of wood: for example, a pair of long benches from a single tree trunk, an unusual chair carved out of the hollow of a tree trunk, or a bird table on top of an interestingly shaped branch rather than a standard pole. Most of the things he made he gave away as gifts to friends and family, but occasionally he was asked to make something special and received payment for his work.

He had always toyed with the idea of setting up his own business and making his hobby into a full-time job, but like many people he thought it was too risky and the opportunity cost always looked too great. He worked full time as an operative in an engineering firm, earning £10 per hour.

One day, while in his local pub, the publican commented on how impressive the wooden benches in Bill's garden looked. Bill explained how he had carved them both from a single tree trunk. The publican asked Bill if he would consider making two much larger pairs for him to place outside the pub. He thought their distinctive rustic appearance would enhance the outside of the pub and provide somewhere for people to sit. Bill was interested and said 'yes' immediately. However, when asked how much he would charge, Bill had no idea what to suggest. The publican suggested £100 each. As £400 seemed a lot of money — a week's wages for Bill — he agreed. It certainly would not take him 40 hours to make four benches, so he thought it must be a good deal.

After this, Bill started to get more and more orders. He never really costed the things he made — as long as the price seemed OK and broadly gave him more than he got at work, he was happy.

Eventually, an opportunity came up to rent a small barn that could act as a showroom and workshop. The rent was cheap and the barn was part of a small group of buildings that housed a craft shop and an antique shop. It was just across the road from a large garden centre and a popular pub. At weekends, the whole area was full of people browsing through the shops and garden centre and visiting the pub. Bill thought it had to be a good idea. He decided on a name for the business (Tribal Woods) and started to move his stock across to the premises. He negotiated with his employer to go part time, working two and a half days a week, leaving him the other two and a half days to create his wood sculptures and open the shop.

The business ticked over but sales never really took off, even over the summer months. One day a group of people were looking at some of the furniture he had made and seemed quite interested. He thought he might be able to make a sale and started chatting to them, explaining that he made each product from a single block of wood. The group were very complimentary and even said that the prices seemed reasonable, given the craftsmanship involved. Bill said, 'Everyone says that, but few people seem to want to buy them.' One of the group said, 'It's a problem coming here. There are so many nice things — here in your shop and in the craft shop and the antique shop — too much to choose from, really. And then, of course, you can go across to the garden centre and see very similar-looking things, obviously not the same quality or individuality, but for about a quarter of the price.'

Bill had not given any thought to competition. He did not think his business had any competitors.

Questions

Total: 41 marks (50 minutes)

1 Define the term 'opportunity cost'. *(2 marks)*

2 Explain four issues, excluding pricing and competition, which Bill should have considered before setting up in business. *(8 marks)*

3 Identify and explain two factors that Bill should take into account in pricing his products. *(6 marks)*

4 Analyse the type of competition that Bill should have taken into account when starting his business. *(10 marks)*

5 Assess how effectively Bill planned and prepared for the launch of Tribal Woods. *(15 marks)*

Unit 2:
Managing a business

Finance

CHAPTER 16

Using budgets

This chapter builds on the ideas introduced in Chapter 14, by looking at how budgets are used to help an organisation to become more efficient. The chapter looks at the benefits and drawbacks of using budgets. Variance analysis — analysing the difference (variance) between budget forecasts and actual results — is explained, and favourable and adverse variance are calculated and interpreted. The chapter concludes by showing how variance analysis can assist an organisation's decision making.

Benefits of using budgets

A firm stands to benefit in several ways from the use of budgets:

- **They provide direction and coordination.** Budgets ensure that spending is geared towards the aims of the business rather than those of the individual, and they can ensure a united approach within an organisation. If budgets are given only to purposes that match the aims of the business, it will be easier for the workforce to understand the fairness of the allocations or targets.
- **They motivate staff.** According to Mayo and Herzberg, teams and individuals are encouraged by the responsibility and the recognition gained from meeting budget targets. Companies may link rewards to the achievement of targets in a budget, thus providing a further source of motivation.
- **They improve efficiency.** By monitoring and reviewing budgets, the business is able to establish standards and investigate the causes of any successes and failures. It can then use this information to improve future decisions. The discipline of working to a limited budget encourages managers to seek more efficient methods.
- **They assess forecasting ability.** Although changes cannot always be foreseen, businesses that can predict the future have significant advantages. Budgeting encourages careful evaluation of future possibilities and realistic planning.

Drawbacks of using budgets

There are, however, a number of disadvantages of using budgets:

- **They are difficult to monitor fairly.** Senior managers will be less aware of detailed expenditure and costs, so they may rely on the honesty of the budget holder in explaining a department or section's budgeting needs. Similarly, if budgetary targets are not met, the senior manager may not understand the reasons for this, and again has to rely on the honesty of the budget holder when explaining the reasons why targets were missed.

- **Allocations may be incorrect.** Budgeting is based on predictions of future events. In all areas of business there will be unforeseen changes, so the budget allocation will not always be right. A cost or expenditure budget that is insufficient will demotivate staff. It will also be difficult to develop the business if there is insufficient money for essential activities. Similarly, an excessively high income or revenue budget may demoralise a manager who cannot achieve it. On the other hand, a low revenue budget could cause complacency.

- **Savings may be sought that are not in the interests of the firm.** For example, to keep within a budget, a buyer may purchase cheaper materials that will lower the quality of the product. In so doing, the buyer may cause consumer discontent and thereby affect the holders of revenue budgets in particular. Sometimes decisions to save money and keep within a budget in the short term (such as by making cuts in new product development or reducing staff levels) can have disastrous long-term effects.

- **Changes may not be allowed for when a budget is reviewed.** External factors outside the control of the organisation may affect budget holders' ability to keep to their plan. The airline industry has needed to increase its expenditure budgets because of terrorist activities; high oil prices have affected firms' heating budgets. Sometimes internal changes, such as a reorganisation, can lead to increased costs or savings that were not originally included in the budget. These changes must be allowed for in any review of the budget.

Features of good budgeting

A good budget should:

- **Be consistent with the aims of the business.** This ensures that managers cannot use the company's finances for projects to boost their own careers or interests, rather than meeting the needs of the company.

- **Be based on the opinions of as many people as possible.** Setting and using a budget is not an exact science, and different people will be able to provide different ideas and expertise. Asking as many people as possible should help the budget holder to come up with a realistic set of targets.

- **Set challenging but realistic targets.** As with any SMART objective, the budget set must be achievable, but only if staff demonstrate a reasonable and expected level of effort and skill in order to reach the target.

DID YOU KNOW?

The mnemonic SMART stands for:
- Specific
- Measurable
- Agreed (or achievable)
- Realistic
- Timed (or time-constrained)

A good objective should meet all of these targets so that it gives staff a sense of direction, offers a realistic challenge and enables staff (and managers) to see if the objective has been reached.

■ **Be monitored at regular intervals, allowing for changes in the business and its environment.** Budgeting allows a business to improve by identifying situations in which targets are being missed or exceeded. In the former case, remedial action can be taken to improve performance. In the latter case, the reasons for beating a target should be looked at, so that other parts of the business can benefit from the good management or work that is taking place. The more often a budget is monitored, the more quickly these actions can take place.

■ **Be flexible.** Although budgets should have a set target, it is crucial that the budgeting process allows for changing circumstances. If a budget allocation is clearly inadequate, because of unforeseen circumstances, it may be necessary to adjust it to a more realistic level.

Variance analysis

An important aspect of budgeting is monitoring and reviewing the actual outcomes in comparison with the budgeted figure (the target). Differences between budgeted and actual figures are known as **variances**. Variance analysis is an essential element of budgetary control.

Calculating variances

A variance is calculated by the following formula:

variance = budget figure − actual figure

Thus a favourable variance is shown when:
■ actual revenue is greater than budgeted revenue
■ actual costs are below the budgeted costs

An adverse (or unfavourable) variance is shown when:
■ actual revenue is less than budgeted revenue
■ actual costs are above budgeted costs

For variance analysis, it is best to use 'F' for favourable variances and 'A' for adverse variances, rather than positive or negative numbers.

Example calculations

1 An expenditure budget allocates £2,000 for stationery expenses, but the actual amount spent is £2,200.

£2,000 − £2,200 = (£200) A

This is an *adverse variance* because costs are £200 higher than the budget and so, other things being equal, the profit will be £200 less than budgeted.

2 An expenditure budget allocates £23,000 for wages, but the actual amount paid in wages is £22,200.

£23,000 − £22,200 = £800 F

This is a *favourable variance* because wages (an expenditure item) are £800 lower than the budget and so, other things being equal, the profit will be £800 more than budgeted.

3 An income budget targets sales income of £56,000, but the actual amount of income received is £55,000.

> £56,000 − £55,000 = £1,000 A

This is an *adverse variance* because revenue is £1,000 lower than the budget and so, other things being equal, the profit will be £1,000 less than budgeted.

4 An income budget targets sales income of £73,000, but the actual amount of income received is £74,800.

> £73,000 − £74,800 = (£1,800) F

This is a *favourable variance* because revenue is £1,800 higher than the budget and so, other things being equal, the profit will be £1,800 more than budgeted.

---

e EXAMINER'S VOICE

Note how a negative variance for an expenditure budget is an *adverse* variance, while a negative variance for a revenue budget is a *favourable* variance.

Similarly, a positive variance for an expenditure budget is a *favourable* variance, while a positive variance for a revenue budget is an *adverse* variance.

---

5 A profit budget targets a profit of £15,000, but the actual profit is £14,100.

> £15,000 − £14,100 = £900 A

This is an *adverse variance* because the profit is £900 less than budgeted.

6 A profit budget targets a profit of £34,000, but the actual profit is £37,000.

> £34,000 − £37,000 = (£3,000) F

This is a *favourable variance* because the profit is £3,000 more than budgeted.

---

e EXAMINER'S VOICE

Use the terms 'favourable' and 'adverse' rather than plus or minus signs when calculating variances. The use of a plus or minus sign can be confusing because, if the actual revenue is higher than the budgeted revenue, this is good for the business. However, if the actual costs exceed the budgeted costs, it is bad for the business. As variance analysis ultimately attempts to look at the overall effect of variances on the budgeted profit, it is more logical to use F (favourable) for any variance that is likely to increase profit and A (adverse) for any variance that is likely to decrease profit in comparison with the budgeted figure. Overall, adding all the Fs and subtracting all the As will give the change in profit.

e EXAMINER'S VOICE

Note that alternative names for an income budget are revenue budget or sales budget. Similarly, an expenditure budget may be described as a cost budget.

Using variance analysis to inform decision making

Example

Table 16.1 shows the variances in the revenue and costs of a fictitious company, Sceptre Paints, a division of HBH Chemicals.

Table 16.1
Budget variances
for Sceptre Paints

	Budgeted income/ costs (£m)	Actual revenue/ costs (£m)	Variance (£m)
Sales of emulsion paint	480	495	15 (favourable)
Sales of gloss paint	220	206	14 (adverse)
Total sales	**700**	**701**	**1 (favourable)**
Raw material purchases	50	56	6 (adverse)
Tins and packaging	14	14	0
Manufacturing costs	88	75	13 (favourable)
Wages and salaries	240	251	11 (adverse)
Administration	96	100	4 (adverse)
Marketing	42	33	9 (favourable)
Distribution and warehousing	31	26	5 (favourable)
Other costs	27	27	0
Total costs	**588**	**582**	**6 (favourable)**
Profit/loss	**112**	**119**	**7 (favourable)**

e EXAMINER'S VOICE

An adverse variance may not be the manager's fault. It could be due to an unrealistic budget or an unpredictable external factor.

After calculating variances the budget holder will interpret their meaning. Adverse variances may show *inefficiency*, where the business has made mistakes. They may also show that *external influences*, such as changes in the market, have made it more difficult for a firm to meet its targets.

A similar logic applies to favourable variances. Favourable variances may show efficiency, indicating that the business has operated well. They may also show that external influences, such as the state of the economy, have made it easier for a firm to meet its targets.

According to Table 16.1, the income of Sceptre Paints shows a favourable variance of £1 million and the costs show a £6 million favourable variance, so overall there is a favourable variance on profit of £7 million. These variances can be interpreted as follows:

- Sales show little difference; it is cost savings that have caused most of the favourable variance. The biggest saving has been in manufacturing costs. The business might have automated its production line or improved efficiency in some way.
- Marketing has kept within budget. Although this is a favourable variance, it may have unfavourable results if it leads to low sales. However, the sales figures do not seem to show a problem, despite a fall in sales of gloss paint.
- Distribution and warehousing expenditure is below budget too. Has the firm delivered in larger batches? Are warehousing costs lower because of lower stock levels? The policies in this part of the business have made significant savings and are worth investigating to see if other divisions can benefit from using the same policies or approaches.

- Although the overall variance is positive, Sceptre Paints should look closely at raw material costs, wages and salaries, and administration, as these are over budget. There may be a valid reason, such as the use of better-quality materials, but the variances could indicate unnecessary spending in these areas.
- Finally, Sceptre should look at the sales revenue to see if the reasons for the good performance of emulsion paints can be applied to gloss paints.

The interpretations of the variances in the example of Sceptre Paints are merely suggestions. In practice, a budget holder should be aware of possible variances and will then be in a reasonable position to explain why they have happened.

> **EXAMINER'S VOICE**
>
> For evaluation questions, move up the skills levels as quickly as possible.

PRACTICE EXERCISE 1 — Total: 30 marks (25 minutes)

1 What is meant by the term 'variance analysis'? *(3 marks)*
2 What is the difference between a favourable variance and an adverse variance? *(3 marks)*
3 Explain three benefits of using budgets. *(9 marks)*
4 Explain three difficulties that a firm might have when trying to operate a budget. *(9 marks)*
5 Explain two reasons why an adverse variance might *not* be a sign of poor management by the budget holder. *(6 marks)*

PRACTICE EXERCISE 2 — Total: 25 marks (20 minutes)

Refer back to the budget variances for Sceptre Paints, shown in Table 16.1 on p. 172. Use the information in the table to answer the following questions.

Questions

1 Select three headings from the Sceptre Paints budget and compile a report to the chief executive of HBH Chemicals suggesting reasons for the variances shown. *(15 marks)*
2 Assume that each line of the Sceptre Paints budget is the responsibility of a different manager. Choose two of these managers and analyse the implications of the variances shown for the two managers whom you have selected. *(10 marks)*

CASE STUDY 1 Frank Roseland, dairyman and newsagent

This case study returns to the story of Frank Roseland, which was introduced in Chapter 14. It takes Frank on to 1 year after he started running the family business.

Frank had just completed the first year of running the family milk delivery business, having taken over from his father (who had not kept very good financial records).

Frank's original attempt at budgeting had not worked out too well. Fortunately, he had reviewed his income and expenditure budgets for the first few months. This

PHILLIP CARR/PHOTOFUSION

had shown him that milk sales were falling slightly faster than he had expected, mainly because a new supermarket had opened on one of the estates to which he delivered. However, this bad news was offset by the results of conversations with customers, who said that they valued his deliveries highly and would be prepared to pay much higher prices.

Frank's milk supplier told him that a competitor, who had charged higher prices, had retired. By increasing his marketing in the area previously served by this competitor, Frank was able to boost milk sales considerably, more than offsetting the decline in customers caused by the opening of the supermarket. Frank had been told that it was normal for milk delivered to the doorstep to be sold at a price that was 60% higher than the cost of purchase. This had seemed high to Frank and so he had budgeted for a lower price. Now he realised that he could actually add on two-thirds (67%) to the cost of his milk.

Newspaper sales progressed reasonably, but sales were lost to the supermarket. Frank did not offer newspaper delivery to his new customers, as his best friend owned the newsagent that served that area.

Frank realised that the future of the business depended on more growth coming from groceries. Towards the end of the year, he contacted some local farm shops and offered a delivery service for their products. Only one farmer responded and Frank earned a lower profit margin on these items because the farmer charged high prices for them. However, within a short period of time these products proved to be very popular with Frank's customers. In the last 2 months of the year, grocery sales started to rise dramatically, mainly because of the fresh products from the farmer.

Frank had underestimated the workload involved in running the business. After only 2 months he decided to employ another part-timer who would collect the newspapers and groceries early in the morning and deliver them to customers. At first, Frank was worried about this decision because it meant that he had to buy another van. However, towards the end of the year, the dramatic increase in grocery sales meant that the second van was used a great deal, as the part-time employee was making far more deliveries.

Frank had been carrying out variance analyses at the end of each month. At the end of the year, Frank sat down and compared his first yearly budget (2009) with the actual outcomes. Frank also set an amended budget for 2010. The results are presented in Tables 16.2–16.4.

Table 16.2 Income budget and actual income for Frank Roseland

| | 2009 | | 2010 |
Source of income	Budgeted income (£000s)	Actual income (£000s)	Budgeted income (£000s)
Milk	160	225	240
Newspapers	18	15	15
Groceries	14	27	57
Total income	**192**	**267**	**312**

Table 16.3 Expenditure budget and actual expenditure for Frank Roseland

| | 2009 | | 2010 |
Item of expenditure	Budgeted expenditure (£000s)	Actual expenditure (£000s)	Budgeted expenditure (£000s)
Supplies of milk	105	135	144
Newspaper purchases	13	11	11
Grocery purchases	9	17	35
Wages	11	20	24
Refrigerator rental	1	1	1
Marketing expenditure	0	4	2
Motor expenses	11	20	24
Administration	4	5	5
Capital costs	0	6	10
Total expenditure	**154**	**219**	**256**

Table 16.4 Profit budget and actual budget for Frank Roseland

| | 2009 | | 2010 |
Item of income/ expenditure	Budgeted profit (£000s)	Actual profit (£000s)	Budgeted profit (£000s)
Total income	192	267	312
Total expenditure	154	219	256
Budgeted profit	38	48	56

Questions

Total: 50 marks (60 minutes)

1 What is meant by a 'profit' budget? *(2 marks)*

2 Calculate the variance on motor expenses for 2009. *(2 marks)*

3 Calculate the variance on profit for 2009. *(2 marks)*

4 Analyse two benefits to Frank arising from his use of budgets in 2009. *(8 marks)*

5 Examine one difficulty that Frank faced in operating his budgets in 2009. *(4 marks)*

6 The actual outcomes in 2009 were very different from the budgets that Frank set. To what extent is this a result of Frank's inexperience in setting budgets? *(18 marks)*

7 Frank has set much higher income and expenditure budgets for 2010. Discuss the reasons for this decision. *(14 marks)*

CASE STUDY 2 Budgeting the Eden Project

The Eden Project is an illustration of a large-scale capital project that managed to be completed without an excessive adverse variance from the projected budget. Many large-scale building projects exceed their capital budgets by considerable sums. The Channel Tunnel and the Millennium Dome are both examples of projects that actually cost more than twice the sum originally estimated.

In contrast, operating budgets (estimates of sales revenue and plans for day-to-day spending on running the business) tend to be much more accurate. Firms find this type of budget much easier to estimate, although ironically the Eden Project's operating budget for its first year was less accurate than its capital

budget. With visitor numbers much higher than expected, the actual sales revenue was 2.5 times the budgeted figure and the £9 million wage bill was more than double the £4 million budgeted figure.

Table 16.5 summarises the main budget headings for the construction of the Eden Project.

Table 16.5 *Eden Project: budgeted and actual costs of construction*

	Budgeted cost (£m)	Actual cost (£m)
Purchase of site and car parks	10.0	10.0
Reshaping the ground	5.0	8.0
Construction of greenhouses (biomes)	20.0	25.0
Soil and plants, including nursery	6.0	5.5
Buildings and exhibits	19.0	19.0
Services to keep it running	6.0	7.0
Design, engineering, legal advice etc.	6.0	9.0
Wages and training prior to opening	2.0	2.5
Total	**74.0**	**86.0**

Originally, the Eden Project was to be funded by grants from the Millennium Commission (50%), the European Union and various regional organisations, and by loans. When it was realised that there would be an 'over-spend' on the original budget, the Millennium Commission agreed to increase its grant from

£37 million to £43 million. The site was opened to visitors before the final completion and visitor numbers were so high (160% higher than the 'best-case' prediction) that the Eden Project found it easy to raise the remaining £6 million needed to pay the actual costs.

Construction work began in October 1998, in a disused china clay quarry the size of 35 football pitches. However, there were unexpected problems, as nobody had ever undertaken such a project before. Matters were complicated by 43 million gallons of water raining into the quarry in the first 3 months, forcing the builders to halt construction for 3 months. Fortunately, specialist help from consultants overcame these problems and the project was completed on schedule in March 2001.

Source: Eden Project website (**www.edenproject.com**).

Questions

Total: 30 marks (35 minutes)

1 What is meant by the term 'budget'? *(2 marks)*

2 a Identify one favourable variance from Table 16.5. *(1 mark)*

   b Calculate the variance between the total budget and the total actual costs as a percentage of the budgeted cost. *(3 marks)*

3 Explain one reason why firms find it easier to estimate revenue budgets than capital budgets. *(4 marks)*

4 Analyse two factors that caused the actual expenditure for setting up the Eden Project to exceed the budgeted figure. *(8 marks)*

5 To what extent did the Eden Project benefit from the time spent on its budgeting? *(12 marks)*

Improving cash flow

In this chapter the causes of cash-flow problems are established and explained. This analysis is then used to scrutinise the different approaches to improving a firm's cash flow: overdrafts and short-term loans, factoring, sale of assets, and sale and leaseback of assets. The chapter also shows the benefits of each of these methods and introduces some alternative solutions to cash-flow problems.

> **DID** YOU KNOW?
>
> It is often suggested that 70% of all business failures are a result of cash-flow problems.

Causes of cash-flow problems

Firms may encounter cash-flow problems for a variety of reasons:

- **Seasonal demand.** The demand for some products and services is seasonal, but companies typically incur costs in producing in advance of the peak season for sales. This causes a significant, but predictable, cash-flow problem for any seasonal business, especially for businesses in industries such as farming, where there is heavy expenditure just prior to the sale of the crop. At this point, the farmer may have gone almost a year without much income. However, because the problem is predictable, it is easy to persuade suppliers to provide credit or to negotiate a bank overdraft.

- **Overtrading.** Firms may become too confident and expand rapidly without organising sufficient long-term funds. This puts a strain on working capital. Businesses often give credit to their customers. Unfortunately, during rapid expansion this means that the business needs to buy more and more materials but lacks money because its customers are not paying it as soon as the goods are sold. This leaves the business short of cash.

- **Over-investment in fixed assets.** Firms may invest in fixed assets in order to grow, but leave themselves with inadequate cash for day-to-day payments. The more successful a small firm, the more eager the entrepreneur will be to purchase new shops or equipment. If such investments are not managed carefully, this can leave the business drained of finance and in danger of cash-flow problems. Equipment and buildings cannot easily be turned back into cash, and in extreme situations the business might be unable to pay its debts, even though it has plenty of assets.

- **Credit sales.** The marketing department will want to give credit to customers, to encourage them to buy, but this can lead to a lack of cash in the organisation if sales are not leading to immediate receipts of cash. This is a difficult situation because organisations will not want to upset their

customers. In the UK, many large firms delay making payment to small firms, possibly believing that the small firm will be reluctant to push too hard to get immediate payment. This problem has eased since August 2002, when legislation was passed to allow a business to claim late payment interest on money that is not paid back on time.

- **Poor stock management.** Organisations might hold excessive stock levels, tying up cash that could have been used for other purposes. There is an added danger that high levels of stock may mean that the stock becomes worthless as it becomes out of date or unfashionable. On the other hand, low levels of stock may limit sales, particularly those resulting from impulse buying. Furthermore, buying large quantities of stock will usually enable a business to benefit from discounts. This may more than offset the costs of carrying high stock levels.

- **Poor management of suppliers.** Cash flow can also be influenced by the credit period given to a business by its suppliers. A well-managed business should be able to negotiate a credit period with suppliers so that the payment from customers reaches the business at the same time as the business is required to pay its suppliers. Good supply chain management also involves negotiating a reasonably low price so that money is not wasted, as well as ensuring prompt deliveries of materials so that customers are not lost.

- **Unforeseen change.** Cash-flow difficulties might also arise from internal changes (e.g. machinery breakdown) or external factors (e.g. a change in government legislation). These could be attributed to management errors or poor planning, but may just be bad luck.

- **Losses or low profits.** Although cash flow and profits are different, the two are linked. A business whose sales revenue is less than its expenditure will usually (but not always) have less cash than one that is making a healthy profit. Furthermore, creditors and investors will be less likely to put money into a business that is not expected to make a profit in the future. Unless a loss-making business can show how it will become profitable in the future, it will find it difficult to overcome cash-flow problems.

FACT FILE

It is not just small or new businesses that face cash-flow difficulties. Massive expenditure on items such as cabling, in readiness for digital communications, led NTL and Telewest to experience significant cash-flow problems. Both of these companies were examples of loss-making businesses with cash-flow problems that survived because they were able to persuade creditors that they would succeed in the long run. However, investors eventually lost faith and agreed to sell the businesses (which had merged) to Virgin Media.

Ways of improving cash flow

Bank overdraft

In order to be agreed by the bank manager, a request for a bank overdraft should ideally be supported by a cash-flow forecast (one indicating that the cash-flow problem is not going to be permanent). This enables the bank manager to see both the need for the overdraft and the prospects of it being repaid. The business will need to pay interest on the amount overdrawn.

Benefits of a bank overdraft

The advantages of a bank overdraft are as follows:

- **Administrative convenience.** Overdrafts are easy to arrange and, once agreed, tend only to need to be confirmed on an annual basis.
- **Flexibility.** An overdraft is flexible, as it can be used to pay for whatever the business requires at the time. In one month it may be used to pay wages; in the next month it may be required to purchase computer software; and in the following month it might help to pay for raw materials.
- **Interest is paid only on the amount owed.** The business with the overdraft only needs to pay interest on the amount of the overdraft that is actually used. Furthermore, it is only paid on a daily basis. For example, let us assume a business has an agreed overdraft limit of £10,000. It has £3,000 in its account but then withdraws £5,000. This means that it goes 'into the red' (needs to use its overdraft agreement), as it is overdrawn by £2,000. The business will only pay interest on the £2,000 and not on the £10,000 maximum that is allowed. Furthermore, this interest will cease on the day that the bank account returns 'into the black' (i.e. into credit). If £2,000 is paid into the account after 3 days, the interest payments will cease at this point. For a business that is constantly going into the red and then back into the black, a bank overdraft may prove to be quite a cheap way of solving cash-flow problems.
- **No security necessary.** Unlike a bank loan, a bank overdraft does not require a business to provide security (collateral). Therefore, if there are difficulties in paying back the overdraft, the bank will not be able to claim the proceeds from the sale of an asset in order to get its money back.

Problems of a bank overdraft

The problems of a bank overdraft are as follows:

- **Variable interest payments.** Overdrafts are based on flexible interest rates, so the interest paid will rise and fall with the Bank of England's base rate. Consequently, it is difficult to budget accurately, as the bank may change its rate of interest on a monthly basis.
- **Higher interest rate.** The rate of interest charged on an overdraft is usually significantly higher than that charged on a short-term bank loan, so an overdraft can prove to be more expensive than a loan.
- **Immediate repayment.** Agreements to provide an overdraft normally allow the bank to demand immediate repayment. Therefore, a business facing

 KEY **TERM**

bank overdraft: an agreement whereby the holder of a current account at a bank is allowed to withdraw more money than there is in the account. The agreement specifies the maximum level of the overdraft.

DID **YOU KNOW?**

Banks sometimes require 'collateral' (or security) if they agree to lend money. This collateral takes the form of an asset, such as the deeds to a property. If the customer does not repay the money, the bank can sell the collateral in order to reclaim the amount that it is owed.

cash-flow problems may suddenly find that it is required by the bank to pay back the overdraft at exactly the time when the business is most vulnerable.

Short-term loan

KEY TERM

short-term loan: a sum of money provided to a firm or an individual for a specific, agreed purpose. Repayment of the loan will take place within 2 years, and possibly much less.

Most short-term loans are provided by banks, although other sources such as venture capitalists and business angels may be used.

Usually, loans are used for fixed assets, so they are not typically a solution to a cash-flow problem that has already occurred. However, a loan may be used to avert a cash-flow problem if the business is expanding quickly. In this situation, stocks of materials may be purchased using a short-term loan. Once the business has produced and sold the products, it is in a position to repay the loan.

Benefits of a bank loan

The advantages of a bank loan are as follows:

- **Fixed interest repayments.** Bank loans are usually at a fixed rate of interest. The interest and repayment schedule is calculated at the time of the loan, so it easy for a business to know whether it can afford to repay the loan. Furthermore, it is easy to budget the loan repayments because a standing order or direct debit is usually established in order to pay the same amount per month over the duration of the loan. This contrasts with an overdraft, where it is difficult to budget accurately because the bank may change its rate of interest every month.
- **Lower interest rate.** The rate of interest charged on a bank loan is usually less than that charged on an overdraft, so it can be a cheaper solution to a cash-flow problem.

Problems of a bank loan

The problems of a bank loan are as follows:

- **Higher interest payments.** Interest is paid on the whole of the sum borrowed. Therefore, if a business has a healthy balance in its current account, this will not help it to reduce the interest payments on the bank loan; such payments will continue to be a fixed sum every month. As a consequence, bank loans can often be far more expensive than an overdraft, even though the overdraft is charged at higher rate of interest.
- **Security.** The business will need to provide the bank with security (collateral). If there are difficulties in paying back the overdraft, the bank will be able to claim back the amount owed by forcing the sale of this asset. If the asset is a vital part of the business's operations, this can cause major difficulties.

Factoring (debt factoring)

The factoring company usually pays the firm about 75% of its sales immediately and approximately 15–20% on receipt of the debt. The firm therefore loses some revenue (about 5–10%, depending on the length of time and current interest rates), which is the factoring company's charge for its service.

KEY TERM

factoring: when a factoring company (usually a bank) buys the right to collect the money from the credit sales of an organisation.

Benefits of factoring

The advantages of factoring are as follows:

- **Improved cash flow in the short term.** This may save expenses such as overdraft interest charges, and in extreme cases the immediate receipt of cash may keep the business alive by allowing it to pay its own debts on time. For businesses offering long credit periods to their customers as a way of boosting sales revenue, the immediate receipt of cash may be essential because it would be impossible for the business to wait a year for payment.
- **Lower administration costs.** Collecting and chasing up debts can be a costly and time-consuming process. The factoring company specialises in this and it is possible that it will be collecting more than one debt from the same firm.
- **Reduced risk of bad debts.** The factoring company takes this risk instead of the original business. However, it does reserve the right to refuse to factor a debt if it considers it to be risky. For this reason, firms such as Comet and Currys (which use factoring companies such as HFC and GE Capital) will contact the factoring company before giving credit to a customer. The factoring companies will have lists of customers who may be a high risk.

- **Increased efficiency.** Factoring can encourage businesses to be more careful with their provision of credit. If a business gains a reputation for having no customers that turn out to be bad debts, then the factoring company will reduce the cost of factoring to that business. This will provide firms with an incentive to be much more efficient in their provision of credit.

Problems of factoring

The main problems of factoring are as follows:

- **Loss of revenue.** The business using a factoring company loses between 5% and 10% of its revenue. Ultimately, this reduces its profit, although it may be possible to increase the price charged to customers where credit terms are being offered.
- **High cost.** The business has to pay a factoring company more for its services than it would have to pay a bank for a loan, as there are administrative expenses involved in chasing up debts. This additional cost should be set against the administrative savings to the business from no longer having to chase up the debts itself.
- **Customer relations problems.** Customers may prefer to deal directly with the business that sold them the product. An aggressive factoring company may upset certain customers, who will blame their bad experience on the original seller of the product.

CHAPTER 17   Improving cash flow

Although factoring involves costs, many large retailers take advantage of this service because large factoring companies can carry out the process of debt collection more cheaply, and pass on their cost savings to the retailer.

 FILE

Why use factoring?

When the Oxford-based company Media Drive set up 4 years ago, it anticipated cash-flow problems. Director Barnaby Smith chose factoring as his solution:

> Factoring obviously imposes a cost on the business but in our experience it was good value when compared to the advantages gained. Factoring means we can access most of the cash owed by customers within 24 hours. Furthermore, over the last 4 years both the fee and the percentage of interest have come down as our business has grown.

 TERM

sale of assets: when a business transfers ownership of an item that it owns to another business or individual, usually in return for cash.

Sale of assets

A business can improve its cash flow by converting an asset, such as property or machinery, into cash. The cash can be used to repay a debt or build up a bank balance.

Benefits of sale of assets

The sale of assets has two main benefits:

- **Income.** It can raise a considerable sum of money, particularly in the case of a large asset such as a building.
- **Profitability.** It is possible that a particular asset is no longer contributing towards the business's overall success. In this circumstance, the sale of the asset will ease the business's cash-flow problem and also enhance its overall profitability.

Sale of assets is most likely to be used as a means of overcoming cash-flow problems when a business is seeking to change direction or move out of a particular market. An unprofitable division of the business may actually be causing the cash-flow problem in the first place, so the sale of the assets related to that division will help the business either by removing the loss-making division or by giving the business a large lump sum of cash.

Problems of sale of assets

The sale of assets involves the following problems:

- **Receiving a low value for the asset.** Assets such as buildings and machinery may be difficult to sell quickly. Usually, a business trying to make a quick sale has to accept a much lower price than its true value. Therefore, selling assets is not usually a good strategy because it can have a damaging effect on long-term profitability.
- **Reduced ability to make profit.** It is a fundamental principle of business that a firm should not sell fixed assets to improve liquidity, as the fixed assets enable it to produce the goods and services that create profit. The exceptions to this rule are when the assets are no longer required (e.g. surplus land) or when the cash-flow situation threatens the survival of the organisation.

Sale and leaseback

Benefits of sale and leaseback

The advantages of sale and leaseback are as follows:

- **Cash inflow.** It will overcome the cash-flow problem by providing an immediate inflow of cash — usually quite a significant amount.
- **Flexibility.** A firm can be more flexible as new and more efficient assets can be leased. This flexibility may also take the form of a greater willingness to relocate if the asset in question is a property. There is a tendency for businesses to be unwilling to relocate from sites that they own.
- **Lower costs.** The ownership of fixed assets can lead to a number of costs, such as maintenance. Many firms lease assets such as machinery and computer software so that the owners are responsible for servicing and solving any problems. In this way, unexpected repair costs are avoided.
- **Greater focus.** Owning an asset can distract a business from its core activity because it has to get involved with additional activities such as property management or organising transport. There is a trend within business in the UK to lease rather than purchase assets, so that businesses can concentrate on their area of expertise.

Problems of sale and leaseback

The disadvantages of sale and leaseback are as follows:

- **Rent.** Assuming that the new owner expects to make a profit from the asset, in the long run the selling business will pay more in rent than it receives from its sale.
- **Reduced assets.** Sale and leaseback reduces the value of the firm's assets that can be used as security against future loans. This can make future borrowing more difficult and lead to higher interest charges.
- **Loss of use of the asset.** The firm may eventually lose the use of the asset when the lease ends, as a competitor may be prepared to pay a higher rental for the lease.

Other ways of improving cash flow

This section describes some more methods by which a firm can improve its cash flow.

 FACT FILE

Ching's Noodles and Tzu

There are many innovative ways of improving cash flow. Ching He-Huang, founder of Fuge Ltd, which runs Ching's Noodles and Tzu, found that she did not have the cash to rent the kitchen that she wanted to start up her business. She used her persuasive powers to negotiate 3 months' free rental. In return, Ching promised the landlady that she would agree to a long lease if the business succeeded. Both Ching and her landlady have benefited as a result.

working capital:
the day-to-day finance used in a business, consisting of assets (e.g. cash, stock and debtors) minus liabilities (e.g. creditors and overdrafts).

Improved working capital control

To stay solvent, a firm must manage its working capital. Working capital management involves careful control of the firm's main current assets (**cash**, **debtors** and **stock**) to make sure that there is enough to pay creditors and make other immediate payments.

Cash management

If a firm is short of cash, it has two main options:

- agree an overdraft with the bank (see p. 179)
- set aside a contingency fund to allow the company to meet unexpected payments or cope with lost income. In industries subject to more rapid change, a higher contingency fund should be kept.

Debt management

Debtors are customers who owe a business money. The first decision to make is whether customers should be given credit. If all sales are for cash, the company will have no debtors but more cash, and this should relieve any cash-flow problems. However, there is a conflict between the desire for sales and profit, and the desire for liquidity and cash. Giving customers credit facilities will encourage them to buy the products (hence helping profit in the long run), but will add to cash-flow problems in the short run, as materials and wages will have to be paid for even though no cash has been received from sales.

The company must evaluate the benefits of an increase in sales and profit potential against the risks of late or non-payment. This judgement will depend on factors such as the policy of rival companies and customer expectations. For example, customers expect to be offered credit for purchases such as furniture and computers, but not for magazines and confectionery.

If it is decided that credit will be given to customers, the company must control its debtors to ensure prompt payment. The main methods are:

- obtaining a credit rating, which will testify to the customer's ability to pay and so minimise the risk of non-payment
- controlling product quality, as a satisfied customer is less likely to delay or dispute payment
- scrutinising the offer of credit, to ensure that its costs do not exceed the profits gained from offering it
- managing credit control, to gain prompt payment from customers

Stock management

Traditionally, companies tended to keep high levels of stocks of both raw materials and finished goods, to guarantee continuation of production and immediate supply to customers. However, many firms now operate **just-in-time** systems that involve low stock levels in order to minimise storage costs. Such systems rely on efficient suppliers and require them to suffer penalties if deliveries are late. Just-in-time companies can operate with lower levels of working capital than other organisations, thus improving their cash-flow situation.

Different departments will view the problem from varying perspectives. From the finance department's perspective, stock should be kept to a minimum because a higher stock level means a lower holding of cash. However, the marketing department will want stocks of finished products to be readily available to meet customer demand. The production department will need stocks of raw materials to make the products. Again, the company must weigh up the relative merits of these different views.

Low stock levels reduce the amount of storage space needed, and the chances of damage, deterioration and obsolescence. High stock levels allow companies to benefit from bulk-buying discounts and to minimise the risk of lost sales and goodwill through failing to meet customer needs.

A business can also improve its cash flow in the following ways:

- It can diversify its product portfolio to create a range that sells throughout the year. For example, Wall's sales of sausages in winter may be balanced by its ice-cream sales in the summer.
- Improved decision-making procedures, planning, monitoring and control, and more thorough market research and intelligence, will help the business to anticipate changes.
- A contingency fund should be set aside to allow the company to meet unexpected payments or cope with lost income.

 FILE

Diversification at Sergio's Pools and Spas

Sergio's Pools and Spas had to find a way to boost business in the winter months, when pool construction and maintenance grind to a halt. The answer was to set up First Response Construction, a business that repairs fire damage. 'Pools are obviously seasonal,' says owner Joe Sergio, 'and most of the house fires happen in winter.' Cash flow is now much more evenly spread throughout the year.

e EXAMINER'S VOICE

When asked to suggest methods of improving cash flow, it is vital to focus on ways of getting hold of cash quickly (e.g. a bank overdraft or sale and leaseback). Suggestions based on increasing profits (e.g. marketing campaigns) invariably worsen cash flow in the short term and so should be avoided.

PRACTICE EXERCISE

Total: 30 marks (25 minutes)

1 Explain three different causes of cash-flow problems. *(9 marks)*

2 Explain two differences between a bank loan and a bank overdraft. *(8 marks)*

3 Explain the difference between 'sale of assets' and 'sale and leaseback'. *(4 marks)*

4 Identify three other ways of solving a cash-flow problem. *(3 marks)*

5 Select two causes of cash-flow problems (you can use examples given in your answer to question 1 if you wish). Explain the best method of solving each of these two causes, justifying your choices. *(6 marks)*

CASE STUDY **Khalid Ahmed's computer peripherals**

Khalid Ahmed was worried. When he had opened up his store, he was the only specialist seller of computer peripherals in town. Now there were five other small shops selling ink cartridges, printers, keyboards, memory sticks, paper and other related items.

Khalid had anticipated the growing popularity of home PCs, but he had not foreseen the dramatic increase in competition. Consequently, his move into a much larger store in 2008 was now proving to be a problem.

The new store had opened up the opportunity to extend his product range to include larger items, such as printers, VDUs and computers themselves. This had helped Khalid to earn far more revenue, but it had also increased his costs dramatically. The profit margin on computers tended to be less than that on software and peripherals. Khalid also found that computer sales were seasonal and this led to cash-flow problems at certain times of the year – particularly from September to November, when he had to buy a great deal of stock in the run-up to Christmas, but had not yet sold the computers.

Khalid had suffered further cash-flow problems because he was forced to offer credit terms in order to

Table 17.1 Cash-flow forecast for Khalid Ahmed, 2009–10

	2009				2010			
	Qtr 1 (£000s)	Qtr 2 (£000s)	Qtr 3 (£000s)	Qtr 4 (£000s)	Qtr 1 (£000s)	Qtr 2 (£000s)	Qtr 3 (£000s)	Qtr 4 (£000s)
Opening balance	2	(4)	(3)	(25)	9	8	17	3
Sales of hardware	20	30	25	75	22	40	35	95
Sales of software and peripherals	60	65	55	75	70	75	65	95
Total inflows	**80**	**95**	**80**	**150**	**92**	**115**	**100**	**190**
Hardware purchases	12	18	30	30	13	24	36	42
Software and peripherals purchases	24	26	22	30	28	30	26	38
Wages*	16	16	16	20	17	17	17	21
Repayment of loan	14	14	14	14	14	14	14	14
Other costs	20	20	20	22	21	21	21	23
Total outflows	**86**	**94**	**102**	**116**	**93**	**106**	**114**	**138**
Net cash flow	**(6)**	**1**	**(22)**	**34**	**(1)**	**9**	**(14)**	**52**
Closing balance	**(4)**	**(3)**	**(25)**	**9**	**8**	**17**	**3**	**55**

*Including annual wage of £28,000 (£7,000 per quarter) paid to Khalid himself.

generate customer interest. He cursed the big rivals such as PC World who had forced him into this position. The use of a factoring company had overcome this problem, although it had led to a reduction in his profits for a while.

Khalid was reluctant to borrow money but realised it would be necessary in order to survive. The lease on his shop, which cost him £30,000 a year, was about to expire and he had discovered that there was a well-located small shop for sale in an area where there was no direct competition. He visited his bank manager with a cash-flow forecast, based on the assumption that he would borrow the £200,000 necessary to buy the shop. He intended to repay the loan within 5 years.

Questions

Total: 50 marks (60 minutes)

1 What is meant by the term 'bank loan'? *(3 marks)*

2 Explain the meaning of the term 'total outflows'. *(3 marks)*

3 How is the 'closing balance' calculated? *(4 marks)*

4 Explain two different factors that might be causing Khalid to experience cash-flow problems. *(6 marks)*

5 The bank manager advised Khalid to take out an overdraft. Explain the reason for this advice. *(5 marks)*

6 How did debt factoring help Khalid's cash flow? *(4 marks)*

7 Khalid decided to use a 5-year bank loan to buy a shop rather than continuing his lease of the previous store. To what extent do you believe that this was a sensible decision? *(15 marks)*

8 Khalid has experienced cash-flow problems in the early years of his business. Do you believe that these problems will occur after the end of 2010? Justify your view. *(10 marks)*

CHAPTER 18

Measuring and increasing profit

Most businesses aim to make a profit. In order to assess the efficiency of the business in achieving this major objective, two profitability ratios are used: the net profit margin and the return on capital. This chapter examines these two ratios in turn, showing how they are calculated and the significance of the results. It then looks at methods of improving profits and profitability, and examines the implications of these methods. It concludes by looking at the distinction between 'cash' and 'profit'.

EXAMINER'S VOICE

This topic is important because Unit 2 (BUSS2) is about improving the performance of a business. These measures can be used to judge (evaluate) whether a business has been successful in its aim to become more efficient.

TERMS

profit: the difference between the income of a business and its total costs. Profit = revenue – total costs.

profitability: the ability of a business to generate profit or the efficiency of a business in generating profit.

Profit and profitability

What is the distinction between profit and profitability? Profit is just a sum (e.g. a profit of £100,000). Profitability relates this sum to the size of the business. A large oil company such as Shell would be disappointed with a profit of £100,000, but for a small corner shop it would be a great achievement. Therefore, to put the £100,000 into a more meaningful form we need to compare it with the size of the business. There are two simple ways to measure the size of a business:

- sales revenue (adding up all the income it receives over a period of time)
- capital employed (adding up all the money that has been invested in the business by owners)

Let us suppose that business makes £100,000 profit in a year by selling £700,000 worth of goods and services over the 12 months. This means that for every £7 of revenue earned, £1 of profit was made. Dividing the profit by the revenue gives a fraction of one-seventh. How does this compare with a smaller business that earns £16,000 profit from sales of £100,000? As a fraction this is 4/25. The easiest way to compare is to convert the fractions to percentages. In the first example, £100,000/£700,000 or 1/7 as a percentage is:

$$\frac{1}{7} \times 100 = 14.3\%$$

In the second example, the percentage is:

$$\frac{4}{25} \times 100 = 16\% \text{ or } \frac{£16,000}{£100,000} \times 100 = 16\%$$

By converting the fractions to percentages, it is much easier to see that the second business has a higher profitability than the first one, albeit only by a small percentage.

The two measures of profitability covered in this chapter relate profit to the size of the firm. In both measures, a high percentage represents a better performance than a low percentage, as businesses want to earn high profits.

Calculating and understanding the main measures of profitability

Table 18.1 shows data on the John Lewis Partnership plc, which also owns Waitrose supermarkets, over a 3-year period.

	Financial year 2006/07 (£m)	Financial year 2005/06 (£m)	Financial year 2004/05 (£m)
Net profit before tax	319.2	251.8	229.3
Sales revenue	5,698.4	5,149.3	4,757.5
Capital investment	2,796.3	2,659.1	2,501.2

Table 18.1 Financial information extracted from the accounts of John Lewis Partnership plc

 EXAMINER'S VOICE

In published accounts it is customary to print the most recent year on the left, nearest to items in the list. This means that the earliest set of figures is on the right.

The usual custom for other sets of statistical data is to have the most recent figures on the right.

In answering any question, make sure that you look at the column headings carefully so that you know exactly which year(s) is being referred to in a particular column.

Calculating the net profit margin

FACT FILE

Net profit and operating profit

Net profit is the profit made from all activities. Occasionally, this can be misleading because a business may make a lot of money by selling an asset that it owns.

Operating profit is profit made from trading (i.e. the main activities of the business). For example, Somerfield has recently sold some of its stores. This would boost net profit but would not be included in operating profit. In this example, operating profit is a better way of measuring how successful Somerfield is at operating supermarkets, and so it is sometimes preferred to net profit as a measure of success.

KEY TERM

net profit margin: this measures net profit (although operating profit can be used) as a percentage of sales (turnover). Net and operating profits are considered the best measure of a firm's profit, while sales turnover is an excellent measure of scale.

The net profit ratio is calculated as follows:

$$\text{net profit margin } (\%) = \frac{\text{net profit before tax}}{\text{sales (turnover)}} \times 100$$

Based on Table 18.1, John Lewis Partnership plc's net profit margins were:

$$2006/07: \frac{319.2}{5,698.4} \times 100 = 5.6\%$$

$$2005/06: \frac{251.8}{5,149.3} \times 100 = 4.9\%$$

$$2004/05: \frac{229.3}{4,757.5} \times 100 = 4.8\%$$

> **FACT FILE**
>
> **Comparing net profit margins**
> Table 18.2 shows the average net profit margin for all UK companies in recent years. Firms with high rates of stock turnover tend to have lower profit margins, as their profit arises from the large number of products sold. Consequently, net profit margin may not be a reliable method of comparison between different industries. However, it is an excellent way of assessing the relative profitability of two firms competing with each other. It is also a good way of seeing whether a business is improving over time.

Table 18.2
Average net profit ratios
for UK firms, 2004–06*

Year	2004	2005	2006
Net profit (%)	4.1	5.0	4.9

Sources: Experian and ONS.

*These years have been selected as John Lewis's financial year ends in January. Therefore, the 2006/07 financial year relates much more closely to 2006 than to 2007.

Interpreting the net profit margins

Method 1: over time

John Lewis has increased its net profit margin from 4.8% in 2004/05 to 4.9% in 2005/06 and finally to 5.6% in 2006/07. This shows that there was a minor improvement between the first 2 years but a noticeable increase in 2006/07.

Conclusion: John Lewis Partnership plc is experiencing a steady, but unspectacular rise in its profitability, as measured by net profit margin.

Method 2: comparison with other firms

This gives a slightly different picture. Across the UK as a whole, the net profit margin for business organisations rose from 4.1% to 5.0% before falling to 4.9% in 2006 (see Table 18.2).

John Lewis's net profit margin rose from 4.8% to 4.9% and finally to 5.6% in 2006/07. This indicates that John Lewis was more profitable than other firms in 2004/05 and 2006/07, but was slightly less profitable in 2005/06.

Conclusion: John Lewis had a bad year in 2005/06, but was slightly above average in terms of profitability.

Note that, ideally, John Lewis will want to compare itself with its competitors. Unfortunately, however, John Lewis is split into two companies: John Lewis, which is a department store, and Waitrose, which is a supermarket.

To enable such comparisons to be made, the business records the performance of these two organisations separately. In 2006/07 Waitrose had a net profit margin of 4.6% and John Lewis had a net profit margin of 7.2%. This difference is to be expected as supermarkets operate in a more competitive environment, making profit by selling high volumes of goods at relatively low profit margins.

John Lewis's net profit margin of 7.2% compared unfavourably with that of Debenhams, which was 10.1%. Waitrose's net profit margin of 4.6% was lower than Tesco's but higher than Sainsbury's margin in that year.

 EXAMINER'S VOICE

Studying measures of profitability can involve working with some large numbers. Do not worry too much about these numbers. As long as you know how to use the formula, your calculator will do the hard work. Make sure you have a calculator with you in the exam room. Once you have let it do the calculations, all you need to do is see which number is higher. In this example, the conclusion that John Lewis did less well than Debenhams can be made because its net profit margin is a lower number.

 FILE

In April 2007, Topshop became the latest high-street store to attempt to improve both its sales volume and selling prices by employing a celebrity. Kate Moss's branded products were an immediate success, with Topshop recording increased sales during the first 6 months of the range's introduction. The brand was also launched in the USA at much higher prices. A Kate Moss mohair jumper on sale for £55 in Topshop was being sold for $198 (£99) in the USA.

Calculating the return on capital

In calculating the return on capital invested, net profit is normally used because this is always declared. However, operating profit is also a good measure of performance. Capital invested is generally considered to be a good measure of a firm's size. It is not a totally reliable guide, as firms are now tending to lease assets rather than purchase them, but it is useful for an entrepeneur to see if his or her return is better than the interest paid by a bank if the money had been saved instead.

Return on capital employed is measured as a percentage using the following formula:

$$\text{return on capital }(\%) = \frac{\text{net profit before tax}}{\text{capital invested}} \times 100$$

Based on Table 18.1, John Lewis Partnership plc's return on capital was as follows:

$$2006/07: \frac{319.2}{2{,}796.3} \times 100 = 11.4\%$$

KEY TERMS

return on capital: ratio showing net profit (operating profit is also used) as a percentage of capital invested.

capital invested: all of the money provided to the business by owners.

$$2005/06: \frac{251.8}{2,659.1} \times 100 = 9.5\%$$

$$2004/05: \frac{229.3}{2,501.2} \times 100 = 9.2\%$$

Table 18.3 Average
return on capital ratios for
*UK firms, 2004–06**

Year	2004	2005	2006
Return on capital (%)	5.4	6.8	6.6

Sources: Experian and ONS.

*These years have been selected as John Lewis's financial year ends in January. Therefore, the 2006/07 financial year relates much more closely to 2006 than to 2007.

Interpreting the return on capital results

Method 1: over time
John Lewis has increased its return on capital from 9.2% in 2004/05 to 9.5% in 2005/06 and finally to 11.4% in 2006/07. This shows that there was a slight improvement between the first 2 years but a noticeable increase in 2006/07.

Conclusion: John Lewis Partnership plc is experiencing a steady rise in its profitability, as measured by return on capital.

Method 2: comparison with other firms
This gives a different picture. Across the UK as a whole, the return on capital for business organisations rose from 5.4% to 6.8% before falling slightly to 6.6% in 2006.

John Lewis's return on capital rose from 9.2% to 9.5% and finally to 11.4% in 2006/07. This indicates that John Lewis was significantly more profitable than other firms in every year between 2004 and 2006. However, it confirms the suspicion that 2005 was not such a good year as the return on capital increased only slightly, whereas most firms enjoyed a much larger increase in that year.

Conclusion: John Lewis had a relatively muted success in 2005/06, but was noticeably above average in terms of return on capital in the other 2 years.

Significance of return on capital

This calculation looks at the percentage return on a sum of money invested in a business. It is therefore an excellent means of comparison. In effect, it says that money invested in John Lewis earned a return of over 11% in 2006/07. What is the opportunity cost of this money? The next best alternative might have been to put it in a bank. This would have earned about 5–6% interest at the time. Therefore, it can be seen that during this period John Lewis was a better investment than putting money into a bank. (However, you need to consider that money in a bank is safe.)

Would it have been better to put the money into Debenhams instead? Debenhams' return on capital was 6.2%.

Conclusion: John Lewis was a better investment than Debenhams. This seems to conflict with the conclusion on the net profit margin. By having two ratios, we are getting a clearer picture overall. Debenhams is better at converting sales revenue into profit. However, John Lewis is better at converting investors' money into profit.

Methods of improving profits and profitability

Businesses have many aims. John Lewis is a classic example — one of its aims is to reward its employees as much as possible by paying them a bonus. In 2006/07 employees received a bonus that equalled 18% of their pay. However, this bonus depends on the business making a good profit. Most businesses aim to make a profit, even if it is not their primary aim.

There are many ways of increasing profit. However, the three most basic methods are:
- increasing the price
- decreasing costs
- increasing sales volume

Other methods of improving profits or profitability tend to fall broadly within these categories.

Increasing the price

If a business increases the price of a product, it will widen the profit margin and therefore each product sold will generate more profit. This strategy will be particularly effective if the product is a necessity or has no close substitutes, as customers will be willing to pay the higher price. However, the strategy of increasing the price must be treated with caution if there are many close competitors for the product and the higher price may lead customers to switch to rival products or stop buying the product entirely. In this situation, it is possible that the price rise may cause a fall in demand that is so great that the higher profit margin will be offset by a dramatic fall in quantity.

For example, suppose that the profit margin is £10 per unit and 100 units are sold — the total profit in this case will be £1,000. An increase in price of £2 will mean that profit margin increases to £12. However, if only 80 units are then sold, the total profit will be £960, and so the price increase has actually led to a *fall* in profit.

In situations where there are many competitors, it may actually be more profitable to *cut* the price. Using the above example, if the firm decides to decrease the price by £2, the profit margin falls to £8 per unit. If this lower price leads to an increase in the quantity demanded from 100 units to 140 units, the profit will increase from £1,000 to £1,120 (£8 × 140 units).

 EXAMINER'S VOICE

A more detailed treatment of the impact of price on the quantity demanded is provided in Chapter 32, where the **price elasticity of demand** is discussed. At that point, it would be useful to refer back to this chapter and link the two ideas together. Price elasticity of demand will enable you to provide more sophisticated responses to questions about price changes.

The Sheffield
College

 FILE

Branding and profitability

How easy is it to increase price without losing customers? Research by *The Grocer* magazine in 2006 confirms the view that 'branding' is the key to success. In the food industry, profitability was much higher for food producers such as Kellogg's and Jordans, which provide branded products. Those firms that produce own-label products for supermarkets have much lower profitability, although their profitability is slightly higher than those businesses that provide the basic food commodities before they are processed (see Table 18.4).

The survey also shows that small producers of branded products work at much lower levels of profitability than larger ones. However, for unbranded products and basic food commodities there is a much smaller difference between the profitability of large and small firms.

Table 18.4 *Profitability of food suppliers, 2006*

	Average of all firms	Firms with sales over £500m p.a.	Firms with sales under £500m p.a.		Average of all firms	Firms with sales over £500m p.a.	Firms with sales under £500m p.a.
Branded	12.9	14.4	8.0	Branded	29.7	34.6	17.0
Own labels	4.9	4.5	5.3	Own labels	17.6	18.5	16.8
Commodities	4.5	5.0	2.4	Commodities	9.6	9.5	10.1

(a) Net profit margin (%)   *(b) Return on capital (%)*

Source: *The Grocer*, 14 July 2007.

 EXAMINER'S VOICE

A common mistake made in examinations is to assume that increasing sales revenue will always increase profit, while a fall in sales revenue will always decrease profits. This is not necessarily the case. The price that a business sets should aim to increase profits more than increase sales. Some niche markets work on this principle. Making a few products at a high price may bring in less revenue than a mass market, but the profit is higher because the business does not need to make a large number of products.

Decreasing costs

If the business can cut its direct costs, such as wage levels or raw material costs, then the profit margin will increase. This means that each product will yield more profit and, assuming that there is no change in demand, this will increase the total profit. In most cases, changes in costs will probably not affect the level of demand, so this strategy will be successful in improving profits and profitability. However, if the change in costs leads to a decrease in quality or efficiency, the demand for the product may fall. This could happen if costs are being cut because inferior raw materials are being used, or if the workers who accept a lower wage are less efficient than those being paid a higher wage.

Similar benefits can be obtained by reducing overheads, such as rent, office expenses and machinery costs. Once again, the business must be careful that cutting these costs does not damage sales. For example, a retail outlet may be reluctant to move to premises with a lower rent if the new location is less accessible to customers. In this case, the savings in costs may be much lower than the decline in sales revenue caused by the unfavourable location.

> **e EXAMINER'S VOICE**
>
> The business concepts in this chapter are ideally suited to evaluative questions. The BUSS2 examination focuses on improving efficiency in order to increase profits. Virtually every topic in the BUSS2 specification relates to ways in which either:
> - price can be increased, or
> - costs can be decreased, or
> - sales volume can be increased
>
> Look out for these links as you study the remaining chapters on the other functional areas:
> - people
> - operations management
> - marketing
>
> This chapter can be used to bring together all the topics covered at AS. On completion of the A2 course, it would be sensible to read this chapter again to check your understanding of how the different functional areas can improve profitability.

> **FACT FILE**
>
> **Cost cutting?**
>
> In March 2006 over 200,000 gallons of crude oil leaked from a corroded BP pipeline in Alaska. American politicians have accused BP of cost cutting. BP officials have rejected the accusations, but the company has lost revenue as the oilfield has been partially closed until pipelines are replaced.
>
> Source: Litterick, D. (2007) 'BP Alaska oil spill blamed on cuts', *Daily Telegraph*, 1 May.

Increasing sales volume

If costs and price remain the same, it is still possible to increase profits by increasing the volume of products sold. This may occur simply because demand increases as the product becomes more established in the market. However, it may be due to the actions of the business, such as marketing or product development.

Other methods of improving profit/profitability

Some other methods of improving profits are noted below, but this is not an exhaustive list:

- **Investment in fixed assets**. Purchasing new equipment, buildings or vehicles can enable a business to expand its scale of operation and possibly improve both the efficiency of production and the quality of the product.

> **FACT FILE**
>
> **Bestway**
>
> Sir Anwar Pervez is someone who focused on sales volume rather than profit margin. The former bus conductor started a convenience store in 1963 but moved into cash-and-carry wholesaling in 1976. At the time, wholesalers were making reasonable profit margins; Sir Anwar thought he could manage by halving the margins. Within 9 years he had six warehouses. His warehouses now operate on a tiny net profit margin of 1.5%, but with sales of £1.7 billion a year this means a £25 million profit. With other activities, the Bestway group makes £73 million. Sir Anwar is now the UK's 138th richest man.

As a result, the business may be able to increase its profits by achieving higher sales volume, charging a higher price and cutting its costs.

■ **Product development.** A business can introduce new, unique products in order to attract more customers. New products often carry higher prices because they are different from established brands, so the business can gain extra profits by selling more items and charging a higher price at the same time.

■ **Marketing.** Successful marketing strategies, such as a clever advertising campaign or sponsorship of a popular organisation, can encourage customers to buy more of the business's products. Furthermore, a great deal of marketing is intended to increase the value of the product to the customer, and so may encourage customers to pay a higher price. Although marketing adds to the costs of the business, these extra costs should be offset by the additional revenue generated, so profit should increase.

■ **Human resource strategies.** The staff of an organisation are invariably its greatest asset. Careful selection, recruitment and training of staff, and strategies that motivate the workforce should lead to greater efficiency. This may lead to greater output, higher-quality products and better customer service, all of which should contribute to higher profits.

Table 18.5
Private limited companies with the biggest profit margins

Rank	Private limited company	Activity	Margin (%)
23	Spreadex	Spread-betting operator	52.02
61	First Oil	Oil and gas producer	45.89
40	BES Consulting	Asbestos risk consultancy	41.76
38	Castlebeck	Care-home operator	38.87
68	RP Valves	Valve distributor	38.29
53	Mactaggart and Mickel	Housebuilder	37.72
79	Moneysupermarket.com	Financial website operator	34.43
15	Aquilaheywood	Financial software developer	34.34
20	Duck and Cover Clothing	Clothing manufacturer	30.85
16	4D Interactive	Dating services provider	30.26

Operating profit and directors' pay as a proportion of sales.

Distinction between cash and profit

Profit is calculated by subtracting expenditure from revenue. It is easy to assume that a profitable firm will be cash rich, but this is not necessarily true. Profitable firms may be short of cash for the following reasons:

■ If the firm has built up its stock levels, its wealth will lie in assets rather than cash. These stocks may not be saleable in the short term.

■ If the firm's sales are on credit, its wealth will be in debtors rather than cash. The firm may have agreed with its debtors that they need not pay for a given time period. Although this helps marketing, it may damage cash flow.

■ If the firm has used its profit to pay dividends to shareholders or repay long-term loans, it may be short of cash.

- If the company has purchased fixed assets, this will have involved a large outflow of cash, but in the accounts the 'cost' of these fixed assets is spread over a number of years. Thus, in the year in which the fixed assets are purchased, the recorded 'costs' will be much lower than the actual loss of cash, leading to a potential crisis. (In practice, major purchases of fixed assets are often supported by loans that are repaid in future years.)

In the long term, a business must make profit in order to survive. A firm that continually records losses will find it difficult to acquire cash, as sales revenue will be lower than expenditure, and creditors and investors will be reluctant to give the firm credit or loans, or buy shares.

However, even profitable businesses may face difficulties if they do not plan their cash flow carefully. For example, a firm that purchases assets may expect to make profit from these assets in the future, but cash payments for the assets could lead to the firm being unable to pay suppliers or workers. This could lead to **liquidation**, with the firm being forced to close and sell its assets in order to make these cash payments.

The most liquid asset that a business can possess is cash. However, items such as stock can often be sold quickly and therefore turned into cash. All firms, however profitable, must manage their cash and their liquid assets (which includes those items that can be converted into cash most easily) to remain liquid and guarantee their survival.

KEY TERM

liquidity: the ability to convert an asset into cash without loss or delay.

PRACTICE EXERCISE Total: 35 marks (30 minutes)

1 What is the formula for calculating return on capital (%)? (3 marks)

2 What is the formula for calculating the net profit margin (%)? (3 marks)

3 Explain why return on capital invested is considered to be a good way for an investor to assess the desirability of his or her investment. (4 marks)

4 The following data are available for a business:
- sales revenue — £10,000
- capital invested — £6,000
- net profit before tax — £1,000

Calculate:
a the net profit margin (3 marks)   b the return on capital (3 marks)

5 Explain how a business might increase its profit by:
a increasing its price (4 marks)   b decreasing its price (4 marks)

6 Analyse two possible problems that might occur if a business tried to increase its profit by cutting its costs. (6 marks)

7 What is the difference between 'cash' and 'profit'? (5 marks)

197

CASE STUDY Improving profitability at Cadbury

A radical reshaping of Cadbury Schweppes' confectionery business is expected to lead to the axing of more than 5,000 jobs.

Cadbury has plans to make savings in certain problem areas. Businesses in Nigeria, Russia and China face cost savings, some of which will come from closing manufacturing operations. Trade unions have objected to the fact that some of the closures are in order to relocate production to Poland, where wages and other costs are lower.

It is thought that the biggest focus on cost cutting will be on overheads, marketing expenditure and general administrative costs. According to Todd Stitzer, Cadbury's chief executive, 'The organisational structure has become too complex.' Cadbury's administrative costs account for some 20% of sales turnover, compared with only 12% for some of its competitors. Some of these cuts will come in the UK. Cadbury has already announced that it is to quit its head office in Mayfair and move to a cheaper site in Uxbridge, West London.

Cadbury's attempts to improve profitability are also being threatened by rising raw material costs, especially milk prices. However, Cadbury is not solely focused on costs. Despite its overall cuts in marketing, it has extended its advertising budget. The cost-cutting exercise has been focused more on spending on its sales team than advertising.

Following a series of awareness-raising outdoor posters, the recent launch of the second phase of its £6.2 million marketing campaign opened with a quirky advert for Dairy Milk, featuring a drumming gorilla. The advert was launched on 31 August 2007 and was scheduled to run for 4 months. The agency had expected it to be seen an average of 10 times by 84% of the adult population. However, it soon received a cult backing, so that by November 2007 it had been seen over 6 million times on the internet. The market research agency YouGov reports a 20% increase in approval of the Cadbury's brand, which had been damaged by health scares in the previous year. Within 9 weeks of the launch of the advert, Cadbury reported a 9% increase in sales of Dairy Milk. Annual sales of Cadbury's Dairy Milk are currently £350 million.

Sources: Laurance, B. (2007) 'Cadbury sheds 5,000 jobs in drastic revamp', *Sunday Times*, 17 June; 'Cadbury Dairy Milk launches gorilla TV ad campaign', www.talkingretail.com.

Questions

Total: 36 marks (45 minutes)

1 Identify three different examples of cost cutting by Cadbury. *(3 marks)*

2 Analyse two examples of cost cutting where there may be unfavourable consequences for Cadbury. *(6 marks)*

3 Manufacturers of supermarket own-label brands have an average net profit margin of 4.9%. Why is Cadbury able to achieve a much higher net profit margin of 12%? *(4 marks)*

4 Assume that there is a 40% profit margin on Dairy Milk. Using this margin and data from the article, calculate the increase in annual profit that Cadbury will achieve from its gorilla advertising campaign, if the 9% increase in sales of Dairy Milk is maintained for a year. Show your working. *(7 marks)*

5 Cadbury has introduced a number of strategies to improve profitability. Select the two strategies that you believe will be the best in helping Cadbury to increase its profitability. Justify your choices with fully reasoned arguments, contrasting them with the strategies that you believe will be less successful. *(16 marks)*

Unit 2:
Managing a business

People in business

Improving organisational structures

This chapter looks at the key elements of organisational structure, including levels of hierarchy and spans of control, workloads and job allocation, delegation and communication flows. Workforce roles including supervisor, team leader, manager and director are considered. Finally, the chapter examines how organisational structure affects business performance.

Organisational structure

KEY TERMS

organisational structure: the relationship between different people and functions in an organisation — both vertically, from shop-floor workers through supervisors and managers to directors, and horizontally between different functions and people at the same level.

organisation chart: a diagram showing the lines of authority and layers of hierarchy in an organisation.

organisational hierarchy: the vertical division of authority and accountability in an organisation.

levels of hierarchy: the number of different supervisory and management levels between the shop floor and the chief executive in an organisation.

An organisation's structure is usually illustrated by means of an **organisation chart**, which shows the connection between people in an organisation. The **organisational hierarchy** refers to the levels of authority and accountability in the organisation. Each line linking two different levels of the management hierarchy represents a relationship where instructions are passed downwards, and reports and feedback are passed upwards within the organisation. Because lines are used to show the link between an employee and his or her supervisor or manager, it is customary to describe the person immediately above someone in the organisation chart as his or her **line manager**. Thus in Figure 19.1, supervisor B's line manager is the production manager for product A. This reporting system from the top of the hierarchy down to the bottom is called the **chain of command**. A formal hierarchy, such as that illustrated in Figure 19.1, has a clear vertical chain of command.

Figure 19.1
Traditional
organisation chart

Organisation charts show:

- the design of the organisation, including the chain of command
- how different functions and divisions fit together
- who is answerable to whom
- the span of control in each division
- the official channels of communication

Figure 19.1 is a traditional structure that divides an organisation into functional areas, including marketing, production, human resource management and finance. Within each function there are a number of layers of hierarchy. For example, the marketing function has two levels, whereas the production function for product A has three levels.

Span of control

If a manager has many subordinates answerable to him or her, the span of control is said to be wide. If a manager has relatively few subordinates answerable to him or her, the span of control is said to be narrow. Normally, the greater the degree of similarity in what a group of workers does, the wider the span of control can be. This is because if people are doing more or less identical jobs, it is likely to be easier to manage them. This explains why there is a narrow span of control at more senior levels of management, but shop-floor supervisors have wider spans of control. In Figure 19.1 the span of control for senior managers is narrower than for the shop-floor supervisors.

Relationship between span of control and levels of hierarchy

Traditionally, organisations have tended to have tall hierarchical structures, i.e. many layers of management, each with a narrow span of control. More recently, hierarchies have become flatter, meaning that the number of layers

KEY TERM

span of control:
the number of subordinates whom a manager is required to supervise directly.

DID YOU KNOW?

Some theorists suggest that the span of control should be between 3 and 6; others suggest between 6 and 12. However, such generalisations are unhelpful, since they ignore the characteristics of the group that is being supervised.

to a halt. Therefore, if responsibility is delegated, it is important to ensure that appropriate authority is also delegated. It is equally important to lay down clearly the limits to a subordinate's authority: for example, that a subordinate does not have the power to hire and fire in his manager's absence. Passing on authority is an issue that many managers find difficult, but if sufficient authority is not transferred, delegation will be unsuccessful.

■ **Accountability.** Despite delegating responsibility and authority, the manager is still accountable, both in law and in fact. He or she has chosen to delegate tasks to a subordinate, has recruited and trained subordinates, and has made the decision that the subordinate is capable of exercising power efficiently. Thus accountability remains firmly at the top of the organisation structure.

Improving the effectiveness of delegation

The following factors are likely to improve the effectiveness of delegation:

■ Delegation should be based on mutual trust between the manager and the subordinate.

■ It is important to select the most suitable person to delegate to — someone who will be able to complete the task efficiently and effectively. The person should be appropriately skilled, trained and informed about the particular task for which he or she will be responsible.

■ Interesting and challenging tasks should be delegated as well as the more routine ones. Managers should not delegate tasks simply because they dislike doing them (e.g. because the tasks are dull or difficult) or because they are overburdened with work.

■ The tasks and responsibilities to be delegated need to be explained clearly in order to avoid subordinates making mistakes or feeling unsure or insecure because of a lack of information. An effective support system should be provided — one that allows the subordinate to question and discuss issues connected with the delegated tasks. This should improve understanding and ensure that subordinates have the skills necessary to carry out their tasks.

■ When delegating responsibility for carrying out a certain task, managers must also delegate the authority to carry it out and communicate this to others in the business, in order to avoid difficulties such as someone else questioning the authority of the subordinate. The limitations of the subordinate's authority should be made clear too.

■ It follows that managers should avoid interfering with delegated tasks unless it is evident that things are going seriously wrong. They must relinquish control in order to ensure that subordinates feel they are trusted and that the manager has confidence in them.

Advantages of delegation

Delegation has the following advantages:

■ **Management time.** Delegation is necessary in all organisations because there is a limit to the amount of work managers can carry out themselves. Delegation reduces the stress and burdens of management, and frees up time for managers to concentrate on more important strategic tasks.

DID YOU KNOW?

Research has shown that taking the above six factors into account can improve the success of delegation fourfold.

- **Motivation.** Delegation empowers and motivates workers. It provides subordinates with greater job satisfaction by giving them a say in the decision making that affects their work and by demonstrating trust in their abilities.
- **Local knowledge.** Subordinates might have a better knowledge of local conditions affecting their area of work and therefore might be able to make better-informed decisions.
- **Flexibility.** Delegation may allow greater flexibility and a quicker response to changes, since if problems do not have to be referred to senior managers, decision making should be quicker.
- **Staff development.** By giving subordinates the experience of decision making, delegation provides a means of grooming them for higher positions and is thus important for management development purposes.

Limits to delegation

Delegation has the following limitations:

- **Small firms.** In some small firms, managers delegate little — often because they do not have the staff to delegate to or because they have set the business up on their own, are used to controlling all aspects of the operations and are therefore reluctant to relinquish control.
- **Customer expectations.** Often, customers want to see the manager in charge, regardless of the fact that responsibilities may have been delegated further down the hierarchy.
- **Attitudes and approach of management.** The leadership style in an organisation will largely dictate the extent to which responsibilities are delegated down the hierarchy.
- **Quality of staff.** The extent to which responsibilities can be delegated will be influenced by the quality and skills of the staff who are employed.
- **Crisis situations.** In emergency or crisis situations where decisions need to be made quickly, delegation is less likely and is often less effective.
- **Confidentiality.** Where there is a need for confidentiality or extreme security, less delegation is likely to take place.

> *e* **EXAMINER'S VOICE**
>
> Always remember to address questions in context, i.e. make sure that your answers relate clearly to the precise organisation that you are considering. This will assist you in gaining marks for application.

PRACTICE EXERCISE 2 — Total: 20 marks (15 minutes)

1 Explain the term 'delegation'. *(2 marks)*

2 Distinguish between the terms 'responsibility', 'authority' and 'accountability'. *(6 marks)*

3 Explain two factors that are likely to make delegation effective. *(6 marks)*

4 Explain two limitations to the delegation of responsibility in business. *(6 marks)*

CASE STUDY 2 Peter's problems

Tuesday

Peter Smith is the sales manager of a textile firm in Lancashire. He is currently working on the draft of a document that will detail the current performance of the firm's various products in each of its sales regions, together with forecasts, based on market research findings, for the next 3 years. So far he has drafted some rough notes, identified the information he needs, and asked his secretary to collect the information and have it ready for him first thing on Thursday morning, so that he can work on it on Thursday and Friday. The document will form the basis of a presentation he is due to make next Tuesday at the board meeting.

Peter's real passion is for selling, but since his promotion to sales manager, he finds that he does less and less of this and spends an increasing amount of time looking at figures, justifying performance and attending board meetings, none of which he particularly enjoys.

As well as a secretary, Peter has an assistant, Sam, who helps him in travelling around to meet the regional sales team and generally coordinating the regions. Sam is keen to take on more responsibility; he is good with figures and would like to be more involved in the planning and reviewing process, which is mainly Peter's responsibility. At present, Sam feels a little constrained by the fact that he spends most of his time on the road travelling.

Wednesday

At a local business forum meeting, Peter learns of a conference in Germany that will focus specifically on the long-term potential in eastern Europe for the types of product his firm produces and sells. The 3-day conference starts tomorrow. Peter feels that he needs to go, but he is aware of the important board meeting next Tuesday when he is due to present the document, which he has not yet really started producing. He decides that this is the right time for Sam to step in — Sam has always said that he wants Peter to delegate more tasks to him, so here is his chance.

Peter arrives back at the office at 3 p.m., with 20 minutes to spare before his next meeting, which will

go on until late in the evening. He calls Sam in and tells him that he will be away for the next 3 days in Germany. He explains that he wants Sam to cancel all his commitments for Thursday and Friday, and to compile the document that Peter will need for the board meeting next Tuesday. Peter gives Sam his rough notes and explains the information that he has asked his secretary to get ready for early tomorrow morning. He tells Sam that he will check the document on Monday and will talk to him about it then. After this he dashes off to his meeting.

Sam is stunned. He has a number of appointments booked for the next 2 days, which are important and which he is reluctant to cancel. However, although producing the document is rather daunting, he is keen to have a go and therefore follows Peter's instructions, rescheduling his appointments.

Thursday

Sam arrives at the office early and goes to Peter's secretary for the information. She has half of the information, but says that the rest is with another manager who wants to speak to Peter before releasing it. Sam rings the manager to explain the task he has been set, but the manager refuses to provide him with the information, saying that it is confidential and that Sam needs Peter's authorisation before he can have access to it.

Friday

Sam does his best to produce the document. However, he is not particularly happy with it and knows there are significant gaps in it owing to the lack of information. He has tried on a number of occasions to contact Peter in Germany, but has been unable to get hold of him. He is also aware that his lack of experience and limited skills in terms of report writing mean that the document does not show the information in the best possible light.

Monday

Peter does not turn up until 2 p.m., having attended a meeting all morning. He finds Sam's report on his desk, together with a note. He ignores the note and scans the document. He then calls Sam into his office. 'This is awful — there are all sorts of gaps in the information and the format is wrong. I can't find the slides for the presentation either...'

Questions
Total: 40 marks (55 minutes)

1 Define the term 'delegation'. *(2 marks)*

2 Explain the terms 'responsibility' and 'authority' in relation to delegation. *(6 marks)*

3 Briefly explain two possible reasons why Sam would want Peter to delegate more tasks to him. *(6 marks)*

4 Managers rely heavily on effective delegation. Analyse this statement in the context of the above case study. *(10 marks)*

5 To what extent was Peter's failure to delegate authority the main cause of the difficulties that Sam faced in completing the report? *(16 marks)*

Communication flows

 TERMS

communication: the process of exchanging information or ideas between two or more individuals or groups.

internal communication: the exchange of information that takes place within an organisation (e.g. at departmental meetings, in team briefing sessions and in memos to staff).

external communication: the exchange of information that takes place with individuals, groups and organisations outside the business (e.g. via advertising material, telephone calls to suppliers and letters to customers).

Effective communication offers organisations a number of benefits:

- It allows the organisation to make more informed decisions based on better-quality information.
- It makes it easier to implement change because employees and other stakeholders understand and recognise the need for it.
- It encourages a more motivated workforce and develops commitment to the business from employees at all levels of the organisation.
- It helps to ensure that the business is well coordinated and that all employees pursue the same corporate objectives.

■ It allows the organisation to be more competitive by improving efficiency and identifying opportunities.

Therefore, an organisation that communicates effectively is likely to be more in touch with consumers and other external groups, have a more motivated and committed workforce, make better decisions and find it easier to introduce change.

Internal and external communication

Good internal communication is vital to the efficiency and success of a business. It ensures that employees know exactly what they are required to do and that different departments interact effectively. Good communication lies at the heart of effective management and is an essential aspect of successful decision making in relation to coordinating and controlling a business. It ensures that the various parts of a business work together in order to achieve corporate aims and objectives.

All businesses exist in a dynamic external environment. Therefore, it is also important for organisations to communicate effectively with external groups, such as suppliers, customers, investors, pressure groups, the media and the local community. Good communication with external groups allows an organisation to monitor its operations and identify areas for improvements more effectively. For example, by listening to comments from customers, it should be able to monitor changes in the market and improve its products and services. Similarly, by establishing good channels of communication with the local community, it should be able to assess its local reputation and adjust its operations if necessary. Equally, the efficient operation of just-in-time (JIT) processes requires highly effective communication systems with suppliers.

The process of communication

Effective communication will happen only if the information sent is received and clearly understood. Although numerous types of communication might occur in a business context, certain features are common to them all:

■ a **sender or communicator** — the person (or group) who is sending the message
■ the **message** — the topic of the communication
■ a **transmission mechanism** (also known as the process, medium or channel) by which a message is conveyed: for example, by telephone, by memo or in a face-to-face meeting
■ a **receiver** — the person (or group) at whom the message is aimed
■ **feedback** — the response from the receiver, whether written, verbal or even a facial expression, indicating that the message has been understood

Without feedback, the communicator will not know whether the message has been received and clearly understood.

Figure 19.5 illustrates the communication process. For example, if a particular organisation is experiencing a permanent fall in sales, senior management may decide that compulsory redundancies have to be made. It communicates this decision, and the reasons, to the employees of the organisation by individual letters sent to their home addresses and by a series of staff meetings at which senior management explains its decisions. Feedback is via questions posed by employees at the meetings, and employees' subsequent reactions (letters to, and meetings with, management, the trade union response etc.).

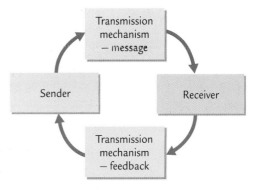

Figure 19.5
The communication process

A message that is not delivered effectively may lead to significant problems for a firm. For example, if the marketing department fails to inform the production department of the estimated demand for a product, insufficient stock may be produced, resulting in disappointed customers and adverse effects on the firm's reputation. Equally, if employees put in a great deal of extra effort in order to satisfy a sudden increase in demand, but receive no praise or recognition for this from senior management, they are unlikely to do the same thing again.

One- and two-way communication

> **KEY TERMS**
>
> **one-way communication:** communication without any feedback (e.g. putting a notice on a notice board, or giving instructions in an authoritarian manner that allows no comment or questions from the listener).
>
> **two-way communication:** communication with feedback (e.g. giving instructions in a manner that allows for questions to be asked or comments to be made, a discussion or a question-and-answer session).

In the context of one-way communication, the communicator can never be sure whether the message has been understood and therefore whether the communication was effective. One-way communication is often associated with autocratic or authoritarian management styles. In contrast, two-way communication ensures that any communication has been fully understood and is therefore more effective. Effective two-way communication is a vital element of democratic management, effective delegation, empowerment and teamworking.

Communication channels

The most effective channels of communication vary according to the information that is being passed on. For example, **team briefing sessions** are usually held at the start of a working day or working week, and are likely to be used as a forum for communication between supervisors and their teams about production targets, new production methods and issues related to the quality of production. Another channel might be a **works council**, which allows

> **KEY TERM**
>
> **communication channel:** the route through which communication occurs.

CHAPTER 19 Improving organisational structures

discussion about company plans between management and employee representatives. This ensures that employees' ideas and suggestions become an automatic element of company decision making.

Communication can take place up and down the chain of command in an organisation, with orders or instructions being passed down the layers of hierarchy, and ideas and suggestions being passed in the other direction. Alternatively, the communication channel might be horizontal across a hierarchy, as in a management meeting attended by the marketing, finance, operations and personnel managers.

Open and closed channels of communication

KEY TERMS

open channels of communication: any staff member is welcome to see, read or hear the discussions and conclusions.

closed channels of communication: access to the information is restricted to a named few.

In the previous example of a firm that is experiencing a permanent fall in sales, the initial discussions about the choice of strategy might be conducted through closed channels such as senior management meetings, with the minutes of the meetings being confidential. However, once the decision has been made, the staff meetings and the subsequent meetings with union representatives would be open, in the sense that all employees would, in the case of the staff meeting, be able to attend. In the case of meetings between senior management and union representatives, employees would have access to the minutes or reports of the meetings.

Formal and informal channels of communication

KEY TERMS

formal channels of communication: communication channels established and approved by senior management, within which any form of communication is regarded as formal (e.g. meetings of departmental heads, personnel department meetings and production team briefing sessions).

informal channels of communication: means of passing information outside the official channels, often developed by employees themselves (e.g. 'the grapevine' and gossip).

Within any business there are both formal and informal channels of communication.

Informal communication channels can both help and hinder formal communications, and for this reason the grapevine is usually recognised by management as extremely important. Rumours of redundancies or a takeover, or the suspension of a senior executive often pass more quickly through informal channels than through established channels; however, such messages may not always be accurate. There have been cases where businesses have even issued 'leaks' on to the grapevine about a possible new development in order to

INGRAM

assess the reactions of employees, and then have made changes based on these reactions before introducing the development to employees along the formal channels of communication. In general, however, the existence of large amounts of informal communication may suggest that the formal communication channels are not operating effectively.

DID YOU KNOW?

Research has shown that the most effective communication requires both formal and informal channels.

 EXAMINER'S VOICE

Students often confuse formal communication with written communication and informal communication with oral communication. Oral communication can be formal (a meeting or an interview) or informal (gossip among staff waiting by the photocopier). Similarly, written communication can be either formal (minutes of a meeting) or informal (a 'private' e-mail about the behaviour of a member of staff).

FACT FILE

Social networks

Buying a coffee machine and water cooler could be the most important investment a company ever makes in its future, for it is at these social hubs of office life that the real business often gets done, as part of a casual chat or chance meeting.

But many managers are unaware that this seemingly pointless social networking does in fact play a crucial part in the way people interact with each other to get work done, according to Andrew Parker, a research consultant with IBM. He argues that official organisation charts underpinning the structure of a company

ignore the hidden social networks that really drive performance. The rapid growth in remote working means it is now even more essential to acknowledge that they are a key factor in business success.

'More often than not, however, important networks don't exist on the formal chart and it can be hard to get busy executives to pay attention to these seemingly invisible structures,' says Parker, co-author of *The Hidden Power of Social Networks: Understanding How Work Really Gets Done in Organizations* (Harvard Business School Press, 2004).

Source: adapted from *Professional Manager*, January 2005.

Vertical and lateral communication

Information can be communicated vertically, both up and down the chain of command, and laterally (horizontally across the chain of command). These different channels of communication are illustrated in Figure 19.6.

KEY TERM

vertical communication: when information is passed up and down the chain of command.

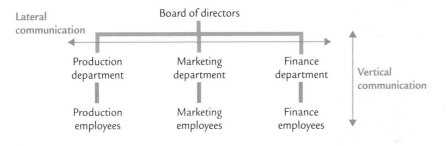

Figure 19.6 Vertical and lateral communication

There are two types of **vertical communication**:

- **Downwards communication** (also known as **top-down communication**) is transmitted from the top of the organisation down to the bottom of the

organisation or from superior to subordinate. This form of communication is generally used to tell employees about decisions that have already been made and to give instructions.

- **Upwards communication** (also known as **bottom-up communication**) is transmitted from the bottom of the organisation up to the top of the organisation or from subordinate to superior.

There is considerable evidence that upwards communication can be of great assistance in decision making. This is because:

- It helps managers to understand employees' views and concerns.
- It helps managers to keep in touch with employees' attitudes and values.
- It can alert managers to potential problems.
- It can provide managers with the information they need for decision making and gives feedback on the effects of previous decisions.
- It helps employees to feel that they are participating, and this can encourage motivation.
- It provides feedback on the effectiveness of downwards communication and how it can be improved.

KEY TERM

lateral communication: when people at the same level within an organisation pass information to each other.

An example of **lateral communication** is a member of the finance department telling the marketing department about the budget available for a sales promotion, or a member of the marketing department informing the production department of the estimated sales for the coming year. However, problems can arise if the different departments fail to understand each other's needs. For example, staff in the marketing department might promise a customer a large sales order within a specified time without discussing with staff in the production department whether they are able to meet the order in time. Thus effective lateral communication is vital for the efficient running of the firm.

How organisational structure affects business performance

Examples of how organisational structure affects business performance can be found in each of the areas covered in this chapter. Reference to these areas is provided below together with some additional relevant points:

- **Organisational hierarchies and spans of control.** Table 19.1 on p. 202 identifies the ways in which different organisational hierarchies and spans of control affect business performance.
- **Clarity of lines of accountability.** When a company's management structure is clear, as shown by its organisation chart, staff should know what

authority has been given to them and by whom. Achievement and recognition of that achievement are likely to produce motivation. Recognition of achievement is more likely if the lines of accountability are clear. On the other hand, if mistakes are made, it is essential to know how they came about, in order to correct them. This can be identified more easily if the lines of accountability are clear. In some instances, clear lines of accountability can be seen as a threat that deters managers from taking decisions in case they turn out badly. This in turn may make them overcautious, to the detriment of the business.

- **Delegation.** Improving the effectiveness of delegation (explained on p. 206) can increase managerial success and hence may improve business performance.
- **Quality circles.** When organisations operate quality circles, this is an important part of the delegation process. The principal function of a quality circle is to identify quality problems, consider alternative solutions and recommend suitable outcomes to management. By delegating the responsibility for identifying problems to quality circles and then taking into account the solutions they put forward, organisations benefit operationally and financially. At the same time, they enrich the jobs of their workers, who appreciate the opportunity to demonstrate their knowledge and talents in a problem-solving environment.
- **Communication flows.** Effective communication leads to more effective decision making, makes it easier to introduce change, improves coordination, encourages a more motivated and committed workforce, and ensures that a business is more in tune with its customers and key stakeholders. All of these are likely to lead to a more efficient and competitive organisation.

Conclusion

The structure of an organisation is influenced by many factors:
- **The size of the organisation.** The larger the organisation, the more complex its structure is likely to be and the more layers of hierarchy, divisions or departments it is likely to have.
- **The nature of the organisation.** The business's structure will depend on whether it is in the manufacturing or service sector, national or multinational, single product or multi-product, and whether it is in an area where tight control, safety or security issues are paramount.
- **The culture and attitudes of senior management.** The structure will be affected by whether the management style is autocratic and controlling, or democratic and participative.
- **The skill and experience of its workforce.** The nature of the workforce — whether the majority of workers do low-skilled, repetitive jobs, or whether they are highly skilled and each do very different jobs — also influences a business's organisational structure.

> ### ℯ EXAMINER'S VOICE
>
> Check that you understand these concepts:
> - wide versus narrow spans of control
> - tall versus flat hierarchies
>
> Always remember to apply your knowledge. Think about the particular business you are being asked about, and relate your knowledge to that business — do not just repeat textbook knowledge without giving it context. For example, if you are considering a small, family-run private limited company, your answer about organisational structure will be very different from an answer you would give about a large multinational plc.

PRACTICE EXERCISE 3   Total: 60 marks (50 minutes)

1 Define the term 'communication'. *(3 marks)*

2 Explain two benefits to a firm of good communication. *(6 marks)*

3 Explain two problems that a firm might encounter if it has poor communication. *(6 marks)*

4 Distinguish between internal and external communication. *(4 marks)*

5 Distinguish between one-way and two-way communication. *(4 marks)*

6 Identify three common features that are involved in the process of communication. *(3 marks)*

7 Identify and explain two channels of communication. *(6 marks)*

8 Distinguish between formal and informal communication. *(4 marks)*

9 Distinguish between vertical and lateral communication. *(4 marks)*

10 Identify and explain four examples of how organisational structure affects business performance. *(20 marks)*

CASE STUDY 3   Mushroom management — don't keep your workforce in the dark

Ragbags is a producer of fine leather handbags. It has grown from a single small factory in Leeds to a much larger manufacturer, with six new production sites throughout the UK and a headquarters based at its original site in Leeds. It sells its products to upmarket department stores and leather retailers only.

Initially, the owner and managing director (MD), Joe Watts, managed the small factory well. His approach was somewhat paternalistic, but he knew everyone and made a point of having an 'open door' policy as far as staff were concerned. All staff, regardless of their position, knew they could see him personally to raise issues and make suggestions about any aspect of their work.

As the company grew, the organisation adopted a more formal structure, with more layers between senior management and the workforce. The organisation chart for the growing company is shown in Figure 19.7.

The new structure meant that some directors were never seen at any one site for months at a time. In addition, issues that staff at one site might be concerned with were never communicated to other sites, and there was a general feeling among staff of being left in the dark. Increasingly, staff spent tea breaks moaning to each other and talking about looking for new jobs. Despite this general feeling of unhappiness, so far there had been no adverse effects on productivity rates and production levels.

Robina Smith was appointed to the business manager's post, which was a new appointment with responsibility for administrative staff and procedures across all sites. Each of the six new sites had an administrative supervisor answerable to her. Robina saw her role as that of a strategic manager and did not feel that 'meeting the troops', as she put it, was an essential part of this — and she thought that it could be done much better by the administrative supervisors. She did, however, believe in communicating with all her staff and she did this regularly — always by e-mail. Every week, staff received endless emails from her about new policies and procedures she was introducing. People ignored many of these e-mails because they knew the policies and procedures would never work.

The administrative supervisors were a bit put out by Robina's approach. They could tell that she was highly efficient and keen to change and update their working practices, but they felt that they should be the ones who communicated changes to their staff. The six of them were required to travel to Leeds once a month for a meeting with Robina, but they had no other opportunity to meet each other or her. It was often difficult to raise issues of concern at these meetings because the agenda, set by Robina, was very tightly structured and the meetings always kept to time.

Production staff at one of the sites were increasingly unhappy about the way their shift-working system was developing. A new system had been introduced recently, but although there had been consultation with the unions and general agreement that it would benefit the company and the workforce, staff did not feel that anyone had really talked it through with them. The production managers at the six sites were in the same position as the administrative supervisors, meeting once per month with the production director at headquarters (HQ). However, they talked to each other a lot on the phone and corresponded by e-mail, mostly complaining about the lack of involvement of senior management in the operations of the six sites, and the failure of anyone at senior management level to take their views and the views of their workers into account.

Joe Watts, the MD, had little idea of the discontent at the various sites. As far as he was concerned, the company was prospering, sales were high and growing, and profitability was excellent. He was currently setting up talks with a group of businesses in Japan to discuss the possibility of selling the company's products in Japanese department stores. The company had recently invested a significant amount of money in improving its ICT, including its communication systems, and all the directors had talked positively about the beneficial impact of this in terms of communication with the different sites.

It came as something of a surprise to Joe when he met Bill Sykes, one of the production managers, by chance at HQ. Bill had been with the company from the start, and Joe knew that he was a first-rate production manager who was loyal and hard working. Bill had come to HQ for one of his monthly production meetings. They started talking and Joe learned that Bill was leaving at the

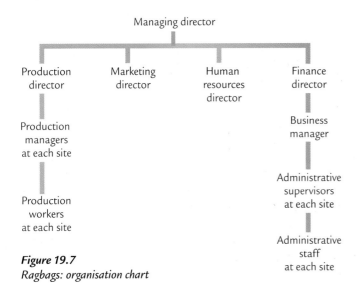

Figure 19.7
Ragbags: organisation chart

end of the month. Joe assumed that Bill had got a promotion and congratulated him on 'moving up the ladder'. Bill said that it was not a promotion, just a sideways move to another firm. Joe was worried. He reasoned that unless it is to do with their personal circumstances, most people do not move sideways to another company unless they are unhappy with their present job. Bill said: 'Quite honestly Joe, I feel that I'm kept in the dark most of the time, and I don't like it so I'm going. The staff don't like it either, but they have no way of telling you.'

Joe decided that he needed to raise this at the next day's senior management meeting. As far as he knew, none of the directors were aware of any problems — which meant the situation was even more serious.

Questions
Total: 20 marks (30 minutes)

1 Examine the communication problems facing Ragbags as it has grown from a single-site producer to a multi-site producer. *(8 marks)*

2 Discuss the possible solutions that might be discussed at the senior management meeting. *(12 marks)*

CHAPTER 20

Measuring the effectiveness of the workforce

This chapter reviews the various methods of measuring workforce performance. It focuses in particular on the calculation and interpretation of measures of labour productivity and labour turnover. It also considers absenteeism and health and safety as measures of workforce effectiveness.

Labour productivity

Calculating labour productivity

Labour productivity is calculated as follows:

$$\text{labour productivity} = \frac{\text{output per period}}{\text{number of employees per period}}$$

Calculation 1: example of a labour productivity calculation

If output in a given month is 20,000 units and 40 people are employed during that month to produce the goods, labour productivity is 500 units per worker (20,000/40).

How to increase labour productivity

Labour productivity may be increased by appropriate **human resource management** (HRM) policies such as:

- the recruitment and selection of suitably skilled and trained employees
- the provision of training to enhance skills and attitudes of existing employees
- appropriate remuneration and non-financial benefits that improve motivation and effort

Other factors that may increase labour productivity include:

- improved working practices
- improved technology and capital equipment

An increase in labour productivity means that output will be increased using the same number of employees. It also implies a lower labour cost per unit (assuming wages stay the same), which might enable the firm to charge a lower price and/or gain a higher profit margin.

KEY TERM

labour productivity: a measure of the output per worker in a given time period.

Calculation 2: example demonstrating that an increase in productivity will lead to an increase in output using the same number of employees

From calculation 1, if improved machinery or new systems are introduced that cause output to increase to 30,000 units using the same number of employees, then labour productivity increases to 750 units per worker (30,000/40).

Calculation 3: example demonstrating that an increase in productivity will lead to lower labour costs per unit

In calculation 1, if labour costs are £1,000 per worker per month, total labour costs are £40,000 per month (£1,000 × 40). The original labour cost per unit is £2 (£40,000/20,000 units).

If labour productivity increases (as in calculation 2), labour cost per unit falls to £1.33 (£40,000/30,000 units).

> **ⅇ EXAMINER'S VOICE**
>
> Many students assume that an increase in labour productivity always leads to an increase in output. This is incorrect. Output per worker (i.e. labour productivity) may have increased, but the firm may be producing the same level of output as before the increase in productivity, while employing fewer workers. Make sure that you are fully aware of the difference between the level of **production** (the total units of output) and the level of **productivity** (units of output per worker).

A business's efforts to increase productivity are likely to be more successful if it ensures that:

- employees recognise why the business needs to increase productivity — for example, because it needs to reduce costs in order to become more competitive and therefore safeguard jobs in the long term
- employees are involved in the changes
- jobs are not lost
- employees gain extra rewards as a result

Where these conditions do not apply, employees may resist attempts to increase productivity. This is particularly the case if they know that the business does not want to increase the total level of output, but simply wishes to reduce costs and maintain output at its original level. Redundancies are then likely as, given the increased productivity, the business will require fewer workers. Similarly, employees may feel that plans to increase productivity may involve a great deal of extra work on their part, and may therefore demand higher rewards. This is why negotiations of both pay and productivity deals often take place at the same time.

Conclusion

In many ways, labour productivity is the most crucial measure of all. There is a direct connection between the productivity of a workforce and the competitiveness of a firm, mainly because labour costs are such a high proportion of total costs for most companies.

FACT FILE

Other factors

It is worth noting that, as a measure of efficiency, labour productivity is really only useful when all other factors are taken into account. For example, the introduction of new machinery could lead to an increase in output, so that the same number of workers is now producing a greater amount of output. This 'increase' in labour productivity is, of course, a reflection not of a more productive or improved work-force, but rather of more productive or improved capital equipment. On the other hand, if the new machinery means that workers have retrained and acquired new skills, it could be the case that the labour force has become more effective.

TOPFOTO

Labour turnover

How to calculate the rate of labour turnover

The rate of labour turnover is calculated as follows:

$$\text{rate of labour turnover} = \frac{\text{number leaving a business over a given period}}{\text{average number employed over a given period}} \times 100$$

For example, if the average number of staff employed in a firm last year was 250 and the number of employees who left the firm last year was 10, the labour turnover would be $(10/250) \times 100 = 4\%$.

KEY TERM

labour turnover: the proportion of employees leaving a business over a period of time — usually a year.

e EXAMINER'S VOICE

The average number of employees can be calculated by adding the number of people employed at the start of the year to the number of people employed at the end of the year and dividing the total by 2. For example, if at the start of the year a firm employed 55 people and at the end it employed 47, the average number it employed over the year would be $(55 + 47)/2 = 51$.

FACT FILE

Stability index

It is important to recognise that although the labour turnover formula allows a business to keep track of the extent of its labour turnover and to benchmark (compare) its own rate with that of similar businesses, it is a rather crude measure. This is because the number of people leaving includes all leavers, even those who left involuntarily owing to dismissal, redundancy or retirement. It also makes no distinction between labour turnover that might be beneficial for the firm and that which definitely is not.

DID YOU KNOW?

The 2007 Recruitment, Retention and Turnover Survey by the Chartered Institute of Personnel and Development (CIPD) suggests that overall labour (or employee) turnover averaged just over 18%.

There is another formula that allows a firm to measure the labour turnover of its more experienced staff. This is called the stability index and is calculated as follows:

$$\text{stability index} = \frac{\text{number of leavers with more than 1 year's service}}{\text{total number of staff in post 1 year ago}} \times 100$$

Causes of high labour turnover

In general, labour turnover indicates how content the workforce is in a firm. If a company's labour turnover rate is increasing, this could be a general sign of worker unrest or dissatisfaction. The causes of labour turnover could be internal or external.

Internal factors

Factors internal to the firm include:
- ineffective leadership and management techniques
- poor communications
- wages and salaries that are lower than those being paid by firms offering comparable jobs in the area
- poor selection procedures that tend to appoint the wrong people to the wrong jobs
- boring/unchallenging jobs that lack career and developmental opportunities
- poor working conditions and unpopular working practices
- low morale and motivation as a result of the above issues

External factors

External factors include an increase in vacancies for more attractive jobs. Other jobs could be more attractive because they are more highly paid, offer better training and working conditions, are more interesting and challenging, are closer to home or offer easier transport links.

FACT FILE

Labour turnover at Euro Disney

Within 9 weeks of the opening of Euro Disney in Paris, 1,000 of the new employees appointed had left, about 50% voluntarily. Unreasonable working conditions, poor communication and lack of cultural awareness among managers were the main reasons given for the staff turnover. The rate of staff turnover at Disney World in Florida is between 200% and 300% per annum.

Problems of high labour turnover

High labour turnover may create problems for a firm, including the following:
- **High recruitment and selection costs** — to replace staff who leave. These include the administrative and management costs incurred in advertising positions, conducting interviews etc. Such costs are likely to be higher for senior management and professional positions.

- **High induction and training costs** — to ensure that new employees quickly become familiar with the practices of the business and learn the necessary skills to carry out their job effectively. This process can take a great deal of time, especially if the job requires specialised skills.
- **A need to redesign jobs** — in some industries where labour turnover is a particular problem, jobs have to be redesigned to keep them as simple as possible, so that it is easier to replace staff who leave.
- **Reduced productivity** — due to the disruption caused by skilled staff leaving and new, usually untrained, staff joining the business. This could result in loss of production or sales, especially if a worker plays an important role in the company or has key knowledge or skills that the business will find difficult to replace.
- **Low morale among existing workers** — as a result of the constant change of work colleagues and the unsettling feelings that this engenders.

Variations in labour turnover

Labour turnover varies by occupation and by industry. According to the CIPD's 2007 survey, the highest levels of turnover (over 22%) are found in private sector organisations, while the public sector has an average labour turnover rate of just under 14%. Successive CIPD surveys of labour turnover show that the highest levels are found in retailing, hotels, catering and leisure (where rates are over 30%), and among other lower-paid private sector services. In the case of hotels, catering and leisure, this high turnover is likely to be related to the fact that this sector typically employs students and seasonal workers, whose turnover is naturally higher. Labour turnover is much higher in less skilled jobs, particularly among sales and customer service occupations, where the average rate of labour turnover is just under 20%, compared with professional occupations, where it is just over 10%.

Whether such differences in rates of labour turnover matter depends to some extent on the overall impact that labour turnover has on quality, costs and the ease of recruitment. For example, in a fast-food restaurant such as McDonald's, high rates of labour turnover certainly lead to higher recruitment and training costs. However, the disruption and effect on the quality of the service have to some extent been alleviated by the fact that McDonald's jobs are designed so that the company can quickly and easily train new recruits, and because many of its staff are students and part-time workers, wages tend to be low.

How to improve labour turnover

Better human resource management (HRM) practices are needed in order to reduce rates of labour turnover. Some of the key areas where improvements may be made are as follows:

- **Monitoring and benchmarking.** Currently, many firms are either not proactive in dealing with labour turnover or unaware of its cost implications. A monitoring system that includes knowing how labour turnover in the firm compares with the industry average, tracking trends in employee turnover over time, and identifying areas, departments and roles in the firm where labour turnover is particularly high, might be useful.
- **Exit interviews.** These are useful to identify problem areas in an organisation and any characteristics that may be common to leavers who have not been with the firm for long. Issues to discuss include the job itself, supervision and management, pay and conditions of work, training and career prospects, and equal opportunities.

 FILE

How reliable are exit interviews?

According to the CIPD's 2007 Recruitment, Retention and Turnover Survey, the key reasons for labour turnover include:

- change of career
- promotion outside the organisation
- level of pay
- lack of development or career opportunities
- retirement
- redundancy

However, the CIPD suggests that the reasons people give for their resignations should be viewed carefully, as they are often only partially true. Although the use of exit interviews is widespread, they are notoriously unreliable, particularly when conducted by someone (e.g. the line manager) who may later be asked to write

a reference for the departing employee. In such instances, employees are understandably reluctant to voice criticisms of their managers, colleagues or the organisation generally, preferring to give a less contentious reason for their departure.

- **Recruitment and selection.** The amount of money spent on ensuring that recruitment and selection procedures are effective will be more than recouped by the savings made from lower labour turnover later on.
- **Induction and training.** High-quality induction training to make the new employee feel like part of the firm is as important as well-directed on-the-job training and supervision. It is important to make sure that the new employee is kept sufficiently motivated and that the work is neither unchallenging nor too demanding.
- **Reducing turnover of long-term workers.** Employees who have been with the business for a long time accumulate a huge amount of **firm-specific human capital**, i.e. knowledge and skills that are of direct relevance to the

firm. If these employees leave, their knowledge and skills also disappear, so it is vital for the firm to try to retain them. This may involve ensuring that some kind of career progression is available to them, and examining their remuneration to ensure it is not out of line with that provided by other businesses offering similar jobs.

 FILE

A missed opportunity?

A spokesman for the CIPD says that 'Most employers are completely unaware of the savings that they might achieve by reducing labour turnover further, even by just a few percentage points. There seems to be no systematic approach to stemming the losses.' At present, only about 7% of human resource departments calculate the cost of labour turnover.

Conclusion

The consequences for a firm of having a high labour turnover are usually negative. The cost of recruiting and training new staff can lead to a weaker competitive position and a fall in efficiency. Evidence suggests that, in general, most firms are either unaware of the costs of high labour turnover or do not have systems in place to monitor or deal with the problem. Better HRM practices are therefore essential.

However, it is worth noting that there is likely to be a 'natural' level of labour turnover which is unavoidable and which may vary from firm to firm. Indeed, some labour turnover may be positive in bringing new ideas, skills, talents and enthusiasm to the labour force. Labour turnover can be healthy if it enables a firm to avoid complacency and an over-reliance on tried and tested ways of working, which may make it inflexible in response to changes in its environment. It can also allow a business to reduce its workforce slowly without having to resort to redundancies — this is often referred to as **natural wastage**.

There is a clear need for a balance to be struck in relation to labour turnover. Aiming for as low a rate of labour turnover as possible is not necessarily the best approach. Knowing how and why the rate of labour turnover is changing is probably as important as the figure itself.

Absenteeism

How to calculate the rate of absenteeism

The rate of absenteeism is calculated as follows:

$$\text{rate of absenteeism} = \frac{\text{number of staff absent on 1 day}}{\text{total number of staff}} \times 100$$

For example, if 21 people out of a workforce of 300 are absent on a given day, the absentee rate is $(21/300) \times 100 = 7\%$.

 TERM

absenteeism: the proportion of employees not at work on a given day.

administering, perhaps, thousands of applications, and the time spent shortlisting, interviewing and assessing
■ the supply of labour — whether there are plenty of potential applicants with relevant skills and experience or whether there are few
■ the culture of the organisation and the extent to which this dictates that internal recruitment and promotion are the norm

Importance of effective recruitment and selection

Ineffective selection can cause increased labour turnover, which in turn leads to additional costs in terms of further advertising, interviewing and training as well as its impact on productivity and employee motivation. Effective recruitment and selection could lead to lower labour turnover, lower costs, improved productivity and more highly motivated employees.

> **DID YOU KNOW?**
>
> In its 2007 Recruitment, Retention and Turnover Survey, the CIPD suggests that the average recruitment cost of filling a vacancy per employee (including advertising costs and agency or search fees) is £4,333, increasing to £7,750 when organisations are also calculating the associated labour turnover costs (including vacancy cover, redundancy costs, recruitment/selection, training and induction costs).

PRACTICE EXERCISE 1   Total: 45 marks (40 minutes)

1 Identify the main stages in the recruitment and selection process. *(6 marks)*

2 Explain two advantages of recruiting an internal candidate for a job and two advantages of recruiting an external candidate for a job. *(12 marks)*

3 Distinguish between a job description and a person specification. *(4 marks)*

4 What is a headhunting organisation? *(3 marks)*

5 Identify and briefly explain three different methods of selecting the best individual for a job. *(9 marks)*

6 Identify and explain two factors that will influence the method of recruitment and selection used. *(6 marks)*

7 Explain the importance of effective recruitment and selection to an organisation. *(5 marks)*

CASE STUDY 1 Searching for stars on the shop floor

Staff development opportunities at Tesco are available for staff at every level. For example:
● The Options Scheme is a development programme for those identified as having the potential to do a bigger or different job. At any one time, 10% of Tesco employees are on this scheme, and in the last 3 years, 50,000 people have been through it.
● The Apprentice Scheme gives staff aged 16–24 years the experience of working in different parts of the business. Tesco's managers coach and assess

candidates and successful apprentices are awarded nationally recognised NVQs.

- Lifelong learning opportunities are available in three core areas: Basic IT, Skills for life (basic English/ maths and English for speakers of other languages) and languages.
- The Debut website, **www.tesco.com/debut**, offers online training and development, financial guidance, discounts and career advice to help 16–24-year-olds through the transition from full-time education to full-time careers.

At Tesco, managers are trained in talent spotting and are expected to have regular meetings with their staff, whose aspirations are carefully considered. They are encouraged to remember what happened when they were spotted and how they were given a chance.

'We make talent spotting an everyday activity for managers,' said a spokesperson from Tesco. 'We show people how to create the right environment for talent to flourish. We want to find the people who are going that extra mile and improving the business. It's essential in a rapidly expanding company.'

All the information that is gathered moves up layer by layer to the board, which gets a complete picture of the staffing resources available. This is matched to a forecast of staffing needs. 'If we know what we have got and what we need, we can take a broad view of where investment in people and training is needed,' said the spokesperson.

Recently when the board reviewed the projections for investment in new stores, it saw that there would be a shortfall in managers. The answer was to accelerate the development of senior team managers. Tesco selected 50 people, 38 of whom were internal

candidates, and sent them on an 8-week intensive training programme designed to fast-track employees to store-manager level. The programme covered weekend and evening work, sessions at Sandhurst military academy, leadership training and all the procedures and policies that candidates were likely to have to deal with.

Having recruited and trained good staff, Tesco wishes to retain them. In 2007 its website included the following information: 'Our retention rate for experienced staff is 84.1%, exceeding our target of 80%. We believe in "growing our own" talent: in the last 3 years we have appointed 27 directors, 200 store managers and 8,000 department managers from within Tesco. Next year, we will appoint over 3,000 new managers in the UK, and want 80% of these to be internal appointments.'

Sources: adapted from an article in the *Sunday Times*, 21 September 2003 and information on the Tesco website (**www.tesco.com**), 1 October 2007.

Questions

Total: 40 marks (50 minutes)

1 Explain Tesco's method of recruiting new store managers. *(4 marks)*

2 Analyse the benefits of Tesco's approach to meeting its staffing needs. *(9 marks)*

3 To what extent do you feel that Tesco's investment in training both of its staff in general and of its new store managers is likely to produce good results? *(12 marks)*

4 Discuss the benefits and the problems that Tesco is likely to face if it continues to recruit the majority of its senior management from within the company. *(15 marks)*

Training

KEY TERM

training: the provision of work-related education, either on-the-job or off-the-job, involving employees being taught new skills or improving skills they already have.

DID YOU KNOW?

It is useful to distinguish between training and development. Training is the process of instructing individuals about how to carry out tasks directly related to their current job. Development, on the other hand, involves helping individuals to realise their full potential. Development covers general growth and is not necessarily related specifically to employees' existing posts.

Training needs

The need for training essentially arises when the knowledge and skills required by the firm exceed or differ from those that workers currently possess. Training is often a response to some sort of change, whether internal or external. Possible changes are:

- the development and introduction of new products
- restructuring of the firm
- the development and introduction of new technology
- changes to procedure, including improvements to customer service
- high labour turnover
- low morale
- changes in legislation

Benefits of training

DID YOU KNOW?

Many business initiatives are constrained by limited finance and training is no different. Thus the broad objective of training and development is generally to ensure the best possible return on the firm's investment in people.

Training offers the following benefits:

- It helps new employees reach the level of performance expected of experienced workers.
- It ensures that employees have the necessary skills, knowledge, attributes and qualifications for the job, both at present and in the future.
- It develops a knowledgeable and committed workforce, with increased motivation and job satisfaction.
- It increases efficiency and productivity, enabling the firm to produce high-quality products and services, which may in turn lead to improved profits.
- It can identify employees' potential and thus increase employees' job prospects and chances of promotion, which may improve motivation.
- It reduces costs in the long term by, for example, reducing the number of accidents and injuries, reducing wastage and poor-quality work, and increasing workers' productivity.
- It encourages employees to deal with change more effectively and to be more flexible — for example, about the introduction of new technology.
- It encourages employees to work towards the organisation's aims and objectives.

- It improves the image of the company. Customers will have more confidence in well-trained staff, and a better image will attract more able recruits.

Induction training

The aim of induction training is to help new employees settle in quickly, in order to ensure that they reach the level of performance expected of experienced workers. It includes familiarising new recruits with the layout of the business, health and safety issues, security systems, key personnel, the hierarchical and departmental systems, the main policies of the organisation, job descriptions, the culture of the organisation, the organisation's history and development, terms of employment including disciplinary rules, employees' benefits and services, and physical facilities. In general, an effective induction programme is likely to:

- reduce labour turnover
- improve employees' understanding of both the corporate culture and the situation in which the organisation is placed
- mean that employees contribute to the organisation more quickly
- increase motivation

> **KEY TERM**
>
> **induction training:** education for new employees, which usually involves learning about the way the business works rather than about the particular job that the individual will do.

External or internal training?

External training, such as joining a college course on business management or supervisory training, is appropriate if there are only a few employees with a specific training need and if the training requirements are not specifically linked to the organisation. External training gives employees the opportunity to meet people from other organisations, allowing an interchange of ideas and a broadening of understanding. It can also make employees feel valued and increase motivation.

Internal training is appropriate if training needs are specific to the individual organisation — for example, if employees need to learn how to use a particular new computer system.

On-the-job or off-the-job training?

> **KEY TERMS**
>
> **on-the-job training:** where an employee learns a job by seeing how it is carried out by an experienced employee (also known as 'sitting by Nellie').
>
> **off-the-job training:** all forms of employee education apart from that at the immediate workplace.

On-the-job training is likely to be cheaper than off-the-job training, as existing employees and equipment can be used. Such training takes place in a realistic environment, therefore avoiding any problems in adjusting between, say, a college environment and a work situation, and there is also no loss of output. However, the quality of training depends on the ability and willingness of the

instructor, and the time available. The employee who is chosen to be an instructor might be unable to teach the proper skills, or might have developed bad habits or short-cuts that are passed on to the trainee. In addition, the work situation might be noisy and stressful, and not conducive to effective learning.

Off-the-job training may be conducted internally — for example, in a conference room — or externally, at a college. Either way, there is less immediate pressure from work. Employees might attend college during working hours through either day release or block release, or in the evening or at weekends. The training will be focused on skills, attitudes and theories that relate to work, and is likely to include generic skills and knowledge that are useful at work, rather than job-specific content.

Off-the-job training often uses specially trained experts to do the teaching. This may result in training being more highly valued by employees, leading to increased motivation. If it is also external, off-the-job training will give employees an opportunity to meet staff from other organisations and to learn about their systems. In general, it is more straightforward to estimate the costs of such training and it is easier to monitor progress. However, it can be expensive and there is a question as to whether the skills learned can be transferred effectively to the actual work environment.

 FILE

How much training?

According to the 2005 Annual Small Business Survey, 41% of businesses had provided or funded training or development, and 59% had not. Larger businesses were more likely to have offered training or development opportunities, with 77% of medium-sized businesses (those with 50 or more employees) stating this was the case. Over half of those that had provided or funded training stated that this training leads to a formal qualification (55%). Three-quarters of businesses had not provided any training or development for their business managers, to improve leadership and management skills. However, this was not the case among the largest businesses (those with 50 or more employees), where only 39% had not trained any of their business managers. Some 14% of businesses indicated that a shortage of managerial skills or expertise was an obstacle to their success.

How can training be evaluated?

Evaluation of training is reasonably easy if the outcome can be observed by, for example, the effective use of a computer system or the production of a product, but it is more difficult in relation to management training courses. In such situations, questionnaires are needed to assess people's views and perceptions before and after the course, and perhaps at a later point. In relation to customer care courses, businesses can use mystery visitors, who act as members of the public to check on how staff are responding to customers after their training. Training can also be evaluated by monitoring improvements in the quality of output, reductions in labour turnover, increases in candidates coming forward for internal promotion, and reductions in accidents, mistakes and wastage.

AQA
AS Business Studies

e **EXAMINER'S VOICE**

As with any area of business, when evaluating, weigh up the evidence and consider the context.

Training and market failure

Much has been written about the efficiency of the 'market'. This is where the forces of supply and demand operate unhindered by government interference. In the labour market, the supply of labour comes from people wanting jobs and the demand for labour comes from organisations wishing to employ people.

Market failure occurs when the interaction of supply and demand fails to allocate resources in the most efficient way or to produce goods that are wanted. Markets also fail when **externalities** such as pollution are not fully accounted for. For example, firms that pollute the atmosphere by their industrial activity fail to pay for their actions and therefore make private profit at the cost of social welfare. In these cases, it is argued that governments should intervene.

A similar analysis can be applied to training and the issue of poaching trained workers. Poaching employees means attracting workers who have already been trained by another business. If company A wants workers with particular skills that can only be acquired with training, it might attempt to poach them from company B, which has already trained its workers in that particular skill. Poaching would mean attracting workers by offering higher salaries. This saves company A the cost of the training process, but means that company B has wasted its resources in training the workers who have now left.

If done widely in an economy, poaching might lead employers to stop or reduce their training of employees. They will realise that it is pointless training employees who then leave the firm, and will consider it more cost effective to hire ready-trained staff. If those staff leave, the firm does not lose out as a result of having paid for their training.

In this way, the market leads to inefficiencies rather than efficiency, and it may be desirable for the government to intervene by, for example, providing tax incentives for organisations that train their own staff. Without some sort of government intervention, such market failure will damage the skill level and therefore the competitiveness of the workforce.

In general, research suggests that firms in the UK fail to invest sufficiently in training and development, viewing training as a cost and failing to consider the long-term benefits to the organisation and to the individual. In addition, training programmes tend to be developed in response to current problems rather than in anticipation of future knowledge and skills requirements.

CASE STUDY 2 Recruitment and training at Starbucks

Careers at Starbucks

Starbucks is a people business. This means that our success depends on your success. We know lots of companies say that, but we can only get to where we want to be with the help and support of the people we hire: our partners. They're our focus and our biggest asset. As a member of our team, you'll get opportunities to develop your skills, further your career, and plan and achieve your goals.

It doesn't stop there, though. We foster a culture of commitment to excellence, and we place a big emphasis on respect for our customers and each other, as well as a dedication to social responsibility. And we don't just say it: we do it every day.

We're looking for individuals who are driven to succeed, who bring passion, integrity, and above all a love of working with people. In addition there is the opportunity to go out and support community projects and charities. If that sounds like you, and the sort of environment you'd flourish in, get in touch with us. We're growing in new and dynamic ways, and we need the ideas and expertise that the right people can bring us.

At Starbucks, we value integrity and embrace diversity as an essential component in the way we do business. These values are reinforced by an uncompromising commitment to equal opportunities. We will not discriminate against anyone applying for a job — or while in our employ — for reasons of gender, marital status, family status, sexual orientation, religion, age, disability, race and membership of the travelling community, or for any other reason. What does this mean in practice? It means that you will always be treated in a fair and unbiased way and that your opportunities to progress will be based on merit alone.

Career paths

Retail opportunities

Do you have experience in providing outstanding customer service? We have a wide range of vacancies, from barista (bar staff) through to store manager level.

Baristas and shift supervisors

Please visit your local store to find out about local opportunities and to complete an application form. The store manager will be able to give you more information about vacancies at his/her store and in the local area.

Assistant store managers, store managers and district managers

Assistant store managers, store managers and district managers oversee the day-to-day operations of each Starbucks location. These positions offer a great career experience for professionals with previous experience in retail management. To learn more about these opportunities and provide your CV and application online, click one of the links below.

Training and education

We guide all new partners through an extensive orientation and fundamental training programme to provide a solid foundation for career advancement at Starbucks. Some of our educational programmes are:

- **Coffee education.** A course focusing on the Starbucks passion for coffee and understanding our core product.
- **Learning to lead.** A three-level programme for baristas to develop leadership skills. The programme also includes store operational and effective management practice training.
- **Business and communication.** The Starbucks Support Centre (SSC) offers a variety of classes ranging from basic computer skills to conflict resolution, to management training.

Total pay (compensation, stock, benefits and savings)

Starbucks' total pay package is referred to as 'Your Special Blend' because it is unique to each partner. Partners who work full time or part time (20 hours or more per week) may participate in a variety of programmes, and make choices based on individual needs and interests.

Depending on the job and personal situation, a partner's total pay package may include:

- healthcare benefits (medical, prescription drugs, dental and vision)
- retirement savings plan
- referral programmes and support resources for child and eldercare
- discounted Starbucks merchandise

And, of course, all partners get a pound of coffee each week.

Source: Starbucks website (**www.starbucks.com**), 1 October 2007

Questions

Total: 40 marks (50 minutes)

1 Explain the likely benefits to Starbucks of its induction ('orientation') training programme. *(4 marks)*

2 Analyse the possible reasons for differences between the recruitment process for a new barista and a new store manager at Starbucks. *(9 marks)*

3 The information provided here is available on the Starbucks website. Discuss how effective the internet is likely to be as a medium for advertising jobs and recruiting staff, compared with more traditional sources. *(12 marks)*

4 Discuss the differences between the types of training that would be most appropriate for developing the effectiveness of a barista and a new store manager at Starbucks. *(15 marks)*

CHAPTER 22

Developing and retaining an effective workforce: motivating employees

This chapter explains various theories that can be used when considering the influences on workforce motivation and the strategies that might be used to motivate employees. Strategies include financial methods, improving job design by enrichment and enlargement, empowering employees and working in teams. Finally, the link between organisational structure and the motivational techniques available to managers is considered.

Theories of motivation

Scientific management and F. W. Taylor

F. W. Taylor (1856–1915) was a US engineer who invented **work-study** and founded the scientific approach to management. He considered money to be the main factor that motivated workers, so he emphasised the benefits of **piecework**, where workers are paid according to how much they produce. He argued that piecework provided high rewards for hard work, benefiting both the worker and the business.

The principles of **scientific management** were laid down in Taylor's book *The Principles of Scientific Management*, originally published in 1911. In it he stressed the duty of management to organise work, using the principles of **specialisation** and the **division of labour**, so as to maximise efficiency. According to Taylor, this was to be achieved by 'objective laws' based on 'science' that management and workers could agree upon. This in turn would reduce conflict between management and workers since, as he saw it, there could be no disagreement about laws based on 'science'.

Taylor believed that the following three methods are the main ways of improving productivity and efficiency:

- **Extreme division of labour**, where a job is broken down into small, repetitive tasks, each of which can be done at speed and with little training. By specialising in a particular task, individuals can quickly become expert at their job, leading to increased productivity.
- **Payment by piecework**, which means payment by results (i.e. payment per item produced). It provides an incentive to work hard but can encourage staff to concentrate on quantity at the expense of quality.

- **Tight management control**, which ensures that workers concentrate on their jobs and follow the correct processes.

Taylor's methods had considerable influence on business, most famously on the **mass production** processes introduced at the Ford Motor Company. However, his influence on the workforce was less successful. Extreme division of labour meant that jobs became more boring and repetitive. The lack of skills needed by workers also led to a loss of power for individual workers. This led to low morale and poor industrial relations, and had some influence on the growth of trade unions.

DID YOU KNOW?

Work-study is the measurement and timing of work processes in order to identify the best method and the most realistic output targets. First, a work-study consultant (or 'time and motion' person) would observe people at work and note down the different actions of which the job was made up, and the sequence of these actions. Then the consultant would assess this to determine whether it was the most efficient method. Each action would then be timed, and the motion and the effort used noted down. The presence of 'time and motion men' quickly became a cause of industrial relations disputes.

To an extent, Taylor saw human beings as machines with financial needs. No account was taken of individual differences or the fact that the approach determined by the time and motion study might not suit everyone. Ideas have moved on considerably since then. Money is obviously vital, but research has suggested consistently that financial rewards alone are not sufficient to create job satisfaction or to improve motivation and productivity.

The human relations school and Elton Mayo

Elton Mayo (1880–1949) was a follower of F. W. Taylor, but his experiments led him to conclude that scientific management could not explain important

aspects of people's behaviour in the workplace. Many of his findings, including the 'Hawthorne effect', came from research he did at the Western Electric factory in Hawthorne, USA, and provided the foundations for the human relations school of management.

Mayo's early research involved trying to measure the impact on productivity of improving the lighting conditions in the Western Electric factory. He followed Taylor's scientific principles by testing the changes in lighting conditions for one group of workers against a control group of workers who worked in a section of the factory with unchanged lighting. Productivity rose in the area where the lighting was improved but, surprisingly, productivity also rose, and by a similar amount, in the area with unchanged lighting.

The results of further experiments conducted by Mayo brought into question Taylor's assumptions about the importance of money in motivating employees, and instead emphasised the importance of **human relations** in the workplace. Mayo's findings suggested the following:

■ Recognition, belonging and security are more important in motivating employees than simply money and working conditions.

■ Work is a group-based activity and employees should be seen as members of a group.

■ Managers need to pay attention to individuals' social needs and the influence of the informal groups to which they belong, since these groups exert significant influence over an individual's attitudes.

■ Managers must communicate with informal groups, ensuring that their goals are in tune with those of the organisation. This could occur by, for example, allowing them to become part of the decision-making process, which would in turn improve worker commitment and loyalty.

■ Increases in output are due to greater communication and improved relations in informal groups.

Important developments resulted from Mayo and the human relations school. These included the introduction of social facilities at work, such as canteens and sports clubs, the appointment of personnel officers whose responsibility was the welfare of employees, and an increase in the quantity and quality of communication and consultation taking place between management and employees.

Figure 22.1 Maslow's hierarchy of needs

Maslow's hierarchy of human needs

Abraham Maslow (1908–70) was a US psychologist whose work on human needs has had a major influence on management thinking. His **hierarchy of needs** suggests that people have similar types of need, which can be classified into a hierarchy. Needs range from lower-level ones, such as the need for food, clothing and shelter, to higher-level ones, such as the need for achievement and self-esteem.

Self-actualisation

Esteem

Social

Safety

Physiological

Maslow's five categories of need, as indicated in Figure 22.1, are as follows:

- **Physiological needs:** the requirements for food, clothes and shelter. In relation to work, this means the need to earn an income in order to acquire these things and have reasonable working conditions.
- **Safety needs:** the need for security and freedom from danger and anxiety. In relation to work, this means the need to have a secure job, a safe working environment, adequate pension arrangements and clear lines of accountability in relation to responsibilities.
- **Social needs:** the desire for friendship, love and a sense of belonging. In relation to work, this means being part of a team, getting along with workmates, and being provided with social facilities such as staff rooms and canteens.
- **Esteem needs:** the need to have self-respect and respect from others. In relation to work, this means the need to receive positive feedback, to gain recognition and status for achievement, and to have opportunities for promotion.
- **Self-actualisation:** the need to fulfil one's potential through actions and achievements. Maslow did not believe that this need could be satisfied fully and thought that people would always strive to develop further and achieve more.

Maslow believed that an unsatisfied need was a motivator of behaviour and that, while it remained unsatisfied, higher-level needs were unimportant. He therefore believed that, starting from the bottom of the hierarchy, each level of need had to be fulfilled before the next level became important. However, once satisfied, a particular level ceased to be important and the next level of unsatisfied need became a motivator.

This theory is intuitively appealing but it can be criticised. In relation to work, it is true that if people have insufficient income to enjoy adequate food, clothing and shelter, they are unlikely to be overly influenced by whether a job is permanent, whether it has good pension arrangements or whether their workmates make them feel welcome. However, once people satisfy their physiological and safety needs, it is questionable whether, for all individuals, social needs come before esteem needs. Many individuals are high achievers and are motivated by this, sometimes to the exclusion of any desire to be part of a team or to get along with their colleagues.

DID YOU KNOW?

Maslow's social needs are similar to the issues raised by Mayo's work and the human relations school.

Needs as motivators

Herzberg's and Maslow's views about needs being the main driving force are similar. Herzberg's motivators correspond with Maslow's higher-level needs, while his hygiene factors correspond with Maslow's lower-level needs. Figure 22.2 demonstrates the link between the two theories.

Figure 22.2 *Links between Herzberg's and Maslow's theories of motivation*

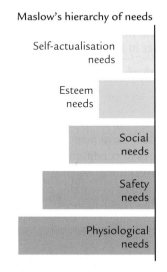
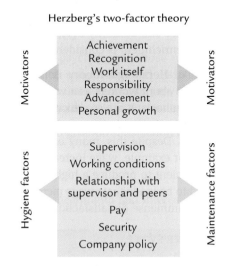

How useful are theories of motivation?

The answer to this question depends on the particular work situation being considered. A traditional manufacturing organisation with a fairly authoritarian approach, a tall hierarchy and routine and monotonous work, may find that money is a great motivator, allowing people to enjoy their social life and home comforts. This supports Taylor's view of what motivates people. It is also likely that in this situation Mayo's informal group influences and Maslow's social needs are important to the worker. Ensuring that Herzberg's hygiene or maintenance factors are appropriate will also be vital to avoid dissatisfaction.

However, in an organisation that employs large numbers of well-educated people with high-level skills, expectations are higher and jobs are more complex. Although rates of pay and working conditions are vital, workers expect more recognition, autonomy, involvement in decision making and empowerment. In other words, they are influenced by Maslow's higher-level needs and Herzberg's motivators are important.

> **EXAMINER'S VOICE**
>
> When you are evaluating, make sure that your conclusion is consistent with the evidence that you have presented and show why it is a natural conclusion from your arguments.

PRACTICE EXERCISE 1   **Total: 50 marks (40 minutes)**

1 Briefly explain the views of F. W. Taylor and the scientific management school of thought.   *(6 marks)*

2 Outline the main problems with these views in relation to motivating employees.   *(6 marks)*

3 What is the 'Hawthorne effect'?   *(4 marks)*

4 Briefly explain the views of Elton Mayo and the human relations school of management. *(6 marks)*

5 Identify and explain the various levels of Maslow's hierarchy of human needs. *(10 marks)*

6 Explain the relevance of Maslow's hierarchy of human needs in a work context. *(6 marks)*

7 Identify four of Herzberg's motivators. *(4 marks)*

8 Identify four of Herzberg's maintenance or hygiene factors. *(4 marks)*

9 Distinguish between the effect of Herzberg's motivators and that of his maintenance or hygiene factors on the motivation of employees. *(4 marks)*

CASE STUDY 1 Herzberg, Maslow and teachers

Despite the huge success of Herzberg's theory, there have been major criticisms of his research. These centre on the fact that the research took place in 1959 and covered a relatively small group of 200 accountants and engineers. A number of studies have tried to replicate the results, usually unsuccessfully.

One example concerned research with US teachers in primary and secondary schools. The findings from this research suggested that in relation to Herzberg's main motivators, achievement ranked as the most important. However, the overall conclusion drawn from the research was that salary was the single most important influence on motivation and satisfaction at work, and that the teachers in the study perceived the amount of salary increase they received to be tied to achievement and the other motivators.

In relation to Maslow's hierarchy of needs, it appeared that the teachers in the study were less satisfied with their personal achievement of esteem (i.e. their self-respect and the respect they earned from others) than with their achievement of self-actualisation (i.e. fulfilling their potential). The research

concluded that fulfilling one's potential (self-actualisation) might provide the basis for self-respect and gaining the respect of others.

The research went on to suggest that this might explain why good teachers were leaving education and moving to other, higher-paying occupations, but also suggested that managers in schools should focus more closely on the esteem needs of teachers.

Questions

Total: 25 marks (30 minutes)

1 This passage shows how theories can always be challenged. Identify and explain other problems with the theories of Herzberg and Maslow, using examples from real organisations wherever possible. *(10 marks)*

2 Discuss how the 'esteem needs of teachers' in schools could be met more effectively by senior managers. *(15 marks)*

CASE STUDY 2 Taylor Wimpey plc

In July 2007, Taylor Woodrow plc merged with George Wimpey plc to form the construction company Taylor Wimpey plc. The following information is adapted from Taylor Wimpey's website.

We want to ensure that our business and employees meet the highest standards of personal and professional conduct. So we respect our customers, our suppliers and each other. As a team, we strive to exceed both our own and others' expectations — and by winning their confidence, we earn their trust. We all share in our commitment to perform and get things done. We do what it takes to deliver the best service to all our customers — within the organisation as well as outside it.

Taylor Wimpey strives to be an attractive company for talented and motivated people in which high levels of personal and company performance are recognised. As a business, we are putting in place initiatives for ensuring an effective working environment and efficient working arrangements, creating personal development opportunities, and promoting a challenging and fulfilling working life. We offer one of the most competitive and attractive remuneration and rewards packages available in our business sector.

We support our people to achieve their potential, and they support us to achieve ours. That is the simple belief that drives our commitment to training and development. Meeting regularly with your manager, you will have the opportunity to discuss your training needs and personal aspirations. Then we will create a tailored training plan that will best meet your needs. For all new employees, we provide a full induction to help you quickly build an understanding of Taylor Wimpey as a business and how we work.

Some skilled tradespeople, such as bricklayers and plumbers, are employed by Taylor Wimpey. However, many are brought in on short-term contracts from other firms while buildings are being erected. Taylor Wimpey encourages internal promotion for staff such as engineers, surveyors and architects, who can become managers.

Performance of the workforce is judged at three levels: individual workers, teams and the organisation as a whole. Individuals are set targets that they agree with their manager. This process also includes discussion of the employee's needs and ambitions. Twice a year, performance is measured against an agreed standard. Salaries and bonus payments are then decided in accordance with the individual's performance. This system of performance-related pay is popular with the workers, who prefer the fairness of a system that is not decided arbitrarily by a manager. Part of the annual pay award is linked to the overall success of the business. The system is designed to encourage all staff to seek responsibility, and employees are encouraged to contribute ideas that will improve the company's efficiency.

Source: adapted from **www.taylorwimpey.com** (30 September 2007).

Questions
Total: 50 marks (60 minutes)

1 Identify and explain why an effective induction and training programme might have a positive influence on the level of motivation of employees. *(6 marks)*

2 Identify and explain one aspect of Taylor Wimpey's approach that corresponds to the ideas of F. W. Taylor. *(6 marks)*

3 Select any one theory of motivation (except that of F. W. Taylor) and discuss the degree to which Taylor Wimpey appears to be using the ideas of that theorist. *(15 marks)*

4 Analyse two benefits that Taylor Wimpey might receive from improving the motivation of its workforce. *(8 marks)*

5 In house building and construction, many of the workers involved in a building project are not employees of the company, but are subcontracted. This means that they are used by the company for a set period of time in order to complete a particular project. To what extent does this make these workers more difficult for Taylor Wimpey to motivate than its own full-time staff? *(15 marks)*

Using financial methods to motivate employees

A range of different financial methods can be used to motivate employees, including time rates, piece rates, performance-related pay schemes, profit-sharing schemes, share ownership and share options schemes, and fringe benefits.

Time rates

Salary and wage payment systems are time-based payment systems. Wages are normally paid weekly and are based on an hourly rate. Salaries are normally paid monthly and are based on an annual rate. Salaries, in particular, are used where it is difficult or impossible to measure work output, and where tasks are complex and involved. Thus payment by time is in a sense a payment for input rather than output. For example, sales assistants in a supermarket are paid a weekly wage for the hours they work, not for the number of goods they sell. Bank tellers are paid a monthly salary; they are not paid on the basis of the number of customers they serve.

Of course, this means that effort is not guaranteed because staff could waste time. However, appraisal and supervision procedures, the need to achieve targets or simply completing the responsibilities of the job can act as a sufficient check. The security provided by time rates may motivate workers, according to Maslow's hierarchy of needs.

Piecework

Paying workers a rate for each item produced is an attractive way of providing them with an incentive to work hard. However, it can cause the following problems:

- It may encourage staff to concentrate on quantity at the expense of quality in order to boost their pay. To some extent, a piece-rate system can reduce the supervision needed to keep workers on task, but greater levels of scrap and reduced focus on quality can cancel this out and simply add to costs.

> **KEY TERM**
>
> **piecework (or piece rates):** payment based on the number of items each worker produces.

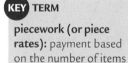

> **DID YOU KNOW?**
>
> Sometimes workers are paid a small, fixed amount of basic pay, which gives some security, and then a piece rate, which gives them the incentive to increase productivity.

- It may mean that the firm's output is heavily influenced by workers' needs rather than customer demand. For example, evidence suggests that piece-rate workers speed up in July and again in December in order to boost their earnings for the summer and Christmas holidays, even though this may not coincide with customer demand patterns.
- Herzberg considered that this type of reward system would reinforce behaviour, with repetitive tasks being emphasised and linked to pay. In this way, piece-rate systems are likely to increase resistance to change because change will tend to slow production in the short term.
- Herzberg also suggested that incentive systems such as piece rates and bonuses are the most ineffective way to reward staff, since such systems do not change an employee's commitment or attitude to work, but simply, and temporarily, change what the worker does (i.e. they cause movement, not motivation).

Performance-related pay

Under a system of performance-related pay (PRP), an employee performing well above average might get a 5% pay rise, while average achievers get only 2%. PRP is usually employed in situations where piece-rate systems are not appropriate because the work cannot be measured in a precise way. Decisions on PRP usually take place following an appraisal that assesses performance and the extent to which individual targets have been met.

There are a number of advantages of using a system of PRP:
- There are direct links between pay and effort.
- It may lead to a reduction in costs as a result of lower levels of supervision, an increase in productivity and an improvement in quality.
- There may be improvements in motivation and a possible reduction in labour turnover and absenteeism.
- It is a useful system for getting staff to work towards company objectives by establishing individual targets at appraisal that are linked to corporate objectives.

However, there are some serious disadvantages:
- It may become a source of conflict among staff who are receiving different bonuses for what they perceive to be the same effort.
- The effect on motivation is debatable because PRP usually represents only a small proportion of salary.
- An important question is how performance can be measured, since PRP is often introduced into occupations where it is difficult to measure performance objectively.
- It can reduce the influence of trade unions and of collective bargaining, as decisions on pay are related to individuals.

Managers often favour PRP because they see it as a means of providing an incentive for staff to improve their performance and commitment, and as a

FILE

Performance-related pay at Lloyds TSB

The 65,000-strong workforce at Lloyds TSB, one of the UK's top four high-street banks, can expect additional financial rewards if they perform well — and the linking of performance with pay has not damaged their view of the company. Tim Fevyer, head of rewards, compensation and benefits for the group, said that in a recent anonymous survey 84% of the bank's employees saw the organisation as a positive place to work.

At Lloyds TSB the way an individual is paid is a mixture of a rate for their ongoing performance —

which reflects what they are worth in the overall marketplace and their competence over time — together with their shorter-term performance, which is assessed against targets agreed with their line manager. Line managers also agree how they can help individuals to attain and exceed these targets. This addresses one of the fears about performance-related rewards — anxiety felt by employees that they are being thrust into direct competition with their colleagues. At Lloyds TSB, employees are competing against their own self-defined objectives.

Source: adapted from Kelleher, J. (2007) 'Bonus plans "add to job satisfaction"', *Sunday Times*, 9 September.

useful control mechanism. PRP is also used extensively to reward senior management and chief executive officers. However, there is little research evidence to support the benefits claimed for PRP as a system for rewarding individuals, and more emphasis is now put on group PRP.

Profit sharing

By relating employees' rewards directly to the performance of the company, profit sharing puts workers in a similar position to shareholders, linking them more firmly to company objectives and avoiding the individualistic approach of PRP systems.

Profit sharing has a number of advantages:

- It may help to reduce problems related to a feeling of 'them and us' between employees and management or shareholders.
- It may lessen resistance to change because the focus is on the profits of the whole organisation rather than an individual's job performance. Financial rewards only result if the organisation as a whole does well.
- If the profit share is large enough, it can provide staff with a personal incentive to keep costs down and productivity up in order to improve profits. For example, at John Lewis, the profit share has at times been over 20% of annual salary.

Problems with profit sharing include the following:

- Unless the profit share amounts to a reasonable proportion of salary, employees are unlikely to consider it a significant incentive and hence it will have little or no effect on motivation and behaviour.
- As it is not linked to individual performance, it might encourage the **free-rider problem**, where certain workers put in less effort, knowing that all employees receive the same rewards.
- Rewards fluctuate with the performance of the company and this can cause uncertainty in financial planning if employees come to depend on them.

 TERM

profit sharing (or profit-related bonuses): a financial incentive in which a proportion of a firm's profit is divided among its employees in the form of a bonus paid in addition to an employee's salary.

DID YOU KNOW?

Research evidence has shown that profit sharing, on its own, has little effect on performance, partly because individuals cannot believe that their own efforts will make a significant difference to the firm's profit level.

■ Large payouts from profits may affect both shareholder dividends and profit retained for investment, with adverse consequences for the firm.

Senior management and chief executive officers are usually given bonuses that depend on profits or other measures of company performance. However, these are normally given as a form of performance-related pay. The assumption is that the performance of these individuals is considered a major influence on company profits and performance.

 FILE

Bacardi-Martini

With a history dating back to 1862, the world's largest rum company has a huge portfolio of familiar brands in the UK, including Bacardi rums, Martini, Bombay Sapphire gin and Bacardi Breezers. In the UK alone, the firm boasts pre-tax profits of more than £16 million.

The Southampton-based firm has a low staff turnover: in the past year, just 38 of the 253-strong workforce left the UK organisation and 16 of those transferred abroad to other divisions within the Bacardi-Martini empire.

The company has developed its own coaching programme, which celebrates the uniqueness of each individual and provides everyone with the opportunity to contribute creatively to the success of the organisation. Furthermore, of the 21 senior managers in the UK operation, 15 were internal appointments, including John Bear, the chief executive, who has been with the business for

22 years. Consequently, employees feel the company is good for their personal growth and say their work is stimulating.

Employees can expect performance-related pay, profit-related pay, free private healthcare for themselves and their families, and childcare vouchers. Maternity pay and leave are well above the statutory minimum, with 18 weeks at full pay. The company offers a variety of flexible working options including job sharing, home working, compressed working hours, reduced hours and flexitime. It also supplies employees with laptops, BlackBerrys and mobile phones to support them in these working patterns.

'We are a family business,' a company spokesman said. 'Our culture embraces not just our employees but also their families. We aim to manage our people as successfully as we manage our brand. Our employees are ambassadors for our company and everyone can make a difference.'

Source: adapted from *The Sunday Times 100 Best Companies to Work For*, 2007.

Share ownership and share options

Share ownership is a means of encouraging workers and managers to identify more directly with company objectives, recognising that their rewards — share value and dividends — are dependent on company performance.

KEY TERMS

share ownership: in this context, a financial incentive whereby companies give shares to their employees or sell them at favourable rates below the market price.

share options: a financial incentive in which chief executives and senior management are given the choice of buying a fixed number of shares at a fixed price, by a given date.

Share options are offered extensively to senior management. As an incentive, chief executives and senior management are often given the option to purchase a fixed number of shares, at a fixed price, by a given date. If the price of the shares on the stock exchange rises above this price, it would be in the individual's interest to buy the shares at the fixed price and sell them at the market price.

Example

As an incentive bonus, in January 2008, Susan Levitt was given a share option by her employer ABC plc, to buy 1,000 shares at £1.20 per share, the share option to be available until January 2010. In January 2008, the shares were trading at £1.00. Susan decided not to take up the share option at that time, as she would be paying more for the shares than they were worth on the market. Since then the company has performed well and shares are now (September 2008) trading at £3.00 per share. Susan decides to take up the share option, buying the 1,000 shares at £1.20 each and then immediately selling them on the stock market for £3.00 each. Susan has therefore paid £1,200 for the shares and sold them for £3,000, making a profit of £1,800 on the deal. If she held the share option until January 2010, she would have to buy the shares for £1,200, regardless of their market value, or forgo the option.

The benefit of share options is that they are believed to provide senior management with the incentive to perform at their very best. However, there are some problems:

- Some people suggest that it is likely to lead to short-termism, i.e. a focus on improving performance when the share option is due, in order to make a profit from the sale of shares, rather than a long-term commitment to improved performance.
- A criticism that has been prominent in the press is that share options can lead to excessive financial rewards in the boardroom, when the workforce may deserve just as much credit as the directors.

 FILE

Share options at M&S

Stuart Rose, chief executive at Marks and Spencer, has nearly doubled his year-end bonus to £2.6 million after returning the once struggling retailer to health. The M&S boss earned a total of £3.6 million for the year, including a £1 million salary, which increased in January from £950,000. His bumper bonus is equal to 250% of his basic pay and he was also awarded 594,395 share options potentially worth £4.2 million, based on the company reaching a target share price of 706.6p. This adds to Rose's existing share option awards, worth in total

£4.6 million based on today's share price of 670p. The share price is up 73.6% since he first joined the company in mid-2004, when M&S shares were trading at around 380p. The first tranche of Rose's share options will become available for sale next month. Last year, Rose was entitled to a bonus of 150% of his basic salary, which added £1.4 million to his final £2.3 million pay packet. In its recent full-year results, Rose revealed a 28.5% rise in pre-tax profits to £965.2 million as sales increased by 10.1% to £8.6 billion.

Source: www.scotsman.com (8 June 2007).

KEY TERM

fringe benefits: benefits received by employees in addition to their wages or salary.

WHAT DO YOU THINK?

In relation to the fact file about Stuart Rose at Marks and Spencer, interesting questions to consider include:
- Can any one individual make such a difference to the performance of a company as to justify such huge bonuses?
- What is the likely impact of such bonuses on the workforce, who in comparison receive modest bonuses, if any?

Fringe benefits

Fringe benefits are a way of rewarding employees without actually increasing their wage or salary. Common fringe benefits include discounts when buying the firm's products, subsidised meals, the provision of sports facilities, a company pension scheme, a company car and private medical insurance.

These benefits add to the cost of employing labour, but are expected to pay for themselves by encouraging staff loyalty and commitment, and also by reducing labour turnover. Substantial fringe benefits are more common at senior management level, which in turn leads to conflict between workers and management.

Money as a motivator

Is money a major motivator? It is obviously important, but most evidence suggests that it does not motivate people particularly well in the long term. Ask yourself why so many wealthy people continue to work when financially they have no need to. Perhaps their reasons are related to Maslow's self-esteem and self-actualisation needs.

Money as a motivator can also lead to serious problems for both individuals and organisations:

■ Rewards fluctuate with the performance of the company and this can cause uncertainty in financial planning if employees come to depend upon rewards.

■ If financial incentives are high and based firmly on quantity, quality may be sacrificed in the drive to produce or sell more, with serious long-term consequences for organisations. This is easy to understand in a manufacturing situation where actual products are being made, but it is also apparent in the service sector. For example, the substantial monetary incentives provided to salespeople in the financial services sector (pensions, mortgages and insurance) to encourage them to increase the sales of these products has resulted in customers finding, years later, that they had been sold inappropriate products for their particular needs and had as a consequence lost large amounts of money. Complaints have been made to the ombudsman over the misselling of pensions, mortgages and insurance by financial services companies, resulting in huge customer relations problems that have seriously affected their reputations.

■ If rewards are based on individual performance, it can cause conflict between employees, especially where an individual employee's contribution cannot be measured objectively and employees are doing the same job.

There are, however, several reasons why financial incentives are used:
■ Firms want to overcome or at least reduce resistance to change. By paying bonuses to those who retrain or learn new systems, a firm is likely to be able to implement change more easily.
■ Many managers still see money as a major means of control.
■ Firms are looking to meet short-term goals, and financial rewards are successful at encouraging what Herzberg termed 'movement'.

 FILE

Staff motivation at Whitbread

'Happy employees mean happy customers,' says Alan Parker, chief executive of Whitbread, the hospitality company which owns brands such as Costa Coffee, Premier Travel Inn and David Lloyd Leisure. 'The company encourages everyone to have as much responsibility as possible. This helps staff to feel fully involved and to believe they can make a valuable contribution to its success.'

Staff have strong relationships with their managers and talk openly and honestly with them. Teams pull together to achieve their targets and go out of their way to help each other. Consistently strong performances are rewarded, with managers and staff receiving bonuses if their unit is performing well. Annual awards carry prizes such as a long weekend in Dubai. Benefits can be brand specific: for example, David Lloyd Leisure employees are given free membership for themselves and a friend. Whitbread gives all those who have 3 months' service a 25% discount card to use across the brands. Staff can also join the 'share save' scheme, allowing them to save up to £250 a month for 3 or 5 years. After this period, the money is converted into Whitbread shares at the price they were when the saving began. Considerable increases in share value mean employees have recently been reaping handsome rewards.

Source: adapted from *The Sunday Times 100 Best Companies to Work For*, 2007.

---

e EXAMINER'S VOICE

Try to consider the reasons for wanting to motivate staff. Is it to increase production or is it to improve job satisfaction? Remember Herzberg said that 'A reward once given becomes a right', meaning that employees can get used to financial rewards and take them for granted.

PRACTICE EXERCISE 2   Total: 50 marks (40 minutes)

1 Explain what 'time rates' are and why they are usually used to pay clerical and administrative workers. *(6 marks)*

2 Explain the meaning of 'piece rates' (piecework). *(3 marks)*

3 Identify and explain two problems a business might encounter as a result of using piece rates to pay its employees. *(6 marks)*

4 Explain the term 'performance-related pay'. *(3 marks)*

5 Briefly explain two advantages and two disadvantages to a business of using performance-related pay. *(8 marks)*

6 Identify and explain one advantage and one disadvantage to a business of using a system of profit sharing to reward employees. *(6 marks)*

7 Identify and explain one advantage and one disadvantage to a business of using share ownership as a means of providing financial incentives for employees. *(6 marks)*

8 What is a share option? *(3 marks)*

9 State three examples of fringe benefits that a business might offer its employees. *(3 marks)*

10 Explain two problems that might result from using financial incentives to motivate employees. *(6 marks)*

CASE STUDY 3   TGI Friday's

TGI Friday's began as a 1960s New York singles bar. It was expanded by Dallas-based Carlson Restaurants and opened in the UK in 1985 after the franchise was bought by Whitbread.

The corporate identity is strictly enforced: kitchen staff replicate pictured dishes, every outlet has a US diner look, and Jan Dalton, a typical manager, who works at the Kingston-upon-Thames branch, aims 'to create a consistent, good-value meal and great experience every time'. Four out of five staff feel that they contribute to the firm's success. They wear efforts on their sleeves, with metal pins given for meeting the company values of balance, enjoyment, excellence and integrity. 'People respond to a bit of personal recognition. They might joke about it, but they all wear them,' says Dalton.

Managers have the independence to set up their own reward schemes, offering free beer or a weekend's use of their company car, and 68% of staff think they have good benefits compared with other companies in the industry.

Salary is tied in with tests. Pay for many hovers around the minimum wage, but bar staff can almost double their pay by passing tests to join the elite '100 club' for top-grade bartenders. Waiters keep tips, which can be significant, sharing a proportion with cleaners and kitchen staff. There is an emphasis on internal promotion. The firm offers a 'share save' scheme and a buy-four-shares-get-one-free scheme (25% of staff own shares). Other benefits include financial assistance with healthcare, insurance and education.

Source: adapted from **www.tgifridays.com** and *The Sunday Times 100 Best Companies to Work For*, March 2003.

Question   15 marks (20 minutes)

To what extent do TGI Friday's motivational techniques depend on financial incentives and how might you judge how effective they are?

CASE STUDY 4 Richer Sounds: 'all singing from the same hymn book'

Making work fun is a concept that the UK's largest hi-fi retailer, Richer Sounds, takes very seriously, according to Julie Abraham, its stock control director. 'I spent 4 years with IBM, where everybody did everything "properly". I came here, and people wear jeans and shorts in the summer. I wasn't sure if it was going to work for me but you just get hooked.' Julian Richer, the founder and chairman, was 19 when he opened his first store in 1978. He now has more than 50, as well as mail order and internet services. The Richer approach aims to achieve unparalleled customer service through highly motivated staff (or colleagues, as they are known).

Although the company has changed dramatically over the years, Richer still maintains a presence and ensures that his employees are kept motivated. 'We all know what we're working for and how our work fits in,' says Lol Lecanu, the marketing manager. 'Everybody is singing from the same hymn book, and the company made me understand my role and how I have an impact on the company.'

Communication is excellent, with all staff having ample opportunity to give feedback at seminars, suggestion meetings and branch dinners. Teresa Chapman, Richer's personal assistant, says: 'You can speak to people at all levels. If anyone wants to see Julian, he'll see them as soon as he can. That's policy.' The business has a very open communications policy to ensure there is always awareness and discussion among colleagues. Results and performance of stores and of individuals, for example, are regularly measured and examined. This means that colleagues are very much aware of how they are performing and that their efforts are being noticed.

Salaries are high for the retail industry and the perks are also impressive: the loan of holiday homes in locations such as St Tropez and Venice; trips in the company jet; free massages, facials and pedicures at Christmas. There is even a take-your-pet-to-work scheme.

Colleagues are encouraged to take on new responsibilities, and promotion from within is the norm; the majority of head office staff have worked on the shop floor. 'The beauty of Richer Sounds is that it is willing to recognise people's potential, and allow them to develop into a role that they may not have previously considered,' says Lecanu.

When it comes to motivating staff, Richer is a great believer in measuring performance and then recognising and rewarding achievement. All customers, for example, are asked to rate the quality of the service they have received; salespeople who are rated 'excellent' receive a bonus, while those rated 'poor' are penalised. Each colleague's rating is measured regularly and performance is discussed. Colleagues are also encouraged to contribute to the suggestions scheme, which has a cash bonus for each idea. It has been remarkably successful, producing on average 20 suggestions a year from each employee.

The results of the approach taken by Richer Sounds are impressive: as well as its incredibly high sales per square foot, Richer Sounds has extremely low rates of labour turnover and absenteeism.

Sources: adapted from www.richerstudentzone.co.uk; *The Sunday Times 100 Best Companies to Work For*, 2 March 2003; and Gillespie, A. (1998) 'On the Richer scale', *Business Review*, Vol. 5, No. 2.

Questions
Total: 50 marks (60 minutes)

1 Identify and explain two types of financial incentive used by Richer Sounds to motivate its workforce. *(6 marks)*

2 Identify and explain two non-financial incentives used by Richer Sounds to motivate its workforce. *(6 marks)*

3 Analyse possible advantages and disadvantages of giving managers the independence to set up their own reward scheme. *(8 marks)*

4 Salaries at Richer Sounds are relatively high for the retail industry. Evaluate the extent to which this is what motivates its staff. *(15 marks)*

5 Discuss whether it is easier to motivate workers with financial incentives in the short term rather than in the longer term. *(15 marks)*

Non-financial methods of motivating employees

Job enrichment

Herzberg suggested that only job enrichment is likely to provide long-term job satisfaction. An enriched job should ideally:

- introduce new and more difficult tasks and challenges at different ability levels, some of which might be beyond the employee's experience to date
- give individuals a complete unit of work — in other words, a meaningful task rather than a repetitive part of a larger process, as advocated by Taylor
- provide regular feedback on performance so that the employee knows immediately how well he or she is performing
- remove some of the controls over the employee while retaining accountability
- increase the accountability of the individual for his or her own work

Such systems have been introduced into many manufacturing organisations, most famously Volvo, Honda and Toyota, all of which completely reorganised their factories so that groups of workers could take charge of producing complete units of work and then check the quality of their own work. Not only did this give workers opportunities to satisfy their social needs, but also, as they were able to manage their own time and work, they had autonomy and responsibility for decision making.

The advantages of job enrichment include the following:

- It develops workers' unused skills and presents them with challenges.
- It allows workers to make greater contributions to the decision-making process.
- It enhances workers' promotional prospects.
- It motivates workers by ensuring that their abilities and potential are exploited, and that individuals gain a high degree of self-control over the setting of goals and the identification of how to achieve those goals.

However, job enrichment has the following problems:

- Although many workers will relish the challenges, others might find the whole process intimidating and may simply feel that it places additional pressure on them that they do not want.
- It could be seen simply as a way to delegate responsibility down through the hierarchy and to reduce the number of employees by **delayering** (removing one or more layers of hierarchy from the management structure of the organisation). In this sense, it could be viewed as an attempt to get more out of workers while paying them the same rate.

- It may be costly and benefits may only be achieved in the long term, as when reorganising the shop floor and retraining the workforce in a manufacturing business.

■ Not all jobs lend themselves to enrichment. For example, refuse collection offers little scope for greater responsibility and challenges.

Job enlargement

job enlargement: increasing the scope of a job, either by job enrichment or by job rotation.

In theory, job enlargement motivates workers by giving them greater recognition, improving their promotion prospects and increasing the feelings of achievement arising from the job itself. However, if enlargement is not used carefully, a firm can demoralise its workforce by giving them excessive workloads.

Jobs may be enlarged either through job enrichment or through job rotation:
■ **Job enrichment** is where the job is expanded vertically (known as **vertical extension**) by giving the worker more responsibility (see p. 264).
■ **Job rotation** is where the job is expanded horizontally (known as **horizontal extension**) by giving the worker more tasks, but at the same level of responsibility.

Job rotation is a systematic programme of switching jobs to provide greater variety. Essentially, it gives workers more varied work to do, but at a similar level of challenge. For example, a shop worker might spend 2 hours on the checkout, 2 hours filling shelves and another 2 hours in the warehouse.

Using job rotation gives a firm several advantages:
■ It is intended to relieve the boredom of the work and has the useful side-effect of ensuring that if one person is absent, others can cover the job without difficulty.
■ Workers may be more motivated because of their wider range of skills, and they will become more flexible.
■ There may be a greater sense of participation in the production process.

However, job rotation has the following disadvantages:
■ Retraining costs will increase and there may be a fall in output because there is less specialisation.
■ It could be seen as simply involving a greater number of boring tasks, but with a reduction in the social benefits of working, since groups will be constantly changing.

Empowering employees

empowerment: giving employees the means by which they can exercise power over their working lives.

Whereas delegation might provide the authority for a subordinate to carry out a specific task, empowerment implies a degree of self-regulation and the freedom to decide what to do and how to do it. For example, large retail chains often not only delegate responsibility to local store managers, but also empower them to make judgements about what products to promote and what stock to carry.

Empowerment can be achieved through informal systems or through the more formal system of **autonomous work groups**. These provide workers with autonomy and decision-making powers, and aim to increase motivation

while also improving flexibility and quality, thus adding value to the organisation.

Empowerment involves:

- recognising that workers are capable of doing more
- making workers feel trusted and confident to carry out jobs and make decisions without supervision
- recognising workers' achievements
- creating an environment where workers wish to contribute and to be involved

With such systems in place, empowerment is likely to lead to improved motivation, reduced labour turnover, reduced absenteeism and, in turn, an increase in productivity. However, the cost of training workers to take on responsibility and make decisions could be great, and managers need to be good delegators if the process is to work effectively. In addition, there is a risk for the employer in providing a level of autonomy that may mean employees' actions are difficult to check effectively. There have been many examples of fraudulent activities in financial organisations where employees have been empowered. Nick Leeson and Barings Bank is a classic example of this.

 FACT FILE

Dirty dealings at Barings Bank

Barings Bank, Britain's oldest and one of its most prestigious banks, was told on 24 February 1995 that huge trading losses in the Far East had wiped out its capital base. It was insolvent. Either a buyer had to be found or it would have to cease trading. Barings stood to lose over £600 million on dealings carried out by one man — Nick Leeson, a 28-year-old trader based in Singapore. The losses exceeded the £540 million of capital built up by the bank since 1762.

This happened because Barings switched from a traditional, centrally managed, low-risk operation to one in which bright young traders were empowered to push for higher profits. Organisations need a culture that is understood by all staff, but one Barings employee was reported as saying, 'There were gung-ho aggressive stock-brokers on the one hand against myopic blue-chip bankers on the other.'

Although there are many good reasons for empowering staff by delegating authority to them, the Barings collapse shows the risks of delegating in a laissez-faire manner, with neither the controls nor the checks to ensure that staff are using power responsibly.

Source: adapted from Marcousé, I. (1995) 'Lessons from Leeson', *Business Review*, Vol. 2, No. 1.

From a more cynical viewpoint, empowerment could be seen simply as a way of delayering and therefore cutting costs, i.e. removing a layer of management and delegating responsibility and authority further down the hierarchy. In a similar manner, it could be argued that workers are being given more responsibility but the same amount of pay.

Working in teams

Teamworking contrasts with systems where individual workers take on smaller, more fragmented processes, characterised by a high division of labour.

A team of people working on a larger task, such as making a complete car rather than just a door, will need to be multi-skilled, well trained and motivated by more than the piece-rate rewards received by workers carrying out a single, repetitive task.

By using teamworking, an organisation gets a more motivated, flexible workforce that can cover absences more easily. When accompanied by other techniques such as job rotation and/or job enrichment and some degree of decision making, teamwork can enhance motivation and/or relieve boredom.

Teamworking can be linked to the theories of Mayo (group norms) and Maslow (social needs).

> **KEY TERM**
>
> **teamworking:** a system where production is organised into large units of work and a group of employees work together in order to meet shared objectives.

WHAT DO YOU THINK?

All individuals are different and the motivational factors that influence individuals will change over time depending on their particular circumstances. Some important questions raised by this chapter include:

- Will increased job satisfaction always lead to increased productivity? Individuals may be happier in their jobs and more ready to accept change, but no more productive than before.
- Does less division of labour mean less control and, if so, is this a problem?
- Is it only factors at work that motivate individuals in a work context? Individuals' higher-level needs may be satisfied outside the workplace and the only thing they may want from work is their wage or salary.

Links between organisational structure and the motivational techniques available to managers

Organisational structure, which was examined in detail in Chapter 19, can have a significant influence on the motivational techniques available to managers and on the level of motivation of employees. Some of the issues are examined below.

FACT FILE

Motivation problems at BT

Tom Alexander heads a long line of former BT employees who realised their potential — and fortunes — only by moving elsewhere. The 47-year-old was deputy commercial director of BT Cellnet, the group's former mobile division, when he was approached by Sir Richard Branson's Virgin group with a plan for a 'consumer-focused youth-orientated mobile business'. While he recognises that BT equipped him with valuable skills, like other BT employees who went on to excel outside the company, he recalls being frustrated by the bureaucracy at the former state-owned monopoly. He says, 'The organisation was very layered, with all these different grades and hierarchy, and, as a result, it was really difficult to make progress.' The structure of BT, he says, 'stifled talent and protected weak people'.

Source: 'How BT launched and lost a thousand stars', *The Times*, 17 May 2006.

> **EXAMINER'S VOICE**
>
> Note how interlinked all these issues are. For example, the levels of hierarchy and spans of control determine the extent of delegation (whether delegation is effective is another issue); communication is influenced by the structure of the organisation. When analysing or evaluating a business situation, remember to consider just how much one issue impacts on another or how a decision in one area can have repercussions in many other areas.

Levels of hierarchy and spans of control

Whether the organisational structure is tall or flat can influence promotional opportunities, the extent of delegation, the amount of responsibility each employee has, the chain of command and thus how quickly decisions are made, and the quality of communication. All these factors need to be taken into account by management when deciding on motivational techniques to use. For example, in a flat organisation with wide spans of control, effective delegation could empower employees by providing them with more autonomy and responsibility, resulting in improved motivation. In a tall organisation, good communication will be crucial in maintaining high levels of motivation.

Lines of accountability

If lines of accountability are clear, it is much easier to recognise achievement and therefore to reward it, which should lead to improved motivation.

Delegation and empowerment

The process of delegating tasks can be a way of motivating and empowering employees, by allowing them to exercise some power over their working lives and providing them with a degree of freedom to decide what to do and how to do it. However, empowerment can only occur if delegation is effective.

Communication

Good communication is important in motivating employees. It can make employees feel valued and an important part of the organisation. Motivational theories recognise the importance of effective communication in raising morale. Any organisation that tries to empower its employees and thus extend their roles and authority needs to ensure that effective communication systems are in place to support this.

It is important that employees understand the objectives of their organisation, how their own job contributes to meeting these objectives and how well they are performing their job and hence contributing to the success of the organisation. Regular feedback on performance, both formal and informal, is an important aspect of employee motivation. By communicating effectively in this area, management is likely to have a much more focused and committed workforce.

Just as good communication can increase employee motivation, well-motivated employees are likely to communicate more readily with management by suggesting ideas, listening to advice and contributing their opinions, and to be more willing to participate in decision making. Demotivated workers, on the other hand, are often reluctant to communicate with managers.

Flexible working

A YouGov Survey in 2007 suggests that allowing employees to work more flexibly can lead to the following benefits: improved staff motivation, increased

EXAMINER'S VOICE

Good communication is likely to mean that employees are praised for their efforts, which might, in accordance with Maslow's hierarchy, meet their ego needs and thus improve motivation. Similarly, good communication can help to make employees feel involved and meet their social needs. Effective feedback is one of Herzberg's motivators.

productivity, improved client service, reduced absenteeism, improved company resilience against transport problems, better-quality job applicants, and improved candidate perception of company.

 FACT FILE

Beaverbrooks

At Beaverbrooks, the jewellery retailer chain, employees feel valued and respected, and say their suggestions are acted upon. Their managers regularly express appreciation when they do a good job, and talk openly and honestly with them, trust their judgement and care about them as individuals. 'You constantly get praise and there's no hierarchy between people. You feel that we're all equal,' says one of Beaverbrooks' sales assistants. Staff are impressed that Mark Adlestone, the chain's managing director, knows everybody by name and staff feel comfortable enough to phone him personally with any concerns. In fact, employees are

encouraged to have direct contact with any executive by phone or e-mail. One employee says: 'I feel I have an input in how things change and feel that, if necessary, I could approach the company director about anything, personal or professional.'

The company develops internal candidates to fill management roles and nearly all managers and assistant managers have been promoted from within. A flexible benefits package includes the option to buy extra holiday, private healthcare for employees and their families, childcare vouchers, life assurance and an employee assistance programme.

Source: *The Sunday Times 100 Best Companies to Work For*, 2007.

PRACTICE EXERCISE 3 — Total: 70 marks (60 minutes)

1 Identify two problems for a business that might result from a low level of motivation among its employees. *(2 marks)*

2 Explain the terms 'job enlargement', 'job enrichment' and 'job rotation'. *(6 marks)*

3 Explain two advantages to a business of introducing job enrichment. *(6 marks)*

4 Explain two problems that a business might encounter as a result of introducing job enrichment. *(6 marks)*

5 Explain how job enrichment is linked to the motivation theories with which you are familiar. *(6 marks)*

6 Explain one advantage and one disadvantage to a business of introducing a system of job rotation. *(6 marks)*

7 Explain the term 'empowerment'. *(3 marks)*

8 How might the empowering of its employees benefit a business? *(4 marks)*

9 Explain two benefits of teamworking to a business. *(6 marks)*

10 Explain the possible links between a firm's organisational structure and the motivational techniques available to its management. *(10 marks)*

11 To what extent might effective communication and feedback influence employee motivation and a firm's performance? *(15 marks)*

CASE STUDY 5 **Honda puts staff first**

Honda, established in Japan in 1948 by Soichiro Honda, is the world's largest manufacturer of motorcycles and engines, and the seventh-largest producer of cars. A

British subsidiary was launched in 1965. The head office is in Slough, and there is a £1.2 billion manufacturing operation in Swindon. Strong team spirit and a

can-do attitude are key features of life at Honda UK.

The company's principles are simple. Staff are told, 'Your growth is the key to Honda's growth.' Martin Sanders, general manager of power equipment, says that constant opportunities and high levels of responsibility keep people with the firm. 'Mr Honda's philosophy was that you work first for yourself and then for Honda,' he says. 'We employ people more than specialists, and the global company provides advice and assistance — but delegates decisions to local management.' He says that it is a strong culture; there is little rigid procedure or hierarchy, but there is a powerful team spirit and sense of empowerment.

Honda offers an excellent benefits package comprising profit-related pay, a contributory pension scheme, family healthcare and the opportunity to take part in a yearly health check.

Motivation appears to be strong, the workforce is a happy one and the turnover rate is half the industry average. In the *Sunday Times* 2003 survey, 77% of Honda's staff believed that the company gave them opportunities to learn and grow, and 86% felt they could make a difference.

Source: adapted from *The Sunday Times 100 Best Companies to Work For*, 2003 and 2005.

Questions

Total: 30 marks (40 minutes)

1 Explain how Honda's organisational structure might have a positive impact on the motivation of its workforce. *(5 marks)*

2 Consider how 'a powerful team spirit and sense of empowerment' might benefit Honda UK. *(10 marks)*

3 Using your knowledge of motivation, discuss how effective Honda's approach to its staff is likely to be in producing a successful company. *(15 marks)*

CASE STUDY 6 Teamwork

Results from a *Sunday Times* survey of medium to large companies suggests that teamwork is missing from many places of work and that instead companies often actively encourage an atmosphere of competition. Although the intention is to use such competition as a motivational technique, it also creates conflict. The survey suggests that when employees feel that interdepartmental conflict exists, there is also evidence of intimidation and managers ordering rather than listening to their workforce. Consequently, employees do not feel fully involved at work and do not feel they can make a difference.

Hydrock, an engineering consultancy firm, is unusual

in that its employees feel that teams are working well together. Brian McConnell, managing director, says that avoiding competition has been a priority. 'We see division as a potential threat, because we have seen other companies' teams being organised so that they compete against each other, even at the expense of other departments. We discourage people from becoming competitive.' He states that the firm does not provide financial incentives that encourage regional teams to compete, 'and that becomes more important as we grow because we know the company can become a lot stronger if we all work towards a common goal.'

Source: *The Sunday Times 100 Best Companies to Work For*, 2007.

Questions

Total: 30 marks (40 minutes)

1 Consider any one of the businesses included in case studies in this chapter. To what extent is encouraging groups of employees to compete with each other likely to improve workforce motivation and have a positive impact on the performance of a business? *(15 marks)*

2 The case study suggests that financial incentives and working towards a common goal are incompatible. To what extent might this be true? *(15 marks)*

Unit 2:
Managing a business

Operations management

CHAPTER 23

Making operational decisions

This chapter introduces the concept of operations management and the issues involved. Different operational targets are introduced, covering cost efficiency, quality and capacity utilisation, with particular emphasis on the importance of unit costs as a measure of operational efficiency. The remainder of the chapter scrutinises capacity utilisation, with specific reference to dealing with non-standard orders and matching production and demand.

Operations management

Providing the 'right' goods or services means providing 'what the customer wants'. This may therefore vary between customers — for example, it may mean quality and price to one customer, but convenience and flexibility to another.

Identifying operations issues

Customers have many requirements, so operations management looks at a variety of issues. The following issues are all aspects of operations management that are covered in the AQA AS business studies course:

1 deciding on the location of a business in order to meet the needs of the business and its customers
2 choosing the mix of resources to use in production
3 managing capacity utilisation
4 organising stock control to meet the needs of customers quickly and cheaply
5 ensuring high quality of goods and services in an organisation
6 providing excellent customer service in order to meet customer expectations
7 working closely with suppliers in order to improve efficiency
8 using technology in order to improve business operations

Issue 1 (location) has already been discussed in Chapter 9, in the context of a small business start-up. Issue 2 was studied in Chapter 3. Issues 3 and 4 are considered during the remainder of this chapter. Issues 5–8 are examined in Chapters 24–27.

Operational targets

As operations management is concerned with getting the right goods or services to the customer, operational targets measure the efficiency with which this overall aim has been achieved.

Three examples of operational targets are considered in this chapter:

- unit costs
- measures of quality
- capacity utilisation

Unit costs

In Chapter 11 we looked at the relationship between output and costs. In order to be competitive in the marketplace, a business will try to reduce the cost of each unit that it produces.

The unit cost is also known as the average cost (AC) or average total cost (ATC). For example, if a business produces 20 units of output at a total cost of £50, the average (or unit) cost is £50/20 = £2.50.

Remember that total costs = fixed costs + variable costs.

In Chapter 11 we saw how total costs increased as output increased. However, we can now look at the impact on average or unit costs. Table 23.1 is the same as Table 11.2 from Chapter 11, but with a fifth column added that shows the unit cost (or average cost).

In this example, the most efficient level of output is 120,000 because this is the output at which the unit cost is at its lowest (£1.42 per unit).

KEY TERMS

operational targets: the goals or aims of the operations function of the business.

unit cost: the cost of producing 1 unit of output. It is calculated by the formula:

$$\text{unit cost} = \frac{\text{total cost}}{\text{units of output}}$$

WHAT DO YOU THINK?

In Chapters 11 and 12 we assumed that fixed costs remain the same, regardless of the level of output. This is an assumption of breakeven analysis. However, in real life a firm will eventually need to spend more on fixed costs as output increases because, for example, additional machinery may be needed. Similarly, it is unlikely that variable costs will always be the same (e.g. £1 per unit, whether 20,000 or 120,000 units are produced). As output grows, a firm may be able to bulk-buy materials, reducing variable costs per unit. On the other hand, if the firm gets much larger, it may need to buy some of its materials from more expensive suppliers.

Can you think of any other reasons why the assumptions made about fixed costs and variable costs may not always be true?

Table 23.1 *Monthly costs and output for a magazine producer*

Units of output (000s)	Fixed costs (£000s)	Variable costs (£000s)	Total costs (£000s)	Unit cost (average cost per unit)
0	50	0	50	–
20	50	20	70	3.50
40	50	40	90	2.25
60	50	60	110	1.83
80	50	80	130	1.63
100	50	100	150	1.50
120*	50	120	170	1.42

*Assume that 120,000 units is the capacity — the maximum possible output.

EXAMINER'S VOICE

Although breakeven analysis is based on the assumptions made in Chapter 12, calculations of unit costs over different levels of output may take other factors (e.g. new fixed costs or bulk buying) into account.

Comparing operational efficiency with competitors

In an industry in which competition is based on prices, it is vital for a business to achieve the lowest unit costs. Look at Table 23.2.

Table 23.2 *Unit costs of four different companies*

	Units of output	Fixed costs (£)	Variable costs (£)	Total costs (£)	Unit costs (£)
Company A	40	200	160	360	9.00
Company B	80	300	300	600	7.50
Company C	100	500	600	1,100	11.00
Company D	150	600	675	1,275	8.50

The most efficient company is B (£7.50 per unit). The least efficient company is C (£11.00) per unit. *On the basis of unit costs only,* company B has the best chance of success because it has the lowest unit cost (average cost).

Unit costs and labour productivity

In Chapter 20 we looked at labour productivity. Labour productivity has a significant impact on unit costs, particularly in businesses that use a great deal of labour as a factor of production.

Table 23.3 shows the link between labour productivity and unit costs in four different firms.

A	B Units of output (per week)	C Number of employees	D Labour productivity (column B/column C)	E Wage costs* (£) (column C × £400)	F Wage costs per unit (£) (column E/column B)
Firm W	400	2	200	800	2.00
Firm X	660	4	165	1,600	2.42
Firm Y	750	5	150	2,000	2.67
Firm Z	1,080	6	180	2,400	2.22

Table 23.3 *Labour productivity and unit costs in four different firms*

* Column E assumes that each firm pays its employees £400 per week.

The higher the labour productivity, the lower the wage cost per unit (assuming each firm pays the same wage level). Firm W has the highest labour productivity and the lowest labour costs per unit. Similarly, firm Y has the lowest labour productivity but the highest labour costs per unit. Although there are other costs to include, it will be difficult for firm Y to match the overall unit costs of firm W when there is such a big difference in labour costs per unit.

WHAT DO YOU THINK?

From Table 23.3 it might seem obvious that a firm will try to reduce wages in order to lower its labour costs (and thus its unit costs). Why might this not be the best approach to adopt?

Measures of quality

There is no single, agreed measure of quality. Quality is defined as 'those features of a product or service that allow it to satisfy (or delight) customers'. As 'quality' depends on people's opinions, there will be different views about what it means. Listed below are some examples of measures of quality and a brief comment on the logic behind their use. Please note that this is just a sample of quality measures — a good quality measure will be geared towards the specific needs of the individual firm.

- **Customer satisfaction ratings.** A survey of customers can reveal customer opinions on a numerical scale (e.g. 1 to 10) or using qualitative measures (e.g. excellent — very good — good — etc.). As the purpose of a product or service is to satisfy the needs of the customer, this is an excellent way of measuring whether quality has been achieved.

- **Customer complaints.** This calculates the number of customers who complain (it is sometimes measured as a percentage of the total number of customers). Although it might seem to take a negative view, it is a good way of measuring whether a company has problems that it needs to rectify. It is said that one unhappy customer can damage a company's reputation far more than satisfied customers can boost it, so companies need to concentrate on preventing customer complaints.

- **Scrap rate.** This calculates the number of items rejected during the production process as a percentage of the number of units produced. It shows the business whether its production methods are working effectively, guiding it towards areas that might need improvement. Rejected products will also lead to higher costs.

- **Punctuality.** This calculates the degree to which a business delivers its products (or provides its services) on time. It is often measured as a percentage:

$$\text{punctuality (\%)} = \frac{\text{deliveries on time}}{\text{total deliveries}} \times 100$$

This measure is used by many businesses, especially those involved in transporting goods (e.g. haulage firms) or customers (e.g. rail franchises).

Capacity utilisation

Calculating capacity utilisation

Capacity utilisation measures the extent to which the company's maximum possible output is being reached. It can be calculated using the following formula:

$$\frac{\text{capacity}}{\text{utilisation (\%)}} = \frac{\text{actual output per annum (month)}}{\text{maximum possible output per annum (month)}} \times 100$$

A company capable of producing 3,500 units but actually producing 2,800 units is working at 80% capacity:

$$\frac{2,800}{3,500} \times 100 = 80\%$$

It could increase production by 700 units or 20%. This is known as its **spare capacity**.

Capacity utilisation can be measured over any chosen time period. For some organisations it may be most appropriate to calculate it on a daily basis, but weekly or monthly calculations may be more relevant to other firms.

There is no one ideal target percentage, but many people believe that 90% capacity utilisation is a sensible level. At 100% there is no scope for mainten-

KEY TERMS

capacity: the maximum total level of output or production that a business can produce in a given time period. A company producing at this level is said to be producing at full capacity.

capacity utilisation: the percentage of a firm's total possible production level that is being reached. If a company is large enough to produce 100 units a week, but is actually producing 92 units, its capacity utilisation is 92%.

ance and repair, to respond to sudden orders or to deal with emergency situations that may occur. However, every percentage point below 100 represents 'unused' resources and higher fixed costs per unit produced.

Link between capacity utilisation and other operational targets

Although capacity utilisation is a target in its own right, it is also important because of its impact on the other operational targets:

Table 23.4 Fixed costs per unit at different levels of capacity utilisation

- **Capacity utilisation and unit costs.** The higher the level of capacity utilisation, the more efficiently a business is using its resources. If a business has a factory, it will incur fixed costs, such as rent, regardless of the level of output. Let us assume that the factory has fixed costs of £120,000 per annum and can produce 10,000 items at full capacity. Table 23.4 shows the link between capacity utilisation and the fixed costs per unit. It can be seen that high capacity utilisation means much lower unit costs. At 50% capacity utilisation, the fixed costs per unit are twice as high as the figure when capacity utilisation is 100%. Below 50% the fixed costs per unit increase dramatically, as capacity utilisation falls.

Level of output (units)	Capacity utilisation (%)	Fixed costs (£)	Fixed costs per unit (£)
10,000	100	120,000	12.00
9,000	90	120,000	13.33
8,000	80	120,000	15.00
7,000	70	120,000	17.14
6,000	60	120,000	20.00
5,000	50	120,000	24.00
4,000	40	120,000	30.00
3,000	30	120,000	40.00
2,000	20	120,000	60.00
1,000	10	120,000	120.00

- **Capacity utilisation and quality.** To some extent, the reverse logic applies when looking at quality. If the business is working at full capacity, there is no scope for additional activities, such as regular maintenance of machinery or ensuring that staff are not overworked. Consequently, the closer a business gets to 100% capacity utilisation, the more likely it is that quality problems will develop. However, it should be noted that very low levels of capacity utilisation may also damage the quality because the workforce may become demoralised by the perceived lack of success of the business.

Taking these two other measures of operational performance into consideration, many businesses recognise that a level of 90% capacity utilisation is an ideal balance.

Managing capacity utilisation

In terms of capacity utilisation, there are two types of situation that a firm needs to manage:

- under-utilisation of capacity (also known as excess capacity or **spare capacity**)
- capacity shortage

These two situations must be managed in radically different ways. As spare capacity is the more normal situation, this will be looked at first, starting with the possible reasons why it occurs.

KEY TERMS

under-utilisation of capacity: when a firm's output is below the maximum possible. This is also known as *excess capacity* or *spare capacity*. It represents a waste of resources and means that the organisation is spending unnecessarily on its fixed assets.

capacity shortage: when a firm's capacity is not large enough to deal with the level of demand for its products. This means that certain customers will be disappointed. Further sales may be lost if unhappy customers decide not to buy from the firm again or if negative publicity results from the firm's failure to supply.

Causes of spare capacity

There are several reasons why a firm may be operating below its maximum possible output:

- **New competitors or new products entering the market.** For example, it has become increasingly popular to open coffee shops in recent years, in response to higher demand. However, the growth of competition has been so high that in some places there is now excess capacity in the market, so the average turnover for each outlet has begun to fall, although overall demand is still rising. A similar situation has occurred with pizza restaurants.
- **Fall in demand for the product due to changes in taste or fashion.** McDonald's has been forced to close some of its restaurants because of a fall in demand caused by many consumers wanting more varied and healthy food.
- **Unsuccessful marketing.** Benetton grew rapidly in the UK, partly as a result of brand awareness created by its advertising. Its decline coincided with negative publicity related to some of the controversial images that it used in its posters.
- **Seasonal demand.** The tourist industry must build facilities to accommodate visitors at peak times of the season. Attractions such as Alton Towers therefore have excess capacity during the winter months. During the working day, organisations such as cafés and fitness clubs also have varying levels of spare capacity.
- **Over-investment in fixed assets.** There was a boom in travel agencies in the 1980s and 1990s as more and more people took holidays abroad. However, as the internet expanded and people found it to be an easy way of booking holidays, the need for high-street travel agents declined. The result was spare capacity in the industry, although this has been eased by the closure of stores.
- **A merger or takeover leading to duplication of many resources and sites.** The integration of Vue and Ster Century Cinemas meant that some towns had two cinemas both providing the same service and unlikely to be reaching full capacity. Usually, such a business will sell off smaller sites to overcome this problem.

Operations management

EXAMINER'S VOICE

The financial calculations involved in a non-standard order are fairly straightforward. Consequently, non-standard order decisions in an examination are likely to require consideration of the operational factors. If an exam question is asked on this topic, look at the issues concerning capacity utilisation. Is the business in need of an additional order or will the additional output create problems? How flexible is the business in terms of adjusting its capacity in the particular case study? These issues may be of special significance.

Ultimately, the firm will need to balance these operational issues with the financial consequences. If the profit to be made is large, the above factors may not be significant. If the financial benefits are small or non-existent, these factors may dominate the decision-making process.

FACT FILE

Capacity in electricity generation

Electricity generation is an industry in which capacity utilisation is a major issue. At peak times in the year (such as after the Queen's Speech on Christmas Day or at the end of a particularly exciting episode of *EastEnders*), huge demands are placed on the national grid as everybody rushes to the kitchen to make a cup of tea. However, at off-peak times, such as the middle of the night, there is low demand for electricity and most power stations are not needed. It is also difficult to store electricity — less than 5% of all electricity is supplied from 'stock'.

To reduce this problem, the national grid came up with an imaginative solution. At Llanberis in Gwynedd, Wales, the largest man-made underground chamber in the world was created in order to generate electricity. Built into the side of a mountain is a pumping station and electricity generation plant. Water flows from a mountain-top lake down through the plant and this is used to generate electricity. The water then flows into

PHOTODISC

a lake at the bottom of the mountain, from where it is pumped back to the lake at the top. The plant, which opened in 1984, is able to generate more than 10% of the UK's total electricity.

In terms of physics, the plant is highly inefficient — pumping the water back to the mountain-top lake uses up more electricity than the plant is able to generate from the water flowing down through the mountain. However, from a business viewpoint it is efficient. At night, when capacity utilisation of the national grid is low, electricity from other power stations is used to pump the water back to the top. Then, at peak times, when there is a shortage of capacity, the water flows down the mountain, adding 10% to the national supply of electricity.

A similar business principle is used in Niagara, on the border between Canada and the USA. During the day, hydroelectric power is generated by diverting over 50% of the natural flow of water from the Niagara river into power stations. At night (when the tourists have gone home) this is increased to more than 75% (leaving less than 25% to cascade over the falls), so that even more electricity can be generated. In recent years this scheme has not been enough to prevent major power cuts in New York, a consequence of the shortage of capacity in the USA's electricity industry. It has even been suggested that Niagara Falls could be turned off at night (by diverting all the flow of water through the power stations) to help the situation.

High levels of capacity utilisation mean that electricity supplies are vulnerable if problems occur. Until the 1980s, the respective governments owned electricity

generation in the UK and USA. Since privatisation, electricity has been run by limited companies seeking to make profits for their owners. A consequence of this has been a reduction in levels of spare capacity. In the UK,

spare capacity has fallen from 28% to 16% since privatisation. In the USA, it has fallen from 15% to 3%.

Source: based on an article by Steve Connor in the *Independent*, 16 August 2003, and various other sources.

PRACTICE EXERCISE

Total: 55 marks (45 minutes)

1 Table 23.6 shows the variable costs of two companies. **Both companies have fixed costs of £300.**

*Table 23.6
Variable costs of
two companies*

	Units of output	Total variable costs (£)
Company A	60	160
Company B	80	300

Using 'unit costs' as a measure of operational efficiency, indicate which company is the more efficient. Show your working. *(6 marks)*

2 a Identify three ways in which a firm might measure the quality of its operations. *(3 marks)*

  b Select one of your answers to part (a) and explain why it is a good measure of quality. *(3 marks)*

3 In order to improve operational efficiency, Tesco introduced a number of cost-saving measures. One measure was to try to increase the amount of stock carried by each lorry. The average lorry can carry a maximum of 26 pallets of stock. Tesco increased the average load from 22.5 pallets to 24 pallets per trip.

  a Calculate the capacity utilisation before the increase in the average load. *(2 marks)*

  b Calculate the percentage of spare capacity after the changes. *(2 marks)*

4 Explain two implications of under-utilisation of capacity for a business. *(6 marks)*

5 Explain three factors that might create high levels of capacity utilisation. *(9 marks)*

6 What is meant by 'capacity shortage'? *(3 marks)*

7 What percentage is considered to be an ideal capacity utilisation? *(1 mark)*

8 Explain the meaning of 'rationalisation'. *(3 marks)*

9 How can subcontracting help a business's capacity utilisation problems? *(5 marks)*

10 What is meant by a 'non-standard order'? *(3 marks)*

11 Analyse three ways in which a business might increase its capacity to supply a non-standard order. *(9 marks)*

CASE STUDY 1   Center Parcs is out of the woods

On 6 September 2007 Center Parcs learned that it could finally build its fifth UK resort after a long battle for planning permission.

The planning process cost the company £1.5 million, but it is hard to overestimate the importance of adding

a new site to the four existing UK resorts. The last one was added in 2002.

The company runs at almost 100% occupancy and is frequently criticised for its high prices and charges, so further price rises were not an option in order to reduce

capacity utilisation. 'It will be worth £70 million per annum to us,' said Center Parcs boss, Martin Dalby. The new venue in Bedfordshire will cost about £200 million to build, with construction scheduled to start in January 2009 and an opening planned for 2010. Difficulties in getting planning permission for such large-scale operations in the countryside mean that it is unlikely Center Parcs will ever open a sixth site. Any further increases in demand will need more inventive solutions.

Dalby recognises that the product needs to evolve: 'We've done it four times now and we know exactly how it works. The core ingredients of Center Parcs will be exactly the same, but we will modify the style of the restaurants and the shops so they will be more contemporary. It is in our leisure activities where the innovations will come. For example, squash courts — which were popular when the first Center Parcs opened — are less in demand these days. Attractions such as spas are far more popular now.'

Center Parcs knows its market well. Sales were £250 million last year and capacity utilisation was 94% — as good as it gets in the holiday industry. That was not a freak occurrence either; the business has been achieving a figure of more than 90% for some years.

Despite its popularity, Center Parcs regularly attracts criticism that its prices are too high and that it exploits parents by ramping up fees in the school holidays. A 3-night weekend stay for two adults and two children in the autumn half-term was advertised for between £709 and £1,800, depending on the accommodation chosen. The equivalent break 2 weeks later in mid-November costs between £449 and £630. However, the fact that 60% of turnover comes from repeat business is an indicator that there are more than a few satisfied customers. The business places a great deal of emphasis on the quality of its provision and has spent over £100 million in the last year on improving the accommodation and facilities in its existing parks.

The quality of the facilities means that unit costs are high, but these costs can be passed on to the consumer in the form of higher prices. There is a possibility that the opening of a fifth park will make it necessary to reduce prices, but the company is confident that its overall profits will be greatly improved once the park opens in 2010.

Source: based on an article by Matthew Goodman in the *Sunday Times*, 7 October 2007.

Questions

Total: 40 marks (50 minutes)

1 What is meant by the term 'unit costs'? *(3 marks)*

2 Explain two benefits for Center Parcs of having high capacity utilisation. *(6 marks)*

3 Center Parcs achieves annual sales of £250 million a year with capacity utilisation of 94%. Assuming that the remaining 6% of holidays could be sold for the same price, what would Center Parcs' annual sales revenue be if it operated at 100% capacity utilisation? *(4 marks)*

4 Center Parcs could increase its capacity by increasing the amount of accommodation provided at one of its existing sites. Why might it be reluctant to take this approach? *(4 marks)*

5 Analyse how Center Parcs uses its pricing policy to improve its capacity utilisation. *(7 marks)*

6 Operational efficiency can be measured through unit costs, quality and capacity utilisation. To what extent do you believe that quality is the most important measure of operational efficiency for Center Parcs? *(16 marks)*

CASE STUDY 2 Design for 2012 Olympic Stadium unveiled

Case Study 2 can be tackled individually, but it is ideally suited to a team working together to share ideas.

Yesterday saw the unveiling of the winning design for London's Olympic Stadium.

The innovative stadium design was praised for its post-Olympics potential. The plan has been to pioneer a state-of-the-art piece of engineering that will allow the stadium to have an 80,000 capacity — the size needed to house the Olympics. However, after the event it will transform into a stadium with a capacity of just 25,000 people. To allow this to happen easily, 25,000 permanent seats will be sunk into the ground, while the remaining 55,000 (temporary) seats will be erected in removable tiered circles above the ground.

The decision to create so much temporary seating was based on the experiences of previous Olympic countries which have been left with stadiums that have become white elephants, as they were too large for everyday sporting activities, but still incurred high maintenance costs. Currently, the plan is to convert the eventual 25,000 capacity stadium to an athletics stadium that will suit the needs of UK athletics. This capacity would be well in excess of current attendances at athletics events in the UK. There is also the possibility of it becoming a future home for a football team (Leyton Orient has been suggested as a tenant, following the rejection of the idea by Tottenham Hotspur and West Ham).

Building is set to be completed by 2011. To ensure both the cost effectiveness and the environmental sustainability of the project, the temporary seating is being surrounded by walls made of fabric. Talks are

LONDON 2012

being held to investigate whether these can be turned into souvenirs to generate an additional source of revenue. Further revenue will be generated by the temporary seating, which will be sold off after the Olympics have taken place.

Critics claim that this innovation has not prevented the budgeted cost of the stadium rising to the current estimate of £496 million, in comparison with the £280 million that was estimated in 2004.

Advocates of the design salute it as an innovative way of solving a major capacity utilisation problem; critics point out that the costs work out at just under £20,000 per seat.

Source: adapted from an article by Emily Dugan in the *Independent*, 8 November 2007, and other sources.

Question

20 marks (30 minutes)

Most stadiums built for previous Olympics have suffered from low capacity utilisation after the event has taken place. To what extent do you believe that the London proposal is a good solution to this problem? In answering this question, you are encouraged to introduce your own possible solutions, but cancelling the Olympics is not allowed.

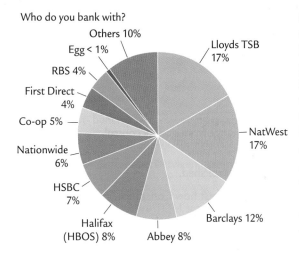

Who do you bank with?

However, despite this trend, the distance of customers from their nearest branch is still a key consideration. This issue should please NatWest, which has focused its advertising on customer service and its claim to be opening, rather than closing, branches.

Unfortunately for NatWest, this message may not be coming across more generally. It is ranked sixth out of the 11 banks in the poll. The most impressive bank is the Co-op. It came first in the survey and has always marketed itself as a niche, ethical bank. The Nationwide is in second place. It is the only mutual (non-profit-making) bank on the list. This implies that non-profit-making banking is still a favourite of customers. The Halifax and Abbey are both former mutual (non-profit-making) organisations and came third and fourth.

However, high rankings do not necessarily translate into big business. The Co-op and the other leaders suffer from the inertia of customers in the sector, which prevents them moving accounts. A large proportion of customers use a particular bank because they cannot be bothered to move, or they choose a bank on the basis of a recommendation from family or friends.

Source: Populus survey and an article by Alexis Ashman in *The Times*, 25 July 2007.

Question

20 marks (30 minutes)

Study the article and Figure 24.1. Based on this information, to what extent is 'quality' the main reason why customers use a particular bank?

CHAPTER 25

Developing effective operations: customer service

This chapter introduces the concept of customer service. The meaning of customer service is explored, including an examination of methods of meeting customer expectations. The need for monitoring and continual improving of customer service is studied. The chapter concludes by looking at the benefits to a business of providing high levels of customer service.

What is customer service?

> **KEY TERMS**
>
> **customer service:** identifying and satisfying customer needs and delivering a level of service that meets or exceeds customer expectations.
>
> **customer expectations:** what people think should happen and how they think they should be treated when asking for or receiving customer service.
>
> **customer satisfaction:** the feeling that the buyer gets when he or she is happy with the level of customer service that has been provided and the degree to which customer expectations have been met by the provider of the service.

Customer expectations are based on:
- what people hear and see
- what customers read and what organisations tell them about their service
- what happens during the customer experience
- what has happened to them in previous customer service experiences

The greater the customer expectations are built up by these factors, the higher the level of customer service that must be provided in order to meet the customers' desires.

What do customers want?

A major challenge in providing customer service is that different customers have varying expectations of a business. As a consequence, most businesses formulate their own measurements of customer satisfaction so that they can identify factors that are relevant to their particular customers.

The Institute of Customer Service (ICS) has attempted to develop a national customer satisfaction index (CSI) in order to identify the main factors that customers expect from a supplier in the UK. The ICS found that customers had ten top priorities which determined the level of customer satisfaction:

- the overall quality of the product or service supplied
- the friendliness of the staff dealing with the processing of the good or service
- the efficiency with which problems and complaints were handled
- the speed of service or delivery of the product in comparison with the promises made
- the helpfulness of staff in general
- the effectiveness with which enquiries were handled, particularly the initial contact with the business
- the extent to which customers felt that they were being treated as a valued customer
- the competence of staff in completing their tasks
- the ease with which the business transaction was conducted and completed
- the extent to which the customer was kept informed of developments

These priorities were built into a survey in which customers were asked to rate organisations in response to 20 questions, all related to the level of customer service.

Findings of the ICS survey

According to the ICS, many businesses investigating customer service look at issues that are important to the organisation's managers, rather than the people who matter — the customers. According to Robert Crawford, ICS director: 'Customers base their evaluation of suppliers of goods and services on whether they have received the results that they expected. Therefore company surveys must be based on the same criteria.'

According to the ICS report, service businesses, such as hairdressers, and professional services, such as architects, are best at satisfying customers. The public sector and utilities services (such as electricity suppliers) are worst at doing this.

According to Crawford, 'Service businesses satisfy customers more than organisations in other sectors because they:

- treat people as valued customers
- are friendly and have helpful staff
- offer good value for money
- handle problems and complaints well
- make it easy for customers to do business with them.'

The survey also highlights the importance of employee satisfaction. Typically, the more satisfied employees are, the more highly motivated they are to provide a good service and the higher the level of customer satisfaction that results.

However, there is another piece of logic at work. Higher customer satisfaction also produces higher employee satisfaction. This is because employees prefer working for companies that deliver high levels of customer service and which therefore have relatively low levels of problems and complaints.

Figure 25.1 shows the overall results of the ICS survey for UK firms; Figure 25.2 shows the levels of customer satisfaction for different sectors of the UK economy; and Figure 25.3 shows the best and second-best UK retailers in terms of customer service, together with the retail sector average and worst scores.

Figure 25.1
Average scores for customer satisfaction in the ICS survey of UK firms, 2007

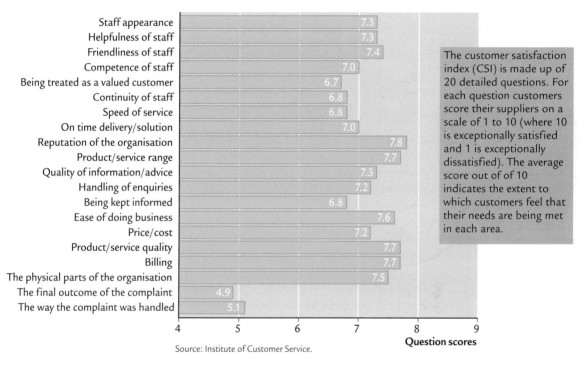

The customer satisfaction index (CSI) is made up of 20 detailed questions. For each question customers score their suppliers on a scale of 1 to 10 (where 10 is exceptionally satisfied and 1 is exceptionally dissatisfied). The average score out of of 10 indicates the extent to which customers feel that their needs are being met in each area.

Source: Institute of Customer Service.

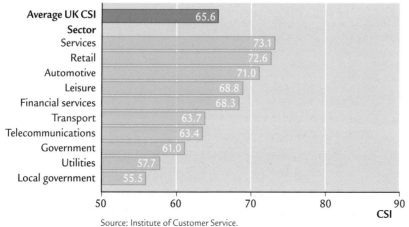

Figure 25.2
Customer satisfaction index for UK industries, 2007

Source: Institute of Customer Service.

Figure 25.3 Extract from the customer satisfaction index for the UK retail sector, 2007

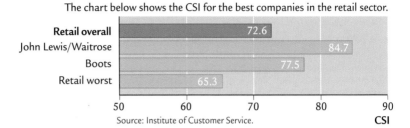

The chart below shows the CSI for the best companies in the retail sector.

Source: Institute of Customer Service.

The ICS report reveals significant variations between different industries. A number of specific conclusions were drawn from the survey:

- Customer satisfaction with the overall quality of the product or service (the indicator that is seen to be the most important of the 20 tested) is highest in the services trade and lowest in local government.
- The survey revealed that being treated as a valued customer is one of the least satisfactory areas, and yet one that is probably easier to improve than other areas.
- Not surprisingly, the handling of customer complaints was the area in which the lowest levels of satisfaction were recorded. However, the more surprising conclusion was that customers whose complaints were handled well became more loyal customers than those who never experienced a problem in the first place.
- The larger the business, the less likely it was to provide good customer service. British Airways was the only organisation that topped the chart for its particular industry in both size and level of customer service.

Customer experience

Table 25.1 shows the top ten organisations for customer service according to the ICS survey. As this is a national survey, small local firms are grouped together according to their trade (e.g. hairdressers).

Table 25.1 The top ten organisations for customer service in the UK, 2007

Position	Organisation	Customer service score (maximum = 100)
1	Ambulance service	88
2	John Lewis Partnership/ Waitrose	85
3	Local hairdressers	81
4=	Local restaurants	78
4=	Local electricians	78
4=	Volkswagen	78
4=	Toyota	78
4=	Nationwide	78
4=	Portman Building Society	78
4=	Boots	78

Source: Institute of Customer Service.

Methods of meeting customer expectations

An organisation needs to ensure that it meets the expectations of its customers. This can be achieved through a series of steps:

1 Conduct market research to find out what the customer expectations are so that customer service targets the right factors.
2 Introduce relevant training in customer service into the organisation so that the workforce can meet and surpass customer expectations.
3 Set up quality procedures and set quality standards so that the organisation is geared towards the needs of its customers.

4 Monitor performance against these standards so that high quality and good customer service are maintained.

We will now look at each of these steps in more detail.

Market research

The standard for 'quality' is set by the customer, who is therefore the best place to start. Primary market research can be used to gather comments from consumers. Feedback from the market can guide a business towards making the improvements to products and services that are needed to keep its customers satisfied.

Secondary market research can be gathered from organisations such as the Department for Business, Enterprise and Regulatory Reform (BERR), which provides data on the factors and features that are most valued in the market-place. Other sources of secondary market research are surveys such as the UK customer satisfaction index (see p. 301), the annual CompariSat survey provided by FDS International and YouGov's BrandIndex, which measures the reputation of brand names. These surveys may provide useful data on how a business's customer service is judged in comparison with its competitors. This secondary market research can give small businesses, which may not be included in these surveys themselves, an idea of what they need to do to match market leaders.

 FILE

London Underground

Market research done by London Underground has revealed that hot, stuffy trains are a major cause of customer dissatisfaction. In response, London Underground is spending £150 million on a programme called 'Cooling the Tube', which will be introduced by 2012. One of the current favourite solutions is for tube trains to carry huge blocks of ice that will cool the air flow.

Training

As indicated in Chapter 24, any quality initiative needs to involve training of the workforce. If customer satisfaction is based mainly on the quality of the actual good or service being provided, the techniques indicated in Chapter 24 will be used. In addition, companies may provide specific training in customer care. Awarding bodies such as Edexcel and the London Chamber of Commerce and Industry (LCCI) provide vocational qualifications at levels 2, 3 and 4 in

customer care. The ICS provides professional qualifications in customer care, with over 200,000 people in the UK having gained a professional qualification in customer service.

Use of quality control or quality assurance

The ways in which systems of quality control and quality assurance can improve customers' satisfaction by meeting or exceeding their expectations are discussed in Chapter 24.

Monitoring quality standards

Any business that subscribes to a quality standard, such as ISO 9001, must regularly monitor its activities to ensure that it is still meeting the standards that have been set. In addition, an independent auditor will monitor the business's progress against the standards on an annual basis, to ensure that standards are being maintained. This discipline will normally be sufficient to ensure that high-quality customer service is maintained once the business has established its quality procedures.

 FILE

Cross-industry comparisons

Improving customer service does not necessarily involve making comparisons with a business in the same industry. When Amancio Ortega, Spain's richest man and the founder of fashion retail-chain Zara, wanted to introduce a system of rapid distribution in order to improve customer service, he ignored the textile and fashion industries and examined DHL, the courier company.

Monitoring and improving customer service

Different businesses have different views of what their customers expect, so it is important for each firm to develop its own, individual approach to monitoring customer service.

A summary of different measures used by certain businesses is provided in the fact file.

 FILE

Monitoring customer service in practice

Sainsbury's — mystery shoppers
Along with many other organisations, Sainsbury's uses mystery shoppers. These individuals visit a store and act like a normal shopper. The mystery shopper is briefed on the customer service targets of the organisation and so will take actions such as asking the location of certain products, recording the time taken in the checkout queue, assessing the friendliness of the staff and noting any products that are not in stock. In this way, an objective and detailed assessment of performance is achieved.

Enterprise Rent-a-Car — ESQi
Enterprise uses ESQi — the Enterprise Service Quality index. Only two questions are asked:

- How would you rate your last Enterprise experience?
- Would you rent from Enterprise again?

Enterprise has found that this simple survey guarantees an excellent return. The company has learned that customers who answer 'completely satisfied' to the first question are three times more likely to become repeat customers than those who said that they were only 'somewhat satisfied'.

Source: www.times100.co.uk.

3 mobile phone company — scanning blogs
Companies such as 3 scan people's blogs on the internet in order to discover what customers are saying about their products. The most recent comments are then investigated to see if problems can be rectified. The company also makes contact with customers in order to resolve problems and invites the (by now satisfied) customer to post a blog on the company website.

National Express — text messaging
National Express, the coach company, invites passengers to send text messages containing their feedback while travelling on the coach. A company called Fizzback collects these data, passes them on to National Express and delivers a response. If the rating is not high, the customer is asked if they want the company to call them. On occasions, this has led to immediate action, such as repairs to air-conditioning being made, before the coach has reached its destination.

Source: adapted from Ilett, D. (2007) 'How to find out what's being said about you', *Financial Times*, 13 June.

Constant monitoring of factors likely to cause dissatisfaction is a vital tool for businesses, as this process can help them to stop problems before they become widespread and develop an awareness of the factors that customers value most.

Benefits of high levels of customer service

To a large extent, the benefits gained from high levels of customer service are the same as those arising from providing high quality. Therefore, these benefits are noted only briefly below; a more detailed analysis is provided in Chapter 24.

- **Impact on sales volume.** High-quality service that exceeds the expectations of customers will lead to increased demand for the goods and services provided by a business.
- **Creating a unique selling point (USP).** The quality of customer service can be used as a USP in order to enhance a company's uniqueness and individuality.
- **Impact on selling price.** The unique selling point will enable a business to charge higher prices and thus earn higher profits.
- **The firm's reputation.** Companies with a reputation for good customer service are likely to gain repeat business and have a solid base of loyal customers.

In addition to the factors highlighted in Chapter 24 there are additional benefits of having high levels of customer service, as outlined below:

- **Employee motivation.** Good customer service may help to motivate the workforce, as good relations with customers can make the workplace a happier working environment.
- **Reduced costs.** Costs may be reduced because there are likely to be fewer complaints to handle.
- **Trade between businesses.** In some cases, organisations will insist on proof of high levels of customer service, such as testimony from other customers, before agreeing to trade with a firm.
- **Public relations.** Positive publicity arising from good customer service can be used for public relations (PR). In marketing terms, PR is highly valued by customers because it is seen to be an objective comment on the business's strengths, rather than the business merely paying for adverts to promote itself. Richard Branson has greatly enhanced customers' views of Virgin through his skilful use of PR. In contrast, BAA (which owns Heathrow, Gatwick and Stansted airports) has found its reputation damaged by its difficulties in persuading the media that some of its problems (such as shoddy conditions at Heathrow, security delays and environmental issues) have been caused by external factors outside its control.

DID YOU KNOW?

Public relations (PR) is a term that refers to activities by a company that receive favourable publicity and may feature in news articles. This favourable publicity enhances the company's reputation because it is seen as a news item rather than paid-for advertising. It is used a great deal in marketing because it raises awareness of a company in a favourable way (and may not cost anything).

- **Strengths and weaknesses.** The process of monitoring customer service can reveal the strengths and weaknesses of the business. As a result of this monitoring, steps can be taken to overcome the weaknesses and build on the strengths. Ultimately, this will lead to further improvement in customer satisfaction.

FACT FILE

Secrets of good customer service

Albert Schindler, founder of Schindler Promotions Ltd, offers five secrets of good customer service:

- Get to know your customers individually if possible.
- Provide a more creative personalised service than your competitors.
- Remember the saying: 'The customer is always right.'
- Be honest with your customers.
- Educate your staff to be as concerned about your customers as you are.

PRACTICE EXERCISE

Total: 45 marks (35 minutes)

1 What is meant by the term 'customer service'? *(3 marks)*

2 What is meant by the term 'customer satisfaction'? *(3 marks)*

3 Identify four examples of customer expectations. *(4 marks)*

4 Explain two reasons why retailers have a higher level of customer satisfaction than local government. *(6 marks)*

5 a Why are large firms less likely to provide the best customer service in a sector? *(4 marks)*
   b Explain one reason why British Airways is able to provide the best customer service, despite being the largest airline in the UK. *(3 marks)*

6 Explain how customer service can be improved through the following:
   a market research *(4 marks)*   b training *(4 marks)*   c quality standards *(4 marks)*

7 Analyse three benefits of good customer service. *(10 marks)*

CASE STUDY Finger on the satisfaction pulse

Customer satisfaction is an important measure for any brand.

Since 2004, FDS International has undertaken CompariSat, a study of 1,800 UK consumers and how they rate customer satisfaction for a range of organisations. This survey gives a useful insight into perceptions of factors such as value for money, product quality, product range, innovation, customer loyalty and trust.

One obvious feature in this year's results is the presence of four out of five of the UK's leading supermarkets in the top ten companies overall. In a highly competitive market sector with tight margins and a high number of transactions with customers each year, the need to deliver consistently high quality across a range of customer satisfaction indicators is vital.

Figure 25.4 shows the scores of the top ten companies in the UK for customer satisfaction, according to CompariSat's survey. Waitrose topped the poll in overall satisfaction across all sectors, followed by ASDA in second place and Amazon in third.

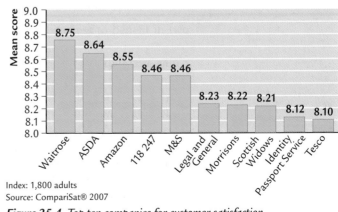

Index: 1,800 adults
Source: CompariSat® 2007

Figure 25.4 Top ten companies for customer satisfaction

an organisation such as a wholesaler that has been given credit by the manu-facturers supplying it, it will not be under pressure to get cash quickly. Therefore, it can offer credit terms to its buyers.

In summary, credit is most likely to be offered when buyers might face cash-flow difficulties because the end product takes a long time to sell. Payment terms are less likely to be needed if the final product brings in sales revenue quickly.

 FILE

Payment terms in the newspaper industry

Newspapers are a good example of payment terms being suited to the needs of the industry. Newspaper publishers are large organisations that are unlikely to be experiencing cash-flow problems. Therefore, they offer credit terms to the wholesalers, which are smaller, but still substantial businesses, The wholesalers will be willing to offer payment terms to the newsagents. Typically, a newsagent is given 1 week's credit, paying at the end of the week for the newspapers received over the 7 days. These may not seem to be generous payment terms, but because newspapers are sold daily for cash, it means that the newsagent will receive money for newspapers sold on Monday or Tuesday, but not have to make any payments for them until the following weekend. A small newsagent, which might otherwise suffer cash-flow problems, may be greatly assisted by the payment terms offered.

DID YOU KNOW?

Sale or return is an example of a type of payment term. If a retailer is reluctant to stock a product because it believes that it may not sell, the supplier might be willing to offer the product on a sale or return basis. This type of agreement means that:
- if the product is sold, payment is given to the supplier immediately
- if the product is not sold, it is returned to the supplier

Sale or return agreements put all of the risk on to the supplier and none on to the retailer. For this reason, the payment terms will be different. Items sold on sale or return will be more expensive to buy, reflecting the fact that the supplier is the one taking the risk.

Quality

As society becomes more affluent, consumers become much more selective. In many industries, price competitiveness is being superseded by quality considerations. Therefore, quality is a critical factor to consider when choosing and working with a supplier. A more detailed treatment of the benefits of high quality is presented in Chapter 24 but, in summary, quality enables a business to:
- increase the volume of its sales
- increase its selling price and probably its profit margin
- create a unique selling point (USP)
- enhance its reputation, and its customer and brand loyalty
- reduce its manufacturing costs through elimination of waste

In order to reap these benefits, a business needs to work closely with its suppliers, both to maintain the quality expected by customers and to achieve consistency of quality.

In the case of a retailer, the quality of the produce on sale is directly related to the quality of the materials provided by the supplier. For example, if the apples supplied by a greengrocer are of high quality, this will reflect positively on the reputation of the greengrocer. However, if fault is found with these apples, customers will not blame the farmer because they will be unaware of the origin of the apples. Instead, customers will blame the person who sold them the apples — the greengrocer.

In some cases, blame may be apportioned to both the retailer and the manufacturer. For example, a fault with a branded electrical product may be seen to be the responsibility of both the manufacturer that made it and the retailer that sold it.

 FILE

Quality and 'own-brand' labels

The growing use of 'own-brand' labels by supermarkets and other retailers is leading to a situation in which faulty supplies often damage the reputation of the retailer far more than the manufacturer, as the name of the manufacturer may not be known to customers. This places even more importance on 'quality' when dealing with suppliers, as mistakes by suppliers may damage the reputation of the retailer.

For manufacturers, it is arguably even more important to ensure that the supplier is providing high-quality components and materials. A substandard product on a supermarket shelf can be easily removed. However, a substandard component in a finished product can cause untold damage as the whole of the product may need to be scrapped or recalled. In recent years, there have been a number of occasions where whole batches of motor vehicles have been recalled because of a fault in one component. This issue not only costs money in recalling the cars, but can also cause a great deal of damage to a manufacturer's reputation.

To summarise, the significance of quality depends on the product in question. For an economy brand that is sold on the basis of its low price, quality will be relatively unimportant. However, if the retailer or manufacturer is promoting the product on the basis of its quality, then the product itself and its components must meet high standards.

The onus is on the supplier to provide proof that it can maintain high quality standards. Usually, buyers will visit suppliers in order to assess whether their quality control or quality assurance procedures are satisfactory. The achievement of a recognised quality standard such as ISO 9001 or BS 5750 is the most important factor here. A supplier that provides proof of a British or International Standard is more likely to be given contracts. Quality standards

that have been authenticated by an independent body, such as the British Standards Institution (BSI), will almost certainly be accepted as proof of quality by potential buyers. A supplier that has acquired a quality standard must regularly provide proof that it is maintaining its level of quality. Quality standards therefore provide reassurance to a buyer that a supplier will continue to maintain consistently high quality.

Capacity

Capacity is the maximum possible output of an organisation. An organisation needs to be reassured that a supplier can provide the quantity of materials that it requires. Therefore, this is another factor to consider when deciding whether a particular supplier should be used.

Capacity will be critical if the supplier is providing a unique component or material that cannot be obtained from other sources. If the supplier does not have sufficient capacity to supply, the buyer's business will suffer as a result of its inability to meet its customers' requirements. This might seriously damage the reputation of the buyer. Buyers need to reassure themselves that the supplier can meet the quantity that the business requires, both now and in the foreseeable future.

Many large organisations prefer to buy in bulk from one or two suppliers, so that they can benefit from bulk-buying discounts. This requires high capacity in order to meet the needs of the buyer.

However, if the supplier provides a component or material that can be sourced from other suppliers, its capacity may be less critical. There is a growing tendency for large organisations to spread their risks by getting supplies from many sources. For example, supermarkets are beginning to promote the fact that they buy locally made products in different areas of the country. Consequently, capacity may be less of an issue, although there will still be an expectation that the supplier has enough capacity to meet the needs of all of the stores in a certain area.

If an organisation is concerned about a supplier's inability to supply enough products because of its lack of capacity, it may encourage the supplier to increase the scale of its operations. Sometimes, the organisation may provide financial assistance to help the business extend its factory, but in many cases a contract with a major buyer is enough to help a supplier persuade a bank to lend it the money needed to increase its capacity.

Reliability

In this context, reliability is the extent to which the supplier meets the requirements of the buyer. Typically, it can be measured by the percentage of deliveries made on time or the degree to which a supplier meets the terms of the contract to supply. Organisations give a high priority to the reliability of their suppliers, so reliability will be a vital factor in almost every situation.

If the buyer is a manufacturer, an unreliable supplier can lead to the whole production line grinding to a halt if a crucial material or component is not available. If the buyer is a retailer, a lack of produce can affect its reputation. Customers will blame the retailer if they are unable to buy a product that they expected to be able to purchase in the shop.

When negotiating terms with a potential supplier, a business should always examine the supplier's track record for reliability before agreeing a contract. The contract between the business and its supplier will also contain clauses emphasising the importance of prompt delivery and outlining any compensation payable to the business if the supplier proves to be unreliable (e.g. failing to deliver on time).

There has been a growing movement towards just-in-time methods in recent decades. The ultimate aim of just-in-time is to reduce or eliminate the need for businesses to hold large amounts of stock.

> **KEY TERM**
>
> **just-in-time:** a system where items of stock arrive just in time for production or sale.

This has had significant implications for the relationship between organisations and their suppliers. Previously, businesses held high levels of stock and therefore an unreliable supplier might have had relatively little impact — supplies could be taken out of the stock being held. With just-in-time methods, little or no stock is held, so the reliability of the supplier is a critical factor.

Just-in-time also has implications for quality. There will not be enough time to check the quality of a product when it is delivered, so it is vital that the supplier provides a product that meets the needs of the consumer.

In August 2007, the Co-operative Group became the first UK business to manufacture its own prescription drugs in China. A spokesman indicated that this was to improve reliability and flexibility, by allowing it 'to have greater control over its supplies'. Many organisations like to guarantee their supplies by owning suppliers. For example, the Co-operative Group is the UK's biggest farmer, and this enables it to supply its own stores.

Flexibility

There may be situations when an organisation needs to make radical changes to its orders from suppliers. Examples include:

- sudden changes in demand for a product
- the liquidation of a rival supplier, leaving buyers short of a product or component
- negative publicity concerning the ingredients or components of a product, or the way in which the product is manufactured
- transport difficulties preventing the delivery of supplies from other sources

In these circumstances, an organisation will want its suppliers to be flexible enough to adapt to the changing circumstances. For example, a supplier that regularly provides 10,000 components a week may be asked to provide

the same time, this shift has created more jobs in administration and planning.

> **FACT FILE**
>
> **New technology at Barclays Bank**
>
> In late 2007 Barclays is planning to introduce its 'wave and pay' cards in London, combining a traditional credit card with Oyster transport payment and a contactless card for small items. For transport and payments under £10, the card is 'waved' over a scanner, rather than the customer entering a PIN.
>
> The company is to axe 1,000 out of 1,850 jobs from its processing centre in Poole, Dorset, as a result of increased automation of its systems. Cheques previously dealt with by hand will be processed by computers.
>
> Source: *Independent*, 11 May and 10 July 2007.

- **Multi-skilling.** Technology is allowing companies to benefit from the multi-skilling of staff, creating jobs that are less rigidly defined and adaptable to changes in the workplace. It has also been a key factor in the development of many small businesses operating from home or small premises.
- **Changes in working practices.** ICT offers greater flexibility in terms of the place of employment. It is encouraging teleworking (i.e. people working from home and other locations, and keeping in contact through ICT). Occupations such as market research, design and software development can all be based away from the office. This can motivate staff by giving them more independence and responsibility, while reducing hygiene factors such as travel time and expense. However, projections that the typical office will cease to exist are probably unrealistic, as many teleworkers find that they miss the social aspects of working alongside colleagues. Moreover, some teleworkers find it difficult to separate work from leisure — a major factor in causing stress.

Benefits of using technology in operations

The use of technology has grown because it offers many advantages to businesses. Some of the main benefits are summarised under the following headings.

Reducing costs

- The use of technology to replace manual systems in areas such as planning, office work, manufacturing and stock holding has greatly reduced labour costs, in some particular jobs eliminating the need for workers altogether.
- ICT can be used in production planning in order to devise the most cost-effective way of manufacturing a product.
- Reductions in waste allow a business to reduce unnecessary costs, thereby improving its competitiveness.

■ Use of the internet in particular enables businesses to locate away from expensive sites. In the financial services industry, for example, trans-actions are invariably conducted remotely by internet, by telephone or through an automated teller machine (ATM). Banks and insurance companies have been able to cut back on both staff and expensive high-street premises.

Improving quality

■ Computer-based quality assurance systems can overcome the possibility of human error and also provide more rigorous scrutiny of quality. This benefit applies particularly in situations where people are unable to monitor quality because of a hazardous environment or because the level of precision needed cannot be achieved by human beings.

■ ICT enables business to understand customers' requirements more fully. As a result, businesses can adapt their products to include those features that customers perceive to be important.

Reducing waste

■ Stock control systems ensure that orders are placed at the most appropriate time so that excessive stock levels do not build up. This means that there is less chance of stock becoming out of date, damaged or pilfered, so stock wastage is reduced.

■ Integrated systems of stock control can identify branches holding stock that is needed by other branches. Transferring one branch's excess stock to a branch in need of that item can also be effective in reducing the possibility that stock will not be sold.

■ Arguably, the most significant waste reduction provided by technology is that of time. Many business activities can be carried out much more quickly with the appropriate technology, which therefore greatly improves the efficiency of the business.

Increasing productivity

■ Machines can work at a much faster and more consistent speed than a workforce without the benefit of such technology. As a result, output per head is considerably increased by technology.

■ Computerised systems allow organisations to keep much closer control over their stock levels, reducing the need for time-consuming manual checks and therefore reducing wage bills.

■ ICT may be used to plan the most efficient approach to production. This enables the business to use its resources most effectively and reduce costs.

Other benefits

■ **Flexibility.** Technology enables businesses to provide an immediate response to consumers' demands. Production lines can be adjusted to change the product being produced; salespeople can make immediate contact with the

company's headquarters to adjust plans to suit a customer, while in a face-to-face meeting with that customer.

- **Financial monitoring.** ICT greatly improves the budgeting process. The speed of processing data and the ability to access more information directly enable businesses to plan their budgets more rigorously. Alternatives can be scrutinised to make sure that the budgets are allocated efficiently. Perhaps the greatest benefit to the budgeting process is in budgetary control. With every item of expenditure being recorded on an integrated ICT system, it is possible to monitor actual expenditure against the budget in order to identify areas of inefficiency. This helps the firm to take prompt action to resolve any problems.

- **New and better products and services.** New products/services can be made available and higher-quality products/services can be produced through new technology. Businesses will thus benefit by improving customer satisfaction levels.

- **Better working conditions.** Technology can lead to improvements in the working environment, through factors such as reductions in the level of noise and greater control over temperatures in the work area.

Issues in introducing and updating technology

The use of new technology can also cause problems. An organisation will need to weigh up the pros and cons before deciding on whether it should introduce or update its technology.

- **Resistance to change.** People are often concerned by change. ICT can lead to job losses for workers in traditional skilled crafts. This causes stress for existing workers, as they will fear for their future. Consequently, productivity may fall.

- **Lower morale.** ICT can undermine group morale by breaking up teams. If job losses are involved, morale may fall because workers are concerned for colleagues who have been made redundant. Again, productivity may fall as a result.

- **Cost.** For many businesses, the most significant problem is the cost of new technology. Not only is it expensive to introduce, but it also needs regular updating and servicing. In some situations, it may be more cost-effective to employ less advanced techniques, to avoid constant expenditure on updating technology. For some organisations, the cost of technology can make the business uncompetitive and thus threaten its survival.

- **Keeping up with change.** Technology changes constantly, so hardware and software need to be updated regularly. Staff will also have to undergo frequent training, again adding to costs and threatening efficiency if a business is unable to keep up with the pace of change.

- **Lower barriers to entry.** ICT helps international communication, so businesses can gain from the opportunities offered by the opening up of world markets. However, ICT poses a threat to some firms, as it reduces

some of the barriers to entry in certain industries. Consumers can use the internet to compare prices, so ICT has the potential to force prices and profits down, especially in high-wage economies such as the UK.

DID YOU KNOW?

New technology and the music industry

The music industry is an example of a trade that is suffering from internet technology. Global sales of music peaked in 1999 and have fallen every year since. A combination of music piracy and illegal file swapping is blamed, with only a small fraction of the decline arising from legitimate downloading.

EMI cut its workforce by 1,500 in 2003 and 2004, and further cuts in its 7,000 workforce are planned in 2007 and 2008 with a view to cutting costs by another £150 million a year.

e EXAMINER'S VOICE

Be cautious when answering any questions relating to the benefits or problems arising from technology. The question will probably be asked from the perspective of the business, but it may require a different focus, such as that of an employee, department, customer or supplier. This may radically alter the arguments that are relevant.

Remember that technology affects all businesses, even those that do not use it directly. The extent of the impact depends on the situation. In the examination, you should look at the case study for any indications of benefits or problems that have arisen. You should also identify the manner in which any new technology is used. Ultimately, the impact of new technology will depend on how well the business has introduced and used it.

PRACTICE EXERCISE
Total: 40 marks (35 minutes)

1 What is meant by the term 'technology'? *(3 marks)*

2 What is meant by the term 'information communication technology'? *(3 marks)*

3 What do the initials EPOS stand for? *(2 marks)*

4 Distinguish between CAD and CAM. *(4 marks)*

5 Identify three ways in which robots can be used in a business. *(3 marks)*

6 Analyse two advantages to a retailer of using technology in its stock control. *(8 marks)*

7 Analyse two benefits of technology to a car manufacturer. *(8 marks)*

8 Explain three ways in which the use of information technology might create difficulties for a firm. *(9 marks)*

CASE STUDY **Automation for dishwashers**

Dishwashers are not only replacing people in the kitchen, they are also replacing them on the production line.

Bosch Siemens is a business that manufactures high-quality dishwashers, aiming its products at customers who value quality, reliability and durability above price competitiveness. One of its unique selling points is that it offers guarantees for 10 or more years on some of its dishwashers.

The company relies increasingly on automation for the manufacture of its dishwashers. It faced a particular problem of trying to install pads to deaden the sound of the dishwasher. The solution involved four robots working together as two pairs. One of the robots picks up the dishwasher unit while the second robot applies the pad to the rear panel. Unlike previous systems, each robot can work with 100% precision, if necessary adjusting the position of its gripper before attaching the pad to the dishwasher.

The production process requires the robots to bend at an angle of 90°, a movement that caused great discomfort to production line workers before the robots were introduced. Further discomfort had been caused by the high temperatures involved in the process.

The robots are also programmed to pick up any defects in materials or in the dishwasher, ensuring a high-quality finished product.

Bosch Siemens has reaped a number of benefits from the introduction of the robots:

- gentler handling of the components, which eliminates waste
- greater reliability in the accuracy of the process
- improved quality in the final product
- greater productivity, achieved most significantly by the 100% availability of the robots — this contrasts sharply with the limited hours of availability of the workforce
- improved working conditions for employees — in addition to coping with the high temperatures, an individual employee previously had to lift, without any mechanical aids, materials with a cumulative weight of 7 tonnes per shift

It was necessary for employees working with the robots to undergo suitable training. However, Bosch Siemens believes that the high cost of introducing the new technology will be recovered as a result of greater profitability within 2 years.

Source: **www.bara.org.uk**.

Questions

Total: 25 marks (30 minutes)

1 Outline one reason why employees may oppose the introduction of robots on Bosch Siemens' dishwasher production line. *(3 marks)*

2 Explain two reasons why employees may support the introduction of the robots. *(6 marks)*

3 Bosch Siemens identified a number of benefits to the business arising from the introduction of the robots. Evaluate the major advantages to Bosch Siemens of introducing these robots. *(16 marks)*

Unit 2:
Managing a business

Marketing and the competitive environment

CHAPTER 28

Effective marketing

This chapter examines the purposes of marketing, particularly from the perspective of the organisation. It contrasts consumer marketing and business-to-business marketing. The concepts of niche marketing and mass marketing are introduced, and their benefits and drawbacks are studied and contrasted.

Purposes of marketing

KEY TERM

marketing: the anticipating and satisfying of customers' wants in a way that delights the consumer and also meets the needs of the organisation.

This definition provides an introduction to the purposes of marketing:

- **Anticipating customers' wants.** The first stage of marketing is to conduct market research in order to discover the wants of customers and the factors that influence those wants. Detailed analysis of market research and the need for a business to understand its markets is provided in Chapters 5 and 6.
- **Satisfying customers' wants in a way that delights customers.** An organisation will decide on suitable marketing techniques in order to ensure that customers are delighted. The approach used by organisations to achieve this aim is known as the **marketing mix** (the 'four Ps'). An organisation will plan a suitable **product**, charge an attractive **price**, put the product into the right location or **place**, and use **promotion** to make customers aware of the product. The marketing mix is examined in detail in Chapters 29–33.
- **Meeting the needs of the organisation.** Ultimately, marketing is intended to enable a business to satisfy its own wants. A business will have **corporate aims and objectives** (the goals and specific targets of the organisation as a whole). Having decided on its corporate aims and objectives, the organisation will then decide on suitable aims and objectives for its marketing activities or the marketing department.

Marketing objectives

KEY TERM

marketing objectives: the goals of the marketing function in an organisation.

A business's **marketing objectives** are the goals of the marketing department. These goals must be consistent with the goals of the organisation as a whole. For example, one of Sainsbury's corporate objectives is to increase the amount of Fair Trade products that it sells. In order to achieve this objective in 2007, Sainsbury's decided to set itself a marketing objective to raise the profile of its Fair Trade range by buying all of its bananas from Fair Trade sources.

Organisations can use the marketing mix in order to achieve their marketing objectives.

e EXAMINER'S VOICE

Define your terms at the beginning of your answer. At AS, marks are awarded for correct definitions of the terms used in the questions. Defining terms also helps to make your answer relevant.

Types of marketing objective

Marketing objectives depend on the aims and priorities of an organisation. They can be categorised as follows.

Size

Size can be measured by sales or market share. The objective may be expressed in terms of:

- a specific level of sales volume (e.g. Nestlé trying to maintain KitKat's sales volume of over 4 million bars every day)
- a percentage rise in sales revenue (e.g. Nokia trying to achieve a 10% rise in sales income in 2008)
- a target percentage market share (e.g. Ford targeting a 15% share of the UK car market)
- market leadership or a certain position in the market (e.g. ASDA and Sainsbury's fighting to be the second largest supermarket in the UK)

Market positioning

This is concerned with a company's appeal to particular market segments. Examples include:

- rugby league trying to appeal to more women
- Starbucks targeting younger age groups
- Setanta bidding for Premiership football in order to increase its appeal to sports fans who would otherwise mainly watch Sky

Innovation/increase in product range

Examples are:

- Ben & Jerry's introducing unusual flavours and names of ice cream in order to maintain its reputation for individuality
- Apple introducing the iPhone both to penetrate a new market and to enhance its reputation for innovation and design

Creation of brand loyalty/goodwill

Examples are:

- O_2 negotiating an exclusive agreement with Apple that allowed O_2 to be the only network provider to offer the new iPhone
- McDonald's aiming to maintain the golden arches as the most widely recognised corporate logo in the world
- Specsavers aiming for a set percentage of 'repeat' customers
- Lush being able to set a premium price in comparison with other soap retailers

Security/survival

Examples include:

- Woolworths trying to maintain a presence in the high street
- Lotto trying to make sure that its overall sales, which fell by 5.5% in 2007, do not fall further

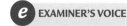

Conclusion

Although many customers perceive marketing to be linked to their needs, the most fundamental reason for marketing is to meet the needs of the organisation. However, this is not an easy task. The wide range of marketing objectives shows how complicated they can be to achieve.

This process is further complicated by the existence of competitors, whose marketing will aim to prevent rivals from achieving their marketing objectives.

Consumer marketing vs business-to-business marketing

There is a tendency to regard marketing as an interaction between a business and individual consumers. All of the examples cited in the previous section would fit into the category of consumer marketing. However, if we take the product back one stage, we can see that this is not the only type of marketing. Retailers such as Woolworths and ASDA will be involved in business-to-business transactions when deciding which products to stock. Business-to-business marketing of this type is very different from consumer marketing.

The main features of business-to-business marketing are as follows:

- **Larger transactions.** Transactions are much larger, with perhaps millions of pounds worth of products being bought and sold in one transaction.
- **Specialist buyers and sellers.** Buyers and sellers will be specialist employees of organisations, and will therefore have much greater knowledge and understanding of the products being exchanged.
- **Quality.** The buyer's reputation will often depend on the quality of the product being sold by the seller, so there is much greater emphasis on quality and related factors, such as after-sales servicing and maintenance.
- **Informative advertising.** Promotions and advertisements tend to be much more informative rather than persuasive, as buyers will base their decisions on factual information.
- **Pricing.** The importance of pricing depends very much on the nature of the market. If there is a wide choice of suppliers, low prices may be critical in securing the deal. However, if there is only one supplier, the seller can set a much higher price.
- **Buyer–seller relationships.** Relationships between buyers and sellers are much more critical. In some cases, an organisation's systems will depend on replacements and additions being compatible with earlier purchases, such as in a computer or security system. There is often a delicate balance between the need for profit and the need to maintain goodwill and good relationships with a customer. News of poor customer service will tend to be publicised and become well known more quickly in business-to-business transactions than in consumer marketing.

KEY TERMS

business-to-consumer (B2C) marketing: where a firm targets individual consumers with its product.

business-to-business (B2B) marketing: where a firm sells its product to another business.

Niche and mass marketing

A critical decision for many businesses is whether to aim for a narrow range of customers or a broad range. Both niche and mass marketing strategies can meet most of a business's marketing objectives.

Niche marketing

One example of a business aiming its product at a particular market segment is Build-A-Bear Workshop, a shop that offers custom-made, personalised teddy bears, complete with birth certificates, personal taped messages and customised clothing.

Niche marketing is an attractive proposition for small firms, as there may be little competition in their segment. However, many firms involved in niche marketing are owned by, or are divisions of, larger organisations. EMAP, one of the UK's largest magazine publishers, produces mass-market publications but even its top sellers, such as *FHM* and *The Garden*, are aimed at specific segments. Niche markets are served more obviously by *Kerrang!*, *Pregnancy & Birth* and *Period Living & Traditional Homes*.

Some niche markets are based on exclusive or high-quality products (e.g. Ferrari) or are located in remote areas, where higher prices can be charged because of the inconvenience for consumers of finding a substitute. But many niche markets focus on lower-priced goods (e.g. Poundstretcher), possibly because larger firms are put off by the low profit margins.

> **KEY TERMS**
>
> **niche marketing:** targeting a product or service at a small segment of a larger market.
>
> **mass marketing:** aiming a product at all (or most) of the market.

Advantages of niche marketing
Niche marketing offers many advantages:

- **Less competition.** There may be fewer competitors, as large companies are not attracted to a relatively small market. For example, there is only one magazine about orienteering, a minority sport, because the potential readership is too low to interest large businesses with high overheads. The lack of competition enables firms to gain enough customers to earn a decent profit. In some niche markets, the lack of competition may help firms to charge a much higher price for their products. Selling relatively few products at high profit margins may enable these firms to achieve good profits.
- **Costs.** The lack of scope for cost reduction by producing on a large scale may mean that small firms can compete more effectively in a niche market. Usually, large, mass-market firms can produce goods at low unit cost because they can afford more efficient machinery or can buy in bulk at a discount. In a niche market, there may be too few customers for a large business to gain these advantages. Therefore, a small firm may be able to match the costs of larger rivals in a niche market.
- **Small-scale production.** The limited demand may suit a small business that would lack the resources to produce on a large scale. A sole trader, for example, would only be able to produce enough products for a small market niche.

- **Tailor-made products.** A business can adapt its product to meet the specific needs of a niche market, rather than compromise between the needs of many different groups of consumers. Tailor-made products, designed to meet the specific needs of a customer, are quite common in niche markets. This makes the product much more attractive to the customer. It not only increases demand but also allows the firm to charge a higher price. The product will have a **unique selling point** (USP).
- **Targeting customers.** It can be easier for businesses to target customers and promote their products effectively when they are only selling to a certain type of customer. The content of advertisements can be designed to appeal to the specific market segment being targeted. Furthermore, the media used can be selected according to the market segment. For example, children's toys are advertised during children's television programmes, using messages and images that attract children's interest.

> **DID YOU KNOW?**
>
> Although more specific targeting is usually an advantage of niche marketing (e.g. *FHM* and *Bliss* magazines have a clear idea who their readers are and how to reach them), this is not always the case. The Build-A-Bear Workshop has found it difficult to reach its customers, who do not fit into the usual market segments. For instance, the firm has been surprised by the number of teenage boys buying bears for their girlfriends — a behaviour pattern not identified in its early research.

Disadvantages of niche marketing

There are, however, some disadvantages of niche marketing:

- **Lower profits.** The small scale of the market limits the chances of making a high profit. Even if a high price can be charged, the lack of customers will reduce the total profit made. In addition, unit costs tend to be higher relative to larger competitors, again reducing the potential for high profit margins. If a niche is large enough for a small business to make a reasonable profit, it is likely to attract competition from other businesses. If a number of businesses are sharing relatively few customers between them, they may find it difficult to survive, particularly if these firms compete fiercely for their customers.
- **Changes in demand.** Small businesses in niche markets can be vulnerable to changes in demand. Niche markets are specialised, so firms operating in them are not able to spread their risks. For this reason, a decline in interest among consumers may threaten the firm's existence, as it has no other products to fall back on. Larger, mass-market firms are able to avoid this risk by producing a wide range of goods and services.
- **Market entry.** An increase in interest among consumers may be enough to attract larger firms into the market. Holland and Barrett identified health foods as a market niche many years ago, but the company has not grown quickly. This is because, as the demand for health foods increased, the large supermarkets decided to offer many more health foods. In rapidly changing

times, it is likely that firms in niche markets will make high profits only in the short term, unless they can continue to react quickly to changes.

Niche marketing at Ben & Jerry's

Ben & Jerry's ice cream tries to emphasise its reputation for niche marketing by sponsoring, in the firm's own words, 'the world's weirdest champion-ships', in keeping with its 'irreverent personality and quirky approach to life'. Lauren Nola, brand manager, commented on Ben & Jerry's sponsorship of three world championships: bog snorkelling, conkers and toe wrestling. 'We are delighted to lend a hand to each of these wacky events and are looking forward to another season of world record breaking bizarreness.' Ironically, Ben & Jerry's is owned by Unilever, one of the UK's largest companies.

Source: www.benjerry.co.uk.

Mass marketing

Examples of mass-market goods are petrol and baked beans. Within a mass market there is only limited scope for targeting. For instance, there is little scope to modify petrol to appeal to a niche market, although cars can be modified to run on environmentally friendlier fuel. There are more variations to baked beans, aimed mainly at children, but most baked beans are sold in the mass market.

Advantages of mass marketing

The advantages of mass marketing are as follows:

- **Large-scale production.** With mass marketing, production on a large scale is possible, which will help to lower costs per unit through factors such as bulk buying. This should improve profit margins, particularly as many businesses will not be large enough to compete in the mass market.
- **High revenues.** The sheer volume of customers enables companies to earn huge revenues. The chemicals industry in the UK is worth over £36 billion per annum. There are roughly 500 UK chemical firms with sales turnover in excess of £5 million per year.

- **Barriers to entry.** Mass marketing allows businesses to use the most expensive (and usually the most effective) marketing. Not only does this help to eliminate smaller rivals, but it can also act as a barrier to entry for new firms. For over 50 years, the soap powder industry has been dominated by two large companies with huge marketing budgets. This has limited the opportunities for new firms to break into the market, as they cannot afford the advertising budgets required.
- **Research and development.** In industries such as pharmaceuticals, it is necessary to appeal to large, profitable mass markets in order to be able to fund the research and development costs needed to introduce new products. It is estimated that discovering a major new pharmaceutical product and bringing it to the market costs a business about £400 million.
- **Brand awareness.** Mass marketing increases brand awareness. This not only assists sales of the branded product but can also help to break down consumer resistance to new products. Firms such as Cadbury's and Coca-Cola can use their high level of brand awareness to encourage customers, who are often reluctant to try new products if they do not recognise the name.

Disadvantages of mass marketing

The disadvantages of mass marketing are as follows:

- **Fixed capital.** High fixed capital costs are incurred, such as the purchase of large factories, extensive and expensive machinery, and other assets such as delivery lorries. This will prevent many businesses from ever operating in the mass market.
- **Changes in demand.** Businesses in mass markets are vulnerable to changes in demand. A fall in demand will lead to unused spare capacity, increasing unit costs. As the pace of change accelerates, this is becoming a much greater problem because customers want the latest products. Small, niche market firms will be less affected as they will not have spent so much on their factories.
- **Effects of standardisation.** It can be difficult to appeal directly to individual customers because mass-market products must be designed to suit all customers. As a result, prices tend to be lower, reducing the opportunities for high profits.
- **Competition.** Mass-market organisations are much more vulnerable to low-cost competition from abroad, as the UK cannot match wage levels and other costs in these countries.
- **Adding value.** In mass markets there is less scope for adding value. As customers' incomes increase, there is a growing tendency for them to want high-priced, unique products. This trend is helping niche marketing but making it harder for businesses that concentrate on the mass market.

Through careful market research, businesses in mass markets can reduce these risks, but there is always a danger that demand for their products will fall. Consequently, such firms must regularly examine their products in order to ensure that their goods continue to suit the market.

Product differentiation in the mass market

In order to compete in a mass market, a business needs to make sure that its product is different from competitors' products. If consumers value this difference, it will benefit the firm in two ways:

- increased sales volume
- greater scope for charging a higher price

In a mass market, product differentiation will usually be achieved by employing elements of the marketing mix (see Chapters 30–33). Examples include:

- Design, branding and packaging to improve the attractiveness of a product.
- Clever promotional and advertising campaigns to boost image and sales. Are Nike sportswear and trainers of better quality than their competitors' products, or are they just marketed more effectively?
- Different distribution methods. Avon cosmetics differentiated itself by selling cosmetics directly to the customer; Amazon differentiated itself through internet selling, without the use of a traditional shop outlet.

> **KEY TERM**
>
> **product differentiation:** the degree to which consumers see a particular brand as being different from other brands.

FACT FILE

Product differentiation in radio broadcasting

Radio is adapting to the needs of niche markets. In Easter 2007, theJazz started to broadcast a mix of pre-bebop, swing and Latin music, attracting 334,000 listeners in its first week. BBC 6 Music caters for rock fans and BBC 7 concentrates on drama and comedy classics. *Smash Hits* could no longer survive in magazine form but has reinvented itself as a radio station with 1 million listeners.

However, the mass market still exists in radio, with Radio 2 attracting over 13 million listeners a week to the broad range of programmes offered.

Source: article by Adam Sherwin in *The Times*, 17 August 2007.

FACT FILE

Product differentiation through branding

At one time, Quaker Oats manufactured all of the porridge for UK supermarket own labels. Although the contents were identical, consumers still felt more secure buying the Quaker Oats brand, which sold at a higher price. Similarly, General Motors used the Vauxhall brand name in the UK and the Opel name in Germany to sell identical cars because these brand names were preferred by UK and German customers respectively.

Many mass-market firms achieve product differentiation through **product proliferation**. This occurs when a variety of products are produced to serve different tastes. In some cases, this can mean significantly different products, such as IPC magazines producing *Woman's Own*, *Loaded*, *Ideal Home*, *Uncut* and *NME*. However, the need for mass production in order to cut costs will limit the number of different products that can be offered.

FACT FILE

What's in a name?

Over many years, 'blind taste tests' suggested that consumers preferred Pepsi to Coca-Cola (when they could not see the brand name), but Coca-Cola always sold in higher quantities because people preferred the brand.

PRACTICE EXERCISE

Total: 40 marks (35 minutes)

1 What are the three purposes of marketing? *(6 marks)*

2 Identify four marketing objectives. *(4 marks)*

3 Distinguish between consumer marketing and business-to-business marketing. *(4 marks)*

4 State four examples of niche markets. *(4 marks)*

5 Why might a magazine publisher target a niche market? *(4 marks)*

6 Is it inevitable that businesses in a niche market will be unable to break into a mass market? *(6 marks)*

7 Explain three benefits of mass marketing. *(9 marks)*

8 What is meant by 'product differentiation'? *(3 marks)*

CASE STUDY Lush Cosmetics

Lush Cosmetics was originally set up in 1978, supplying cosmetics to The Body Shop. However, an ill-fated venture into mail order led to its collapse.

Lush recommenced trading in 1994, producing
5 soaps, shampoos, cosmetics and related products. This time it decided to open its own retail outlets, selling directly to consumers rather than doing business-to-business marketing, as it had with The Body Shop. It has been so successful that, in addition to manufac-
10 turing all of its own products, it has set up almost 100 stores in the UK alone. Overseas, there are over 270 franchises in more than 40 different countries.

Lush focuses on its range of products. Each bar of soap, shampoo etc. contains fresh (not synthetic)
15 ingredients, ranging from the predictable (aloe vera, lemon and tea tree oil) to the peculiar (Belgian chocolate, almond shells and marigold petals). In this way, Lush sees itself as operating in a niche market rather than in a mass market. Products are not
20 tested on animals. For its overseas franchises, the products are manufactured locally to guarantee freshness.

Marketing is mostly by word of mouth and through an in-house magazine, which has also been used to re-
25 establish a mail-order service. The nature of the ingredients means that the location of a Lush shop can usually be detected by smell from a considerable distance (depending on the wind direction). This can also help to encourage con-
30 sumers to visit the shops.

Over 200 products are made, with the range changing constantly according to demand. Unsuccessful products are quickly eliminated and there is constant
35 research aimed at producing new products. The product range is updated every 3 months. Consumers and press reports are used to provide marketing slogans, such as 'Lush is
40 like the AA, pretty vital in a crisis' and 'It's better to bathe in sweets than to eat them'. Interest is also aroused through unusual product names such as 'Honey I Washed the Kids' and 'Sex Bomb'. Staff are encouraged to spot celebrities, and a list of famous
45 names, and their Lush purchases, is regularly updated on the company website.

With typical product prices at about £2.10 for a 100 gram bar of soap, Lush achieves high profit margins. The ingredients of a bar of soap can cost
50 as little as 50p.

Source: www.lush.co.uk.

Questions

Total: 55 marks (65 minutes)

1 What is meant by the term 'business-to-business marketing' (lines 7–8)? *(3 marks)*

2 Distinguish between a 'niche market' and a 'mass market' (lines 18–19). *(6 marks)*

3 Analyse two reasons why Lush introduces new products every 3 months. *(8 marks)*

4 Analyse two reasons why Lush might have decided to open its own shops when it relaunched in 1994. *(8 marks)*

5 Lush changed from business-to-business marketing to marketing directly to consumers. Evaluate the main differences between business-to-business marketing and consumer marketing for Lush. *(10 marks)*

6 Discuss the difficulties faced by Lush as a result of its decision to produce a range of 200 different products. *(10 marks)*

7 Evaluate the benefits for Lush from operating in a niche market. *(10 marks)*

Decline

If the business sees a decline in sales for its product as temporary, it should continue to use extension strategies. Once decline is seen as inevitable, however, the firm can 'milk' the product. By cutting advertising expenditure, it may be able to achieve high profits for a period of time. Eventually, the firm should take the product off the market, but only if it has ceased to be profitable. The sales of most national newspapers are currently in decline but they can still generate a profit. If their rivals leave the market first, it is even possible that their sales will recover.

Problems of predicting the product life cycle

The product life cycle is of limited use in strategic planning because the exact life span of a product is never known. In industries that experience relatively few changes, the life cycle can be easier to predict, but it is more useful in explaining past events than future trends. The confectionery market is relatively stable, with some products having extremely long lifetimes. Recent sales figures suggest that the Mars Bar may have entered its decline phase, but this could just be a temporary fall — only time will tell.

It is important to predict life cycles in order to assess whether a product launch is feasible. A record label knows that a record will need to make a profit within months of its launch; a bus company can expect its bus services to take much longer to make a profit.

DID YOU KNOW?

Product life cycles are getting shorter. Although the exact lengths are impossible to predict, consumers are constantly striving for new products and are less loyal to brands than they were in the past. This means that businesses need to plan shorter, more intensive promotional campaigns and spend more time on developing new products. Higher prices will be needed to compensate for the higher costs and lower sales figures.

FACT FILE

Oxo cubes

Oxo cubes were introduced in 1910, but in the 1950s they went into an apparently terminal decline. Analysts suggested that the product was too old-fashioned to survive. Rather than accept this advice, Oxo repackaged the product and started to promote it heavily. Product variations and highly successful advertising campaigns have kept Oxo in maturity for a further 50 years. Ironically, one of the main reasons for the repackaging was to save costs — the expensive tin containers, which turned out to be the main cause of consumers' dislike of the product, were replaced by cheaper, paper packaging that presented a more modern image.

Financial implications of the product life cycle

There is a tendency to look at the product life cycle purely in terms of its implications for marketing. However, it is also important for the business to monitor a product's life cycle from a financial perspective.

Figure 30.2 (see p. 361) shows a typical product life cycle and the pattern of cash flow that arises. The dangers of releasing a new product are clear, as it

can be sold for twice as much as music recorded in state-of-the-art Western studios.

Music sales are plummeting throughout the world, with the 10% drop in the UK over the past year being much less than the decline in sales in countries such as the USA, France and Canada. Virgin Megastores lost £50 million in 2007 and Richard Branson has decided to get out of the industry. Those recordings sold have smaller profit margins — downloading a single track now costs 79p against the £4 that a CD single cost in 1999.

There is still money to be made in the music industry. In recent years, interest in live music has increased dramatically. Attendances at shows last year rose by 11% and by the end of 2007 450 music festivals would have taken place in the UK. Last Monday, Ticketmaster reported that 20,000 tickets for the Spice Girls' first reunion concert at London's O2 arena in December sold out in 38 seconds, with 1 million fans registering to buy. Three weeks earlier, more than a million people clamoured for seats at the forthcoming Led Zeppelin reunion. Glastonbury Festival disposed of its 135,000 weekend passes to this year's event within 2 hours, taking more than £21 million in the process. Ticket prices, particularly for A-list artists, have soared as the prices of CDs have tumbled. You could have bought Madonna's entire recording catalogue for less than half the cost to see her perform at Wembley Arena last summer, when the best seats in the house went for £160.

The nature of the product has changed. In the 1960s and 1970s, bands such as the Beatles used live performances to increase consumer awareness and thus help to sell records. With factors such as new technology and changes in consumer tastes, and the willingness of competitor bands to undertake more concerts, the product has completely transformed. Records are now used to help performers earn the big money from concerts and fan paraphernalia sold at gigs and through websites.

In the light of these changes, the probability is that music fans are now spending more money on their passion than they were in the heyday of the CD. Fans have rediscovered an ancient truth — that music is the root of communal experience as much as it is something that goes on between your ears.

Source: adapted from Sandall, R. (2007) 'The day the music industry died', *Sunday Times*, 7 October.

Questions

Total: 45 marks (55 minutes)

1 Radiohead have identified three separate products arising from their activities:
  a recorded music
  b sales of concert tickets
  c fan paraphernalia, such as T-shirts and signed photographs, sold at gigs and through websites
  Classify each of these three items in terms of their place in the Boston matrix, explaining
  the reasoning behind your decisions.   *(9 marks)*

2 With reference to your answers to question 1, analyse the implications of the recent changes in
  these items on the likely financial success of:
  a the band itself   *(6 marks)*
  b record stores such as HMV   *(6 marks)*

3 Discuss the main factors that have changed the ways in which bands and recording artists, such
  as Radiohead and Madonna, can profit from their 'product'.   *(12 marks)*

4 Evaluate the main reasons why some of the long-established, older bands are finding that they
  can extend their product life cycle.   *(12 marks)*

CASE STUDY 2 How the low-powered Wii moved the big boys aside

Coming up to its second Christmas, the Nintendo Wii is still in short supply in some markets, including the UK. While electronic products are supposed to fall in price once they have become established on the market, the Wii has got more expensive. Its rival – the Sony PlayStation 3 – has been forced to cut its price in order to remain competitive.

You can pay as much for a 729 MHz processor Wii as you can for the more technically advanced 3.2 GHz Sony product. Shigeru Miyamoto, Nintendo's top game designer, clearly got it right when he said that 'Power isn't everything.' The main problem with the Wii is that Nintendo has never been able to keep up with the demand. It has increased its manufacturing base twice from 800,000 per month to 1.8 million, producing more than 20 million Wiis a year. Worldwide, the Wii has already sold as many units as the Xbox 360, in spite of giving Microsoft a year's start.

The secret of the Wii's success has been to focus on different market segments. The traditional market for games – 15- to 24-year-olds – is dominated by Sony and Microsoft. Nintendo has had huge success in its traditional market – younger children. The ease of playing the Wii has also attracted other, mainly older family members. Wii games do not require the same level of precision and practice, so they appeal much more to casual game users, rather than those who play games frequently.

The difficulty facing all the main console producers is the shortening of the product life cycle. Early consoles, such as those produced by Nintendo and Sega, dominated the market for more than 10 years before requiring a major update. As technology and consumer expectations have increased, updates have been required more frequently. The PlayStation is now on its third edition and yet the original PlayStation was introduced only 12 years ago – although some might consider the PlayStation 2 and PlayStation 3 to be extension strategies rather than new products.

Fortunately for the three main competitors, the vast expense required to introduce a new console means that rival products do not appear very frequently in the market. Currently, it is believed that Microsoft will need to replace the Xbox 360 soon, as its technology is beginning to look dated and Microsoft has tended to be slower to overcome faults. With the Nintendo Wii still in its growth stage and the Sony PlayStation 3 in maturity, there is less pressure on these two companies to devote the huge resources needed to launch a new product.

Source: adapted from articles by Jack Schofield in the *Guardian*, 6 and 13 December 2007.

Questions

Total: 30 marks (40 minutes)

1 Explain two extension strategies that Sony might use for the PlayStation 3. *(6 marks)*

2 Explain one possible advantage for Nintendo arising from its inability to produce enough Wiis to meet the demand. *(4 marks)*

3 Analyse two implications for Nintendo of the fact that the product life cycles for games consoles are becoming shorter. *(8 marks)*

4 Discuss the reasons why the Nintendo Wii can match the Sony PlayStation 3, despite the fact that it is technically inferior. *(12 marks)*

CHAPTER 31

COMPANY PROFITS

23%

sale

Using the marketing mix: promotion

This chapter introduces the concept of promotion. The overall aims of promotion are introduced through the AIDA model and the different elements of the promotional mix are examined. The chapter concludes by studying the main factors that affect the choice of promotional mix adopted for a certain product or service.

DID YOU KNOW?

Promotion is often categorised in two ways:
- **above-the-line promotions** — advertising through media (newspapers, television, radio, the cinema and posters)
- **below-the-line promotion** — all other promotions, such as public relations, merchandising, sponsorship, direct marketing, personal selling and competitions

EXAMINER'S VOICE

Do not confuse advertising and promotion. Advertising is just one element of promotion, although it is often the key element in the promotional mix of a product.

The distinction between the two will become clearer as the chapter describes the other elements of the promotional mix that can be used alongside or instead of advertising.

KEY TERM

promotion: in the context of marketing, the process of communicating with customers or potential customers. Promotion can also describe communication with other interested groups, such as shareholders and suppliers.

What is promotion?

Promotion and advertising can be **informative** or **persuasive**. Informative promotion is intended to increase consumer awareness of the product and its features. Persuasive promotion is intended to encourage consumers to purchase the product, usually through messages that emphasise its desirability.

Aims of promotion

Promotion has many different purposes. A popular model that is used to demonstrate the different aims of promotion is **AIDA**. This is a mnemonic that stands for Attention, Interest, Desire, Action, and describes the process of a successful marketing campaign.

- **Attention.** The first step in a promotional strategy is to get the attention of the consumer. Attention raising is mainly an attempt to improve awareness of the name and product among the target audience. Typically, advertising at this stage is used to make people aware of the product or service, but it does not aim to provide them with detailed information.

- **Interest.** Promotional campaigns are usually drip-fed over a period of time, using various forms of media, in order to gain the interest of consumers. After hearing a brand name repeatedly, consumers are more likely to trust it. The intention is to make consumers want to find out more about the product. The choice of media, messages and images will be based on the interests of the target market.

- **Desire.** Having gained the consumer's interest, promotions may change in nature to provide the consumer with more specific reasons for purchasing the product. This often involves informative advertising, such as giving the technical specifications of a piece of equipment. However, in some markets, desire is fuelled by imagery. In such cases, promotions will be persuasive rather than informative.

- **Action.** The final and crucial step is converting desire on the part of the consumer into the action of purchasing the product. Point-of-sale displays, special offers and competition entries are popular methods of achieving this aim. In the case of goods that are 'impulse buys', promotions in the shop itself are much more likely to be successful.

AIDA should be seen as an integrated whole. A brilliant shop display is unlikely to be successful if earlier stages have been missed and the consumer fails to recognise the item being displayed. Similarly, attention, desire and interest may not convert into action if the product cannot be located in a store.

FACT FILE

How important is media advertising?

Media advertising is popularly seen as the most significant form of promotion, but the AIDA model puts it into perspective. It is unlikely that a consumer's decision to purchase something will be based on advertising alone, especially if it is not a printed form of advert. Television, radio and cinema campaigns are usually meant to bring people's *attention* to a product, raising their *interest*. As a general rule, it is the more detailed informative promotions that create *desire*, and brochures and merchandising activities that trigger *action*. However, as with so many business issues, there will be plenty of exceptions to this rule.

DID YOU KNOW?

A classic example of a successful 'attention' campaign was the Amy campaign in 1984. A poster of a young girl appeared on bus shelters across the country accompanied by the sentence 'I'm Amy and I like slugs and snails.' After a time without any further information, the national media picked up on the story, and they tried to discover who Amy was and what she was meant to be promoting. Eventually, market research revealed that 75% of the UK population had heard of Amy. At this point it was revealed that Amy was promoting the idea of using bus shelters for poster advertising. With 75% awareness achieved, advertising agencies began to recognise the effectiveness of this (previously unpopular) method of advertising. This style of attention or awareness raising is known as a 'teaser campaign' and has been used successfully by organisations as diverse as the government and Orange.

Elements of the promotional mix

Public relations (PR)

The public will recognise that an advert is designed to sell a product, and will therefore be wary of the messages being sent. However, an article in a newspaper that praises a product can raise awareness in a cost-effective way. If Jeremy Clarkson can be persuaded to test drive the new Porsche on television, it can help Porsche to sell more cars. Newspapers may publish a 'press release' from a business if the story is considered newsworthy, so firms will often try to find a human interest story connected to their product. Successful PR relies on the reaction of the media to the story being put forward by the firm. As a result, it is more unreliable than most other forms of promotion, but it is extremely cost-effective when it works.

Branding

Brands can add value to a product and a firm. Consumers are much more likely to buy Coca-Cola than Panda Cola, simply because of the name. When Nestlé bought Rowntree Mackintosh, it paid a sum that was more than double the value of the company's tangible assets (e.g. machinery). In effect, Nestlé paid over £6 billion just to get hold of famous brand names such as KitKat and Yorkie. However, if one product in a brand gains a bad reputation, it can affect customers' loyalty to all the products with the same brand identity.

Merchandising

Kellogg's tries to persuade retailers to offer more shelf space (e.g. by producing variations of basic cereals); Procter & Gamble has a special team that advises small retailers on the most attractive way to display its products; Tic Tac produces displays that persuade consumers to buy at the point of sale.

Both manufacturers and retailers try to maximise sales by using psychological research. To improve the shopping environment in supermarkets, pleasant smells (e.g. fresh bread) are pumped around the building and colourful displays of fresh produce are placed near the entrance. Merchandising is well suited to 'impulse buys', but because merchandising works at the point of sale, it is effective only if other methods are successful in enticing customers to the point of sale.

Sales promotions

Popular sales promotion methods include competitions, free offers, coupons, 'three for the price of two' or BOGOF (buy one, get one free) offers, introductory offers, product placement (featuring a product in a film), credit terms and endorsements by famous personalities.

 TERMS

promotional mix: the coordination of the various methods of promotion in order to achieve overall marketing targets.

public relations (PR): gaining favourable publicity through the media.

branding: the process of differentiating a product or service from its competitors through the name, sign, symbol, design or slogan linked to that product/service.

merchandising: attempts to persuade consumers to take action at the 'point of sale' (PoS) (also known as the 'point of purchase', PoP).

sales promotions: short-term incentives used to persuade consumers to buy a particular product.

direct selling: the process of communicating directly to the individual consumer through an appropriate form of communication (e.g. postal system or telephone).

advertising: the process of communicating with customers or potential customers through specific media (e.g. television and newspapers).

FACT FILE

Orange Wednesday

Luke Mitchell, a consultant for Reach Students, an agency specialising in promoting to students, believes that Orange has developed an excellent promotional mix:

A great example of an effective mix is Orange Wednesday's two-for-one cinema ticket offer. It is delivered via mobile phones. Students love it and it's easy to understand why: it brings together three things that are close to their hearts. Firstly, they are massive filmgoers with 92% of them going at least once a month. Secondly, they are probably the heaviest users of mobile phones and new technologies. Thirdly, they relish freebies.

In the case of business-to-business promotions, approaches such as offering credit terms or providing 'hospitality' (invitations to attend an event or a meal) are often used as sales promotions. Sales promotions are an excellent way of providing a boost to sales, especially when a product is new to the market or would not have been purchased otherwise. If the consumer enjoys the product, it can mean that a new loyal customer has been gained. Promotional price cuts are often used to persuade consumers to try a product for a short time, in the hope that they will then become loyal customers. However, the cost-effectiveness of promotions needs to be assessed carefully. They often provide only a short-term boost and in many cases they allow customers to purchase more cheaply a product that they would have bought anyway.

Direct selling

This takes four main forms:

- **Direct mail.** This describes promotions that are sent directly to the customer. It is growing rapidly as a form of promotion. Databases are becoming more detailed, so businesses are able to discover an increasing amount about their customers. Organisations such as supermarkets, in particular, have used loyalty cards to obtain information on buying habits. This has enabled them to target direct-mail offers for certain items to specific consumers. (The 'junk mail' contains less junk because the offers are more likely to interest the person who has been targeted.) Internet links are also used.

- **Telephone.** As many households block or throw away 'junk mail', many companies have resorted to making telephone contact, often initially disguised as market research but then transforming into attempts to achieve a sale. Although these tactics are often resented by customers and can be blocked, companies have found them to be quite successful because many people are reluctant to be rude to a telephone caller. However, they can create a negative image of a company.

- **Door-to-door drops.** These are promotions that are delivered directly to houses. They are often delivered with the local free newspaper and can be highly cost-effective and targeted. IKEA, for example, delivers its catalogues in August and September, the beginning of the run-up to Christmas. Postcodes that provide the highest sales are identified through sales records, and houses in these postcode areas are targeted to receive the catalogue.

- **Personal selling.** This is considered to be a crucial element in the final action to buy by consumers. In general, high labour costs have led to a decline in door-to-door selling, but for durable items such as housing, cars and household goods, the role of the individual salesperson is crucial. In these cases, customers may value the expertise or details provided by the sales-person. Personal selling is particularly important in commercial marketing, where a company's sales force contacts other firms that are seen as potential customers.

In general, direct selling – particularly telephone contact — is often seen by consumers as an invasion of privacy, so businesses must use it with caution.

Advertising

The main media chosen for advertising are outlined on the following pages, with a brief comment on their use.

Television

Television has the advantage of being memorable, as it can present both moving images and sound. It is ideal for mass-market, fast-moving consumer goods. Although the cost of television advertising is relatively high when considered against the number of viewers reached, the cost per thousand (CPT) can be quite low.

With the increase in the number of television channels and more specialisation of programmes, often with a narrow focus in terms of audience make-up, television advertising is also becoming more suited to niche market products.

> **KEY TERM**
>
> **cost per thousand (CPT):** an indicator used commonly in the advertising industry to assess and compare the expense of different forms of promotion.

> **FACT FILE**
>
> **Television advertising**
>
> Although television advertising has experienced some decline, it still remains an effective medium. Slogans such as 'Beanz meanz Heinz' and 'A Mars a day helps you work, rest and play' are remembered long after the firm stops using them.
>
> A recent research project by tvWORKS, matching advertisements seen on television to purchases of goods by households, revealed the increases in sales shown in Figure 31.1.

> **DID YOU KNOW?**
>
> Programmes such as *Coronation Street* and *Emmerdale* gained the nickname of 'soaps' because traditionally they were watched by housewives who decided which soap powder the family should use. As a result, the advertising slots during these programmes became the most popular times for companies that wanted to advertise their soap.

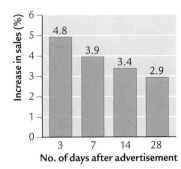

Figure 31.1
Effect of television advertising on sales

Radio

Radio advertising is increasing in popularity, as it is flexible enough to target a small local area as well as national markets. Radio advertising tends to be cheaper than many other media, so it is ideally suited to job advertisements in the local area and local events, such as fairs. Mass-market companies also use radio advertising, as the low cost per advert means that a wide spread of local radio stations can be used to achieve national coverage at a reasonable overall cost.

Cinema

Cinema advertising can be targeted to specific audiences. For example, the advertisements placed during a Disney film will be different from those featured during a horror film. Cinema advertising can also be used to promote complementary activities such as a restaurant or nightclub to be visited after watching the film.

 FILE

Cinema advertising

Cinema is an excellent medium for reaching the youth market, as the following information shows.

In comparison with the overall population, those who visit the cinema are:
- over two-and-a-half times more likely to be aged 15–24
- 30% more likely to be from social classes A and B
- equally likely to be male or female

This latter factor is important, as cinema is the only major form of media that captures an even mix of males and females.

Source: http://business.pearlanddean.com/audience.html.

National newspapers

Although sales of national newspapers have declined, the most popular newspapers, such as the *Sun*, are still read by millions of people daily. Consequently, national newspapers remain a popular medium. Advertisements can be placed on pages that relate closely to the interests of the readership, thus increasing the effectiveness of the advertisement. This aspect of newspaper advertising is particularly prevalent in weekend newspapers, where magazine supplements featuring interests such as fashion, travel and personal finance contain advertisements related to those features.

Posters

Posters are a highly flexible medium and can be used for mass-market products or be geared towards certain market segments. In places where customers are likely to be waiting for a period of time, such as the London Underground, detailed informative advertising can be provided. In general, however, posters are a persuasive form of media, usually geared towards trying to gain initial attention or interest in the product or service.

Magazines

Most magazines in the UK tend to be specifically targeted at a focused audience. Consequently, they are ideal media for promoting niche market products, although magazines are also used by mass-market companies trying to boost sales in a particular market segment. The use of colour in magazines and the high quality of print enhances their effectiveness as an advertising medium. In some cases, there is an additional benefit that magazines, such as *Reader's Digest*, remain in circulation long after their date of release, often

being used by doctors' and dentists' surgeries as reading material for patients who are waiting for appointments.

Internet and other electronic media

Both of these media are excellent methods for reaching customers. Although internet users may not always be aware of it, they are constantly exposed to promotions while surfing. Furthermore, the advertisements on internet pages are invariably specific to the material on that page, so internet advertising can be a cost-effective way of reaching target audiences at a time when they are expressing an interest in a particular topic or product. Electronic media, such as electronic displays and text messages, can be even more focused, being sent only to individuals who are known to be interested in a product or service.

Regional newspapers

Local or regional newspapers tend to be significantly different from national newspapers in terms of advertising. Advertisements tend to concentrate on goods and services that are sold on a local basis, rather than nationally. Particular products that lend themselves well to local newspaper advertising include new and second-hand cars, property, local entertainment and job opportunities.

Sponsorship

Sponsorship means giving financial assistance to an individual, event or organisation. For example, sponsorship of popular football teams can generate a great deal of publicity for companies. Sponsorship can also be targeted towards a particular audience, as with O_2's sponsoring of the O_2 Arena in London, a venue that puts on events that are often geared towards the company's target market. Sponsorship can enable organisations that face advertising restrictions to reach customers, and it often improves goodwill when it is seen to be supporting a good cause (e.g. sponsorship of litter bins). It can also give a company access to attractive events such as Wimbledon, performances at the Royal Albert Hall and Grand Prix races. The company can then pass on invitations to customers or suppliers, and build goodwill and closer links. However, sponsorship can be unpredictable. An unexpectedly good cup run for a rugby team or a scandal involving the person sponsored can affect the results.

Trade fairs and exhibitions

Although some exhibitions are popular with the general public, most exhibitions and trade fairs are used to target other businesses. They can be used to 'network' (get to know people in other businesses), but more importantly they are used to demonstrate products to potential customers, and to provide detailed information and brochures. At exhibitions, customers can test and order products, so they can be vital to the success of some firms, especially in industries where new products are being developed constantly.

 **EXAMINER'S VOICE**

Be aware of the costs of advertising. Relatively few companies can afford television advertising, so they choose media that they can afford and that are appropriate for their situation.

Book publishers are aware that in-store posters and displays have always been a vital part of the promotional mix. In recent years the shops have taken advantage of this situation by charging publishers to display their books prominently. Example of charges made by Waterstone's are as follows:

- £45,000 for one book to appear in the window and front-of-store displays, and in Waterstone's national press and television advertisement campaign
- £17,000 to be one of two titles promoted as the 'offer of the week' for 1 week in the run-up to Christmas
- £500 for an entry in Waterstone's Christmas gift guide, complete with a bookseller review

Similar charges are made by other leading booksellers, such as Borders and WH Smith. A spokesman for the latter said, 'Our premium promotion spaces are oversubscribed, which suggests that publishers feel that they are getting value for money.'

Anthony Cheetham, chairman of Quercus books, a small independent publisher, said: 'It's not a system you can opt out of. If Smith's offer you one of their slots and you say no, their order doesn't go down from 1,000 copies to 500 copies — it goes down to 20 copies.'

Should bookshops be allowed to make these charges?

Source: adapted from Hoyle, B. and Clarke, S. (2007) 'The hidden price of a Christmas bestseller', *The Times*, 18 June.

Influences on the choice of promotional mix

When deciding what form of promotion to use, a business will consider the following factors:

- **Objectives of the campaign.** If the firm is trying to introduce a new product, it will focus on using media that raise awareness, such as television. If it is aiming to provide information, the internet or newspapers will be more relevant.
- **Costs and budgets.** Small businesses cannot justify the use of a television campaign because of the expense involved. For these businesses, local radio or newspapers are a better choice. Media companies calculate the cost per thousand (CPT) to show how much it costs to get a message to 1,000 consumers. National companies find it much more cost-effective to use national newspapers and television, as one advert can reach a large number of people. The marketing budget allocated to the manager will influence the media that can be used. Ryanair is a large firm, but its relatively low marketing budget prevents it from using television advertising in the way that its rivals do.
- **The target market.** Lord Leverhulme, formerly of Unilever plc, is famously quoted as saying: 'Half of what I spend on promotion is wasted. The trouble is I don't know which half.' Firms will spend more eagerly on a medium that reaches their target market. Channel 4 advertisements have a higher CPT because many of the channel's programmes are targeted towards specific groups of people. For the same reason, magazines and local media can be more effective than national media.

FILE

Pot Noodle — Fuel of Britain

The effectiveness of advertising can depend on the ability of an advert to capture the imagination of its audience. In 2006 Pot Noodle released its 'Fuel of Britain' campaign featuring noodles being 'mined' in Wales. Brand awareness increased considerably and there was a significant rise in sales. Television viewers were encouraged to visit a related website to reinforce the message. Despite over 80 objections of racism at the expense of the Welsh to the Advertising Standards Authority, the campaign continued and led to a 104% improvement in the number of viewers regarding the brand in a positive way. Of all snack brands, only Walkers Crisps were regarded more favourably by the target market — predominantly 14- to 34-year-old males.

- **The balance of promotions in a campaign.** Advertising must be planned along with other promotions to maximise effectiveness. As seen in the AIDA model, advertising usually introduces a campaign, while more specific methods of promotion, particularly merchandising, complete the process. However, the effectiveness of sponsorship can be enhanced by having advertisements running at the same time, such as Barclays plc advertisements during a Barclays Premiership football match.
- **Legal factors.** Restrictions on the use of media, such as limits on alcohol advertising on television, may encourage firms to use different media. Businesses that cannot use television and newspapers use the internet for word-of-mouth advertising, to bypass these restrictions.
- **External factors.** Changes in the overall wealth of the country and the social and political environment can all influence promotions. Customers will usually be more receptive to promotions if they are experiencing higher living standards. The style of the promotions and the images and messages used must also fit in with society's views. For example, more restrictions are now being placed on advertisements that are targeted at children because of changing views about what is acceptable in this area.

 FILE

Targeting children

Food manufacturers have been criticised for targeting their advertising at children through the cinema, the internet and social networking websites such as Bebo. Examples such as the 'Kids Zone' on McDonald's website and Coco Pops adverts before the most recent Harry Potter film have been cited as evidence of this trend. Since 1 January 2008, Ofcom has banned television adverts that promote sugary, salty or fatty foods during programmes targeted at children under the age of 16.

EXAMINER'S VOICE

Remember that promotion is not just advertising. Advertising is one element of promotion, but there are many others involved. Business organisations use a wide range of promotional methods in order to raise awareness. Do not underestimate the importance of below-the-line promotions.

WHAT DO YOU THINK?

Sony Ericsson mobile phones show no distinct variations in the age of users, except for a significant drop among people over the age of 55 and a huge fall among over-65-year-olds. Heavy users are low watchers of television, but visit the cinema and use the internet frequently. They are more likely to see outdoor advertisements and are more than twice as likely as the average UK resident to have visited the Science Museum in London in the last year. Other popular activities among Sony Ericsson mobile users are 'visiting Italy', 'going to the Motor Show' and 'taking risks'.

How could Sony Ericsson use this information to plan a promotional campaign?

PRACTICE EXERCISE
Total: 70 marks (60 minutes)

1 What is the difference between 'promotion' and 'advertising'? *(6 marks)*

2 What does the mnemonic AIDA stand for? *(4 marks)*

3 What is an 'impulse buy'? *(2 marks)*

4 Which media would you select in order to advertise the following? In each case justify your choice.
  a a job vacancy for a checkout assistant in Woolworths *(3 marks)*
  b a new CD by a well-known pop star *(3 marks)*
  c a new model of a car *(3 marks)*

5 Explain one benefit and one problem of direct selling. *(6 marks)*

6 What is meant by 'PoS' (or 'PoP')? *(2 marks)*

7 Explain one benefit and one problem of merchandising. *(6 marks)*

8 Explain the difference between sponsorship and public relations. *(4 marks)*

9 Identify two products that might use exhibitions or trade fairs as a form of promotion. *(2 marks)*

10 Identify three examples of sales promotion. *(3 marks)*

11 Briefly explain one advantage and one disadvantage of using the following media for advertising:
  a television *(4 marks)*   **b** cinema *(4 marks)*   **c** radio *(4 marks)*   **d** internet *(4 marks)*

12 Analyse three factors that an organisation should consider when planning its promotional mix. *(10 marks)*

CASE STUDY 1 **The year advertising turned digital**

The charts on p. 379 illustrate the use of advertising media in the UK:
- Figure 31.2 illustrates the total amount of money spent on UK advertising from 2000 to 2007.
- Figure 31.3 shows a forecast of the percentage share of advertising spending achieved by the main forms of media in the UK in 2007.
- Table 31.1 shows forecast growth rates in different advertising media for 2008, provided by two leading industry forecasters.

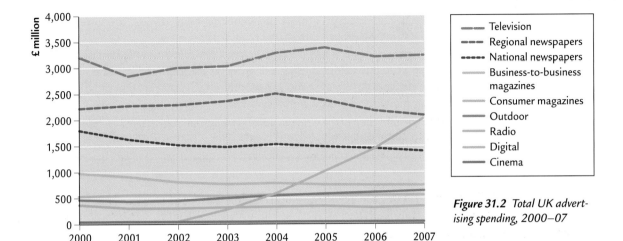

Figure 31.2 Total UK advertising spending, 2000–07

Source: GroupM

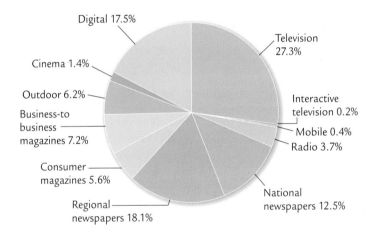

Figure 31.3 % share of advertising spending, 2007 forecast

Table 31.1 Forecast growth rates in selected advertising media, 2008 (%)

	Forecast by Zenith	Forecast by GroupM
Internet	+25.6	+30.8
Television	+2.2	+0.9
Newspapers	+1.1	–2.8
Magazines	+0.1	–0.4
Radio	+1.9	+2.0
Cinema	+1.8	+3.0
Outdoor	+6.0	+5.9
Total	**+6.2**	**+6.0**

Internet search is expected to contribute up to three-quarters of all advertising revenue growth during 2008, while traditional media stagnate. GroupM predicts that advertising will grow by 6% in 2008, but without the contribution from Google and other search engines, the rate of improvement across other media would be only 1.5%.

Internet advertising will also come close to overtaking television advertising in 2008, emphasising how quickly the new medium has become a mainstream means of promotion. This year internet spending is predicted to hit £3.4 billion, up from £2.6 billion in 2007, on Group M's estimates.

Five sources of good news for advertising

- Beijing Olympics, creating an increased awareness of the London Olympics in 2012
- Increased use of colour in newspapers
- Electronic outdoor billboards replacing traditional posters
- Continued strength in luxury goods spending
- Programming revival at ITV

Despite an expected recovery in ITV's fortunes, forecasts suggest limited growth in television advertising. GroupM predicts television revenues of £3.57 billion, up 0.9%, although Zenith-Optima, its rival, is forecasting a rise of 2.2%.

Zenith also suggests an increase in colour advertising will make newspapers a more attractive proposition. Adam Smith of GroupM disagrees: 'There is a notion that just by turning black and white into colour you turn lead into gold. Where do you go when everything is in colour? Colour may be a mild stimulant, but nothing more.'

The magazine market is likely to come under yet more pressure as men favour the internet over magazines.

Both GroupM and Zenith agree that radio advertising will grow by 2%, citing an increase in sponsorship and promotion, and the fact that radio works well with the internet.

Source: adapted from an article by Amanda Andrews in *The Times*, 2 January 2008.

Questions

Total: 25 marks (35 minutes)

1 Choose any two of the 'five sources of good news for advertising' and briefly explain why they will benefit the advertising industry. *(6 marks)*

2 Analyse two reasons for the increase in popularity of the internet for advertising purposes. *(8 marks)*

3 Analyse the implications of these changes for:
 a ITV   *(5 marks)*   **b** a car manufacturer   *(6 marks)*

CASE STUDY 2 Lara Croft: 'Legend'

The seventh game in the Lara Croft, Tomb Raider series, 'Legend', was released in 2006 for the PlayStation and other games consoles. This game was critical to Eidos, the owners of the brand. The previous 2 years had seen a critical mauling of the 'Angel of Darkness' game and poor performance of the latest film, starring Angelina Jolie.

In order to revive the brand it was decided to give greater credibility by focusing on public relations (PR), rather than paid-for promotions. The objectives of the campaign were as follows:

- to create significant coverage across different media sectors
- to achieve the number one position in the market for console games, at launch
- to re-establish brand credibility with consumers and the media

A new model, Karima Adebibe, was introduced as the new face of Lara. The agency in charge of the campaign, THBC, adopted a strategy similar to that of unveiling a new supermodel for an underwear or cosmetics brand. Their human interest story, featuring Karima's rags-to-riches story — she was previously employed as a checkout assistant at Topshop — was central to the campaign.

THBC was also successful in securing exclusive articles in the press on Valentine's Day, Lara Croft's birthday, and the agency worked on a campaign to shortlist Lara in the Great British Design Quest, organised by the BBC. This campaign was so successful that Lara Croft was placed in the top ten British cultural icons of all time, alongside the Spitfire, the red phone box and the eventual winner, Concorde.

The culmination of the PR campaign saw articles covering a double-page spread in the *Sun*, and full-page articles in the *Star*, the *Evening Standard* and *Metro*. Other media coverage included appearances by Karima

on BBC News, Sky News and Radio Five Live, as well as regional radio broadcasts and news articles in both national and regional newspapers.

The publicity created by the successful PR campaign was then supported by Eidos sales teams visiting retailers across the country, in order to encourage pre-orders.

As the launch date approached, greater focus was placed on the tabloid press, notably the *Sun* and the *Daily Star* and men's magazines such as *FHM*, *Zoo* and *Nuts*. However, articles were also featured in the quality press, such as the *Sunday Times* magazine and the *Sunday Telegraph*.

The result was that the 'Legend' game reached number one on release in the UK and retained that spot for over 2 months.

Having primarily used PR for the initial launch, subsequent marketing promotion has varied in accordance with the format of the game. In late 2006/early 2007 the 'Legend' game was launched for mobile phones. This launch was supported by extensive outdoor posters, direct mail and online media, with only a small focus on PR. A competition awarding a prize of a visit to Machu Picchu in Peru was also featured. The most recent release of the game, on 7 December 2007, has been for the Nintendo Wii. Given the different nature of the Wii's target market (a greater focus on younger children and adults), this campaign has centred on print media such as newspapers and magazines, with a particular focus on girls' lifestyle publications. There has also been a greater focus on in-store posters and events and, for the first time, 'Legend' has been promoted through a 3-week television campaign across both terrestrial and multichannel media.

Grant Tasker, UK product manager at Eidos, expects the game to remain in the top ten for a lengthy spell and is hoping that its launch will attract more consumers to buy Wii consoles.

Sources: uTalk; **www.mcvuk.com**; **http://forums.eidosgames.com**

Questions

Total: 45 marks (55 minutes)

1 Explain why it was important for Eidos to restore the reputation of the Lara Croft brand name. *(6 marks)*

2 Indicate how a game like 'Legend' can help to sell a console such as the Nintendo Wii. *(4 marks)*

3 To what extent did Eidos succeed in achieving the targets for its initial campaign? *(8 marks)*

4 Evaluate the reasons for deciding to launch 'Legend' through focusing mainly on the use of public relations (PR), rather than other elements of a promotional mix. *(12 marks)*

5 Evaluate the reasons why the launch of 'Legend' for mobile phones and for the Nintendo Wii differed so significantly from the original promotional mix for the PlayStation. *(15 marks)*

CHAPTER 32

Using the marketing mix: pricing

This chapter focuses on price. It examines pricing strategies, such as price skimming, penetration pricing, price leaders and price takers. Consideration is given to two pricing tactics: loss leaders and psychological pricing. The chapter then analyses influences on pricing decisions, focusing primarily on the price elasticity of demand. The determinants of the price elasticity of demand are considered, along with its significance and the difficulties in measuring it. The chapter concludes by showing the effects of price changes on total revenue.

Pricing strategies

There are five main pricing strategies.

Price skimming

In price skimming a high price is set to yield a high profit margin. This price is often used during the introduction of a product, when it appeals to **early adopters** — people who want to be among the first to purchase a new product. Such consumers will pay for the status of being an early adopter.

In the long term, firms use this strategy for products that they hope will 'skim the market'. This means appealing to a more exclusive, up-market type of customer. Chanel, Harrods and Bang & Olufsen are brands that employ this pricing strategy. The objectives in these cases are to maximise value added or profit margins and to establish a prestigious brand name.

KEY TERMS

penetration pricing: a strategy in which low prices are set to break into a market or to achieve a sudden spurt in market share.

price leadership: a strategy in which a large company (the price leader) sets a market price that smaller firms will tend to follow.

price taking: a strategy in which a small firm follows the price set by a price leader.

predator (or destroyer) pricing: a strategy in which a firm sets very low prices in order to drive other firms out of the market.

Penetration pricing

In effect, penetration pricing is the opposite of price skimming. Low prices are set to break into a market or to achieve a rapid growth in market share. Many firms use this strategy when a product is first released or to entice new customers. For example, credit card companies often make introductory offers in order to gain new customers. In this way, they increase their market share and possibly increase brand awareness.

Price leadership and price taking

In price leadership a large company (the price leader) sets a market price that smaller firms (price takers) tend to follow. Large retailers such as Currys and manufacturers such as Ford influence prices for electrical goods and cars in this way. In some industries, such as petrol, price leadership may be shared among a few major firms. Small firms will usually follow because a lower price could trigger a **price war**, while a higher price will mean that they lose customers. By becoming the established brand leader, a firm can ensure that prices are set at a level that suits it and discourages price competition.

Predator (or destroyer) pricing

In this strategy, a firm sets very low prices in order to drive other firms out of the market. For example, cut-price airline fares have led to some small airlines closing or being taken over by competitors. If predator pricing acts against the consumer interest (by eliminating choice), it can be ruled illegal, but this is often difficult to prove. The sole objective is to reduce the number of competitors in the market.

KEY TERMS

pricing tactics: pricing approach or techniques used in the short term to achieve specific objectives.

loss leadership: a tactic in which a firm sets a low price for its product(s) in order to encourage consumers to buy other products that provide profit for the firm.

psychological pricing: a tactic intended to give the impression of value (e.g. selling a good for £9.99 rather than £10).

Pricing tactics

Pricing tactics are adopted in the short term to suit particular situations. There are two main pricing tactics.

Loss leaders

Some firms, such as supermarkets, set low prices for certain products in order to encourage consumers to buy other, fully priced products. Cheap bread and milk (at the back of the supermarket) will lead customers through the store, during which time they may buy many other products from which a greater profit is made. (In practice, 'loss leaders' are often sold at reduced profit margins rather than at a loss.) Manufacturers use loss leaders too — the main product may be a loss leader, but the accessories can create the profit.

Psychological pricing

Psychological pricing is intended to give an impression of value (e.g. £3.99 instead of £4, or £99 rather than £100). Although a few retailers, such as Marks and Spencer, do not use this approach any more, the frequency of its use suggests that firms believe that it does attract extra customers.

Paintballing is an industry that uses this technique in a slightly different way. The full-day fee at the local paintball venue may be £30. This price encourages customers and provides them with everything that they need to 'destroy' their enemies, including 100 paintballs. However, the average 'paintballer' uses 500 paintballs a day and additional paintballs can add between £30 and £80 to the price.

Influences on the pricing decision

Two main influences are examined:

- the costs of production
- the price elasticity of demand

Costs of production

All the pricing strategies and pricing tactics described earlier rely on setting a price that customers find acceptable. However, a business also needs to ensure that it makes a profit, so the price of a product must be high enough to cover costs (unless a loss leader or predator pricing approach is being used). To make sure that the price suits both the customer and the business, businesses often use **cost-plus pricing**.

In cost-plus pricing the price set is the average cost of a product plus a sum to ensure a profit. For example, a clothes retailer typically adds 100% to the wholesale cost of purchasing a dress, while a pet food manufacturer adds 30% to the manufacturing costs when selling to a supermarket chain. Thus a dress purchased wholesale by a retailer for £50 is sold to the customer for £100; a tin of cat food that costs 30p to make is sold for 39p. The percentage added on to the average cost is known as the **mark-up**.

In determining what percentage mark-up to add to its costs, a business must remember that it needs both to make profits and to appeal to the market. If the percentage added on is too low, it may mean a lost opportunity to make profit; if it is too high, it will reduce sales. The percentage added on depends on a number of factors:

- the level of competition
- the price that customers are prepared to pay
- the firm's objectives — for example, whether it is aiming to break even or maximise profit, or aim for a high market share

Price elasticity of demand

KEY TERM

price elasticity of demand: the responsiveness of a change in the quantity demanded of a good or service to a change in price.

The formula for calculating the price elasticity of demand is:

$$\text{price elasticity of demand} = \frac{\%\ \text{change in quantity demanded}}{\%\ \text{change in price}}$$

Price elasticity of demand can be elastic, inelastic or unitary:

- **Elastic demand.** If the percentage change in price leads to a greater percentage change in the quantity demanded (ignoring the minus sign), the calculation yields an answer greater than 1. This indicates that demand is relatively responsive to a change in price.
- **Inelastic demand.** If the percentage change in price leads to a smaller percentage change in the quantity demanded, the calculation yields an answer less than 1 (ignoring the minus sign). This indicates that demand is relatively unresponsive to a change in price.
- **Unit (or unitary) elasticity.** This name is given to the situation where both percentage changes are the same, giving an answer of (–)1. In theory, the price change is exactly cancelled out by the change in quantity demanded, so sales revenue stays the same.

> **DID YOU KNOW?**
>
> A fall in price usually leads to a rise in demand; a rise in price usually leads to a fall in demand. Thus price elasticity of demand is usually negative. Because it is negative (apart from in exceptional circumstances), it is customary to ignore the negative sign. Therefore, a figure of 0.5 means that a 1% rise/fall in price leads to a 0.5% fall/rise in the quantity demanded.

Example calculations

Calculation 1: price falls from 25p to 20p, leading to an increase in quantity demanded from 200 to 220 units.

$$\frac{\% \text{ change in}}{\text{quantity demanded}} = \frac{\text{change in quantity demanded}}{\text{original quantity demanded}} \times 100$$

$$= \frac{(220 - 200)}{200} \times 100 = \frac{+20}{200} \times 100 = +10\%$$

$$\% \text{ change in price} = \frac{\text{change in price}}{\text{original price}} \times 100$$

$$= \frac{(20 - 25)}{25} \times 100 = \frac{-5}{25} \times 100 = -20\%$$

> **DID YOU KNOW?**
>
> Price elasticity of demand is often referred to as just 'elasticity of demand'.

$$\text{price elasticity of demand} = \frac{+10}{-20} = (-)0.5$$

An elasticity of 0.5 means that demand is inelastic, because the percentage change in price leads to a smaller percentage change in quantity demanded.

> **e EXAMINER'S VOICE**
>
> It is worth spending time on price elasticity of demand. Examiners like it because it can test many skills and usually produces a range of answers. However, be wary of using raw data to calculate elasticities, as the changes in demand will also have been influenced by other factors apart from price.

In practice, it is impossible to isolate changes in price from other factors that influence demand, although firms try to estimate the price elasticity of demand because of its potential usefulness. In theory, elasticity is based on the assumption that 'nothing else changes' when price (or income) changes. In reality, it is unlikely that a firm such as Tesco will do nothing (or that there will be no changes in external factors) if ASDA changes its prices.

Calculation 2: price rises from £11 to £13, leading to a decrease in quantity demanded from 76 units to 52 units.

$$\frac{\text{\% change in}}{\text{quantity demanded}} = \frac{\text{change in quantity demanded}}{\text{original quantity demanded}} \times 100$$

$$= \frac{(52 - 76)}{76} \times 100 = \frac{-24}{76} \times 100 = -31.6\%$$

$$\text{\% change in price} = \frac{\text{change in price}}{\text{original price}} \times 100$$

$$= \frac{(13 - 11)}{11} \times 100 = \frac{+2}{11} \times 100 = +18.2\%$$

$$\text{price elasticity of demand} = \frac{-31.6}{+18.2} = (-)1.7$$

An elasticity of 1.7 means that demand is elastic, because the percentage change in price leads to a larger percentage change in quantity demanded.

Determinants of price elasticity of demand

The factors influencing the price elasticity of demand are as follows.

Necessity
If a product is essential, consumers will still buy similar quantities even if the price is high. However, a reduction in price will not tend to encourage buyers to purchase much more, as they will have already satisfied their need at the higher price. The more necessary a product, the more *inelastic* is the demand.

Habit
Some products are habit forming. Typical examples are cigarettes, chocolate, alcohol and watching television. In effect, a habit means that the product or service becomes a necessity to that individual. This means that cigarette manufacturers can increase the price of their product and demand will stay roughly the same. The stronger the habit, the more *inelastic* is the demand for the product.

Availability of substitutes
If there are no alternatives to a product, a consumer is likely to buy a similar quantity if the price changes.

> **DID** YOU KNOW?
>
> A major reason for the high prices of some habit-forming products (notably petrol, alcohol and cigarettes) is the excise tax charged by the government. The government places heavy taxes on these (inelastic) goods, knowing that people will continue buying them (and so pay taxes). If the government taxed goods with elastic demand, it would not raise as much money.

However, if there are many alternatives, customers will switch to a close alternative. The impact will also depend on consumer tastes: for example, how close the alternative is seen to be. Some buyers may see beef as a close alternative to pork, but other customers will not see them as substitutes.

The greater the availability of close substitutes, the more *elastic* is the demand, as small price rises will encourage consumers to buy the alternatives. This can be seen in the market for petrol. In remote rural areas or at motorway service stations, prices tend to be higher than they are in cities, where it is easier to find an alternative supplier. Thus demand at any particular garage is more elastic in cities than it is in the countryside.

In the long term, demand becomes more elastic as consumers search out and switch to alternative products.

Brand loyalty

Firms attempt to create brand loyalty by various means, such as the quality of the product, advertising and other forms of promotion. In addition to increasing sales volume, the creation of loyal customers will also influence people's reactions to price changes. A consumer who insists on wearing Armani clothing will not be put off by a higher price. The greater the level of brand loyalty, the more *inelastic* is the demand.

Proportion of income spent on a product

Consumers will be less concerned about price rises if a product takes up only a small percentage of their income. For example, a 20% increase in the price of a box of matches will only be 2p or 3p, so the consumer is unlikely to change the number of boxes bought (demand is *inelastic*). On the other hand, buying a car will use up a large amount of income, so consumers will be affected by small percentage changes in price. This factor will make the demand for cars more *elastic*.

Income of consumers

Rich people are less worried about price rises than poorer individuals. Thus they (as individuals) are going to have more inelastic demand for the products that they buy. David Beckham may pay hundreds of pounds for a haircut, but most consumers would try to find a cheaper alternative if this was the price advertised by their local barber or hairdresser. For this reason, businesses often target rich people. The prices of brands bought predominantly by wealthy consumers can be increased without affecting sales a great deal, so their demand is *inelastic*. Shops in exclusive areas can often set higher prices because their customers are less conscious of price.

Overall, the elasticity of demand will be determined by a combination of these factors.

WHAT DO YOU THINK?

Firms prefer their products to have price-inelastic demand. A business will not just accept that its products are price elastic or inelastic, but may take steps to change customers' views. How can a firm make demand for its products more inelastic?

e EXAMINER'S VOICE

Application is not just about including the company's name in your answer. If your answer makes as much sense without the company name as it does with it, then you are probably showing the skill of analysis rather than application.

Significance of price elasticity of demand

The importance of price elasticity of demand can be seen by looking at its influence on sales revenue and profit, following a change in price. A business planning a change in price as part of its marketing mix will want to be able to predict the effects of such a price change. The effect of price elasticity of demand on sales revenue and profit depends on whether demand is elastic, inelastic or unitary.

Inelastic demand

If demand for a good is inelastic, when its price rises the quantity demanded falls by a smaller percentage. This means that the impact of the price increase outweighs the relatively small percentage change in demand, so sales revenue increases. For example, a 50% rise in price from £1 to £1.50 leads to a smaller (20%) fall in sales from 100 to 80 units. Price elasticity is −0.4.

Sales revenue increases from (£1 × 100 = £100) to (£1.50 × 80 = £120). Does this mean extra profit? The answer is yes. The total costs of producing 80 units will almost certainly be lower than those of producing 100 units, so costs will tend to fall at the same time as revenue increases. Thus a price rise always increases sales revenue and profit if demand is price inelastic. Similarly, a price fall leads to lower sales revenue and profit if demand is price inelastic.

Elastic demand

If demand for a good is elastic, when its price rises the quantity demanded falls by a larger percentage. This means that the impact of the price increase is outweighed by the relatively large percentage change in demand, so sales revenue decreases. For example, a 20% rise in price from £1 to £1.20 leads to a larger (50%) fall in sales from 100 to 50 units. Price elasticity is −2.5.

Sales revenue decreases from (£1 × 100 = £100) to (£1.20 × 50 = £60). Does this mean a decrease in profit? The answer is not necessarily. It will be cheaper to produce 50 units than 100, so costs will fall as well as income. If costs fall by more than income, profit will still be improved. But if costs fall by a smaller amount, profit will fall. Thus a price rise always decreases sales revenue if price elasticity of demand is elastic, but the effect on profit depends on cost savings. The chances of more profit are higher if there is a high profit margin on the good.

In the case of a price fall, the sales revenue of a good with a price-elastic demand always increases. However, the quantity demanded rises and so production costs also rise. Consequently, it is impossible to predict the effect on profits without knowing about the costs of production.

Unitary elasticity

If demand for a good is unitary, sales revenue is the same whether price rises or falls. A price rise would then be advisable if the business is aiming to

increase profit, because this means a lower volume of sales would be required, which would enable production costs to fall. However, the business may not increase price if it has other aims, such as increasing its market share.

The impact of price changes on sales revenue is summarised in Table 32.1.

Table 32.1
Effect of price changes on sales revenue

	Price elasticity of demand (PED)		
Price change	PED > 1 (elastic)	PED = 1 (unitary)	PED < 1 (inelastic)
Price increases	Sales revenue falls	Sales revenue unchanged	Sales revenue rises
Price decreases	Sales revenue rises	Sales revenue unchanged	Sales revenue falls

Using price elasticity to interpret the market

Price elasticity of demand can be used to interpret the market, as the example in Table 32.2 shows.

	Product X	Product Y
Price elasticity of demand	(−)4.0	(−)0.3

Table 32.2 *Price elasticity of demand data*

The following conclusions about products X and Y might be inferred from the data.

Conclusions for product X

■ Price elasticity of demand is (−)4.0 (very elastic). A change in price leads to a proportionally larger change in quantity demanded. This product is not a necessity and is likely to have many close substitutes.
■ It is possibly a cheap, low-quality substitute for other products in a very competitive market, and is likely to be purchased by consumers who cannot afford a better alternative.

Conclusions for product Y

■ Price elasticity of demand is (−)0.3 (inelastic). The product is a necessity or has few close substitutes.
■ It probably has few close substitutes and may be habit forming, or appeals to consumers who can afford higher prices.

Marketing strategies for product X

■ Charge a lower price to increase sales revenue, but not if the company is operating on low profit margins.
■ Consider repositioning the product in order to appeal to higher income sectors *or*, if profit margins are reasonable, the company may keep the product unchanged. It may act as a cash cow, and in periods of fierce competition price cuts should enable the company to generate high sales volumes.

Marketing strategies for product Y

■ Increase price as there will be a relatively small fall in demand, creating a rise in sales revenue from a lower level of output.
■ Aim for high 'value added' to increase profit margins.
■ Safeguard the product's exclusive image.

Price discrimination

Firms can use price elasticity of demand to practise **price discrimination**. Price discrimination involves charging a higher price to some customers for the same product or service because they are prepared to pay such a price. Typical examples are train fares and charges for telephone users. Consumers who use peak-time trains or phones are willing to pay the higher price because they value their

use so highly at those times (when their demand is price inelastic). People who are less desperate to use the service at that time can receive it more cheaply during off-peak periods (their demand is price elastic).

> **EXAMINER'S VOICE**
>
> Watch out for the wording of the question, such as whether price has increased or decreased. Price-elastic demand for a product means that a price *cut* leads to an increase in sales revenue (but a price *increase* has the opposite effect).

Difficulties in calculating and using price elasticity of demand

Price elasticity of demand can be very unreliable because of the difficulties involved in calculating it. Price elasticity of demand calculations assume that 'other things remain equal' while price changes. In practice, this does not happen.

The main difficulties in calculating (and using) elasticity of demand are as follows:

- **Other factors not 'remaining equal'.** There might have been significant changes in the market, affecting the level of demand independently of price. For example, consumer tastes might have changed; new competitors might have entered the market or previous competitors might have left it; technological change might have influenced the market; or the image of the product might have changed.
- **Competitors' reactions.** Changes in price may provoke a reaction from rival firms, which may try to match the change or modify their marketing in response to the change. This reaction may not always be the same. For example, in some markets competitors are more likely to match a rival's cut in price than they are to match a rival's increase in price.
- **Consumers' reactions.** Consumers may react differently to increases in price than to decreases. For example, a decrease in price might not encourage consumers to buy more, but an increase may tempt them to buy from competitors.
- **Market research.** It may be difficult to use secondary market research to calculate elasticity, as the planned change in price may be different from anything experienced in the past. At the same time, consumers may be unable to predict how their spending will be affected by price changes, and so primary surveys may be unreliable.

Marketing and the competitive environment

391

Even the company's own actions may reduce the reliability of any calculations. Firms often promote their price reductions and so brand awareness (and thus the quantity demanded) may increase for this reason rather than because of the price cut.

PRACTICE EXERCISE 1   Total: 35 marks (30 minutes)

1 What is meant by the term 'psychological pricing'? *(3 marks)*

2 The following costs apply to a product: wages 50p, raw materials 60p, other costs 70p.
  a What price would be set if cost-plus pricing were used and a mark-up of 100% were chosen by the business to set the price? *(3 marks)*
  b Wages rise by 10% and the mark-up is reduced to 80%. Calculate the new price. *(4 marks)*

3 Explain two reasons why a company might use price skimming and state two real-life examples of this strategy. *(8 marks)*

4 Explain two reasons for penetration pricing by a business. *(8 marks)*

5 What is the difference between a 'price leader' and a 'price taker'? State one example of each. *(6 marks)*

6 What is meant by a 'loss leader'? *(3 marks)*

PRACTICE EXERCISE 2   Total: 40 marks (35 minutes)

1 What is meant by the term 'price elasticity of demand'? *(4 marks)*

2 State whether each of the following factors will make demand price elastic or price inelastic:
  a It is habit forming.
  b There are many substitutes.
  c It is aimed at a wealthy market segment.
  d Advertising has created brand loyalty.
  e The product is a necessity.
  f It takes up a small percentage of consumers' incomes. *(6 marks)*

3 The price of an item rises from £20 to £21. Sales of the item fall from 4 million to 3.9 million per annum.
  a Calculate the price elasticity of demand. *(4 marks)*
  b Based on your answer in (a), indicate whether demand is price elastic or price inelastic. *(1 mark)*

4 How should a business market a product that has price-inelastic demand? *(5 marks)*

5 To what extent can a business influence the price elasticity of demand of one of its products? *(10 marks)*

6 Discuss the reasons why it would be more difficult for a computer manufacturer to use price elasticity of demand than it would for a company marketing pencils. *(10 marks)*

CASE STUDY 1 Shakeaway

Shakeaway is a retailer specialising in unusual flavours of milkshake. The business opened in Bournemouth in 1999 and now operates ten outlets in the south of England, focusing mainly on tourist resorts and upmarket towns. It realises that future expansion may be based in less affluent areas.

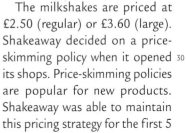

The stores offer approximately 150 different milkshakes, with flavours such as apricot, Bakewell tart, Bourbon biscuit, Parma violets, Toblerone and Trebor extra strong mints. These are blended with ice cream and milk to create the finished product. This culinary experience can be improved further by adding products such as bran, wheatgerm, flake and marshmallows. Jelly Tot fans can choose a Jelly Tots milkshake topped with Jelly Tots.

At present this is a niche market, as most other providers of flavoured milkshakes have not ventured far beyond strawberry and chocolate. However, more direct competition is entering the market in the form of businesses such as 'Shakes' and 'Shaker Maker'.

In response, the business has diversified slightly into hot drinks (including hot milkshakes) and confectionery, but 90% of its sales come from milkshakes.

The milkshakes are priced at £2.50 (regular) or £3.60 (large). Shakeaway decided on a price-skimming policy when it opened its shops. Price-skimming policies are popular for new products. Shakeaway was able to maintain this pricing strategy for the first 5 or 6 years of its existence, with profit margins increasing each year. However, in recent years its price rises have not kept pace with the increases in its costs. There are worries that it may need to change its strategy away from price skimming in the near future.

An initial proposal to use psychological pricing to set a price of £1.99 for the regular milkshake was rejected because it was felt that this would reduce profit levels rather than increase them.

The cost of ingredients for a typical, regular milkshake is estimated at 90p. Labour and other costs are estimated at £330 per day, during which an average of 500 milkshakes would be sold.

Sources: various, including **www.shakeaway.com**.

Questions

Total: 40 marks (50 minutes)

1 What is meant by the term 'price skimming' (line 31)? (3 marks)

2 a Calculate the average cost of production of a regular milkshake. (5 marks)

   b Shakeaway uses a cost-plus pricing method. Use your answer to part (a) to calculate the percentage that Shakeaway adds on to the average cost in order to set its price for a regular milkshake. (4 marks)

3 Examine why Shakeaway rejected the idea of psychological pricing (lines 40–43). (8 marks)

4 Shakeaway believes that demand for its milkshakes is price inelastic. Analyse two reasons why this might be true. (8 marks)

5 Discuss possible factors that may lead to Shakeaway being forced to change its strategy of price skimming. (12 marks)

CASE STUDY 2 The marketing mix at Ryanair

Ryanair is a classic example of a business that uses price as the key element of its marketing mix. However, price cannot work in isolation from the rest of the four Ps. In order to maintain its policy of long-term low
5 prices, Ryanair has also needed to look closely at product, place and promotion.

Ryanair based itself on the highly successful model established in the USA by Southwest Airlines, a company that had been operating low-cost flights in
10 the USA since the 1960s. Ryanair's chief executive, Michael O'Leary, attempted to create a low-cost airline by examining every element of Ryanair's activities, in order to cut costs in the way that Southwest Airlines had.

Product

15 O'Leary started by eliminating 'frills' and 'unnecessary' expenditure.

● Travel agents were eliminated, based on the idea that Ryanair's customers would not then be paying
20 towards the costs of their city-centre premises and trained staff.

● Internet bookings were introduced, saving approximately 15% per booking.

● Bookings do not require paperwork at the airport;
25 customers just need to provide a booking reference and their passport.

● Seats are not allocated to passengers; they are taken as passengers board the plane.

● The previous two factors reduce administration costs
30 further, but the main bonus is time savings. The turnaround time on Ryanair planes is 25 minutes

on average – half that of British Airways (BA). This means that the planes are more productive and can make more journeys per day.

● Free meals are not provided – customers must pay 35 for any food they require. Not only does this save costs (especially on staffing and cleaning because passengers eat and drink less), but it also provides an additional source of profit that can be used to keep prices low. 40

Some examples of Ryanair's cost savings have been less well received by customers. Its customer care department employs six staff (one-tenth of BA's equivalent staff, based on staff per customer) and Ryanair does not offer some facilities that are provided 45 free by other airlines. However, these features reinforce the company's USP.

Unfortunately, it is also restricting expansion plans. O'Leary has decided against expansion into the USA because long flight times would make it impossible to 50 replicate many of the company's cost-saving measures, such as quick turnaround of planes and avoiding overnight hotel bills for pilots and aircrew.

Place

A key element of Ryanair's strategy is that it only flies to 55 popular destinations, giving it more security of custom. This policy meant that when Ryanair took over Buzz, many of Buzz's flights were removed, where Ryanair considered the destinations to be lacking in popularity. More recently, Ryanair has tried to take over Aer Lingus 60 in order to eliminate competition on some routes.

A major cost saving for Ryanair has arisen from the locations that it has chosen. By using Stansted airport, Ryanair estimates that it saves £3 per customer in comparison with Heathrow. Some of this saving arises 65 from the relatively strong bargaining position of Ryanair. It is vital to Stansted's success as an airport and can therefore negotiate lower charges.

Ryanair also saves money by using secondary rather than 'main' airports in other countries. This means 70 lower costs for Ryanair that can be passed on to customers, softening the blow that the airport is further from the customer's intended destination than

they had hoped. In some cases, airports have been so keen to attract Ryanair that they have paid the company to choose that airport. The airport's revenues will increase from retailing activities in the airport as passenger numbers rise.

Promotion

Ryanair keeps advertising to a minimum, relying on newspaper advertisements and posters rather than more expensive television adverts. Simple messages reinforce the philosophy of low cost, low price. As an economy measure, advertising agencies are not used. As a result, there have been some controversial promotions attacking competitors or presenting issues insensitively.

Recognising the benefit of joint activities, Ryanair takes a percentage of any bookings made through its website (typically car hire and hotel bookings). It has also allowed its planes to be used as flying billboards, advertising products such as Kilkenny beer. These ancillary revenues provide 14% of the firm's profits.

Price

Given the vital role of safety in the airline industry, Ryanair has not economised on aircraft — it only uses Boeing 737s. However, shrewd timing of aircraft purchases (just after the Gulf War and again during and after the Iraq War) to coincide with excess supply has brought Ryanair some bargains. Unconfirmed estimates suggest that some of the Boeing 737s have cost the company less than half the normal £34 million price tag.

Ryanair has adopted the following pricing policies:

- Its normal pricing is based on cost-plus pricing in order to secure some profit. Typically, the first 70% of seats are sold on this basis. Special offers are often one-way — an example of psychological pricing, as customers believe that they will pay less than they actually do. This psychology also applies to baggage — Ryanair is much more likely to charge its customers for the baggage they carry, which can often increase the price of a flight quite substantially.

- Unlike traditional airlines, which sell any remaining empty seats at a low price (enough to cover variable costs), Ryanair uses price discrimination. The airline's view is that anyone seeking to book a flight at the last minute is probably in desperate need and therefore likely to be willing to pay a higher price. Thus the final 30% of the seats are sold at higher prices.

- At times, short-term, very low promotional prices are charged. These could be seen as penetration pricing (to increase market share), but some analysts see them as predator prices, used to drive away competition. In practice, many of these promotional flights are one-way only and so the savings for customers are less significant than they originally seem (unless the passenger does not want to return).

Ryanair's marketing has been highly successful. In terms of passenger numbers, it is Europe's second largest airline (after Lufthansa) and the market leader among budget airlines.

In the year ending 31 March 2007, Ryanair prices increased by 7%, but passenger numbers increased by 22% as many budget airlines were unable to keep their price rises as low as Ryanair. However, factors such as customer concerns over air pollution, higher airport taxes and large queues in airports have subsequently led Ryanair to predict that it will miss its 2007/2008 target of 5% growth by 2%. In response, Ryanair launched a price war in May 2007, coinciding with news that easyJet, a major rival, was struggling to maintain its profit levels. Ryanair is selling 10 million one-way flights to Europe for £10, £15 or £20, including air passenger tax.

Sources: *The Money Programme*, BBC2, 4 June 2003; articles by Steve Hawkes in *The Times*, 9 May and 5 June 2007; and an article by Nic Fildes in the *Independent*, 20 June 2007.

Questions

Total: 66 marks (80 minutes)

1 What is meant by 'cost-plus' pricing (line 105)? *(3 marks)*

2 Explain how Ryanair's 'joint activities' have helped it to keep prices low (line 88). *(6 marks)*

3 Explain how Ryanair uses 'psychological pricing'. *(5 marks)*

4 Explain two ways in which Ryanair cuts costs in order to keep prices low. *(6 marks)*

5 Is Ryanair likely to be a price leader or price taker? Justify your view. *(4 marks)*

6 Analyse the long-term benefits to Ryanair of using penetration-pricing methods. *(8 marks)*

7 Analyse the possible reasons why Southwest Airlines did not attempt to bring its low-cost approach to Europe before Ryanair used the idea. *(6 marks)*

8 Ryanair charges low prices to early customers and higher prices to people who book flights later, because it believes that demand for early flights is price elastic whereas demand for late flights is price inelastic. Analyse the reasons for this difference in price elasticity of demand over time. *(6 marks)*

9 Discuss the potential difficulties faced by Ryanair in trying to maintain its low-price policy in the future. *(10 marks)*

10 In 2006/07 Ryanair increased prices by 7% but passenger numbers increased by 22%. This suggests that the price elasticity of demand for Ryanair flights is +3.14. Explain why this calculation is almost certain to be incorrect, and discuss the reasons why it would be impossible for Ryanair to calculate accurately the price elasticity of demand for its flights. *(12 marks)*

CHAPTER 33

Using the marketing mix: place

The role of place in the marketing mix is established in this chapter. The chapter starts by examining the importance of the location of the retailer and placement in the point of sale. It then studies the need to ensure that a product or service is available in as many different locations as possible and is distributed as efficiently as possible. The alternative distribution channels (and their merits) are contrasted, along with the key factors influencing the choice of distribution channels.

Importance of location

There is a saying in business that the three factors most critical to a firm's success are 'location, location, location'. An important part of 'place' is making sure that you operate in the right location. This involves several elements:

- **Convenience.** For major purchases, such as cars, people may be prepared to put time and effort into researching the best deal and locating their ideal product. However, for most products, convenience is crucial. An individual will not want to spend much time trying to find the cheapest litre of milk. Furthermore, for a minor purchase such as a bottle of milk, the cost of travelling to purchase it from a cheaper source may outweigh the advantage of buying from the local convenience store, where the milk costs more but travel costs are much lower. Even supermarkets have discovered that convenience is vital. Despite their different reputations, product ranges, pricing policies and promotional techniques, supermarkets' own research has found that the convenience of their location to customers is the most important factor.

- **Accessibility.** The place of purchase must be easy to reach by usual forms of transport. The further the store is from the town centre, the less likely it is that consumers will find time to visit. However, in some areas the town centre shops may not have an advantage over remoter locations if it is difficult to park and traffic jams are a regular occurrence.

- **Cost of access.** Out-of-town shopping centres that provide free car parking have an advantage over town centre shops in some cases. Some councils are now restricting the building of out-of-town shopping centres because their low access cost for shoppers using cars has led to a decline in town centres, damaging the attractiveness of the town centre and increasing the overall level of pollution. Businesses such as Currys are tending to close town centre locations in favour of out-of-town shopping centres, and supermarket expansion is largely taking place outside town centres.

EXAMINER'S VOICE

Remember to apply your answers to the organisation in the question. Where would the target customers shop and where would they expect to find the product or service featured in the question?

 FILE

The Midlands Riviera?

For residents of Birmingham, beach holidays have never been convenient. Following successful projects in Paris and London, Birmingham is now planning to create two city-centre beaches. The city council is planning to create 'Plage Brum', spending £50,000 on sand, parasols and palm trees. Meanwhile the Bull Ring, Birmingham's main shopping centre, has plans for a £150,000 beach and related entertainment.

Source: *Guardian* online, April 2007.

■ **Reputation.** This is vital for certain goods and services. Doctors in Harley Street and fashion houses in Knightsbridge benefit from the prestige attached to such addresses, both in the volume of sales and in the price they are able to charge. In many communities there are shopping areas geared towards upmarket shops. Sir Philip Green is focusing more effort on Topshop stores, as Topshop's reputation has improved lately, and less effort on other Arcadia stores such as Dorothy Perkins and Burton.

 FILE

Jeeves of Belgravia

Jeeves of Belgravia is an up-market dry cleaners, based in the West End of London. It is able to use its name and reputation, partly arising from its trading area, to charge higher prices than the other branches of the business. These trade under the name of Johnson Service – the company that took over Jeeves of Belgravia when it bought Sketchley, the former owners of Jeeves of Belgravia.

■ **Localisation.** Some retailers tend to locate close together for consumer convenience. In such cases, any new retailer in that line of business would be strongly advised to choose the same location. Electrical retailers often locate close to each other, despite the fact that it might seem wiser to be in a unique location. This is because customers like to compare prices for major purchases such as washing machines. If two or three electrical retailers are located close together, this will enable the customer to compare

 FILE

Store design

Store design and layout are also vital for success. Marks and Spencer has recently opened its first 'green' store in Bournemouth. The new design uses 25% less energy and has cut carbon emissions by 90% compared with its previous Bournemouth store.

House of Fraser is changing strategy in a different way. Most of its new stores will be less than half the size of its existing stores and will focus on fashion items. Don McCarthy, chairman of House of Fraser, said: 'There are certain cities, such as Cambridge, where we don't think we can have a big store – but we could have a smaller fashion store.'

products and prices quickly and efficiently. The customer is then unlikely to travel to other locations to examine isolated retailers. Localisation is also common in the case of estate agents, clothing and shoe shops, and solicitors.

Placement in the point of sale

Market research into groceries indicates that 70% of buying decisions are made in-store and that a shopper is exposed to 1.6 pieces of in-store marketing every second.

It is evident that sales of products can be increased by the careful placing of products in the point-of-sale outlet. Some examples of this practice, based on supermarket placements, are as follows:

- similar products, such as biscuits, being placed together, so that shoppers can make comparisons and more easily tick off their purchases if they are using a shopping list
- supermarkets and greengrocers arranging brightly coloured, attractive fruit and vegetable displays so that they are visible from outside the store
- impulse buys, such as sweets, being placed by the checkouts to catch people's attention while queuing
- popular products, such as Kellogg's Corn Flakes, being given greater shelf space so that they are more likely to be seen and so that the store is unlikely to run out of stock
- loss leaders being scattered around the store, with some placed well away from the entrance, in order to encourage shoppers to walk around the whole store
- standard, everyday purchases, such as bread, being placed at eye level, so that shoppers will find them easily
- complementary products being placed in close proximity, such as cooking sauces being located close to pasta and rice

Supermarkets sometimes rearrange their store layout. Although this can upset customers in the short run, it is often done to force them to look around the whole store. This can draw their attention to new goods that they may not previously have been aware of, or interested in.

Placement also applies to direct selling. Catalogue shops, such as Argos, and internet sites, such as Amazon, put considerable effort into how products are arranged in their catalogue or website, to make it easy and attractive for shoppers to use.

Number of outlets

Persuading retailers to stock products is often crucial to success. The more outlets that stock the product, the more sales a business can generate. For impulse buys, in particular, the number of outlets is vital. Some 37% of mint eaters drive while eating mints.

Given the limited space in most garage shops, mint producers see place as important. If only one type of mint is stocked, that will be the one purchased, unless the consumer has a very high level of brand loyalty. Therefore, persuading the garage to stock your product in preference to a rival's can be vital.

Businesses can take a variety of measures to increase the number of outlets stocking their products:

■ **Promotional campaigns.** Retailers may be persuaded to stock a product by advertisements in trade magazines. Promotions aimed at consumers may increase demand and so persuade a shopkeeper that he or she needs to stock that product, rather than lose customers. For this reason, manufacturers always keep retailers informed of any future marketing campaigns.

■ **Providing extra facilities or attractive displays.** For example, in the frozen food market, manufacturers provide free freezers in return for agreements to stock the firm's frozen foods. In small stores, the lack of space means that this arrangement can also help to exclude rival frozen food manufacturers. Häagen-Dazs achieved large increases in sales by supplying upright freezers. These saved floor space compared with the usual chest freezers, and were seen as more attractive by customers. For these reasons they were preferred by both retailers and customers.

■ **Offering high profit margins to retailers.** Retailers want to use their space as effectively as possible. Supermarkets have been persuaded to devote more space to non-food items because they can make higher profit margins. Tesco outsold all the UK's bookshops in sales of the latest Harry Potter book — an item that carried a higher profit than its usual stock.

■ **Paying generous commission to sales staff.** This gives the sales force the incentive to persuade retailers that they should stock the products. Sales staff are often paid low basic hourly rates with high commission rates. Commission is a percentage of the order that they secure from the retailer.

■ **Increasing brand variety.** Firms such as Heinz and Birds Eye may gain extra shelf or freezer space (at the expense of competitors) if they bring out new ranges of products. With their wide ranges, Heinz and Birds Eye are able to secure more space for their products in the shop. However, if the sales of a product are too low, retailers may decide not to stock it. Heinz Salad Cream found itself in this situation when sales became too low and some supermarkets decided not to stock the product; this was partly caused by customers preferring Heinz Mayonnaise.

■ **Getting sole brand deals.** In some trades, notably pubs and clubs, producers try to secure a deal to sell only their version of a product. By giving large discounts for bulk buying, companies such as Pepsi-Cola may persuade a pub to make Pepsi the only 'Cola' drink served. This approach tends to occur where there is a captive audience. Supermarkets are unlikely to agree to this because customers might choose to go elsewhere if their favourite brands are not stocked.

■ **Investigating alternative outlets.** Increased sales may be achieved by discovering new retailers or ways of selling. Some coffee shops have located in larger stores such as Homebase or bookshops such as Borders, while vending machines have become more popular in recent years.

 FILE

Vending machines

For impulse buys, place is particularly important. The decline of small convenience stores has threatened sales of impulse purchases. Companies such as Mars have responded by placing vending machines in public places to increase the chances of impulse buying. In the UK, Mars has lost market share to Cadbury and Nestlé. However, through owning Klix and Flavia drinks machines, Mars has obtained more knowledge of the vending market and has used this to its advantage.

In the UK there are over 1 million vending machines, generating sales in excess of £3 billion per annum. The top three chocolate brands sold through vending machines belong to Mars — the Mars Bar, Twix and Snickers. However, vending machines are much more important for sugar-based sweets, with Fruit Pastilles and Starburst leading the way. At a time when confectionery sales generally are slowing down, vending machine sales are growing by 10% per annum.

Integrating place with other elements of the marketing mix

No aspect of the marketing mix can work in isolation from the other three Ps, and place is no exception. The following example illustrates the importance of integrating the marketing mix — in this case, focusing on place and product.

Integrating place and product: the case of the didgeridoo

Where on earth would you buy a didgeridoo? Australia would be a good place to start, but where would you find one in the UK?

The didgeridoo is a product that is growing in popularity, but retailers need to identify the key features of the didgeridoo that make it an essential item for certain individuals. Recognising the key features that appeal to different consumers helps a business to maximise sales. So what is a didgeridoo to its potential customers, and where would you buy one?

■ To some, the didgeridoo is a musical instrument. Musicians will pay in excess of £200 for a didgeridoo that has been correctly crafted from a termite-infested eucalyptus tree — but it will need to pass the 'boing' test to be suitable as a musical instrument. These consumers will naturally seek out a didgeridoo in a music shop, but the limited demand may make it difficult for manufacturers to persuade shops to stock them.

■ Other customers see the didgeridoo as a spiritual object or a lifestyle statement, as evidenced by the number of sellers at certain festivals. Ideally, potential sellers should reserve a pitch at festivals such as WOMAD.

■ For some buyers, the didgeridoo is an item of ornate decoration, to be artistically placed against a wall. For these customers, craft shops are the best location.

- More socially responsible consumers see the didgeridoo as a way of supporting aboriginal craftsmen and their traditional way of life. These customers are usually targeted by direct mail or internet suppliers.

Place is critical to the marketing of didgeridoos, as there is limited scope for promotion. A magazine, *Didgeridoo*, which was published four times a year, has now ceased trading and so most promotion takes place at the point of sale (often websites).

DID YOU KNOW?

D. C. Thomson, publishers of the *Beano* and *Dandy*, are planning to convert their comic strips, such as 'Dennis the Menace', into digital slideshows that can be sent to mobile phones, complete with sound effects. This is in response to growing numbers of children owning mobile phones and making fewer visits to newsagents.

Types of distribution channel

Movement of a product from the manufacturer to the consumer in international trade may involve additional agents, but most domestic distribution involves one of three methods, as shown in Figure 33.1.

A summary of the role of each organisation in the distribution channel is presented below.

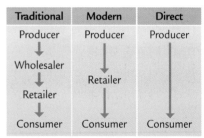

Figure 33.1 *Channels of distribution*

Producers

The job of producers (or manufacturers) is to make the product.

Wholesalers

The main task of wholesalers is to buy in bulk from the manufacturer (producer) and sell in smaller quantities to the retailer. The existence of wholesalers can benefit both manufacturers and retailers:

- Wholesalers help producers by purchasing their stock of finished goods as soon as it is produced, and storing it until consumers want it. This means that producers save on storage costs. By paying immediately, wholesalers can also help the cash flow of producers. This reduces producers' risks — if a product does not sell, it is the wholesaler's problem. Delivery costs are also reduced, as each producer can send a range of products to the wholesaler in one delivery.
- Retailers can also benefit from lower delivery costs, as the wholesaler stocks products from many different manufacturers and will usually deliver the order. This allows the retailer to compare products and prices in order to get the best deals. Retailers may also gain from credit terms being offered by the wholesaler.

Despite these benefits, the role of wholesalers has declined. Wholesalers charge for their services, usually by 'marking up' the price that they pay the producer for the goods in order to cover their costs and make a profit. Large supermarkets tend to buy directly from the producers in bulk, and receive deliveries either straight from the producer or via their own warehouses. Wholesalers have tried to prevent their decline by supporting the small retailers that still use them. Organisations such as the Society for the Protection of the Average Retailer (SPAR) have helped retailers to get together to share orders, in order to keep prices competitive.

Retailers

The main roles of the retailer are to serve the needs of the customer by providing:
- convenience — a 'place' that is easily accessible to consumers
- advice — knowledge to help the consumer reach the right buying decision
- financial assistance — retailers often provide credit terms or accept payment in a form that suits the consumer's needs
- after-sales support — for durable products, the quality of the guarantees or after-sales service can be crucial

Where a shop is not necessary to perform these roles, it is possible for a producer to sell directly to the consumer. Catalogues can provide convenience, financial assistance and after-sales support, eliminating the need for the retailer. Screwfix Direct, for example, has used the internet successfully to sell DIY equipment directly to consumers and tradespeople. Customers do not really want to scrutinise the product in detail before purchasing it. In the holiday trade, where travel agents add 15% to the costs, direct selling from holiday providers has grown considerably.

Consumers

Consumers are the individuals (or businesses) that purchase the finished product for their own use. The distribution channel used must meet their needs and lifestyles. With more consumers experiencing less leisure time, convenience has become more important.

 FILE

Tilda and Patak's

Two UK companies founded by Asian immigrants, Tilda and Patak's, are now selling rice and curry in India. As the Indian economy has developed, an increasing number of Indians have the money to be more selective but not the time. As a consequence, many middle-class Indians are buying branded, pre-packaged rice because they are too busy to visit traditional markets. This has opened up an opportunity for brands such as Tilda and Patak's to extend their distribution to include India.

Factors influencing the method of distribution

The final choice of distribution channel depends on the following:

- **The size of the retailer.** In general, large retailers will want to bypass the wholesaler, for reasons already given.
- **The type of product.** For a perishable product being sent to a limited number of retailers, it may be desirable to bypass the wholesaler, but for items such as newspapers there is more need for a wholesaler. Figure 33.2 shows an example where three manufacturers each supply ten local shops through a wholesaler. This involves a total of 13 journeys: three from the manufacturers to the wholesaler, and ten from the wholesaler to the retailers. If each manufacturer had to supply each retailer directly, this would require a total of 30 (3 × 10) journeys. Similarly, delivering 12 different newspapers to each of 100 newsagents would involve 12 × 100 = 1,200 journeys. With a wholesaler, only 12 + 100 = 112 journeys are needed.

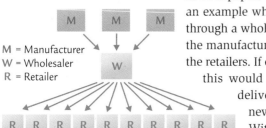

M = Manufacturer
W = Wholesaler
R = Retailer

Figure 33.2 *Distribution through a wholesaler*

- **Technology.** With significant advances in technology, more and more products are being sold through the internet, effectively bypassing the wholesaler and retailer. It is estimated that within the next 5 years, online sales of groceries will exceed the sales of all of the supermarkets outside the big four of Tesco, ASDA, Sainsbury's and Morrisons. The music industry has already become dominated by internet sales. Luxury fashion retailer, Net-a-porter.com, was set up in 2000. By 2007 its sales had reached £37 million per annum, and it is currently ranked 42 in terms of turnover in the *Sunday Times* list of private limited companies.
- **The geography of the market.** In a remote rural area, it is less likely to be cost-effective for a manufacturer (producer) to deliver directly.
- **The complexity of the product.** The product may need direct contact with the producer or an expert retailer.
- **The degree of control desired by the manufacturer (producer).** In order to control quality and protect their reputation, some firms deliver directly to selected retailers only. For example, Tyrrell's, Nike and Levi's have prevented retailers such as Tesco from selling their goods.

 FILE

Zara

Place is an important weapon in the armoury of Zara, the Spanish clothing retailer. Zara controls both the production and retailing of its clothes. In this way it can provide much more flexibility. Half of Zara's clothes are produced within 15 days of design, so Zara's fashion experts can copy a fashion idea and produce it within a short time.

Store managers are allowed to make their own decisions on stock, so the individual shops can meet local needs. A few copies of each item are distributed directly to each shop and additional orders of those that sell well can be delivered quickly. This has kept Zara at the forefront of fashion retailing for the general public. In Spain, customers queue up outside stores when a delivery is expected — a phenomenon dubbed as 'Zaramania' by the Spanish press.

Another advantage for Zara is the impact that its policy has had on customers. Because the whole stock of a shop is likely to be turned over in a few weeks, customers know that they must quickly purchase an item that they admire, as it is unlikely to be there for long. It also means that customers visit the shop more regularly, as totally new styles of clothes arrive constantly.

FACT FILE

Claire's Stores is a US multinational with annual sales in excess of $1.48 billion in 2007. Although the vast majority of the stores are in the USA, most of the new stores planned are situated in Europe. Sales revenue per square foot (a common measure of success in retailing) averages $504 per square foot overall, but in Europe figures exceed $850 per square foot. This has helped the European stores to achieve higher profit margins than those in the USA.

Source: www.clairestores.com.

EXAMINER'S VOICE

Read the wording of the question carefully. It can be tempting to use an answer to a question that you have already practised, but you must resist this temptation if the wording is different. Time spent checking the meaning of the question is time well spent — a few seconds of planning can save you 10 minutes of wasted effort.

GROUP EXERCISE

In order to further your understanding of product placement, visit and examine the following point-of-sale places:

- a food retailer
- a clothing retailer
- a catalogue
- a website offering direct sales to visitors

What conclusions can be drawn about the layout of the places that you visited? Explain why products were located in certain places or displayed in a certain way. What changes to the layout would you recommend and why?

PRACTICE EXERCISE — Total: 40 marks (35 minutes)

1 What is meant by the term 'place' in the context of the marketing mix? *(4 marks)*

2 Explain two reasons why the location of a store is so important. *(6 marks)*

3 Why do manufacturers of 'impulse buys' see place as an important factor in the marketing mix? *(6 marks)*

4 Explain two ways in which a company such as Birds Eye can increase the amount of space that retailers provide for its products. *(6 marks)*

5 Why has the role of the wholesaler declined in recent years? *(6 marks)*

6 Describe two services that a retailer provides for its customers. *(6 marks)*

7 Explain two factors that influence the method of distribution chosen for a product. *(6 marks)*

CASE STUDY Distribution at Tesco

Terry Leahy, chief executive of Tesco, recognises that scope for growth in large-scale groceries in the UK is limited by the level of competition and by government regulations on mergers. This opinion was reinforced
5 by the Competition Commission's refusal to let Tesco bid to take over Safeway in September 2003. Indications of how distribution channels and place have been used to improve performance include the following:

10 ● The company has delivered over £300 million of efficiency savings by simplifying distribution, and operating more frequent deliveries has reduced delivery and storage costs. Constant review of distribution has led to recent job cuts, with 400 redun-
15 dancies being announced at a distribution centre in Milton Keynes in September 2007.

● Tesco acquired T&S Stores, a leading convenience retailer. These shops, which serve local community needs, have helped to increase Tesco's share of the
20 convenience retail market to 7%.

● Tesco achieves over 250,000 weekly orders through its internet retailing activities. This is the fastest expanding element of Tesco's business.

● Sales of non-groceries have increased dramatically, rising much faster than sales of food items. Tesco is 25 now the fourth largest electrical retailer in the UK and the ninth largest clothing retailer. It sold more copies of the final Harry Potter book than any other retailer.

● Tesco's property division has purchased substantial 30 amounts of new land. Tesco is Europe's biggest property company, owning property valued at £28 billion in 2007. In addition, it is estimated that 50% of land suitable for additional supermarket development over the next 5 years is owned by 35 Tesco, ensuring that Tesco's market share is likely to grow still further.

● Tesco has built up a substantial chain of hyper-markets in over 12 different countries. Overseas operations now account for almost half of its selling 40 space and a quarter of its sales revenue.

Source: www.tesco.com.

Questions

Total: 40 marks (50 minutes)

1 What is meant by the term 'distribution channels' (line 7)? *(3 marks)*

2 Explain one possible reason why Tesco might have decided to enter the convenience retailing market. *(4 marks)*

3 Analyse two problems that Tesco might face in its international retailing which are unlikely to cause such difficulties in its UK operations. *(9 marks)*

4 Discuss whether Tesco should continue to expand its internet retailing activities. *(12 marks)*

5 Based on your own understanding of Tesco and the factors described in the article above, to what extent do you believe that 'place' has been the most important element of Tesco's marketing mix? *(12 marks)*

CHAPTER 34

Marketing and competitiveness

This chapter introduces the concept of market conditions, examining the features and level of competition in different markets. These market conditions are also examined through Porter's five forces model. The link between market conditions and the marketing mix is scrutinised. The determinants of competition and methods of improving a business's competitiveness are then examined.

The business environment

Businesses operate in a competitive environment. The nature of this competition varies from industry to industry, but almost all firms face some level of competition. The number of competitors, for example, dictates the extent to which a business can raise or lower its prices, and the amount of advertising it is likely to undertake.

Markets and market structure

Some markets are highly competitive with many small businesses operating in them, each selling only a small proportion of total market sales. Other markets tend to be dominated by a few large firms, each selling a significant proportion of the total market sales. The size of a market is measured either by volume (the number of units sold) or by value (the money spent on all the goods sold).

In practice, defining the nature of a market is quite complex. For example, is British Gas in the gas provision market or in the fuel provision market? This will determine whether it sees itself as competing only against other gas suppliers or against all fuel suppliers, including those supplying coal, electricity and oil. Similarly, do newspapers compete only with other newspapers or with all other news sources, including the internet, radio, and cable and satellite television? The managing director of Waterman Pens is famously quoted as saying, 'We are not in the market for pens, but executive gifts.' Thus he redefined the company's competitors as Dunhill and Rolex, rather than, or in addition to, Parker and Bic.

KEY TERM

market: a place where buyers and sellers come together.

Market structure and the degree of competition

In general, four different market structures explain the broad range of competitive environments in which most firms operate. These range from monopoly

KEY TERM

monopoly: in theory, a single producer in a market, but in practice a firm with a market share of 25% or more.

situations where, in theory, there are no competitors, to perfect competition where there are many competitors.

Monopoly

The potential danger of monopolies is that they exploit the consumer. If there is little or no competition in providing a particular product or service, and therefore few or no alternative supplies of it, monopolists could charge high prices and offer poor service, and they might simply waste scarce resources by being inefficient.

Where monopolies exhibit or are likely to exhibit any of these characteristics, the government investigates them and can require them to change their behaviour and subject them to large fines. When the former nationalised utilities, including gas, electricity and water, were privatised, regulators such as Ofwat and Ofgas were appointed to control them, in order to ensure that they did not abuse their monopoly position.

Before the 1980s, the UK had a number of true monopolies in the form of the nationalised industries, including British Coal, British Gas, British Steel, British Rail and other utilities such as electricity and water. All these industries were privatised and opened up to competition, so that in the UK today true monopoly situations are rare.

However, businesses with more than 25% of the market continue to exist because it is extremely difficult for a new firm to enter the market of a monopolist owing to high barriers to entry. These barriers to entry include:

- the high capital costs required to set up a new business in markets in which existing firms are monopolies
- patents that allow existing firms to 'monopolise' the market legally
- the loyalty of customers to existing firms
- the need to achieve large cost savings quickly in order to be able to charge a competitive price

 FACT FILE

Airport competition

Pressure is being put on the government to introduce more competition in airports. Currently, BAA has a monopoly in the London area, as it owns Heathrow, Gatwick and Stansted airports. Critics believe that facilities at these airports compare unfavourably with those at other international airports because there is little incentive for BAA to spend money on improving facilities when it is almost guaranteed that customers in the London area will use one of its airports. BAA also owns a number of regional airports.

KEY TERM

oligopoly: a market dominated by a small number of large businesses, known as oligopolists.

Oligopoly

Oligopoly markets may seem to be extremely competitive because each producer competes fiercely in order to maintain or increase its share of the particular market. However, if one oligopolist reduces its prices, the others

Monopsony means a single buyer, as opposed to a monopoly, which is a single seller. A single buyer of a product has a great deal of power over the supplier of the product. For example, it can force the supplier to lower prices, it can delay payment or it can impose stringent quality standards, and the supplier can do little in response since there are no alternative buyers with which to trade. This situation often emerges in practice when a small firm, such as a pig farm making its own sausages, sells all of its products to a large firm, such as one of the major supermarket chains. In 2007 the Competition Commission investigated whether supermarkets were taking advantage of their position as 'monopsonists' by forcing down the prices that they offer their small suppliers. It found that this was the case with some of the supermarkets' practices.

follow suit and so no firm gains. Similarly, a business that increases prices may lose market share, as the other oligopolists may not copy this strategy. Therefore, rivalry usually takes the form of **'non-price' competition**, such as special offers and advertising.

Cartels are illegal in the UK, but they are often difficult to detect. If they are found out, legal action can be taken to force the firms involved to change their behaviour and a fine of 10% of revenue can be imposed. In September 2007, the government conducted an investigation into milk prices set by the main supermarkets and discovered that they were colluding in fixing the prices for consumers. At the time of writing (January 2008), the investigation has not been fully concluded but some supermarkets and suppliers have been fined £116 million. The Competition Commission estimates that, over a 3-year period, consumers paid over £270 million more than was necessary for their milk.

Predicting the behaviour of oligopolies is complex because each firm is aware that whatever action it takes will result in a reaction from its competitors. It must therefore guess this possible reaction and take it into account before undertaking any action itself.

As markets mature and successful firms take over or merge with less successful firms, more markets inevitably become oligopolies. Then, as with monopolies, oligopolies continue to exist because of high barriers to entry.

Monopolistic competition

Monopolistic competition can result from the development of brand names or local reputation. For example, a hair salon might have an excellent reputation and a loyal clientele, which enable it to charge higher prices than other hair salons in the vicinity. A local café or bar might have developed a reputation as the 'place to be' for 18–25-year-olds, even though its prices are much higher than the pub next door.

It is easy for a new firm to enter this type of market because the set-up costs tend to be relatively low and the nature of the market is such that there is a constant flow of businesses.

KEY TERM

cartel: a group of firms that come together to agree price and output levels in an industry.

Many oligopolies are in fact monopolies under the government's 25% market share definition.

KEY TERM

monopolistic competition: where a large number of firms are competing in a market, each having enough product differentiation to achieve a degree of monopoly power and therefore some control over the price they charge.

Perfect competition

Under perfect competition, all the sellers produce homogeneous (identical) products and are 'price takers', meaning that they accept the ruling market price. The buyers all have perfect knowledge: for example, they know the price being charged in the market. There is perfect freedom of entry into and exit from the market for businesses.

Like the theoretical monopoly of a single firm, perfect competition is rarely evident in practice and tends to be simply a model against which the behaviour of firms in the real world can be compared.

EXAMINER'S VOICE

When you answer case-study questions about particular market situations, try to decide what type of market structure is evident (e.g. whether oligopolistic or monopolistic competition). Then apply your knowledge of the characteristics of the relevant market structure in answering the question (e.g. how a particular market structure will affect the profitability and likely success of the firm, and how it might affect the firm's objectives and strategy).

Table 34.1 *Market conditions*

Table 34.1 summarises the different types of market conditions in which businesses operate.

Characteristic	Perfect competition	Monopolistic competition	Oligopoly	Monopoly
Number and size of firms	Many and small	Many and small	Few and large	One, in theory*
Nature of product	Identical	Differentiated	Differentiated	Unique
Examples	Foreign exchange market, stock market, fruit and vegetable market	Hairdressers, plumbers, cafés and insurance companies	Supermarkets, banks and motor vehicle manufacturers	Nationalised industries (pre-1980s), Royal Mail (for letters)
Barriers to entry	None; it is easy to enter or leave the market	None; it is easy to enter or leave the market	High barriers to entry	High barriers to entry
Effect on business	Price takers Cost efficiency needed for survival No real scope for marketing Very low profit margins	Some control over price Cost efficiency is important unless the firm has a strong USP Benefits from marketing Low profit margins	Non-price competition High overheads High profit margins but aim to achieve USP through branding High spending on promotion Collusion can occur between firms	Price setter Can become complacent Power depends on importance of the product and its alternatives High profit margins

*In theory, a monopoly is a single producer; in practice, a monopoly is a firm with a market share of 25% or more.

Porter's five competitive forces

An alternative or additional way of analysing market conditions is to draw on Michael Porter's idea of **competitive forces**. Some firms struggle to survive

or are forced out of business, while others prosper, grow and become profitable. Why? Michael Porter identified five features of markets that determine how a successful business might cope with its competitors. These are shown in Figure 34.1.

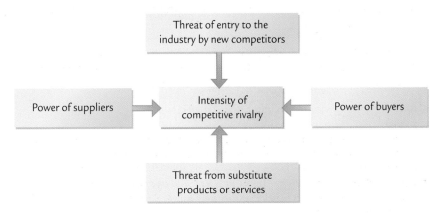

Figure 34.1 Porter's five competitive forces

When using this model to analyse a firm's position, the following questions should be asked:

■ **Intensity of competitive rivalry.** Are there a large number of small firms competing fiercely in the market, or are there a few large firms controlling the market?

■ **Threat of entry to the industry by new competitors.** Can new firms enter the market in response to high profits or are there significant barriers to entry? These might include patents, contracts tying wholesalers or retailers to existing manufacturers, and the need for a large capital base.

■ **Threat from substitute products or services.** Is the product unique and in high demand, or are there substitute products produced by other firms that can be used as alternatives?

■ **Power of suppliers.** Are the firm's inputs supplied by a single firm or cartel such as the Oil Producing and Exporting Countries (OPEC) or by a large number of competing suppliers?

■ **Power of buyers.** Does the firm sell to a single powerful buyer, such as a major supermarket chain, or to a large number of individual customers?

Porter's model can be used to assess a firm's strategy in an attempt to create the right conditions for it to have a clear competitive advantage over its rivals. If, for example, a supplier has too much power over a firm, one possibility is for the firm to find alternative sources of supply. Equally, if the firm currently sells to a single buyer, its strategy might be to find more buyers in order to reduce the power of any one buyer.

Competition

All firms in the UK operate in a competitive environment of some sort, but this has not always been the case. Before the 1980s, a number of large state monopolies or nationalised industries existed that had no competition. It is therefore useful to consider the advantages and disadvantages of competition with other organisations.

The advantages of competition are based on the fact that, in order to gain market share, firms need to offer the cheapest or the best-quality products to customers. This usually means that they try to:

- improve efficiency
- improve cost-effectiveness
- improve the quality of products and services
- reduce waste by attempting to become more efficient

However, the disadvantages of competition include the following:

- If competition is based on price, product quality might be sacrificed.
- Huge resources are devoted to competing with other firms. An example of this is advertising, which uses resources that could be spent on producing cheaper or better products.
- Some businesses will inevitably be forced out of the market, with the economic and human consequences of redundancy and unemployment.
- The competitive process tends to mean that successful businesses take over, or merge with, unsuccessful ones. This in turn leads to the existence of a smaller number of larger and larger businesses: in other words, to the growth of more oligopolies and to increasing concentration rather than competition.

DID YOU KNOW?

The **degree of concentration** refers to the number of firms that produce and sell a given proportion of the market share in an industry. For example, if the largest three firms in an industry have 60% of the total market share compared with another industry in which the largest five firms have 10% of the total market share, the former industry would be considered as heavily concentrated compared with the latter.

WHAT DO YOU THINK?

The granting of a patent generally guarantees a monopoly for 20 years. This could be seen as a reward for the research and development undertaken by the company and as allowing the company time to enjoy a return (which could mean huge profits) on its investment. Without such patent-related monopoly power, much research and development might never take place.

If people demand a particular product, is it unfair for a company to charge them a high price? Does it depend on the nature of the product and whether it is a basic necessity or a luxury?

Impact of market conditions on the marketing mix

Market conditions can be linked with most marketing activities. The marketing mix may need to be adapted to the market situation (e.g. non-price competition for oligopolies), and the length of the product life cycle may depend on the level of competition. Similarly, links can be made with operational issues. For example, bulk-buying discounts are more accessible for monopolists than for firms in competitive situations, but are less possible if there is spare capacity.

Monopoly and the marketing mix

Product

With only one organisation in the market, there is little need for new product development. Consequently, most monopolists spend relatively little on the product aspect of the marketing mix, unless they operate in a competitive international market. An illustration of this situation is BT — when it had a monopoly of telephone services in the UK, only one style of telephone handset was available to its subscribers.

Price

Monopolies are price leaders/setters and can take advantage of the lack of competition in the market to set high prices. This is particularly true if the product is a necessity with inelastic demand. However, a lower price would need to be charged if a monopolist was producing a good with price-elastic demand.

Promotion

There are high barriers to entry in monopoly, so it is unlikely that new competition can emerge. Therefore, promotion will mainly be informative — geared towards ensuring that customers are aware of the product and its benefits — rather than persuasive. Once a customer recognises the need for the product, it is guaranteed that they will buy it from the monopolist as there is no alternative supplier.

Place

This is a relatively important element of the marketing mix under monopoly because customers are less likely to purchase products or services that are not conveniently located. Traditional monopolies, such as telecommunications, gas and water supply, put considerable effort into making sure that their products and services reached as many houses as possible. Once access had been gained, little effort was then required to persuade customers to use their products and services.

Oligopoly and the marketing mix

Product

The product is crucial to success in an oligopolistic market because product differentiation is the way in which a unique selling point can be achieved. Therefore, oligopolists are some of the businesses that spend the most money

on research and development and market research in order to modify continually their goods and services to suit the needs of the customer.

Price

Although price wars are a feature of oligopolistic markets, particularly when firms are using penetration pricing in order to increase market share, price does not tend to be the main element of the marketing mix for an oligopolist. Ultimately, price wars cause all oligopolists to suffer from a fall in profit, so most of the emphasis is on product differentiation. Price-fixing agreements are technically illegal, but there is a suspicion that in some oligopoly markets, firms are reluctant to cut prices and so they tend to remain relatively high.

Promotion

Promotion is important in oligopolistic markets because it is one of the major ways in which product differentiation and unique selling points can be achieved. In some oligopolistic markets, such as soap powders, as much as 30% of costs can take the form of promotional expenditure. The level of promotional expenditure may be inversely related to the uniqueness of the product. For example, bottled waters may need considerably more promotional expenditure in order to differentiate brands than motor vehicles, where the differences between products may be more apparent.

Place

Place is also important in oligopolistic markets, as there will be many competing brands. Consumers will prefer easy access to the product. For a specific oligopolist's version of the product, this is most easily achieved by making it widely available in as many different outlets as possible.

FACT FILE

Marketing in the electronic media industry

As competition has become tougher in the electronic media industry, firms have responded in different ways. BT has launched 'video on demand', Carphone Warehouse has offered integrated telephone and internet services, and Virgin Media believes it has achieved a USP by offering four services on one bill.

Monopolistic competition and the marketing mix

Product

Product is vital in monopolistic competition, as it is the critical way in which a business can make its marketing mix different from the competition. However, the vast number of competitors in this market makes it difficult to achieve a completely distinctive product.

Price

With many small firms competing together, there is limited opportunity for cost savings, for example through bulk buying. Therefore, firms usually accept that prices tend to be similar and use other mechanisms to compete.

Promotion

The need to be price-competitive is likely to limit promotional budgets in monopolistic competition. Therefore, promotion is less significant in monopolistic competition than in markets such as oligopoly.

Place

Place can be important under monopolistic competition because transport and distribution costs may form a significant element of total costs. In farming, for example, many products are distributed locally in order to reduce costs.

Perfect competition and the marketing mix

To a large extent, perfect competition is a theoretical model rather than one that exists in the real world. Since all products are identical and firms are price takers, there can be no distinction between products and prices among different firms competing in a perfect market. Consequently, there is no point in promoting a product that cannot be distinguished from its competitors. Place therefore appears to be the vital element. Customers will tend to purchase from the nearest supplier, rather than spend time and effort locating a product that is less conveniently sited. However, in theory, there are no barriers to access for any firm in perfect competition.

Competitiveness

The success of a firm depends greatly on its ability to match or surpass the products/services offered by its competitors. The UK government has set up a special Competitiveness Unit to examine ways in which UK firms can improve their performance both domestically and in overseas markets. One of the key conclusions of the Competitiveness Unit was that the government should increase competition within markets, to ensure that businesses become more efficient.

> **KEY TERM**
>
> **competitiveness:** the ability of businesses to sell their products successfully in the market in which they are based.

Determinants of competitiveness

The main determinants of competitiveness for a particular firm, according to the Competitiveness Unit, are:

- **Investment in new equipment and technology.** Machinery and computers can improve the speed, reliability and quality of products, and still provide flexibility. Labour and other costs can be reduced.
- **Staff skills, education and training.** A skilled and educated staff will be more adaptable and flexible, able to cope with change more readily, and possess more creativity and innovative talents.
- **Innovation through investment in research and development.** The pace of change requires companies to update and broaden their product range constantly. Product life cycles are becoming shorter, and new ideas must be incorporated into products.
- **Enterprise.** The entrepreneurial skills of the owners and their desire to become their own bosses create a culture of independence, hard

work and flexibility, which helps to supply the needs of larger organisations while providing alternative products and services. In larger firms, owners try to encourage the development of an entrepreneurial approach by rewarding innovation and risk-taking.

Other factors determining competitiveness, and which are within the control of a business, include:

- **The effectiveness of the marketing mix.** A well-planned marketing mix, suited to the needs of the business, can greatly improve its competitiveness and therefore its ability to gain sales in the face of competition.
- **Incentive schemes for staff.** Motivated staff work more effectively, take on more responsibility and identify more closely with the aims of the organisation. Consequently, a well-rewarded workforce will contribute towards a successful business.
- **Improvements to operational procedures.** Improvements to factors such as factory layout, the location of the organisation, stock control and the processes used in the factory or outlet can all reduce unit costs. These changes will improve both the profitability and competitiveness of the firm.
- **Quality procedures.** Effective quality procedures can both reduce the unit cost of production by improving the efficiency of the process, and improve the quality of the product itself. This will enhance the reputation of the product in the eyes of consumers, thus increasing sales revenue.
- **Financial planning and control.** A well-organised finance department can ensure that clear targets are set, challenging managers to improve their efficiency. Furthermore, effective monitoring of progress can also improve efficiency by making sure that any problems are quickly detected and rectified.

Methods of improving competitiveness

EXAMINER'S VOICE

The AQA AS business studies specification states that methods of improving competitiveness *include* marketing, reducing costs, improving quality and staff training.

These four headings illustrate just four methods, but it should be noted that they are drawn from the four functional areas of a business, i.e. marketing, finance, operations management and people management. There is a brief development of each of these factors on p. 417 to illustrate how they might help to improve competitiveness.

However, in the examination you should focus on the issues affecting competitiveness for the particular business in the case study. The case study may include some of the four factors, or it may include reference to some of the factors listed in this chapter as factors determining competitiveness. In addition, it may consider other factors that are not listed in this chapter. Virtually every aspect of business studies that is covered in this book has an impact on the competitiveness of a business. Any question about factors influencing competitiveness should be seen in this light.

Marketing

A business uses market research in order to develop a product or service that satisfies the needs of its target market. Once the product has been produced, a pricing strategy or tactic is used to set a price that both pleases its customers and achieves the business's financial targets. The promotional mix will be geared towards the interests of the target market in a cost-effective way, and cost-effective distribution efforts must be made in order to place the product in convenient outlets.

Reducing costs

Careful financial planning and control can help to meet this target. Cost reduction also requires cooperation with operations management and human resources management, in order to make sure that any product is made as cost-effectively as possible. For products that have price-elastic demand, low costs enable the business to keep the price very competitive and thus increase sales significantly. However, even if the product is price inelastic, low costs will help the business by allowing it to achieve high added value.

Improving quality

As living standards have improved, quality has become more important to consumers. Improving quality can help the business to increase both sales volume and the selling price of its products and services, as high quality will provide much greater customer satisfaction and help to create a USP. Quality improvements can also take place in the production process itself. This will help to reduce waste and make the production process more cost-effective.

Staff training

A well-educated and trained workforce can provide a number of different benefits. Greater labour productivity can be achieved, thus reducing the cost of the product or service. Well-trained staff are more likely to identify innovative ways of making a product and are more likely to be able to produce high-quality products and identify defective goods, thus preventing flawed products from reaching the consumer. Finally, a well-educated workforce tends to be more flexible and adaptable. In the modern business world, where change is becoming increasingly rapid, this can be a significant asset for a business that is trying to stay ahead of its competitors.

GROUP EXERCISE

Select one business that has recently experienced a change (improvement or deterioration) in its competitiveness. Investigate the main factors that appear to have led to the changes in its competitiveness.

1 Distinguish between the theoretical definition of a monopoly and the legal definition. *(4 marks)*

2 Describe the main characteristics of a market that is an oligopoly. *(4 marks)*

3 Why is it often difficult for new firms to set up in monopoly or oligopoly markets? *(4 marks)*

4 What are the main characteristics of perfect competition? *(4 marks)*

5 Analyse the ways in which a firm's marketing mix might be influenced if it is operating under conditions of:
   a oligopoly *(8 marks)*
   b monopoly *(8 marks)*

6 What is meant by the term 'competitiveness'? *(3 marks)*

7 Analyse four ways in which a business might improve its competitiveness. *(15 marks)*

CASE STUDY 1 Market conditions in the UK milk industry

The big four supermarkets have been involved in a cartel with dairy companies to fix the prices of milk, butter and cheese, according to the Office of Fair Trading. A 3p increase in the price of milk was allegedly agreed between the supermarkets, possibly to ensure high profit levels. With most purchases of milk taking place in supermarkets, there is little chance of competition forcing down prices if the main supermarkets are all charging the same price. Although the market for groceries fits the description of oligopoly, with a few firms dominating, the legal definition of monopoly defines the largest supermarket (Tesco) as a monopoly because it has a 31% market share. As the major buyer of milk, some would describe it as a monopsonist.

A similar situation exists at the processing level. The supply of dairy produce is dominated by a few suppliers such as Arla, Dairy Crest, Lactalis McLelland, the Cheese Company and Wiseman. However, as these oligopolists sell many of their products to larger oligopolies in the form of the main supermarkets, they are in a much weaker bargaining position.

The bottom of the chain is clearly the farmer. As shown in Figure 34.2, milk prices paid to farmers have fallen by a third between 1996 and 2007, at a time when prices paid by customers have risen by 15%. With many small suppliers and no real distinction between

the milk produced by different farmers, it is arguably the nearest there is to a perfectly competitive market in the UK. Consequently, farmers are price takers with little control over price.

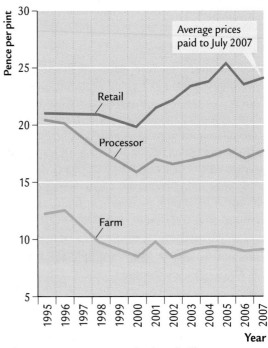

Figure 34.2 *Average cost of a pint of milk*

The price per pint being paid to farmers was increased from 9p a pint to 12p a pint in October 2007, 1 month after the OFT investigation ended but 2 months before it published its initial report. For many farmers this news has come too late, as half of them have left dairy farming in the last decade. In 1997 there were 28,000 dairy farmers in the UK; in 2007 the figure stands at 14,000. Cynics see two reasons behind the price rises for farmers:

- an attempt by processors and supermarkets to gain favourable publicity at the time of publication of the report
- a recognition that such low prices are threatening the supply of milk, potentially forcing up the prices that processors and supermarkets will have to pay in the long run

Source: adapted from an article by Valerie Elliott in *The Times*, 21 September 2007, and other sources.

Questions

Total: 40 marks (50 minutes)

1 Why would Tesco be defined as a 'legal monopoly'? *(3 marks)*

2 Explain why milk retailing and milk processing would be seen as 'oligopoly' market conditions but dairy farming would be seen as an example of 'perfect competition'. *(6 marks)*

3 a What is meant by a 'cartel'? *(3 marks)*
b Why might oligopolists, such as milk retailers, agree to form a cartel? *(4 marks)*

4 Study Figure 34.2 and the article. To what extent are the information provided and the events taking place consistent with the view that farming is an example of perfect competition and milk retailing an example of oligopoly? *(10 marks)*

5 Using Porter's five forces model, evaluate the reasons behind the changes that have taken place in the dairy industry between 1996 and 2007. *(14 marks)*

CASE STUDY 2 Surf's up — social networking sites

For Facebook, 2007 was an unmitigated triumph. In the last 6 months alone, it doubled its user base from 29 million to a remarkable 58 million active users.

Few deny that social networking sites, where users
5 create personal web pages or profiles and interact with friends, are huge successes. However, all is not well. Last month over 50,000 users signed a petition against Facebook's controversial marketing system, which gives advertisers access to personal data on the site.
10   With little brand loyalty, consumers who flock to its pages would not think twice before upping sticks and going elsewhere. Currently, despite its reputation, Facebook pulls in around $305 million of advertising revenue per annum in comparison with former market
15 leader MySpace's $850 million. MySpace is losing out on users but is able to convert fewer social networkers into much greater revenue for owner, Rupert Murdoch.

MySpace lost its market leadership as users became fed up with its commercialisation, but Facebook may go the same way, as it needs to find a way of converting 20 users to advertising revenue.

CHAPTER 34 · Marketing and competitiveness

With around 40 million members, Bebo is the world's third most popular social network. It has particular appeal to customers aged 15–24, with 4.3 million unique users in this age range, compared with 3.3 million for Facebook. Bebo also has much greater loyalty among the under-15 age bracket, to such an extent that Mars has paid a six-figure sum to advertise 'Skittles' on the site.

Increasingly, advertisers want to know how long websites can keep the customer hooked. This is known as the 'stickiness' of a site. This is another area where Bebo comes up trumps — users spend an average of 33 minutes a day on its site, compared with 28 minutes for Facebook and 23 minutes for MySpace. Bebo also scores more highly on security — a feature that is becoming more valued as users worry about their privacy.

The large social networking sites could learn from 'Gaia'. Gaiaonline.com is a rapidly growing virtual world and social networking site for teenagers, which aims to keep its customers online for as long as possible. Within 4 years of its launch, it has registered 2 million users, quadrupling its numbers in the last year. Gaia's biggest draw is its 'stickiness', achieved by its range of interactive online games. Around 300,000 of its users log in daily, with an average visit of 2 hours a day. This is because the website users are paid for their time online in 'Gaian Gold', a virtual currency that cannot be used as cash but which can be converted into virtual goods and services within Gaia.

Sources: articles by David Crow in *The Business*, 5 May 2007 and 5 January 2008, and other sources.

Questions

Total: 40 marks (50 minutes)

1 a What market condition exists in the market for social network websites? *(1 mark)*
  b Justify your view. *(4 marks)*

2 What is the USP for 'Gaia'? *(4 marks)*

3 Analyse one reason that supports the view that Facebook is the most successful social network site and one reason supporting the view that MySpace is more successful. *(6 marks)*

4 There is 'little brand loyalty' among users of social networking sites (line 10). Analyse two implications of this lack of brand loyalty for Facebook. *(8 marks)*

5 Explain how Bebo tries to differentiate itself from its competitors. *(6 marks)*

6 Select a particular social network website. Based on the information in the case study and your own knowledge, discuss the main factors that determine the popularity and competitiveness of your particular website. *(11 marks)*

The Sheffield
College
Hillsborough LRC
Telephone: 0114 260 2254

Unit 2: Managing a business

Index

Note: page numbers in **bold** type refer to key terms (where these occur more than once only the first occurrence is given).

Index